Jewish History
and
Thought:
An Introduction

Jewish History and *Thought:*
An Introduction

by
MENAHEM MANSOOR

Joseph L. Baron Emeritus Professor
Department of Hebrew and Semitic Studies
University of Wisconsin
Madison

KTAV PUBLISHING HOUSE, INC.
HOBOKEN, NJ 07030

Copyright (c) 1991
Menahem Mansoor
Library of Congress Cataloging-in-Publication Data

Mansoor, Menahem.
    Jewish history and thought : an introduction / by Menahem Mansoor.
      p. cm.
    Includes bibliographical references and index.
    ISBN 0-88125-404-5 : $39.50 -- ISBN 88125-403-7 (paper) :
  $19.95
    1. Jews--History--Outlines, syllabi, etc. 2. Judaism--History-
  -Outlines, syllabi, etc. I. Title.
  DS118.M26 1991
  909'.04924--dc20   91-34985
                                                  CIP

Manufactured in the United States of America

This work is respectfully dedicated to the loving memory of Harry J. and Belle Goodman whose beautiful way of life exemplifies teachings of Judaism — "only to do justice, to love kindness and to walk humbly with your God,"

and

to Sam and Helen Stahl for their love and commitment to Jewish life and learning, and for many years of friendship and encouragement.

תִּפְאֶרֶת בָּנִים אֲבוֹתָם

"The glory of children is their parents" (Proverbs 17:6)

CONTENTS

viii

A WORD OF THANKS

This is to express my sincere thanks and appreciation to all those who helped in the preparation of this work. The faculty-student involvement in planning and writing this work has been a most rewarding and stimulating experience. I have greatly benefited from the keen observations and genuine interest of the students who were partners in this undertaking. The subject matter was sufficient to inspire all of us.

I am particularly indebted to Rita Burns, Jack Edelstein, Warren Green, Mark Mandel, Lois Schlar and David Sorkin who worked from my lecture notes, outlines and other reference materials. At the time (1970-1971) they were all students majoring in the Department of Hebrew and Semitic Studies at the University of Wisconsin. Tom Freeman and Harvey Temkin, also majors in Hebrew Studies, read and edited the first drafts of the book when it first appeared in offset edition in 1972. Their observations have greatly improved its usefulness.

Thanks are also due to Yoav Morahg for word processing the entire manuscript, and to Nadine Shapiro of Madison for her meticulous editing and proofreading of the text and making important observations. My sincere gratitude to Larry Kohn, Emeritus Professor Milton Konvitz of Cornell University, and Professor Zev Garber, at the time, President of the National Association of Professors of Hebrew for reading part of or the entire manuscript and offering insightful suggestions, greatly improving the final product. I also appreciate the cooperation of Steven Lancaster, a doctoral candidate, who entered the last corrections. Finally, I would like to express my warm thanks and appreciation to Project Assistant, Judith Egyes, who shared trials and tribulations with me during the final stages of the book, for checking and editing the entire text, and for the preparation of the Bibliographies and the General Index.

The initial research for this work was supported by grants from the WISCONSIN SOCIETY FOR JEWISH LEARNING in 1970-71. The printing and publication of this volume was assisted by generous contributions from my friends Irwin and Robert Goodman, men of infinite compassion and love, who epitomize all that encompass goodness, friendship, caring and integrity in a society. Their deeds are their monuments.

I also wish to express my gratitude for the support, friendship, hospitality, and encouragement which Pearl and Nathan Berkowitz have always extended to me and my family since our arrival in Wisconsin thirty-five years ago. This served as a tower of strength. Their appreciation of the beauty and meaningfulness of Jewish learning and way of life has been a source of joy and inspiration to me and my family.

To my wife, Claire, our daughter Yardena, her husband Michael Phillip and our son, Daniel, I owe much for their encouragement and support. Claire, in particular, has been my mentor, supporter, and critic. I am profoundly indebted for her patience, constant care, counsel and interest.

It is my hope that the book will prove a worthy tribute to all of them.

Menahem Mansoor
Madison, Wisconsin
May 23, 1991

INTRODUCTION

This work spans Jewish history and thought from Biblical times through the twentieth-century and the establishment of the State of Israel, covering developments that have shaped Judaism, Jewish learning, Jewish religion, and the Jewish people.

This is a personal approach to introduce Jewish history and thought in an outline format to the general lay reader, the teacher, the student and adult study groups. This approach proved most successful in the author's book, *Guide to the Dead Sea Scrolls*, which was published by three publishing firms and had some 13 printings. The present work is based on the author's twenty-year experience in teaching this subject to undergraduates-as a year course-and to adult study groups on the campus and beyond. It is as the title indicates-an introduction. It is essentially a reference work and guide to the general public and to those who wish to study it for personal enjoyment and enrichment. In fact, it has been used successfully as a correspondence course and in independent study by the University of Wisconsin-Outreach Program. It is also the author's fervent hope that it will stimulate the reader to take greater interest and study further.

This book, however, is not meant to be a substitute for the study of the classic Jewish sources themselves. A person wishing to study or consult such sources-most of which are readily available in English translation-should consult *Sources in Translation* in the General Bibliography, Appendix C, at the end of the book. Discussions of Jewish literary masterpieces are adequately included in this work, for the author regards these as the most faithful and comprehensive documentary record of Jewish history, religion and experience.

To help the user, each chapter has the following components:

1. Introductory observation about the chapter under study
2. Detailed outline of the chapter
3. Concluding observations

This book also contains several useful appendices:

1. "History of the Jews," one chapter summary by Ellis Rivkin of the Hebrew Union College, printed here with the author's permission.
2. Chronological charts
3. Extensive bibliographies in Jewish history and thought
4. Glossary of terms

To make the work even more useful, several charts are provided:

1. Hebrew Bible:
   The Division of the Books
   The Hebrew and English Names of the Books
   The Traditional Authorship and Dates
2. Kings of Israel and Judah, with Dates
3. Prophets of the Bible, with Dates
4. The Division of the Books in the New Testament
5. Structure of the Talmud-the Rabbinic Tradition
6. Jewish Calendar and Festivals

Finally, one of the main reasons for writing this book is my earnest desire to share the excitement and the inspiration I have derived from studying and teaching some four thousand years of Jewish history and thought, from the time of Abraham-the founder-up to the present.

If the readers of this book will be stimulated to take greater interest in, and further study our heritage in depth, this author, who has spent more than 30 years teaching and planning this book, will be more than compensated.

I

BIBLICAL AGE I: PATRIARCHS THROUGH THE CONQUEST

In the early part of the second millenium B.C.E.* Abraham, a Mesopotamian shepherd, set out to discover the land which he believed had been promised to him by God.† This land was Canaan, a small, fertile area situated between the Arabian Desert and the Mediterranean Sea. The broken terrain of this land, as well as the variety of groups inhabiting it, discouraged a consolidation of political power. The population of Canaan was, for the most part, Semitic. Canaanites occupied the lowlands, exerting a sufficiently strong influence to assimilate most of the small groups who settled among them. Amorites inhabited the mountainous districts, while the Philistines occupied the southern coastal regions. Smaller nationalities controlled single cities (e.g., the Hivites in Gibeon and the Jebusites in Jerusalem). Stronger foreign powers also exerted influence over the land. The Egyptian Empire maintained military garrisons throughout the area and the Assyrians made frequent attempts to wrest control from Egypt.

Though archaeological discoveries have brought much to light about the world of this time, specific dates for the call of Abraham, the Exodus from Egypt, and the conquest of Canaan are not agreed upon by scholars.

For a chronological listing, see Appendix B, "Chronological Chart," at the end of this book.

A. *Period of the Patriarch (c. 2000-1750)*

1. Based on the Book of Genesis, tradition ascribes the earliest ancestry of the Jewish people to Abraham, an inhabitant of Mesopotamia in the early second millennium. Abraham was part of a large migration of Northwest-Semitic peoples from various lands and backgrounds to the land of Canaan. Procuring tracts of land by peaceful covenant with the Canaanites, Abraham and his descendants, Isaac and Jacob, settled there as seminomadic herdsmen pasturing their flocks.

---

*All dates given in this chapter are B.C.E. (Before the Common Era), often referred to as B.C.

†The four-letter word YHVH is used to designate the special Divine Name of God. It is also called the Tetragrammaton—a Greek word meaning four-lettered. The original pronunciation of YHVH is unknown. (Yahweh or Yehovah has been conjectured.) By the second century B.C.E. it was traditionally no longer pronounced by Jews but read as Adonai, Hebrew for "my Lord(s)."

2. Preserving their patriarchal traditions and ancestral gods, the "children of Abraham" adopted the language, culture, and even to some extent, the religion of the Canaanites.

3. When Canaan fell into hard times, some clans remained. Others (which were to later become the nucleus of Israel) wandered down into Egypt. They settled in the land of Goshen. Eventually, these became state slaves.

4. Though unlike the paganisms of Mesopotamia and the fertility cults of Canaan, the religion of the Biblical patriarchs cannot be described as strictly monotheistic. Abraham, Isaac, and Jacob each had a personal experience with a deity whom he viewed as patron of his clan. When Abraham left his homeland it was at the bidding of this God. While he was wandering in Canaan, that land was promised to him and to his descendants, who would become a great nation and inhabit it. The promise was renewed to both Isaac and Jacob, and later to their descendant Moses, in Egypt. The beliefs of the patriarchs helped to shape the later faith of the people of Israel.

B. *Period of the Exodus (c. 1400-1250)*

1. Moses led the Israelites in rebellion against their Egyptian masters. According to the Biblical account, the dividing of the Red Sea allowed the Israelites, together with a "mixed rabble," to flee Egypt.

2. In the wilderness of Sinai, this group became a people by reason of its covenant with God. This strict monotheism provided the basis for a moral and ethical system.

3. Unsuccessful in attempting to enter Canaan from the south, the Israelites wandered in the desert. During this time they developed into a more cohesive group under the leadership of Moses.*

C. *Period of Conquest*

1. Some of the Israelites settled on the east side of the Jordan River. Joshua, after the death of Moses, mustered the strength of the people to enter the main body of the land. The city of Jericho, in the central

---

*The Torah and the Ten Commandments are discussed elsewhere.

hill country, and the immediate areas to the north and south were taken. The shepherds gave up their wanderings to become farmers.

2. The process of conquest was slow and laborious. The Israelites did not spread to the coastal regions until generations later. Several principal cities were still controlled by Egyptian garrisons, and areas conquered by the Israelites were divided by numerous Canaanite fortresses. These divisions, in addition to geographical divisions and tribal jealousies, made the Israelites vulnerable to foreign incursions.

3. Tribal organization was weak. Towns and villages were, for the most part, independently ruled and judged by elders. (Egypt remained in the background as nominal suzerain over the whole country.) Occasionally, an outstanding figure—usually a military hero—was able to transcend local divisions and unite the tribes against common enemies. These leaders were the Judges. Deborah, a woman, succeeded in forming a temporary coalition of tribes to defeat Canaanite enemies in the north. Gideon led the people to defeat Midianite raiders, and Jephthah stopped the invading Ammonites.

4. Though the religious cult of the Israelites was continually threatened by Canaanite paganism, it proved strong enough to maintain the group's identity. Common enemies forced the development of unity based on the national covenant with God. The universal threat of the Philistines eventually paved the road to nationhood.

BIBLICAL AGE II: THE UNITED MONARCHY

By the end of the period of the Judges, the Israelites who had come into Canaan after the Exodus (c. 1400-1250) had settled into a loose, religiously based confederation of tribes. There was no central government. However, there was a certain amount of cooperation in the maintenance of the central shrine at Shiloh. Only the common threat of the Philistines, at the beginning of the twelfth century, was able to unite the Israelite tribes. The Philistines were from Asia Minor and the Aegean Islands. They were displaced by the toppling of the Hittite and Mycenaean empires in the late thirteenth century. They first moved south and tried to enter Egypt, but were repulsed. They finally settled along the Mediterranean coast of Palestine. There they established five city-states: Gath, Gaza, Ekron, Ashdod, and Ashkelon. Once settled, they decided to conquer Palestine, and so began to raid inland.

This was the situation that Israel faced at the end of the period of the Judges. The Philistines had three distinct advantages over Israel. First, the Philistines alone had a knowledge of iron. Second, the Philistines had chariots and horses. Finally, and perhaps most important for the future course of Israel's history, the Philistines were very well disciplined militarily, and the kings of the city-states were able to cooperate effectively with one another. Israel's tribes would just as soon have fought against one another as with one another. The entire situation demanded strong leadership for Israel.

A. *Aphek and Its Aftermath*

1. The tribes tried to unite against the Philistines' threat. At the battle of Aphek the Israelites suffered a calamitous defeat. Both corrupt sons of Eli the Priest (descended from Aaron) were killed, the Israelite forces were decimated, and the portable Ark of the Covenant was captured by the Philistines.

2. The news of the defeat and the death of his sons caused the death of Eli.

3. Samuel took Eli's place. He was not of the priestly line, but had grown up serving the shrine at Shiloh. He took over the priestly duties and also functioned as a Judge. (Samuel, having already received a revelation from God, foreshadowed the prophet-priest rivalry which was to develop in later years.)

B. *The Reign of Saul (c. 1020-1004)*

1. Saul's kingship began auspiciously: He forced the Philistines back into their own territory. In the process he unified the country.

2. The success of the monarchy did not last.

   a. Saul split with Samuel, ostensibly over Saul's usurpation of priestly duties and disobedience to priestly commands. Samuel's jealousy, compounded by misgivings about the conceit of the monarchy, also played a role.

   b. Saul was not really fit to be king. He was a brave and able warrior and military commander but a woefully inadequate administrator. His court was never more than a military camp. He had no interest in building up the country economically or in protecting it by diplomacy.

   c. His later years were plagued by emotional instability, culminating in periods of deep depression and outbreaks of cruelty. Ultimately, his instability, combined with jealousy, focused on David, the young hero of the nation and a friend of Saul's son Jonathan. That David had married Saul's daughter Michal only made the antagonism worse.

3. David, a court musician, was ultimately driven to seek safety elsewhere. He gathered around him a disorganized band of fugitives and outlaws which he welded into a competent fighting force.

4. Finding his position between Saul and the Philistines untenable, David presented himself and his army to the Philistine ruler of Gath. In exchange for military service, he received protection and even governorship over a subsidiary city.

5. Saul and Jonathan both died in battle against the Philistines. Saul was succeeded by Ishbaal and the country again fell under Philistine control.

C. *The Reign of David*

1. David split with the Philistines and seized Hebron. He was accepted as king over Judea in 1013.

2. Ishbaal was assassinated by his own men and David was accepted as king by the northern tribes in 1006.

3. David subsequently eliminated the Philistine threat and secured his borders. He captured his old refuge of Gath. This done, he reorganized the administration of the country.

4. David's kingship was based on a covenant with his people. His power was limited and public opinion was able to influence him. David's policy was definitely a change from that of the traditional oriental ruler.

5. David made Jerusalem, which he captured from the Jebusites, his capital. There were at least three reasons for this:

    a. It was defensible.

    b. It was centrally located in the kingdom.

    c. It was part of important trade routes.

6. The domestic affairs of his kingdom settled, David set out to acquire an empire. He conquered Edom, Moab, Ammon, and Aram.

7. Absalom, David's son, revolted with a large segment of the population. This group disagreed with David's reforms. Absalom succeeded in capturing Jerusalem, forcing David to flee. In the war which followed, David was able to recapture the country and Absalom was killed.

8. Adoniyah, David's oldest living son, had himself proclaimed king while David was still alive. David had his son Solomon anointed as his successor by Zadok the Priest. When Adoniyah heard of this he surrendered to Solomon. Shortly after this event David died.

D. *The Reign of Solomon*

1. Solomon's reign was, for the most part, peaceful. He ruled by statesmanship rather than military power.

2. Solomon realized the value of Palestine as a land bridge between Asia Minor, Asia, and Africa. With the help of Egypt, he captured Gezer (an important trading city). He began levying tribute from traders in exchange for protection from highwaymen.

3. Literature and art flourished under Solomon. Proverbs and songs (similar to Biblical proverbs and psalms) were some of the main art forms.

4. Solomon embarked on an extensive building program. He fortified many cities (including Jerusalem, Gezer, Megiddo, and Hazor), and he built the Temple. The program required heavy taxation and forced labor, which was viewed by the people as a breach of covenant, and as despotic.

5. Near the end of Solomon's reign, Shishak gained power in Egypt and encouraged Jeroboam, who was agitating in the north.

6. Solomon died (c. 930) and the people gathered at Shechem to select a successor. Solomon's son Rehoboam was chosen. However, he refused to lighten the burden of the people, and the northern tribes revolted under Jeroboam, dividing the kingdom of Israel.

E. *Conclusion*

This period of the United Monarchy was one of the most significant periods in the history of Judaism. For the first time, Israel was a nation-state with a centralized government and a strong sense of unity. Even with all the abuses under Solomon's reign, it was still considered a "golden age." Throughout the periods of the Divided Monarchy, the Exile, and the Diaspora, the period of the United Monarchy would serve as an ideal for Judaism.

BIBLICAL AGE III:
THE DIVIDED KINGDOM AND THE PROPHETIC PERIOD

The period of the Divided Kingdom was both a troubled and a creative time. Israel—the Northern Kingdom—was larger, more powerful, and more prosperous than Judah—the Southern Kingdom. Although intertribal jealousies and threatening foreign powers kept the periods of peace short-lived, the Northern Kingdom lasted two centuries. It was ruled by nineteen kings, many of whom reigned only a few years and some just a few months. The nation was externally strong but internally weak, not only politically but morally. Class distinctions bred injustice and corruption. With little regard for religious obligation, many worshipped at local shrines and bestowed on them their lavish support. This was a token offered to God for guarding the nation from its enemies and supporting the status quo. Despite prophetic demands for true worship and social justice, Israel persisted in her ways. The kingdom was destroyed in 721 B.C.E.* by the Assyrians.

The Davidic dynasty exercised a strong hold on the populace of the Southern Kingdom. Though it, too, knew rebellion and dissension, in comparison with the North it enjoyed internal peace. Judah was small. Its only significance in world affairs was its strategic position between Egypt and Assyria. It, too, was beset with social and religious corruption. As a result, it also had prophets who denounced evil and warned of God's ensuing judgment. The prophetic message, though full of words of doom and destruction, was flavored with touches of pity and consolation. The words of the prophets became the creative force for the future of Judaism.

The kings of Israel and Judah and the literary prophets are listed in Appendix C at the end of this Book.

A. *Israel*

1. Civil War

Not long after Solomon's death (c. 930), Jeroboam led the Northern Kingdom in revolt against Judah. He reigned in Israel until his death in 912. He erected shrines in Dan and Bethel to rival that of Jerusalem.

---

*All dates given in this chapter are B.C.E. (Before the Common Era), often referred to as B.C.

Jeroboam installed golden bull-calf images as visible pedestals for the invisible throne of God. He was succeeded by his son who, soon after receiving the throne, was assassinated by Baasha, one of his army officers. Baasha, in turn, reigned for twenty-four years.

2. The House of Omri (c. 887-843)

   a. Though Omri reigned briefly (c. 887-876), he consolidated his kingdom to some degree. He also engaged in some foreign conquests and alliances. He transferred the capital from Shechem to nearby Tirzah and finally to Samaria.

   b. Omri's alliance with Phoenicia was strengthened by the marriage of his son Ahab to Jezebel, daughter of the king of Tyre. Jezebel's influence during her husband's reign (c. 876-853) and that of her sons Ahaziah (c. 853) and Jehoram (c. 853-843) led to worship of Phoenician gods and a jealous regard for courtly power.

   c. During the Omride dynasty, Israel and Judah were allies in several conflicts with Aram. For a time, the two joined with Aram against an even larger enemy, Assyria.

   d. The forty-year Omride dynasty came to an end when Jehu, one of Jehoram's generals, led a revolt against courtly injustices. This began the second and longest dynasty in Israel's history.

3. Jehu's Dynasty (c. 843-745)

   a. Jehu abolished the Baal worship introduced by Jezebel. Other religious corruptions, however, were to take hold during his dynasty.

   b. With Assyrian help, Aram was no longer a major threat to Israel. Assyria was concerned with her own internal affairs at this time. Trade and industry were revived in Israel. A degree of peace and wealth was realized in the kingdom.

   c. The dynasty of Jehu was unpopular, for the nobility enjoyed wealth and luxury at the expense of the small peasant. Thus, in c. 745 the dynasty of Jehu ended as it had begun—in rebellion and assassination.

4. Civil War

    a. Turbulent, anarchical times followed. Ten kings ascended the throne in a period of five years.

    b. As the Assyrian monarchs Tiglath-pileser III and Shalmaneser V encroached on their neighbors to the west, Israel was forced to pay tribute. Under the rule of Pekah, Israel allied herself with the Aramean, Philistine, and Phoenician powers against Assyria.

    c. The threat to Israel seemed even more evident as Babylon and Damascus fell to the encroaching Assyrian power. At the suggestion of Egypt, Israel's king Hoshea refused to pay the annual tribute to Assyria. In 721 Assyrian forces, led by Sargon II, razed Samaria.

    d. Having won political control, Assyria succeeded in blurring the spiritual identity of the Israelites. The conquerors deported the Israelite nobility to the far corners of the Assyrian Empire and opened the conquered territory to foreign settlers. The Israelites who were deported merged with other peoples. Those left in Israel intermarried. This latter group became the Samaritans. They were named for their district, which was now an Assyrian province.*

B. *Judah*

1. Death of Solomon (c. 930) to the Fall of the Kingdom of Israel (721)

    a. Following the secession of Israel, the Israel-Judah conflict took the form of minor territorial disputes. The tiny Judean kingdom enlisted Syrian help in maintaining its independence.

    b. By the reign of Jehoshaphat (875-851), relations with Israel had improved. The king's son Jehoram married Athaliah, daughter of Israel's King Ahab and his Phoenician wife Jezebel. When Jehoram's son Ahaziah (844-843) was killed, the Queen Mother

---

*The religious beliefs and practices of the Samaritans came to differ widely from those of normative Judaism. The Samaritan Scriptures contain only the Pentateuch (first five books of the Hebrew Bible). Its text, written in old Hebrew script, is at variance with that of the Hebrew Bible. A rival Temple to that of Jerusalem was built on Mount Gerizim. The liturgical calendar, feasts, and practices of the Samaritans differ from those of standard Judaism. Though its membership is small, the Samaritan tradition continues today in Israel.

Athaliah ruled. She was devoted, much like her mother in Israel, to her own interests and gods. Athaliah's corruptions became the cause of a revolt. She was eventually put to death

c. Under the monarchs Joash (837-798) and Amaziah (798-780), Israel's power weakened, thus weakening the position of the subservient Judean kingdom. This invited Syrian aggression. Syria, however, was bought off in order that Jerusalem might not be taken.

d. During the reign of Ahaz (735-720), Judah refused to join the anti-Assyrian bloc with Israel and Damascus. When Judah refused, Northern forces marched on Jerusalem to set up a puppet king. Ahaz appealed to Assyria for protection. In return for military aid, Judah became a tributary kingdom of Assyria, standing between the two great rival powers of Assyria and Egypt. It was during this time that Damascus, and eventually Israel, fell to the Assyrians.

2. From Assyrian to Babylonian Rule

a. Tired of being the battleground of Assyria's skirmishes, Judah, under the leadership of Hezekiah (720-692), joined in an Egyptian-supported revolt against the Assyrian Empire upon the accession of Sennacherib (705). Assyria swooped across Judah and was about to take Jerusalem when peace was made with Egypt. The Assyrian armies withdrew.

b. During the reign of Manasseh (692-638) foreign influence prevailed in Judah. Local sanctuaries were restored, human sacrifices were offered, and alien cult worship took place in the Temple. Conflicting factions arose among the Judeans. Amon (638-637) was assassinated in a rebellion against corrupt policies.

c. Josiah (637-608) set about religious reform. The Temple was purged of foreign influence and local shrines were abolished. Josiah, perceiving the increasing weakness of Assyria and the growing strength of Babylonia, aligned Judah with Babylonian rebels against an Egypt-Assyria coalition. In a confrontation with Egyptian forces, Josiah met his death. His son Jehoahaz was killed by Egyptian forces a short time later.

d. Jehoiakim (608-598), another of Josiah's sons, allied himself with Egypt. In 605 the Egyptian-Assyrian coalition succumbed to

Babylonian power under the leadership of Nebuchadnezzar. In the beginning, Jehoiakim paid allegiance to Babylon. He later withdrew his support. Jehoiakim died as Babylonian troops marched toward Jerusalem.

e. Jehoiachin (598-597), the frightened eighteen-year old son of Jehoiakim, hastened to placate the rulers of Babylon with Temple and palace treasures. As a result, Babylon gave Judah semi-independent but subordinate status. Zedekiah succeeded Jehoiachin. At Egypt's invitation he joined in a coalition against Babylon. In the winter of 588-587, Nebuchadnezzar appeared at the walls of Jerusalem. With the help of Egyptian forces the city withstood the siege until the following winter. Jerusalem was conquered in the winter of 587-586. Zedekiah was taken in chains to Babylon. One month later Babylonian forces looted Jerusalem, burning its principal buildings. Though some of the rural population remained, the wealthy and influential citizens were led off to Babylon.

f. Gedaliah, a devout man in Mizpah, tried to salvage and restore Judaism in Judah. A nobleman from a rival family murdered him and no attempts at recovery were made.

C. *The Prophetic Period*

1. The three centuries between 750 and 450 were politically and religiously turbulent. The classical, or literary, prophets lived during this time.

2. Survey of Hebrew Prophecy

   a. The literary prophets were preceded by men and women with prophetic and sometimes miraculous powers. There is no written record of their oracles.

   b. By the time of Samuel, bands of prophets were organized into guilds. During the monarchy, prophets served as diviners for kings. However, the office of court prophet led to abuse: "False prophets" spoke not the word of God but what was pleasing to the kings and to the people.

   c. As a balancing force, men who were reputed to have been divinely inspired professed God's call to monotheism and attempted to restore morality in the kingdom.

    d. Prophetic utterances were written down by the prophets themselves or by their followers. The longer literary works of the "major" prophets are those of Isaiah, Jeremiah, and Ezekiel, while the shorter prophetic books of the "minor" prophets include those of Amos, Hosea, Micah, Zephaniah, Nahum, Habakkuk, Obadiah, Haggai, Zechariah, Malachi, Joel, and Jonah. All these books, characterized by alternating styles of prose and poetry, are of the highest literary quality.

    e. Rabbinic tradition sets the end of divinely inspired prophecy at the death of the last of the minor prophets, Malachi, in 450.

3. The Troubled Times and the Prophetic Message

    a. With the monarchy, the state replaced the Mosaic covenant as the basis of social obligation. Both Israel and Judah suffered from the loss of tribal solidarity and the development of strong class distinctions. The wealthy, supported by corrupt Judges, could and did take advantage of the poor.

    b. Social disintegration is not without its religious repercussions.

        (1) Although elaborate shrines in Israel were attended by many worshippers, true religious fervor was rare. Local shrines were centers for a mixture of monotheistic and pagan worship. The clergy, being aligned with the state, promoted injustice, Jehu's efforts to rid Israel of the worship of Baal were supported by religious leaders. After the efforts were successfully completed, the religious hierarchy became complacent, allowing the wealthy to gain power at the expense of the poor. Israel's complacency was built on the belief that God would save His people regardless of their lack of faithfulness to the covenant.

        (2) Judah suffered from the same social and economic ills that prevailed in Israel. Judah also experienced religious decay. In the late eighth century, when Ahaz accepted Assyrian political support, he also accepted Assyrian gods into the Temple in Jerusalem. The priests led the official state cult and provided spiritual support and defense of the court. Judah had lost sight of the moral demands of the covenant. The people relied solely on God's supposed promise of national security and the glorious future of the House of David. Assyrian aggression

jeopardized the nation itself and tested their belief. There were those in Judah who trusted blindly and fanatically. Others, like Ahaz, lost faith in God.

c. Prophetic message: The prophets were reformers, issuing a call to monotheism—to an acceptance of God's lordship—and a call to justice and righteousness—a return to the laws of the covenant. In Israel, Amos and Hosea had warned of God's judgment. In Judah, Isaiah and Micah offered an explanation for the national humiliation by Assyria: the lack of faith in God. They recalled the obligations inherent in monotheism. Judah's prophets inspired efforts to rid their nation of foreign cults and at all times announced God's judgment on justice. Most important, they proclaimed to the nation a word of hope which survived the fall of Jerusalem: the hope that there would be a remnant and that God's people would never be destroyed.

III

EXILE AND RETURN

The period of the Babylonian Exile and the Restoration was significant in Jewish history. It changed the emphasis and practice of Judaism, transforming it from a national sect to a worldwide religion. It was also a period of intense literary activity.

The two persons who had the greatest effect on postexilic Judaism were Ezra and Nehemiah. Both were zealous reformers dedicated to renewing and purifying Judaism.

A. *Historical Background*

1. Mesopotamian Campaigns

    a. Israel (the Northern Kingdom) fell to Assyria, the dominant power in 721 B.C.E.* Sargon II (721-705) then ruled from Nineveh, his capital.

    b. Less than a century later, Nabopolassar (626-605) established the Neo-Babylonian Empire and began to threaten Assyria as a rival. He took Nineveh in 612, and overcame Haran in 610.

    c. Assyria appealed to Egypt (under Pharaoh Necho from 609-593) for help, and Necho moved north through the Palestinian corridor in 609.

    d. Judah's king Josiah tried unsuccessfully to stop Egypt and was killed. Necho placed Jehoiakim on the Judean throne.

2. Babylonian Hegemony

    a. Even with Egyptian help, Assyria was unable to regain its strength. After Nabopolassar's son Nebuchadnezzar defeated the Egyptians at Carchemish (605), Babylon became the reigning power.

---

*All dates given in this chapter are B.C.E. (Before the Common Era), often referred to as B.C.

   b. Jehoiakim realized this and paid tribute to Nebuchadnezzar. After three years, however, he rebelled. Nothing happened immediately, but in 598 Nebuchadnezzar began marching west.

   c. Jehoiakim died, and his eighteen-year-old son Jehoiachin ascended to the throne. He had ruled only three months when Jerusalem surrendered (597). The first deportation began.

   d. Nebuchadnezzar placed Jehoiachin's uncle, whom the Babylonian king renamed Zedekiah, on the throne. In 588, under pressure from the pro-Egyptian party in court, Zedekiah rebelled.

   e. Nebuchadnezzar immediately laid siege to Jerusalem. Within a short time, of all the cities and towns in Judah, only Jerusalem, Lachish, and Azekah remained free. They also ultimately fell.

   f. In the month of Av of 586, the wall of Jerusalem was breached and the city was razed and pillaged. The Temple was destroyed and its treasures carried off. Zedekiah was blinded and taken in chains with his court to Babylon.

3. The Exile

   a. Nebuchadnezzar appointed a Judean aristocrat named Gedaliah to the governorship. He was viewed by some Judeans as a puppet. He was betrayed by a member of his own court and killed. This caused even more Jews to go to Egypt and Babylon, thereby hastening the Babylonian Exile.

   b. During the Exile the Jews formed colonies and settled down to live as normally as possible. Many remained farmers as their fathers had been, but some entered commercial occupations. Of these, several attained prominence in the Babylonian Empire.

4. Persian Campaigns

   a. Cyrus of Persia was meanwhile beginning to consolidate his power and expand his territory. He moved north into Asia Minor and subdued the Lydian Empire ruled by Croesus. He then looked back toward Babylon.

b. In 539 the Persians attacked. They defeated Babylon in the decisive battle at Opis on the Tigris River, shifting the center of power in the ancient world to Persia.

5. Persian Rule and the Return From Exile

a. Under Nabonidus, the last Babylonian king, gods of other regions had been brought to Babylon. Cyrus instituted a new policy and reverently returned the idols to their own cities. He also returned the vessels of the Temple which had been taken from Jerusalem. Cyrus also allowed the Jews to return to their land.

b. In 538 the first group (approximately fifty thousand persons) traveled under the leadership of a Jewish noble named Sheshbazzar. A person named Zerubbabel is also mentioned.

c. Some scholars believe that Zerubbabel is just another name for Sheshbazzar; others believe that Zerubbabel is Sheshbazzar's successor. According to one account, Zerubbabel, a grandson of Jehoiachin and therefore of Davidic descent, tried to revive the ceremonial religious practices in Jerusalem by setting up an altar and by reinstating observance of the festivals. He also made efforts to begin the rebuilding of the Temple. After his reign the high priests assumed more religious and political power in Jerusalem.

d. The first thing the returning Jews did in Jerusalem was erect an altar and institute daily offerings.

e. Shortly after this, the Samaritans approached and proposed joint worship. The Jews refused because they viewed the Samaritans as syncretistic, as incorporating other religious practices into the true faith of Israel.

f. Consequently, the rebuffed Samaritans were hostile and obstructionist, interfering as much as possible with the rebuilding of the Temple.

g. Meanwhile, Cyrus installed his son Cambyses as governor of Babylonia. When Cyrus was killed in 529, Cambyses took the throne. Cambyses annexed Egypt to the Persian Empire. Shortly after this, in 522, he died after he had been usurped from the throne.

h. One of Cambyses' officers overthrew the usurper, but this new ruler, Darius, spent the next two years putting down petty rebellions.

i. The Temple was completed in 515, and the Jews continued under Persian rule until Alexander the Great conquered Asia Minor in 334 or 333.

B. *Ezra*

1. Ezra in Babylon

   a. Ezra, a pious Jew who was in Exile, heard that conditions among Jews remaining in Jerusalem were very bad. For example, the city lay unfortified, and intermarriage with gentiles was common.

   b. This news dismayed Ezra, and he petitioned Artaxerxes I to allow him to return with a group of exiles. The Persian emperors generally were very tolerant of their subjects' religions, and Artaxerxes I was no exception.

   c. Not only did Ezra receive permission to return, he was also presented with offerings to buy sacrificial animals for Temple use. In addition, he was given access to the Persian treasury and authorization to set up a legal system to teach and enforce Jewish law and the laws of the king.

2. Ezra in Jerusalem

   a. Most scholars fix the date of Ezra's arrival in Jerusalem at c. 457, during the reign of Artaxerxes I. However, it has also been suggested that the date of his arrival should be placed at c. 397, during the reign of Artaxerxes II.

   b. Ezra immediately required all Jewish men to divorce their foreign wives and abandon the children of such mixed marriages. The issue was not racial purity; rather, Ezra tried to keep the nation of Israel true to the faith and laws of their fathers. It was thought that strict observance of the Law would be less likely with non-Jewish spouses.

   c. Ezra's second act was to read the Law to all the populace. Subsequently, the entire community bound itself in a solemn covenant to observe the Law and keep the commandments. Because of this, Ezra is called the second lawgiver.

C. *Nehemiah*

1. Nehemiah in Persia

   a. Nehemiah, who was cupbearer to Artaxerxes I (465-424), learned of all the difficulties and dangers faced by the Jews in Palestine. The most serious problem was the condition of the walls of Jerusalem: They had not been rebuilt after the city was razed by Nebuchadnezzar.

   b. This troubled Nehemiah greatly. He petitioned the king for a leave of absence. This he obtained, and was even made governor of Judah. His governorship is very significant; it meant that Judah was now separate from Samaria.

   c. Nehemiah was also given permission and funds to improve the Temple and to rebuild the walls of the city and the city gate. One reason for the granting of these favors was that Egypt was growing restless and Artaxerxes wanted Palestine to be friendly.

2. Nehemiah in Jerusalem

   a. On the third night that Nehemiah was in Jerusalem, he rode around the city walls in order to determine the extent of the damage. Then he gathered the priests and elders and discussed the rebuilding project with them. They were enthusiastic. Plans were made to begin the rebuilding.

   b. Antagonistic forces included Sanballat, the governor of Samaria; Tobiah, an Ammonite slave; and Geshem, chief of a tribe in northwest Arabia. These three claimed that rebuilding the walls was an act of rebellion. When these insinuations did not work, Sanballat started guerrilla warfare. It was necessary for those building the wall to arm themselves in order to continue the construction.

   c. Those who were helping Nehemiah build had no income. They were therefore forced to go into debt, sometimes even to the extent of putting their children up as security against a loan. When Nehemiah heard of this he was furious. He called the rich people together and roundly condemned them for taking advantage of the rebuilding of Jerusalem and persuaded them to cancel the debts and return all security.

d. Nehemiah finished the wall in spite of open accusations against him by his enemies and installed his brother Hanani and another man, Hananiah, to rule Jerusalem. Nehemiah returned to Susa to his job as cupbearer. Within a few years, however, he was forced to return to Jerusalem because:

(1) the Sabbath laws were not enforced, and wine presses were allowed to operate on the Sabbath;

(2) intermarriage with non-Jews was occurring at a rapid rate (even the grandson of the High Priest);

(3) Eliashib the High Priest had allowed Tobiah, who opposed the rebuilding of the wall (see above), to live in the Temple itself; and

(4) the Levites were not being paid and had therefore abandoned their Temple duties to return to farming.

e. In a short time, Nehemiah threw Tobiah out of the Temple, restored the Levites, and rectified the other abuses.

D. *Conclusion*

1. This period of Exile and Restoration was very important to the development of Judaism and brought several important changes in Judaism's focus and practice.

a. Prior to the Exile, the religion of the Israelites was Temple centered; it was a national religion of ritual and sacrifice. During the Exile there was no Temple. The institution of the synagogue was established and became very important. This development was later reflected in the rivalry between the Pharisees and the Sadducees in Palestine after the return.

b. The God of Israel was thought to be active outside the confines of Palestine. This contributed to Judaism becoming a universal religion. In postexilic times idolatry was seen by the Jews as bad for all people, not just the Jews. Sabbath observances also became more important during the Exile.

c. One very significant linguistic change occurred during the Exile. Aramaic replaced Hebrew as the vernacular for the Jews. Aramaic had long been the diplomatic language of the ancient world, but only during the Exile did it replace Hebrew. This had an interesting effect; when the Torah was read in the synagogue, it was no longer true that everyone understood the Hebrew. Consequently, there arose a need for an Aramaic translation. It was thought undesirable to abandon the reading of the Hebrew, so each congregation had an interpreter who would give a verbal translation/interpretation of what was read in Hebrew. Eventually, these Targumim (from the Aramaic word meaning "interpreter") were written down. Three exist today, and they shed much light on the language and exegesis of the time. (See Chapter VI, "Ancient Versions of the Hebrew Bible.")

IV

HELLENISM

The Hellenistic period was one of great philosophical and political activity. From the time that Alexander the Great conquered Asia Minor (c. 334-333 B.C.E.*) to the time of the Roman Empire and even beyond, there was a great exchange of goods and ideas. For the first time, people began to think of themselves as citizens of the world. During this time, the Jews, who had recovered from the Babylonian Captivity, revolted against the forced Hellenism of Antiochus IV and formed an independent state. This independence did not, however, last long, for the Hasmonean State fell to the Romans in 63. But a decisive change had been wrought: Judaism was changing from a religion of temple, priest, and ritual to one of synagogue, Rabbi, and law. With this came an emphasis on philosophy, largely as an attempt to reconcile Jewish thought with Greek rationalism.

A. *Historical Background*

1. Alexander the Great conquered Asia Minor c. 334 and proceeded to conquer Palestine in 332. After his death in 323, his kingdom was divided among his generals, among whom were Ptolemy and Seleucus. Palestine, an important trade center and passageway between Egypt and Asia Minor, was hotly contested, but ultimately Ptolemy controlled Egypt and Palestine, while Seleucus controlled Syria.

2. Under the Ptolemies, life was rather pleasant for the Jews in Palestine; as long as they paid their taxes and obeyed the law they were left alone. It was under the Ptolemies that the Septuagint (LXX), or Greek version of the Hebrew Bible, was accomplished. (See Chapter VI, "Ancient Versions of the Hebrew Bible.") In general, there was considerable intellectual development. Some Jews, particularly the upper classes, became Hellenized, speaking and dressing in the Greek manner. Antiochus III (the Great) fought the Ptolemaic ruler c. 200 and took control of Palestine.

3. Under the Seleucids, life was less pleasant for the Jews. The Seleucids tried to force Hellenism on the people. The Jews reacted against it, especially when their spiritual sovereignty was violated. The most

---

*All dates given in this chapter are B.C.E. (Before the Common Era), often referred to as B.C., unless they are denoted C.E. (Common Era), often referred to as A.D.

insistent Seleucid ruler was Antiochus IV (Epiphanes), who ascended to the throne in 175. Considered insane by some historians, he was a fanatical Hellenizer. In his attempts to institute Greek ways, he tried to stamp out Judaism. This attempt culminated in an act that horrified the Jews—he had a hog slaughtered on the altar of the Temple in Jerusalem. He followed this step with orders that hogs be sacrificed on all other Jewish altars. A priest named Mattathias of the house of Hasmon refused to allow this, and the Maccabean Revolt began.

4. Mattathias and his five sons fled to the hills, where they carried on guerrilla warfare against the Seleucids. After Mattathias's death his son Judah (called The Maccabee) carried on the fight against the Hellenists. They were ultimately successful. In 164 the Temple was cleansed and rededicated.

5. When Alcimus (of a priestly family) was appointed to the office of High Priest, he and his supporters felt their goal had been attained, and they ceased to support Judah, who, by now, was seeking political independence as well as religious freedom. Judah's brother Jonathan continued Judah's role and won the support of many who previously were content with religious freedom alone. Alcimus died, leaving the office of High Priest empty. In return for his support of Alexander Balas—who had gained control in the Seleucid Empire—Jonathan was made High Priest. Simon, who succeeded his brother Jonathan as High Priest and Jewish leader, made friends with the Syrian monarch, and the Jews in Palestine were granted independence.

6. The Hasmoneans

   a. John Hyrcanus (135-105), son of Simon (last of Mattathias's five sons), began a policy of territorial expansion, pushing the Second Commonwealth forward on every side. This policy developed Jewish commerce and national prosperity. One faction among the Jews—the Pharisees, or Separatists—were unhappy with Hyrcanus's shift of alliance to their rivals—the priestly family of Zadok, or the Sadducees. They therefore withdrew from participation in the government. (See Chapter IX, "Jewish Sects.")

   b. John's son Alexander Yannai (104-76) extended territorial frontiers. The extent of his Jewish state rivaled Solomon's. However, his many warlike successes only widened the breach between the king and the Pharisaic opposition. His Sadduceean policies and his usurpation of power led the masses to rebel and civil war was waged against him.

c. Salome Alexandra (76-67) succeeded her husband Alexander Yannai. She surrounded herself with Pharisaic advisers, bringing about peace between Pharisees and Sadducees. Salome appointed her elder son Hyrcanus High Priest. He later attempted to succeed her to the throne.

d. Aristobulus (67-63), Hyrcanus's younger brother, waged civil war in a successful effort to seize his brother's position. Both Hyrcanus and Aristobulus appealed to Rome for support in securing power. In support of Hyrcanus, Pompey marched on Jerusalem in 63 and massacred Aristobulus's followers. The price of Roman aid, however, was the loss of independence. Another Hyrcanus, John's grandson, governed the country as a Roman territory.

B. *Intellectual History*

1. Greek intellectual life emphasized rationalism, logic, and science. During this period there was great scientific development, exemplified by such men as Euclid, Archimedes, Hippocrates, and Eratosthenes. In literature the classical epics of Homer gave way to more practical and realistic material, exemplified by Euripides. Aristotle turned away from metaphysical abstraction (Plato) to humanism and natural science. There was an upsurge of interest in history, biography, and even fiction. There was also a great interest in religion.

2. Various types of religions developed during the Hellenistic period, partly as a result of anxiety brought on by a rapidly changing world, and partly because of increased contact with different cultures. There was a great mixing of East and West during this time.

a. City cults: The city-state had been the basic political unit to the Greek world, but after Philip of Macedon (382-336), it began to break down and the Olympian gods began to lose their central position. Worship of them was still carried on, often with much splendor, but they had ceased to be a living force among the people. In response, local rulers began to be looked upon as divine. An example of this is the Seleucid king Antiochus IV, who referred to himself as God.

b. Mystery religions: In their anxiety and confusion at the changing world, some people turned to a number of esoteric cults which had developed. These hinged on secret initiation and rites, some of which reenacted the death and rising of a fertility deity. All stressed the attainment of immortality and mystical union with the divine. One very large and important cult was Mithraism, which later became one of the great religions of the Roman Empire.

c. Chance/fate religions: Some persons were attracted to the belief that all life is preordained and that everything is dependent on the whim of fate. Man, not in control of his will, is therefore not responsible. Curiously, some adherents of this sort of religion still prayed to their gods for deliverance from difficulties even while believing things were predestined.

d. The philosophical schools: The center for philosophical thought was Athens. The chief philosophical problem was that of Platonic dualism, or how to reconcile the spirit and flesh, form and matter. Among the philosophical schools were the Epicureans, the Stoics (perhaps the strongest), the Skeptics, and others. All based their philosophies on logic.

3. Jewish reaction to Hellenism and Hellenistic Philosophy

a. In an attempt to divorce Judaism from all Hellenistic influence, some separatist sects developed; one of the best known is that of the Essenes, who isolated themselves entirely from any polluting influences.

b. Other groups worked out compromises between Judaism and Hellenism. A notable example of this is Philo of Alexandria, the Hellenistic Jewish philosopher who sought to harmonize Jewish thought with rationalistic Greek philosophy.

c. Some groups, such as the Hasidim, advocated armed resistance to the Hellenizers, and the Maccabean Revolt was partly a result of this sort of reaction.

C. *Effects of the Age of Hellenism*

1. The primary result of the Hellenistic period was that Alexander's conquests opened the borders of the ancient world. No longer could a group remain isolated from the intellectual and political trends of the

rest of the world. Naturally, this brought on initial confusion and anxiety, but it ultimately allowed the development of the idea of world citizenship. Alexander visualized a worldwide culture, influenced by East and West alike.

2. This opening of borders brought about greatly increased contact between different groups and cultures, which led to the development of science and philosophy to a much greater degree than had been previously possible. Judaism was influenced by a variety of forces and, in its reaction to these forces, began to develop a distinctive philosophy. More important, Judaism was freed from its geographical boundaries and became a major world religion.

ROME AND JERUSALEM

The few hundred years surrounding the turn of the millennium were most unsettled times in the Palestinian Jewish community, times during which hopes for religious and political freedom loomed large under oppressive Roman policies. Under such rulers as Herod the Great, the Jewish community suffered intensely. Various sects among the Jews attempted to deal with their life situation in different ways. This was an inevitable but weakening force which left distinct and often hostile divisions in the community. Palestinian Jewry united twice in rebellion against Roman oppression, only to be hopelessly defeated. The greatest loss came in 70 C.E. when, suffering from inner discontent and scarcity of supplies, the Jews in Jerusalem witnessed the loss of their city and their Holy Temple. Jewish life in Palestine, though not completely destroyed, had suffered tragically.

A. *Roman Hegemony Over Palestine (63 B.C.E.-66 C.E.)*

1. Hyrcanus II (c. 63-40 B.C.E.) governed Palestine with nominal authority while Antipater, his chief minister, made most of the decisions. Hyrcanus was deprived of any trace of political authority when Antipater appointed his sons Phasael and Herod as local governors in Jerusalem and the Galilee.

2. Herod (37-4 B.C.E.), his aggressiveness having proven him competent, was named prefect over all of Southern Syria and eventually rose to power in Jerusalem also. This ended the Hasmonean rule. Herod married a granddaughter of Aristobulus II (she was also a daughter of Hyrcanus II) to try to dispel opposition to his royal status among the Jews. Nevertheless, excessive internal troubles with the Hasmoneans eventually led him to execute the most powerful Hasmoneans, including his own wives and their relatives. Herod's long reign was in some ways successful and glorious. Because of his friendship with Rome, he enjoyed absolute power at home and peace with his neighboring countries. Through his diplomacy the boundaries of his kingdom were enlarged and the country enjoyed much prosperity. He launched an extensive building campaign, his devotion to Greek and Roman culture being evident in the cities and palaces he built and rebuilt. He reconstructed the Jerusalem Temple in grand proportions. His absolute power and his devotion to Hellenistic culture and Rome, however, made him hated by the entire Jewish population.

3. After Herod's death in 4 B.C.E. his dominion was divided among his sons. Archelaus ruled Judea. In 6 C.E. Augustus deposed Archelaus and the period of Roman procuratorship began in Palestine. In 6 or 7 C.E. the Jews, especially in Galilee, resisted the census undertaken for financial assessment. This uprising, led by Judah, son of Hezekiah, and the Pharisee Zadok, gave rise to a party known as the Zealots who were vehemently opposed to foreign rule. Other factions of this period were the Essenes and the followers of Jesus. (See Chapter IX, "Jewish Sects.") During the early part of the first century C.E., the Roman procurators held strict control over the Jews in Palestine. This rule was not aggressive, so as to avoid any further uprisings. As the years wore on, the procurators became more harsh and unjust, forcing Judea to seethe with rebellion. The last procurator, Florus, appointed in 64 C.E., was the worst of all. His oppression precipitated a full-scale revolt by the Jewish community. Roman armies were dispatched to quell the rebellion, but the belligerent Zealots had gained control among the Jews. These Zealots were now the leaders of those angry with both the Romans and the wealthy Jews who supported Roman rule. Another war for independence had begun.

B. *The Jewish War (66-73 C.E.)*

1. The Roman emperor Nero was determined to put down the Jewish rebellion. He placed Vespasian in command. Meanwhile, defense measures were taken in the northern provinces, especially in Galilee, by the Jews. Josephus, a moderate who had been to Rome and presumably knew Roman tactics, was appointed military governor of Galilee. The lack of organization and his personal lack of resolution allowed the Romans to quickly conquer the towns and villages in Galilee. (See Chapter XIII, "Josephus.") By the end of 67 C.E. all of northern Palestine had either surrendered to the Romans or been annihilated by them. In 69 C.E. Vespasian had control of virtually all of Palestine except Jerusalem, which had been well fortified by its Jewish commanders. Vespasian, who followed Nero as emperor, left the resolution of the Jewish rebellion in the hands of his son Titus.

2. Meanwhile all the friends of Rome had left Jerusalem. All others remaining in the city were won over to the rebellion either by persuasion or force. But moderate and revolutionary Jewish leaders, though they had fortified the city well, were divided among themselves. This greatly weakened their position. Rome besieged the city, which was taken after several months. On the Ninth of Av in 70 C.E., the Holy Temple was destroyed. Fortresses in the vicinity of

Jerusalem were soon taken. The last to fall was Masada—which had been considered impregnable—in 73 C.E.

C. Relationships with Rome (73-135 C.E.)

1. The war-torn land of Palestine slowly revived in the years following the war. The failure of the revolt quelled the activities of the Zealot party. With the destruction of the Temple, the High Priesthood ended and the function of the priestly Sadduceean party came to an end. Though Rome continued to govern and exact taxes, the Sanhedrin (the scholarly assembly which served as both court and legislature) was reconstituted and its Patriarch became the Jewish authority in matters dealing with Rome. Under Pharisaic leadership, the Jewish community in Palestine gradually rebuilt itself. In an effort to foster religious and intellectual life, Johanan ben Zakkai founded a school at Yavneh. The synagogues and their rabbis became the centers of local Jewish life.

2. In 115 C.E. the Jews of the Diaspora (Egypt, Cyrene, and Cyprus), with the aid of Armenians and Parthians, rose in revolt against Trajan in Rome, but were soon put down amidst much bloodshed.

3. Later, in 132 C.E., Hadrian's attempt to turn Jerusalem into a heathen city, and his revision of a law against mutilations of the body (which included circumcision), precipitated a Jewish revolt in Palestine. Under the leadership of Simeon Bar Kokhba, and with the support of the religious leader Rabbi Akiva, Jerusalem was taken from Roman hands. An attempt was made to restore the Temple. However, Julius Severus waged a war of attrition against the Jewish forces. In 135 C.E. the revolt came to an end. Jerusalem was razed, and a heathen city name Aelia Capitolina was established in its place—a city which the Jews were not allowed to enter. Palestine itself lay in ruins. It was at this time that the Romans named the land "Palestine" in order to dilute further the link between the land and the Jewish people.

4. Many influential persons, seeing the futility of the revolt and fearing Roman oppression, had fled to Jewish communities in the Diaspora, especially to Babylonia. The population which had remained during the revolt had been almost annihilated by war. Though Jewish life was nourished in the new national center in the Galilee, Palestine had suffered severely. The center of Jewish life was now Babylon.

V

THE BIBLE AS LITERATURE

The term *Bible* is derived from the Greek *biblion*, meaning "book." The Hebrew Bible is also called *Tanakh* from the initials of the Hebrew names assigned to its three main sections: Torah ("Law," or "Pentateuch"), *Nevi'im* ("Prophets"), and *Ketubim* ("Writings," or "Hagiographa"). The Hebrew Bible is known as the Old Testament to Christians whose Bible contains New Testament writings. The language of the Bible (except for portions of Daniel and Ezra which are written in Aramaic) is usually regarded as classical Hebrew, an ancient Semitic tongue belonging to the same family as Arabic, Aramaic, Syriac, and Ugaritic. It was spoken by the Israelites until about the third century B.C.E.,* after which it was used only for prayer and literary works. In modern times Hebrew has been revived as a spoken language in Israel. The Hebrew script is consonantal, that is, it lacks vowel signs, and is written from right to left.

The land of the Bible was ancient Canaan, a small area on the eastern shore of the Mediterranean Sea. Its capital since about 1000 has been the city of Jerusalem, the site of the ancient Jewish Temple built by King Solomon. The country has also been known as Palestine, from the ancient Philistines who lived in the coastal area. The area of Canaan is generally that of modern Israel.

The people of the Bible are the Hebrews or Jews. They trace their descent from the twelve sons of the patriarch Jacob, who was also called Israel, hence the terms *Israelites, Children of Israel, Land of Israel.* The word *Jew* is derived from the names "Judah" or "Judea," the southern section of the ancient land of Israel. The Bible is a collection of the national and sacred literature of the Jews and has become the heritage of Christianity and Islam as well.

A. *Historical Background of the Bible (Summary and Review)*

1. The Biblical period extends from about 2000 to 450, that is, from the earliest period associated with the patriarchs to the time of Ezra and Nehemiah. No exact chronology for Israelite history is possible prior to 1000.

---

*All dates given in this chapter are B.C.E. (Before the Common Era), often referred to as B.C., unless they are denoted C.E. (Common Era), often referred to as A.D.

2. The Age of the Patriarchs (c. 2000-1750)

   This is the period of history's first empire, ruled by Sargon I of Akkadia, in Mesopotamia. It also marked the birth of the first central kingdom in Egypt.

3. The Sojourn in Egypt and the Exodus (c. 1750-1250)

   a. In the eighteenth century the Egyptian kingdom was overthrown by Semitic invaders (known as Hyksos) from Asia. The descent of the Twelve Tribes of Israel to Egypt is associated with this period.

   b. In the sixteenth century the Hyksos were overthrown by a national Egyptian movement and this event is linked by some to the transition of the Hebrew settlers into bondage. The new Egyptian rulers extended their domination over all of Palestine and Syria.

   c. An exact dating of the Exodus is, as yet, impossible. It is believed to be between 1450 and 1270.

   d. Meanwhile, Mesopotamia was under the rule of foreign nations.

4. The Conquest of Canaan and the Period of the Judges (c. 1400-1000)

   The date of the conquest of Canaan by the Hebrews is variously set at c. 1400 or c. 1250, but in any event, it coincided with the decline of Egyptian power over Palestine. The same period marks the beginning of the Assyrian Empire in Mesopotamia and the arrival of the "Sea People," the Philistines, in coastal Palestine.

5. The United Kingdom of David and Solomon (c. 1000-930)

   A temporary lapse in power of both Egypt and Assyria allowed the Hebrew state under David (c. 1005-965) and Solomon (965-930) to prosper and become the most important state in the eastern Mediterranean.

6. The Divided Kingdom (928-586)

   a. After the death of Solomon, the Hebrew Kingdom was forcibly divided into the states of Israel (the Northern Kingdom) and Judah (the Southern Kingdom).

b. The two states suffered from repeated invasions by the Egyptians (tenth century) and by the Assyrians (from the second half of the eighth century). The latter finally brought an end to Israel in 721.

c. Judah became the vassal of Assyria. Following the downfall of Assyria, Judah was invaded first by the Egyptians and later by the Babylonians, who finally destroyed the kingdom in 586. Jerusalem was destroyed and the inhabitants were taken as captives to Babylon. Thus began the First Exile.

7. Exile and Return (586-445)

a. About 539 the Babylonian Empire was overthrown by the Persians, whose king, Cyrus, permitted the exiled Jews to return to Palestine (538) and rebuild the Temple.

b. The ensuing century saw the struggle between the returning Jews and the Samaritans, who are variously considered to be descendants of Israelites not deported by the Assyrians, or foreign settlers brought by the Assyrians, or a fusion of the two.

c. The rebuilding of the Temple of Jerusalem was completed in 515.

d. A further stage of the restoration took place with the return of more exiles under Ezra and Nehemiah in the middle of the fifth century. This marked the end of the Biblical period.

B. *Contents of the Bible*

1. Torah (Pentateuch, or "Law")

a. To the Jews, the Torah is by far the most important part of the Bible, embodying the Law, which is the essence of traditional Judaism. In fact, the term *Torah* has been loosely applied to the entire body of Jewish sacred literature.

b. Portions of the Torah are read every Sabbath in the synagogue. For this purpose the entire Torah has been subdivided into fifty-four weekly portions, known as *sedrah* or *parashah* ("portions").

c. The Torah or Pentateuch consists of five books: Genesis, Exodus, Leviticus, Numbers, and Deuteronomy.

(1) Genesis and part of Exodus are mainly historical narrative.

(2) The remainder of Exodus and the bulk of Leviticus, Numbers, and Deuteronomy are made up of legal material, and this is why the entire collection is known as Law.

(3) Sometimes the Book of Joshua is added to the Torah. The whole is then described as the Hexateuch ("Six Books").

d. Archaeological discoveries in Mesopotamia have shown that certain events described in the Bible are paralleled in ancient Sumerian and Babylonian documents.

(1) One set of these contains the so-called Gilgamesh Epic. It also includes accounts of the creation and of the flood which resemble the Biblical account.

(2) Scholars have also noted similarities between ancient Babylonian laws attributed to King Hammurabi (eighteenth century) inscribed on a stele (see Appendix D, "Glossary") found in 1901. Whether there is any connection or link between Biblical and Babylonian material is still a subject of controversy.

2. Prophets (*Nevi'im*)

a. Former Prophets (The Historical Books)

The books of Joshua, Judges, First and Second Samuel, and First and Second Kings tell the story of Israel from the death of Moses through the times of Israel's judges and kings until the fall of Jerusalem in 586.

(1) It is interesting to note that practically no records of Israel's history other than the Bible have survived. It must be kept in mind, however, that the historical books of the Bible were written as religious rather than as secular history. Thus, certain kings described in the Bible as "wicked" are known from outside sources to have been very successful leaders.

(2) Postexilic histories are also recounted in the Hagiographa books of First and Second Chronicles, Ezra, and Nehemiah. Chronicles recounts an historical review from earliest times

through the history of the kingdom of Judah. The books of Ezra and Nehemiah contain a history of the Jews from the end of the exile to the second half of the fifth century.

b. Latter Prophets

The Latter Prophets consist of the oracles of the major prophets (Isaiah, Jeremiah, and Ezekiel) and the minor prophets (Hosea, Joel, Amos, Obadiah, Jonah, Micah, Nahum, Habakkuk, Zephaniah, Haggai, Zechariah, and Malachi).

(1) The prophets voiced the religious concept of ethical monotheism, the concept of God as the only ruler of the universe, and the brotherhood of mankind under God.

(2) They emphasized the relationship between God and Israel through the covenant; they brought social, moral, and humanitarian issues to the forefront; some of them described suffering as the result of transgression and planted the idea of "the remnant will return." This last idea gave rise to the messianic hopes of postexilic times.

3. Hagiographa (*Ketubim* or "Writings")

The third section of the Hebrew Bible consists of twelve books of assorted types.

a. The historical books of Ezra, Nehemiah, and Chronicles I and II were discussed above.

b. Several books can be called wisdom literature in that they contain the wisdom of sages on topics concerning the universal problems of life. These wisdom books include Job, Proverbs, and Ecclesiastes.

c. The Book of Psalms is a collection of prayers and hymns.

d. Each of the Five Scrolls (*megillot*) is read in the synagogue on an appointed day: the Book of Ruth (relating to the period of the Judges) on Pentecost (*Shavuot*); Songs of Songs (a collection of love poems) on Passover; Lamentations (elegies on the destruction of Jerusalem) on the Ninth of Av; Ecclesiastes on the Feast of Tabernacles (*Sukkot*); and Esther (relating to the persecution under a Persian king) on *Purim*. (See Chapter XVIII, "Jewish Liturgy.")

e. The Book of Daniel is noted for its apocalyptic tone.

C. *Literary Analysis of Biblical Literature*

1. History, narrative, and biography form the major part of the prose sections of the Bible, particularly the historical books (Joshua to Second Kings, Ezra and Nehemiah, First and Second Chronicles).

2. Laws comprise a significant section of the Pentateuch, including an important part of Exodus and the bulk of Leviticus, Numbers, and Deuteronomy.

3. Several sections of the Bible can be described as classical short stories. Such stories make up entire books, such as Ruth or Esther, or appear within the context of larger works, such as the stories of Joseph (Genesis 37-49), Solomon's Judgment (I Kings 3), Samson (Judges 13-16), and others.

4. Parables and fables (Judges 9, II Kings 14:9), dreams and their interpretation (Genesis 28 and 41), miracles (Exodus 14, I Kings 18), and other folkloristic literature appear throughout the Bible.

5. Prophetic literature consists of oracular poetry interspersed with biographical and autobiographical passages. This is an element of great importance both from the point of view of religion and of literary style.

6. Orations of the prophets and other leaders make up the books of the Latter Prophets, but are also found in the Torah (e.g., Moses' farewell speech in Deuteronomy 33) and elsewhere (Samuel's speech, I Samuel 8:11-20).

7. Psalms, prayers, hymns, songs, and lamentations are among the most significant poetic contributions to Biblical literature. They make up two entire books (Psalms and Lamentations) and also appear within the general context of other books, e.g., the Song of the Crossing of the Red Sea (Exodus 15), Deborah's Song (Judges 5), David's Lament for Saul and Jonathan (II Samuel 1).

8. The entire books of Proverbs and Ecclesiastes are devoted to proverbs and maxims which are of universal rather than specifically Jewish character.

9. Several sections of the Bible (such as the Book of Job and the Song of Songs) are considered by certain scholars to be dramatic, or theatrical, works. However this theory has been challenged.

D. *Influence of the Bible*

1. The Bible surpasses any other written work both in importance and circulation. It has been translated into more than nine hundred languages.

2. It is the basis of three great monotheistic religions—Judaism, Christianity, and Islam.

3. Biblical ethics were and are vital in the development of Western civilization and society.

   a. From the Prophets comes the concept of ethical monotheism with its consequent sharp attacks on social injustice and inequality.

   b. The Sabbath was the first concept of a day of rest, the basis of much labor legislation.

   c. Biblical sanitary codes foreshadowed health regulations.

4. The Bible brought education to masses of common people in many countries.

5. Various scripts, such as Armenian and Gothic, were devised specifically for Bible translations.

6. Translation of the Bible into various European languages had revolutionary effects. For example, Luther's German Bible became the basis for the modern German language, and the King James Version standardized modern English. The English language is sprinkled with adages and idioms from the Bible, such as "by the skin of his teeth" (Job 19:20), "put words in his mouth" (Exodus 4:15), "a man after my own heart" (I Samuel 13:14), and so forth.

7. The Bible has supplied themes for many of the world's greatest artists.

   a. Some works included are Dante's *Divine Comedy*, Michelangelo's *Moses*, Milton's *Paradise Lost*, Mendelssohn's *Elijah*, Haydn's

Creation, Ruben's *Elijah in the Fiery Chariot*, Byron's *The Destruction of Sennacherib*, Saint-Saen's *Samson and Delilah*, and Stravinsky's *Symphony of Psalms.*

b. The titles of two of John Steinbeck's books, *East of Eden* and *Grapes of Wrath*, have biblical backgrounds, as does Irwin Shaw's *The Young Lions* (Nahum 2:13).

8. The Bible was an important influence in the Protestant Reformation and subsequent developments that brought most of the early settlers to America.

a. Pilgrim Fathers and other pioneers consciously shaped their way of life along Biblical lines.

b. The first Thanksgiving feast was modeled after that described in the Pentateuch.

c. Preachers during the American Revolution identified King George III as Pharaoh, Washington as Moses, and the revolutionaries themselves as the Children of Israel.

d. The inscription on the Liberty Bell is taken from the Book of Leviticus 25:10: "Proclaim liberty throughout the land unto all the inhabitants thereof."

e. Negro spirituals, which have greatly enriched American culture, are based, to a great extent, on Biblical themes and phrases: "Joshua Fit the Battle of Jericho," "Go Down Moses," "Dry Bones," and "Swing Low, Sweet Chariot."

THE MAKING OF THE BIBLE

The text of the Bible is the work of many authors in various ages and cultures spanning well over one thousand years of history. Evidences in the Torah, particularly the legal codes, reflect traditions which date back to the Mesopotamian culture of the eighteenth century. In general the Torah is an account of the Patriarchs and tribes in their nomadic wanderings among the deserts and trade routes of the Middle East (c. 2000-1000). The historical and prophetical books cover the period from about 1000 to 538, when the Egyptian, Phoenician, Assyrian, and Babylonian empires surrounded or encompassed the monarchies of Israel and Judah. The last four Biblical books reflect influences from the Persian Empire and the beginnings of Greek influence dating from the fourth century. Thus, the Biblical texts stand as a treasury of information about ancient Middle Eastern cultural and political history.

Exact dates for the original composition of Biblical texts are, in most cases, not known. However, it is known that by the second century, all of the books of the Hebrew Bible were written and generally divided into the three groupings of Torah, Prophets, and Writings (Hagiographa).

The Babylonian Exile and period following it found the Bible, especially the Torah, in a position of great importance to a Judaism trying to survive the loss of the Temple and Temple worship, which had previously been the center of national and religious cohesion. With religion becoming more individualized, the reading and study of the Scriptures became the primary religious expression as well as the religious duty of every Jew. As a result of this, the Scriptural texts became standardized, and the work of accurate transmission emerged as a task of utmost importance. Gradually, schools of Scriptural exegesis were founded and expanded to produce a wealth of post-Biblical Jewish literature and tradition.

A. *Authorship*

1. Traditional view: The Talmud (*Baba Bathra* 14b-15a) ascribes authorship of the Torah to Moses, other books to Joshua, Samuel, David, Solomon, Jeremiah, etc. down to Ezra and the Men of the Great Synagogue. (See table on authorship at the end of this chapter.)

2. Modern Biblical Criticism

   a. During the late nineteenth and early twentieth centuries C.E., a German scholar, Julius Wellhausen, and his school popularized the "documentary hypothesis" on the question of the authorship of the Bible. Based on the use of different names for God, linguistic and stylistic variations, as well as other internal signs of a composite structure, the documentary hypothesis assigns authorship of Biblical texts as follows:

      (1) The J or *Jahwist* document (J for the initial letter in the English divine name Jehovah for Hebrew *YHWH*), allegedly a product of the Southern Kingdom of Judah in about the ninth century. (See Tetragrammaton in the Glossary.)

(2) The E or *Elohist* document (E for the initial letter in the Hebrew divine name *Elohim*), supposedly a product of the Northern Kingdom of Israel in about the eighth century.

(3) The D or *Deuteronomist* document, which it is said, stemmed from King Josiah's religious reform during the late seventh century.

(4) The P or *Priestly* document or code is said to be a reflection of Israel's religious development under Ezra's reform in about the fifth century.

b. According to this view, there were three redactions: the *Prophetic*, which combined the documents J and E; the *Deuteronomic*, which combined JE with D; and the *Priestly*, which combined JED with P, resulting in the Torah substantially as we now have it.

c. Though this documentary theory has been applied primarily to the Torah, corresponding methods have been applied to questions of authorship of the Prophets and Hagiographa. Generally, critics ascribe the latter two Biblical sections to later periods than does traditional view.

3. Current Jewish Thought on Biblical Authorship

a. Concerning the traditional view of Biblical authorship, scholars recognize that the Talmud implies that some of the later authors "edited" rather than "wrote" the books attributed to them. The fundamental assumption implies that the Bible is the product of consecutive additions and editions, the last books being completed in the time of Ezra, and that with the death of the last minor prophets (Haggai, Zechariah, and Malachi), "the spirit of prophecy ceased in Israel."

b. Jewish scholars of recent years have recognized the ingenuity and scholarship of the documentary hypothesis and the permanent residue of truth it has contributed to Biblical scholarship. However, for the most part, the conclusions of Wellhausen's theory have been rejected and the current trend in Biblical criticism is toward greater conservatism. The current view is largely based on recent archaeological discoveries which support the general trustworthiness and substantial historicity of Biblical tradition.

B. *Development of the Hebrew Standardized Text ("Canon")*

1. The word *canon* comes from the Greek word for *measuring rod.* When applied to the Bible, it refers to those books which have come under the measuring rod, or standard of admissibility to the Sacred Scriptures. Thus, those books are called canonical which official religious authorities have designated as inspired by the Divine Spirit.

2. There are various theories regarding the development of the Hebrew Bible.

   a. Some scholars believe that the Law (Torah) received canonical status in the fifth century, the Prophets in the beginning of the second century, and the Hagiographa (Writings) at the Synod of Jabneh (Greek: *Jamnia*; Hebrew: *Yavneh*) about 90 C.E., though it is believed that controversy over some of the Hagiographa continued well into the second century C.E.

   b. Others believe that the Law, Prophets, and Hagiographa developed concurrently and were canonized at the same time.

3. Variations in the number of books as well as the order of their appearance differentiate Jewish, Protestant, and Catholic Bibles.

   a. A group of sacred writings dating from the same period as the Hagiographa, the Apocrypha (see Chapter VIII, "Apocrypha and Pseudepigrapha"), was not considered canonical by the Jews, but was included in Septuagint (Greek translation of the Old Testament). As the Hebrew Bible was further translated and passed on, the Catholic Church retained the apocryphal books as canonical, while the standard Protestant and Jewish Bibles did not include them. Thus, until today, discrepancies in the canons of the Jews, Protestants, and Catholics exist.

   b. The Hebrew Bible is divided into three sections: Torah, Prophets, and Hagiographa. Catholic and Protestant Old Testaments are divided into the books of the Torah, historical books, and wisdom literature. Differences of opinion concerning the categorization of some books have caused the variation in the order of appearance of Old Testament books in Jewish, Protestant, and Catholic Bibles.

   c. Traditionally, the Hebrew Bible consists of twenty-four books. By dividing Samuel, Kings, and Chronicles into two books each and by individually enumerating Ezra, Nehemiah, and the twelve minor prophets, some list the total number of books of the Hebrew canon as thirty-nine. The Roman Catholic Old Testament contains a total of forty-six books—the thirty-nine separate volumes of the Hebrew Bible plus seven separate apocryphal books accepted by Catholics as canonical.

C. *Textual Transmission*

1. As was stated above, a passage in the Talmud (*Baba Bathra*) ascribes the collection, arrangement, and final redaction of the Biblical text to the Men of the Great Synagogue during the Persian Period.

2. Originally, the texts were not uniform and consisted only of consonants with some letters (Waw, Yod, He) being used occasionally as vowel letters.

3. Following the Babylonian Exile, as Hebrew fell into disuse and Aramaic became the daily language of the Jews in Palestine, the need to help the reader with correct punctuation and understanding of words gave rise to an extensive surge of Biblical textual study.

4. The transmission of the text was the responsibility of the scribes (Sopherim), specialists in the copying and linguistic interpretation of Biblical texts.

   a. Tradition has it that the scribes counted letters as they copied Biblical texts to ensure the accuracy and the uniformity of the consonantal text which by this time had become standard.

   b. They indicated *Qeri* (how the word should be read) when *Ketiv* (the written consonantal text) represented an unapproved reading.

   c. They pointed out *Plene* (use of consonants as vowel letters) and defective spellings.

   d. They created a set of notes which clarified difficulties in the text. This set of interpretative aids, known as *Masorah* (tradition), was handed on to later generations of Biblical specialists as a standard for the interpretation of problematic texts.

e. The turbulent era of the destruction of the Temple, the Bar Kokhba Revolt, and the Diaspora interrupted the textual work of the scribes.

5. Between the sixth and the tenth centuries another group of textual specialists (called Masoretes because they based their work on the *Masorah* of the earlier scribes) emerged and became the authoritative group on interpretation of Biblical texts.

   a. Because of the threat of the loss of the correct pronunciation of Scriptural texts, vowel systems for the Hebrew language arose during this period.

   b. Of the three vowel systems, the Palestinian and Babylonian systems were supralinear; that is, vowel markers were inserted above the consonants. However, these systems were gradually replaced by the official acceptance of the Tiberian infralinear pointing in which vowel markers were inserted within and below the consonants (e.g., אֶחָד).

   c. The Masoretes also added a detailed system of diacritical marks which served as accents, punctuation, and musical notes for use in worship services.

   d. Thus, by the tenth century the Masoretes had officially determined the reading, vocalization, and punctuation of the Biblical texts.

6. By the thirteenth century, as Jews, Christians, and Moslems engaged in religious debates, the need arose for a common vehicle of reference to specific Biblical passages. Thus, chapters and verses of the Bible came to be numbered.

7. Today, in synagogue services, the Torah and the scroll of Esther are read from unvocalized, handwritten parchment scrolls.

THE BOOKS OF THE BIBLE:
TRADITIONAL DIVISION OF THE BOOKS

The Law (Torah)

1. Genesis
2. Exodus
3. Leviticus
4. Numbers
5. Deuteronomy

The Prophets (Nevi'im)

6. Joshua
7. Judges
8. Samuel I and II
9. Kings I and II
10. Isaiah
11. Jeremiah
12. Ezekiel
13. The Twelve Minor Prophets

The Hagiographa (Writings, Ketubim)

14. Psalms
15. Proverbs
16. Job
17. Song of Songs
18. Ruth
19. Lamentations
20. Ecclesiastes
21. Esther
22. Daniel
23. Ezra-Nehemiah
24. Chronicles I and II

THE HEBREW NAMES OF THE BOOKS OF THE BIBLE

Nahum	נַחוּם	.21	Genesis	בְּרֵאשִׁית	.1
Habakkuk	חֲבַקּוּק	.22	Exodus	שְׁמוֹת	.2
Zephaniah	צְפַנְיָה	.23	Leviticus	וַיִּקְרָא	.3
Haggai	חַגַּי	.24	Numbers	בְּמִדְבַּר	.4
Zechariah	זְכַרְיָה	.25	Deuteronomy	דְּבָרִים	.5
Malachi	מַלְאָכִי	.26	Joshua	יְהוֹשֻׁעַ	.6
Psalms	תְּהִלִּים	.27	Judges	שֹׁפְטִים	.7
Proverbs	מִשְׁלֵי	.28	Samuel I	שְׁמוּאֵל א	.8
Job	אִיּוֹב	.29	Samuel II	שְׁמוּאֵל ב	.9
Ruth	רוּת	.30	Kings I	מְלָכִים א	.10
Song of Songs	שִׁיר הַשִּׁירִים	.31	Kings II	מְלָכִים ב	.11
Ecclesiastes	קֹהֶלֶת	.32	Isaiah	יְשַׁעְיָהוּ	.12
Lamentations	אֵיכָה	.33	Jeremiah	יִרְמְיָהוּ	.13
Esther	אֶסְתֵּר	.34	Ezekiel	יְחֶזְקֵאל	.14
Daniel	דָּנִיאֵל	.35	Hosea	הוֹשֵׁעַ	.15
Ezra	עֶזְרָא	.36	Joel	יוֹאֵל	.16
Nehemiah	נְחֶמְיָה	.37	Amos	עָמוֹס	.17
Chronicles I	דִּבְרֵי הַיָּמִים א	.38	Obadiah	עֹבַדְיָה	.18
Chronicles II	דִּבְרֵי הַיָּמִים ב	.39	Jonah	יוֹנָה	.19
			Micah	מִיכָה	.20

KINGS OF ISRAEL AND JUDAH AND LITERARY PROPHETS

All dates are B.C.E. (B.C.)*

Kings of Israel		Kings of Judah	
928-912	Jeroboam	930-917	Rehoboam
912-911	Nadab	917-915	Abijah
911-888	Baasha	915-875	Asa
888-887	Elah	875-851	Jehoshaphat
887	Zimri	851-844	Jehoram
887-876	Omri	844-843	Ahaziah
876-853	Ahab	843-837	Athaliah
853	Ahaziah	837-798	Joash
853-843	Jehoram	798-780	Amaziah
843-816	Jehu	780-740	Azariah (Uzziah)
816-800	Jehoahaz	740-735	Jotham
800-785	Jehoash	735-720	Ahaz
785-745	Jeroboam II	720-692	Hezekiah
744	Zechariah	692-638	Manasseh
743	Shallum	638-637	Amon
743-736	Menahem	637-608	Josiah
736-735	Pekahiah	608	Jehoahaz
736-730	Pekah	608-598	Jehoiakim
730-721	Hosea	598-597	Jehoiachin
		597-586	Zedekiah

Literary Prophets			
c. 750	Amos	before or during	
c. 740	Hosea	Exile	Obadiah
c. 730	Isaiah	520	Haggai
c. 730	Micah	c. 520	Zechariah
c. 630	Zephaniah	c. 450	Malachi
c. 611	Nahum	after 500	Joel and Jonah
c. 586	Jeremiah		
early Exile	Ezekiel		
Exile	Habakkuk		

---

*Dates are taken from *The Standard Jewish Encyclopedia,* Cecil Roth, ed. Jerusalem: Encyclopedia Publishing Company, Ltd., 1959, and from M. Mansoor, *General Survey of Hebrew Literature in Translation—The Biblical Period.* Madison: The University of Wisconsin Extension Division, 1959.

TRADITIONAL JEWISH AUTHORSHIP OF
THE BOOKS OF THE BIBLE
(Baba Bathra 14b)

Book	Traditional Author
Genesis	For the Five Books: Moses
Exodus	
Leviticus	
Numbers	
Deuteronomy	
Joshua	Joshua (also last eight verses of Deuteronomy)
Judges	Samuel
I and II Samuel	Samuel
I and II Kings	Jeremiah
Isaiah	Hezekiah and his company*
Jeremiah	Jeremiah
Ezekiel	The Men of the Great Synagogue*
The Twelve Minor Prophets	The Men of the Great Synagogue*
Psalms	David (incorporating the production of the ten elders)
Job	Moses
Song of Songs	Hezekiah and his company*
Ruth	Samuel
Lamentations	Jeremiah
Ecclesiastes	Hezekiah and his company*
Esther	The Men of the Great Synagogue*
Daniel	The Men of the Great Synagogue*
Ezra, Nehemiah	Ezra
I and II Chronicles	Ezra

---

*Transcribed words revealed to others.

VI

ANCIENT VERSIONS OF THE HEBREW BIBLE

The presence of Jewish communities in foreign lands necessitated translation of the Bible into languages other than Hebrew. These translations both preserved the central place of the Torah in the lives of non-Hebrew speaking Jews, and provided the means through which the Torah reached all nations.

For the Jews in exile in Babylon, Aramaic quickly replaced Hebrew as the spoken language. This change was much more gradual in Palestine. With the return of the exiles to Palestine, Aramaic vied with Hebrew for the vernacular use. The result was that Hebrew was retained as the literary language while Aramaic became the popular spoken language, necessitating translation of the Torah for the Aramaic-speaking masses. Thus, probably from the time of Nehemiah, an oral Aramaic translation of the Bible was used in the synagogue along with the reading of the Scriptures in Hebrew. Similar circumstances gave rise to Syriac translations of the Scriptures from about the second century C.E.* (Syriac is an Eastern-Aramaic dialect.)

Alexandria, an Egyptian port, was a prominent cultural center during the Hellenistic period. According to Josephus Flavius, the Jewish historian of the first century (see Chapter XIII, "Josephus"), Jews had settled there since the third century and, by Roman time, constituted a significant proportion of the population. These Jews were bombarded with and immersed in Hellenistic culture, and quickly adopted its language. Hence, when Greek became their lingua franca, a Greek translation of the Hebrew Bible was needed. Therefore, the Septuagint was made. Later on, after it was officially adopted by the Christian Church, the Septuagint was rejected by the Jews.

When the Hellenistic culture was replaced by the Roman, Latin replaced Greek. Christendom's official Latin translation of the Bible, the Vulgate, was carried to all parts of the Roman Empire. It became the basis for virtually all medieval translations of the Bible into Western European languages. Only in the sixteenth century did any scholars return to the original Hebrew as the basis for translation.

It is clear that these early translations were vital after Hebrew was no longer spoken. They are important also to scholars today, both to indicate Hebrew pronunciation in Intertestamental times and to clarify textual problems in the Hebrew Bible. Furthermore, translations from texts other

---

*All dates given in this chapter are C.E. (Common Era), often referred to as A.D., unless they are denoted B.C.E. (Before the Common Era), often referred to as B.C.

that the Masoretic preserve variant textual traditions of the Intertestamental period.

A. *Septuagint*

1. Name

a. Septuagint (Latin) means *seventy*, from the number of scholars (actually seventy-two) said to have been engaged in this translation of the Torah into Greek.

b. The name Septuagint was originally applied to the Torah only, but as the Prophets and the Hagiographa also became translated into Greek, the designation was extended to cover the Greek translation of the entire Hebrew Bible.

c. The Septuagint is often designated as LXX, the Roman numerals for seventy.

2. Background

a. The Letter of Aristeas is a pseudepigraphical work believed to have been written by a second century B.C.E. Egyptian Jew. It describes the legendary origin of the Septuagint—that Ptolemy II, king of Egypt (285-247 B.C.E.), invited a group of Jewish scholars to Alexandria to translate the Scriptures of the Jews into Greek for inclusion in the Alexandria Library. The work was probably written for the purpose of extolling the importance of Greek friendship for the Jews and to point out the contribution the Jews could make to Hellenistic culture.

b. It is likely that the Jewish community in Egypt had been so influenced by Hellenistic culture that they needed a Greek translation, especially for liturgical use in the synagogue.

c. It is thought that initially the translation was oral and accompanied the reading of the Hebrew text, and that later, the translation was written down and gradually took the place of the Hebrew Scriptures among Greek-speaking Jews.

d. The Mishnah Tractate *Sopherim* 1:7 says that the Septuagint is the work of five translators, each of whom apparently translated one book of the Pentateuch.

3. Date of the Septuagint

a. The Septuagint translation of the Torah is thought to have been completed by the middle of the third century B.C.E.

b. The Prophets and Hagiographa were probably translated early in the second century B.C.E.

c. Most of the Hebrew Bible was probably translated into Greek by 150 B.C.E., because the prologue to the Greek translation of Ecclesiasticus (Ben Sira), written in 132 B.C.E., refers to the existence of the Scriptures in Greek.

d. Josephus Flavius refers to the tradition of the seventy translators, as do several early Church Fathers. (See Chapter XIII, "Josephus.")

4. Contents of the Septuagint

a. The Septuagint includes all the canonical works of the Hebrew Bible, as well as a number of apocryphal books.

b. The order of books is different from the Hebrew Canon and forms the basis of the Christian Canon of the Old Testament.

5. Language of the Septuagint

The language of the Septuagint is basically the Hellenistic Greek spoken in the empire of Alexander the Great and his successors, though it also contains many elements of Hebrew. It is usually referred to as Koine Greek (i.e., the commonly spoken and written Greek of this period).

6. Style and Literary Evaluation

a. The Septuagint is obviously the work of many translators of varying skills, ranging from excellent translations to obvious errors, glosses, and emendations. The translation of the Torah is the best though it is not always literal. Amos and Ezekiel are good translations, while Isaiah is an inferior rendition. Jeremiah shows the hands of two translators (chapters 1 to 28 and 29 to 57). Job is rendered into excellent Greek, but has been considerably shortened. Esther and Daniel are lengthened in the translation. Numerous later additions and interpolations are detectable.

b. Several portions of the Dead Sea Scrolls were found to agree with the Septuagint rather than with the Hebrew Bible. While this is not necessarily an indication of the superiority of the Greek version, it indicates that the Septuagint translators worked from a Biblical Hebrew version differing from the traditional Hebrew (Masoretic) text probably in circulation at the time.

7. Use and Influence of the Septuagint

a. Though in the beginning, Palestinian Jewry favored and blessed the making of the Septuagint, the Septuagint fell into disfavor for the following reasons:

(1) It contained divergencies from the traditionally accepted Masoretic Hebrew text.

(2) It was used by Jewish sects at variance with the mainstream of Judaism.

(3) It was accepted as the official Biblical text by the Greek-speaking Christians.

b. The Septuagint eventually served as a basis for the Old Latin as well as for the Coptic, Ethiopic, Arabic, and other Biblical translations.

c. The translation of Hebrew names and difficult words in the Septuagint has been of utmost importance in efforts at reconstructing the Hebrew pronunciation of the Intertestamental period.

B. *Other Greek Translations*

1. Aquila's Translation

a. Aquila is believed to have been a convert to Judaism from Pontus in Asia Minor. In the first half of the second century he made a literal translation of the Scriptures from the Hebrew original which replaced the Septuagint as the Bible of Greek-speaking Jews.

b. In his efforts to remain absolutely faithful to the original Masoretic text, Aquila produced an excessively literal translation. At times, his translation is incomprehensible to anyone who lacks knowledge of Hebrew. Difficult Hebrew words were simply transliterated into Greek letters.

c. Aquila's translation, as well as those of Theodotian and Symmachus, was used by Origen in his revision of the Septuagint, the Hexapla.

2. Theodotian's Translation

a. Theodotian is believed to have been another convert to Judaism from Ephesus in Asia Minor in the late second century.

b. His translation displays a strong Jewish spirit, and although literal, it avoids the excessively literal style of Aquila.

3. Symmachus's Translation

a. The author of this translation is thought to have been a Jew or Samaritan converted to Christianity at the end of the second or the beginning of the third century.

b. His Greek is superior to that of Aquila and Theodotian. He did not use any Greek transliterations of Hebrew words.

C. The Hexapla

1. Origen's *Hexapla* (Greek for "sixfold"), which was done in the early third century, profoundly influenced all subsequent text-critical work. It was intended to establish the true text of the Septuagint for those Christian exegetes who did not read Hebrew. Thus, he provided a common textual basis for exegetical discussions between Jews and Christians.

2. Origen arranged all the available Greek texts according to their literal correspondence with the Hebrew in parallel columns alongside the Hebrew, and a transliteration of the Hebrew into Greek characters. The six columns were (1) the original Hebrew text, (2) a Greek

transliteration of the Hebrew, (3) Aquila's Greek translation, (4) Symmachus's Greek translation, (5) the Septuagint, and (6) Theodotian's Greek translation. In some sections, additional columns were inserted.

3. Utilizing the text-critical signs (obelus and asterisk) of the Alexandrian philologians, Origen attempted to bring the Septuagint into line with the original Hebrew.

4. The original text of the Hexapla was destroyed in the sixth century C.E. at Casesarea; only fragments exist today.

5. The transliteration of the Hebrew into Greek characters is of utmost importance to the study of contemporary pronunciation of Hebrew.

D. *Targum*

1. Name

When Aramaic replaced Hebrew as the spoken language of Palestine, a translator, or *meturgeman*, stood next to the synagogue reader of the Bible and translated the Hebrew text for the congregation. Hence the term *targum* came to be applied to the Aramaic translation of the Bible.

2. Background

  a. After the return of the Jews from the Babylonian Exile, Aramaic became the lingua franca of Palestine. While Hebrew continued to be studied for copying the Scriptures and for religious purposes, a translation of the Hebrew Bible into Aramaic became necessary.

  b. The Targum, like the Septuagint, probably began as an oral translation used in the synagogue together with the reading of the Hebrew text. The Talmud (*Berakhot* 8a) reflects the custom of having the Hebrew read twice and the Targum once in public worship.

  c. In its oral form the Targum was probably both a translation and a partial interpretation of the text, often with Midrashic details enlarging upon the text itself.

3. Date of the Targum

    a. The Talmud suggests that the custom of adding an Aramaic translation to the reading of Biblical texts in worship service dates from the time of Ezra.

    b. It is known that the practice of adding the Aramaic translation during the worship services was customary during the Second Temple Period.

    c. Written Aramaic translations of the Hebrew text existed as early as the first century, though it is believed that the main translations, those of Onkelos and Jonathan (see below) date from the fourth century.

    d. Extant manuscripts generally date from the seventh to the ninth centuries.

4. Contents of the Targum

    a. The earliest Targumim were mostly translations of the Pentateuch only, though the Targum attributed to Jonathan ben Uzziel includes the Prophets and part of the Hagiographa.

    b. Common features of the Targumim were the addition of Midrashic or explanatory material and the avoidance of anthropomorphic elements (the ascription of human attributes to God). "And God came down" is rendered "And the Spirit of God came down," and so forth.

5. Language of the Targumim

The language of the Targumim seems to be halfway between Biblical Aramaic and the Aramaic spoken by Jews in Palestine during the early Christian centuries.

6. Extant Targumim

    a. The Old Palestinian Targum includes not only a translation of the Hebrew text but also considerable Midrashic additions. Different versions of the same Biblical passage found in several manuscripts show that there was no single or authorized version. It is known as the Targum Yerushalmi, or the Jerusalem Targum.

b. Babylonian Targumim

(1) Targum Onkelos: This translation of the Pentateuch is the most ancient and expresses, for the most part, the plain meaning of the text, with only a few interpretations. It is generally dated from about the second or third century. References in rabbinic literature have confused the identity of the translator, Onkelos. Consequently, some scholars believe Onkelos to have been a contemporary of Rabban Gamaliel at Jabneh in Palestine, while others identify Onkelos with Aquila, the Jewish proselyte who translated the Bible into Greek (see above).

Targum Onkelos was accepted by the Babylonian Jews as their official translation of the Pentateuch and therefore is sometimes referred to as the Babylonian Targum. It was probably compiled and edited not by one translator but by a group of scholars. It seems to have been an effort to render as closely as possible the Masoretic text of the Hebrew text into Aramaic. In instances where the Targum deviates from the standard Hebrew text, it appears to have been an effort to avoid anthropomorphisms or otherwise offensive passages.

(2) Targum Jonathan: This Aramaic translation of the Hebrew text is believed to have been compiled about the fourth century. *Jonathan* is either a transliteration of Theodotian, another Greek translator, or the name refers to Jonathan ben Uzziel, a pupil of the famous Rabbi Hillel (first century). Targum Jonathan is a translation of Prophets and part of the Hagiographa, as well as of the Pentateuch. The style of its translation of the Prophets is paraphrase, for the most part. The translation of various Hagiographa is very Midrashic, considerably longer, in some cases, than the real text, and it sometimes shows little connection with the literal sense of the text. It, like Targum Onkelos, was probably a compilation and the product of a group of scholars.

c. The Samaritan Targum: The Samaritan community in Palestine was faced with a problem similar to that of the Jews. Hebrew was replaced by Aramaic as the spoken language. Hence there was need for an Aramaic translation of their Scriptures. No official Samaritan Targum exists and every surviving manuscript shows considerable variation in the text.

d. The Pseudo-Jonathan or Jerusalem I Targum: This is generally a faithful rendition of the Targum Onkelos, but with considerable explanatory material which is absent in the Babylonian Targumim. Though it contains some early elements, it is thought to have been completed only in the Moslem era (seventh century or later).

e. The Babylonian academies accepted Targum Onkelos as the official Aramaic translation of the Pentateuch and Targum Jonathan as the official Aramaic translation of the Prophets. Although Aramaic translations of the Hagiographa exist, they were never officially accepted as the authorized translation. Their unofficial status may be related to the fact that the books of the Hagiographa were not used for liturgical services. Exceptions to this occur with the Five Scrolls (Esther, Ruth, Lamentations, Ecclesiastes, and Song of Songs). Generally, these translations are very Midrashic in character. The exception to this is the official Targum Esther which is almost a literal translation.

7. Use and Influence of the Targum

Rashi and other commentators cited the Targum as an authoritative interpretation of the Hebrew Scriptures.

E. *Peshitta*

1. Name

The Syriac translation of the Bible is called *Peshitta* ("simple") because it was translated directly from the Hebrew or the Septuagint in contrast to the Syro-Hexapla, another Syriac Bible translation which was translated from Origen's Hexapla.

2. Background and Usage

a. Some scholars contend that the first Syriac version was compiled for the Royal House of Adiabene, a kingdom in northwestern Iraq, converted to Judaism in the first century.

b. Though it seems that the Peshitta was originally written for use in certain Jewish circles, by the third century it had become the official Bible of Syriac-speaking Christians. It also served as the official Scriptural text for the Nestorians of Iraq and Persia. (The doctrines of Nestorius were condemned as heretical by the Church Council of

Ephesus in 431. However, they became the official teaching of the Persian [Sasanid] Church which was headed by the Patriarch of Babylon.)

3. Date of the Peshitta

The Peshitta is the work of many translators working in different periods. It was probably begun about the first or second century. The present text appears to be a revision made early in the fifth century.

4. Contents of the Peshitta

    a. The Peshitta contains both the Old and New Testaments, though originally it did not contain the Old Testament books of Esther, Ezra, Nehemiah, Chronicles, and the Apocrypha.

    b. This Syriac translation seems to have been made from a Hebrew or Greek text which differed from the Masoretic text.

    c. Some books of this Syriac translation reflect the influence of the Septuagint, Targum, and Midrashic exegesis.

F. *Vulgate*

1. Name

The best-known Latin translation of the Hebrew Bible is called the Vulgate from the Latin *vulgatus*, meaning "common," as it could be easily understood by common folk.

2. Background and Usage

    a. In the second century, Latin began to replace Greek in the Western world as the language of religion and learning. Hence the need arose for a Latin Bible translation.

    b. The *Vetus Latina* or "Old Latin" translations originated in North Africa, especially Carthage, the most important city of Roman Africa in the second century. At the same time, or shortly after, other Latin translations were made independently in Gaul (France) and provincial Italy.

c. The earliest translations into Latin were oral and were used only in conjunction with the Greek text. Written texts existed by the third century though there was no single authoritative version.

d. In 382 Pope Damasus I commissioned Jerome—who knew both Hebrew and Greek and was the greatest Christian scholar of his day—to compile an official Latin text of the Scriptures. Around 400 Jerome moved to Bethlehem in Palestine to undertake this most important work—a Latin translation of the Bible from the Hebrew. In his work, Jerome benefited from the advice of Jewish rabbis and scholars in Palestine and constantly referred to all existing Greek translations. The Vulgate translation appears to have been made from the standard Masoretic text of the Hebrew Bible. Scholars characterize the quality of Jerome's translation as being generally, though not totally, faithful to the original. His Latin style is elegant.

3. Influence of the Vulgate

a. The Vulgate was not immediately recognized as the official Latin text, and for a long time ranked equal to the Old Latin translation. In fact, Jerome's translation of the Old Testament was initially attacked because he had bypassed the canonical "inspired" Septuagint and had used the original Hebrew which no one in the whole Western Church other than himself could then understand. However, it was declared the official Bible of the Catholic Church by the Council of Trent in 1545 and remained the authoritative Latin Bible until the 1940s when it was replaced by a new Latin version translated from the Hebrew.

b. The Vulgate formed the basis of numerous translations into other Western European languages, especially pre-Reformation French, Italian, Spanish, Irish, and English.

c. Because of the influence of Jerome's Jewish teachers, as well as that of his Greek predecessors in translation, the Vulgate is of value today in that it sheds light on these early sources.

d. The Vulgate was the first book to be printed (1452-1456) by Gutenberg.

G. *Polyglots*

1. Bibles containing the original Hebrew text plus several ancient versions arranged in parallel columns are called polyglots. These have

been important in determining correct readings or meanings of the text.

2. Walton's *London Polyglot* is a standard one which dates from the seventeenth century and contains texts in Hebrew, Samaritan, Aramaic, Greek, Latin, Ethiopic, Syriac, Arabic, and Persian, along with Latin translations.

3. Most modern polyglots simply give the texts in Hebrew, Greek, Latin, and a modern language.

VII

DEVELOPMENT OF RELIGIOUS THOUGHT IN THE SECOND TEMPLE PERIOD

Between 200 B.C.E.* and 100 C.E., the Near Eastern world was the setting for major developments in cultural and political history, as well as in religious thought. The boundaries of Alexander the Great's empire were extensive, yet Hellenistic thought and culture reached to the farthest limits and pervaded all. And it is from the seed of this Graeco-Roman world of the Intertestamental† period that our own Western civilization has developed.

The religious ferment of the period is all too evident in the popularity of mystery cults and chance/fate religions in Greek circles, in the solidification of a number of sects in Judaism, and ultimately in the rise of Christianity. For the Jews, the question was not whether or not to mix with Greek culture, for it was all pervasive and exerted influence in nearly all spheres of life. The question was the extent to which Jews could adapt to take part in Hellenistic culture and still remain distinctive. Though Zoroastrian dualism and Greek trends were officially rejected by the rabbis, their influence on Jewish thought of this period is indisputable.

A major trend in Jewish thought of this period was "otherworldliness." Persian and Greek cultural influences combined with religious persecutions by both Greeks and Romans acted as catalysts for Jewish attempts to escape their unsettled and disappointing surroundings. They grabbed onto eschatological seeds which were only sparsely sown in the Hebrew Scriptures, and apocalypticism became a popular mode of survival in troubled Jewish circles.

Jewish literature of this period—Apocrypha, Pseudepigrapha, and apocalyptic—aptly characterizes it as one of transition. Its major themes include an emphasis on personal piety, reward and punishment, resurrection and immortality, the Messiah, and the Kingdom of God— themes which appear only briefly in the Hebrew Scriptures.

---

*All dates given in this chapter are B.C.E. (Before the Common Era), often referred to as B.C., unless they are denoted C.E. (Common Era), often referred to as A.D.

†The Second Temple period is also known in Biblical studies as the Intertestmental period.

A. *Political and Cultural Background*

1. Influence of the Exile and Postexilic Reforms

   a. The destruction of the First Commonwealth and of the Temple (586), followed by the exile of the Jewish people in Babylon, was the seedbed for drastic changes in Judaism. Preexilic prophets had begun to preach a universalism (in contrast to nationalistic policies).

   b. The people whose Temple had been destroyed sought refuge and foundation for new life in the Torah. Concern for the covenant Law grew out of the prophetic pronouncement that the Exile was occasioned precisely by lack of regard for the covenant. Knowledge of the Torah and concern for its prescriptions concerning Sabbath observance, circumcision, ritual cleanness, etc., became the roads to piety.

   c. It was during this period that the consonantal text of the Hebrew Scriptures was fixed and standardized. It was also then that the extension of the Torah—the Oral Law—was begun. Synagogues were Torah centers where the Law was taught and interpreted.

   d. The postexilic period found many Jews remaining in Babylonia and eventually spreading in other directions also. Too scattered to find a rallying point solely in the Temple, the people clung to the Torah as the focal point of Jewish life.

   e. The reforms begun by Ezra and Nehemiah and continued by the Great Synagogue sought to establish a separatism to balance universalistic tendencies which too often were temptations for lapsing into assimilation. The prescriptions of the Torah were to characterize and set apart the pious Jew from his foreign surroundings.

2. Persian Influence

   a. In postexilic Persian surroundings, the Jews could not escape the influence of Zoroastrianism, the Iranian religion founded by the prophet Zoroaster; probably during the seventh century. Zoroastrianism had apocalyptic tendencies, looking forward to the end which was thought to be near and which was to be followed by a "new age" in which the powers of good would reign.

b. The distinguishing characteristic of Zoroastrianism was its dualism—belief in a cosmic struggle between the powers of good (light) and the powers of evil (darkness). The dualism which permeated Persian thought along with eschatological tendencies is evident in Jewish Intertestamental circles, for example, in the Qumran writings.

3. Hellenism

a. A major influence in religious developments in Judaism during the Intertestamental period was Hellenism, Greek culture and thought which was developed under Alexander the Great and which was fostered even during the Roman period of Jewish history. The subsequent breakdown of Greek city-states, the declining importance of local Olympian gods, plus the universalistic aspirations of Alexander the Great, ironically enough, left room for the emerging importance of the individual.

b. The tolerant policies of the Ptolemies probably exerted as much influence on the Jews as did later Seleucid persecutions. In an atmosphere of toleration, Hellenism was not viewed as a deadly enemy and thus gradually exerted more and more influence as postexilic separatist tendencies in Judaism weakened.

c. The persecutions of the great fanatical Hellenist, Antiochus IV (Epiphanes), clearly marked Hellenism as an enemy to pious Jews. Religious oppression gave rise to the Maccabean Revolt, initially a religious movement strongly supported by the religious Hasidim (Pious Ones). When religious freedom was won, the Maccabean spirit remained and took on nationalistic goals, at which point the support of the Hasidim (who were satisfied with religious freedom) was withdrawn.

d. In the Diaspora (its center was in Alexandria), Greek became the lingua franca of the Jews. The Jewish philosopher Philo sought to harmonize Torah belief with Greek thought. Philo used the Greek language, Greek thought patterns (e.g., the Platonic concept of *logos*), and a common Greek literary technique—allegory—in his work. Greek thought pierced Jewish separatism and left its mark on future abstract, philosophical trends in Jewish religious thought.

e. The Hasmoneans, with increasingly kind feelings for Hellenism, were a disappointment to pious Jews. This disappointment, together with Greek and Roman persecutions, was soothed by apocalyptic trends—beliefs that the forces of good would soon defeat the forces of evil and those who now suffered unjustly would be rewarded in the life hereafter.

4. Roman Rule

When Roman rule replaced Greek rule, the Hellenistic cultural atmosphere remained. Times of toleration alternated with periods of persecution. The difficult times which preceded and followed the First Jewish Revolt against Rome were especially ripe for apocalyptists.

B. *Developments in Jewish Religious Thought*

1. An emphasis on transcendence (i.e., remoteness from mankind and the world) characterized the doctrine of God during this period. The conviction that God's name was too sacred for men to utter led to the practice of avoiding the use of God's name except on special religious occasions.

2. A result of the emphasis on transcendence was the popular belief in a system of angels who served as intermediaries between God and man. Though angels were only occasionally spoken of in the Hebrew Bible, apocryphal, and New Testament books, later rabbinic writings attest to developed systems of angelology and demonology. It is likely that the dualism of Zoroastrianism was the impetus for these personifications of good and evil.

3. Another means of mediation between the transcendent God and His world was the concept of *logos* ("Word" or "Reason"). Evident here is Greek influence, especially that of Philo who attempted to explain God's relation to this world in terms an instrument of creation which he terms *logos*.

4. One of the greatest changes that occurred in Jewish thought during this period was in the concept of the afterlife. There are only a few remote references to such a concept in the Hebrew Scriptures. But for the Jews in this period, victims of political and religious persecution, a life after death in which the righteous would be compensated for the unjust evils they endured in this world was an attractive concept. However, it must be mentioned here that resurrection of the body and immortality

of the soul were Pharisaic doctrines rejected by the priestly Sadducees. (See Chapter IX, "Jewish Sects.")

5. During this period the Biblical concept of the Messiah ("Anointed One") took on new importance. According to the traditional view, the Messiah was to be a national and political figure who would hold power in God's kingdom when it was established. This view was coexistent, and sometimes intermingled, with the view of the Messiah as the "Son of Man," a predominantly transcendental, eternal, and universal Messiah. The latter concept reflects the dualistic view of the universe prevalent at that time. Thus, the Messiah was believed by many to be that eschatological figure chosen by God to exercise the lead role in the coming of the kingdom which would last forever.

6. The Hebrew Bible says little about the origin of sin. Ben Sira, in the apocryphal work Ecclesiasticus, regards Adam as the origin of sin and sin as the very cause of death itself. This concept was further developed by apocalyptic writers. Thus, the world was viewed as an evil place, and mortals of flesh and blood as guilt laden.

7. The development of personal devotion to God is one of the greatest characteristics of the apocryphal period. Private prayers occur frequently in literature of the period and almsgiving came to be important as an act of religious devotion.

VIII

APOCRYPHA AND PSEUDEPIGRAPHA

The Apocrypha consist of the original fourteen books or parts of books which form an historical link between the time of Nehemiah (c. 433 B.C.E.*) and the beginning of the Christian Era. These books reveal important trends in Jewish life and thought just prior to the emergence of Christianity. New concepts, prominent among Jews of this period and only alluded to in the Hebrew Scriptures, are developed fully in the Apocrypha. Written by and for Jews, the Apocrypha were originally in Hebrew and Aramaic. For the most part, it is preserved only in Greek and Latin translations. These historical, didactic, and apocalyptic books are somewhat similar in character to the Hagiographa (Writings) of the Hebrew Bible and are found interspersed throughout the Old Testament in the Septuagint. They were popular in Jewish circles during the Second Temple period, but were later overshadowed by Talmudic literature and eventually cast aside. Preserved primarily by Christians, the Catholic Church adopted the apocryphal works as part of its Old Testament Canon at the Council of Trent (1546 C.E.). In early Protestant Bibles the apocryphal books were grouped together between the Old and New Testaments but later were dropped altogether.

The Pseudepigrapha is a group of works similar to the Apocrypha, but is more highly flavored with apocalyptic thought. The writers of these books often ascribed them to famous Biblical characters.

The historical period from which the Apocrypha emerged was full of momentous political developments in Palestine. With the return from the Babylonian Captivity in 538, Jewish life in Palestine (under the rule of the Persian Empire) assumed a more normal course. Things changed radically with the conquest of Palestine by Alexander the Great in 332. His successors, the Ptolemies and the Seleucids, fought over Palestine. The Seleucids ultimately won. Their harsh rule and forced Hellenism (especially Antiochus IV) led to the Maccabean Revolt, which resulted in the creation of an independent Jewish state in the mid-second century B.C.E. (See Chapter V, "Hellenism.") Independence under the Hasmoneans lasted until the conquest of Palestine by Rome in 63. The tenseness of the political setting from the second century B.C.E. to the second century C.E.—times in which the situation of the Jews was insecure and their future was even more dubious—acted as a catalyst for apocalyptic thought. An attempt was

---

*All dates given in this chapter are B.C.E. (Before the Common Era), often referred to as B.C., unless they are denoted C.E. (Common Era), often referred to as A.D.

made to turn from contemporary realities and to look toward the coming messianic era, which was thought by many to be imminent.

This period also saw the development of sects and parties in the Jewish community, each group attempting to deal with its faith and its historical situation in a different way. (See Chapter IX, "Jewish Sects.") The most important groups were the:

1. Pharisees, pious pacifists who developed and upheld the Oral and Written Law and were opposed to the idea of a *secular* Jewish state;

2. Sadducees, the party of the Jewish priests and aristocracy which introduced Greek culture and ideas into Judaism and rejected Pharisaic interpretation of the Torah;

3. Essenes, an ascetic sect, which believed in communal life and retired into the wilderness; and

4. Zealots, a fanatical sect, which refused to recognize any foreign or secular authorities.

A. *Apocrypha*

1. Name

   a. The expression employed by the rabbis for the exclusion of a book from the Hebrew Bible was *ganaz*, to "store away" or "hide."

     (1) Some "hidden books" were withdrawn from common use because they were believed to be too mysterious and too profound to be communicated. The rabbis were reluctant to include books written after the Exile and those of unknown authors.

     (2) Other "hidden books" were believed to be heretical and thus deserved to be hidden.

   b. In Greek, these "hidden books" were called *Apokryphoi* ("hidden" or "secret").

2. Apocryphal Works

	Approximate Date
a. Additions to Canonical Books	
Daniel—Susanna	175 to 165
Daniel—Bel and the Dragon	175 to 165
Daniel—The Song of the Three Holy Children (with The Prayer of Azariah)	175 to 165
Some Additions to Esther	100
b. Two Romantic Narratives	
Tobit	200
Judith	150 to 120
c. Historical Books	
I Maccabees	100 to 60
II Maccabees	75 to 50
I Esdras	150
d. Wisdom Literature	
The Wisdom of Solomon	40
Ecclesiasticus, or The Wisdom of Ben Sira (Sirach)	200 to 175
A Letter of Jeremiah (Epistle of Jeremy)	c. 70
Baruch and The Epistle of Jeremy	c. 100 C.E.
The Prayer of Manasseh	150 to 100
II Esdras	50 to 250 C.E.

3. Authorship

   a. The only apocryphal book of which the author is definitely known is the Wisdom book, Ecclesiasticus, written by Jesus ben Sira in about 180.

   b. Some works included in the official list of Apocrypha are, strictly speaking, Pseudepigrapha: They are ascribed by their authors to ancient authoritative Jewish leaders such as Solomon.

4. Contents and Ideas

   a. The apocryphal books developed Biblical ideas beyond the original concept.

   b. They introduced a number of religious concepts which have little or no basis in the canonical books.

   c. The most important of these concepts were

      (1) Angels and demons: These are only mentioned in passing in the Bible, but in the Apocrypha they received definite attributes as intermediaries between God and man. Several angels appear by name such as Michael, Gabriel, and others.

      (2) Life after death: This is another idea touched upon only briefly and not explicitly in the Hebrew Bible. It assumes definite shape in the Apocrypha. Men began to believe in an afterlife in which the inequalities of this life would be rectified. This period also produced the idea of religious martyrdom, directly associated with the idea of life after death and resurrection.

      (3) Eschatology: The messianic or latter-days ideas. The Apocrypha goes far beyond the prophets in developing the messianic age, in speaking of omens and supernatural signs which will precede it, and in describing its characteristics. Immortality of the soul and bodily resurrection are clearly defined.

      (4) Original sin: This concept is stressed and developed in the Apocrypha where the origin of sin is traced to Adam.

(5) Wisdom: This Biblical concept is further developed as an intermediate stage between man and the Divine.

(6) Individual prayer: The importance and significance of personal prayer to God is greatly emphasized.

(7) Almsgiving: This idea was developed in the Apocrypha and later became one of the fundamentals of Judaism, Christianity, and Islam.

5. Usage

a. Jews regarded the Apocrypha as pious writing until the period following the destruction of the Second Temple. At that time rabbinic Judaism became normative and the Scriptures and Oral tradition were regarded as the primary foundation of Judaism. Because the Apocrypha was not canonical and did not contain Biblical interpretation or commentary, the Talmudic scholars discarded it as having no direct bearing on Jewish spiritual life.

b. The preservation of the Apocrypha in translation is largely due to the Christian Church.

(1) The early Christian Church, for the most part, used the Septuagint, since Gentile converts did not read Hebrew. Because antagonism developed between the Synagogue and the Church, the Jews abandoned the use of the Septuagint. (See Chapter V, "The Making of the Bible.")

(2) The Old Latin translation of the Bible was made from the Septuagint and thus contained the Apocrypha. Popular opinion in early Christianity regarded the apocryphal writings as equal in value to the Old Testament canonical books.

(3) When Jerome made his famous Latin translation of the Bible, the Vulgate, he included but separated the apocryphal additions to Daniel and Esther, included the Books of Tobit and Judith, but excluded other apocryphal books.

(4) Later scholars reinstated the other apocryphal books among the Old Testament books. Some designated these books as apocryphal while others held them to be canonical.

(5) Early Protestant Bibles grouped the Apocrypha together between the Old and the New Testaments and labeled it as not equal to Scripture, yet holy and worthy to be read.

(6) Since the Reformation, the Protestant inclusion and exclusion of the Apocrypha have not been consistent and have resulted in varied degrees of respect for the Apocrypha among Protestant denominations.

B. *Apocalyptic Literature*

1. Nature of Apocalyptic Literature

   a. Those writings are said to be apocalyptic which deal with subjects beyond the realm of normal human knowledge (e.g., the end of days, existence of spirits, immortality, resurrection, eternal reward, and punishment after death).

   b. In general, these Jewish and Christian works were attempts to encourage the faithful to stand firm under persecution. They promised those who suffered from political or religious persecution that, as a result of God's intervention, their present suffering would be rewarded. These are actually the first records of Jewish and Christian mysticism.

   c. The classical period for apocalyptic literature was between the second century B.C.E. and the second century C.E.

   d. In much of its literature, the Dead Sea sect reflects an almost complete apocalyptic orientation.

   e. Apocalyptic works were written in Hebrew, Aramaic, and Greek.

2. Apocalyptic Writings

   a. Sections of the canonical Book of Daniel are apocalyptic. The New Testament Book of Revelations (see Chapter XI, "The Rise of Christianity") and some sections of the gospels are also apocalyptic.

   b. II Esdras is an example of apocalyptic writing in the Apocrypha.

   c. The pseudepigraphical works, Apocalypse of Baruch and Assumption of Moses, are apocalyptic.

C. *Pseudepigrapha*

1. Name

    a. The name Pseudepigrapha is derived from the Greek. It means "with false title."

    b. This group of writings is so named because of the contemporary practice of ascribing a work to a famous historical personage in order to enhance the book's authority and spiritual stature.

    c. There is some inconsistency in classifying Pseudepigrapha by its Greek name, since some books commonly called Apocrypha are, properly speaking, Pseudepigrapha (e.g., Wisdom of Solomon, Baruch) whereas other books, commonly classified as Pseudepigrapha, are not written under a pseudonym (e.g., Book of Jubilees).

    d. Generally speaking, those books are pseudepigraphic which date from the period of the Apocrypha. They are usually written under a pseudonym and are not included in the Septuagint, the Vulgate, or the Hebrew Bible.

    e. Pseudepigraphic literature is often equated with apocalyptic literature, though not exclusively so, since some canonical works, such as parts of Daniel and the New Testament Book of Revelation are apocalyptic but not pseudepigraphic and some works (e.g., Psalms of Solomon and the Testament of the Twelve Patriarchs) are called pseudepigraphic but are not apocalyptic. Pseudepigraphic works are properly called apocalyptic insofar as they are immersed with such eschatological and mystical concerns as the End of Days, the mysteries of the earth and the heavens, the soul's existence, the function of angels and evil spirits, etc.

2. Pseudepigraphic works include

    a. Psalms of Solomon: a collection of eighteen psalms attributed to King Solomon probably composed between 70 and 40, since they describe Pompey's conquest of Jerusalem (63), his desecration of the Temple, and Pompey's death (48).

    b. Testaments of the Twelve Patriarchs: twelve separate testaments in which each of the twelve sons of Jacob declares the virtues and vices of his own life and then counsels his children to live a life of virtue.

c. Book of Jubilees: a commentary on the Book of Genesis and the first part of Exodus written in the form of a revelation to Moses— evidently intended to remind Israel of its unique calling and to recall its duty to the Law.

d. Apocalypse of Baruch: several apocalyptic works in Greek, Syriac and Ethiopic which were attributed to Baruch and probably written during the second century.

e. Book of Enoch: a collection of various legends and "visions" of Enoch.

f. Assumption of Moses: a work containing a revelation supposedly made by Moses to Joshua relating the coming history of Israel down to the reign of Herod and the messianic era.

g. Ascension of Isaiah: a two-part work containing an account of the martyrdom of Isaiah by King Manasseh and a vision in which Isaiah is carried to the heavens.

h. Sibylline Oracles: twelve quasi-prophetic books written under the pseudonym of a pagan prophetess which are believed to date from sometime between the second century B.C.E. and the fourth century C.E.

3. Authorship

For some time, scholars tended to ascribe the authorship of Pseudepigrapha to the Pharisees. It is also believed that the Pseudepigrapha probably arose among the Essenes or another Second Temple Period Jewish sect which was more involved in the widespread eschatological movement.

4. Contents and Ideas

In summary, the Pseudepigrapha is thematically similar to the Bible and the Apocrypha. It differs in that the Pseudepigrapha concentrates more heavily on apocalyptic hopes, such as the coming of the Messiah, the coming of judgment, and the end of days.

5. Usage

a. Though several apocryphal and pseudepigraphic concepts were later incorporated into the Talmud, contemporary Pharisees actively developed the strong eschatological orientation of these books with the purpose of encouraging the faithful to stand firm under persecution and in the midst of political unheaval.

b. Early Christians, whose views arose from the same general eschatological ferment that produced the pseudepigraphic writings, accepted them not as canonical but as semisacred literature and adapted them to fit their interpretation of the life, mission, and second coming of Jesus. With a few minor changes, the Pseudepigrapha were incorporated into Christian tradition.

APOCRYPHAL LITERATURE

The apocryphal literature dates back to the Second Temple period. It is generally believed that these works were composed between the fourth century B.C.E. and the first century C.E. In Hebrew these works are known as *Sefarim Hitsonim* (the "Outside Books"), since they were not included in the canonization of the Hebrew Bible. Although these works were excluded from the Hebrew Bible, they nevertheless had a significant effect on the Jews and they were popularly read. The influence of the apocryphal literature on Jewish thought is apparent in various Midrashim.

The apocryphal literature consists of four major elements. The first element is the additions to the canonical works. Included in this group are additions to the Book of Daniel and additions to the Book of Esther. It is felt that the additions to the Book of Esther were attempts at putting a religious element into that work. A second major element of apocryphal literature consists of romantic narratives. Two works included in this grouping are the Book of Tobit and the Book of Judith. In addition to being fascinating tales, these works include commentaries on Jewish religious thought. The third element of apocryphal literature includes historical works such as the books of Macabees I and II and I Esdras. These works contain extremely valuable historical information. The final category of apocryphal literature consists of Wisdom Literature. Included in this group are Wisdom of Solomon, Ecclesiasticus, Baruch, Prayer of Manasseh, and II Esdras. These works deal with various religious thoughts and beliefs as they related to the Jewish position in the Intertestamental period.

A. *Additions to Canonical Works*

1. In the Septuagint, the Books of Daniel and Esther contain sections which do not appear in the Hebrew Bible. These sections include three separate additions to the Book of Daniel and additions to the Book of Esther.

2. Content and Significance of Additions

   a.   Additions to Daniel

   (1) Susanna: This well-known narrative was prefixed to the Book of Daniel in the Septuagint and served as an introduction to the book. A beautiful and devout Jewess exiled in Babylon refused the lustful approaches of two Jewish elders. When she did not submit to them, they swore in court that they had caught her in the act of adultery. Susanna pleaded her case to the Lord and, as she was being led to her execution, was saved by a young lad, Daniel, who gained permission to question the two witnesses separately before the assembly. When their testimonies conflicted under Daniel's questioning, Susanna was freed and the two elders executed. This is a fine literary narrative teaching purity, trust in God, and efficacy of prayer.

   (2) Bel and the Dragon: In the Septuagint, Bel and the Dragon, as two separate stories, come after the end of the Book of Daniel (Chapter 14 in the Vulgate). In both of these old detective stories Daniel appears as the destroyer of heathen idolatry and religious beliefs.

   The first narrative tells the story of how Daniel dispelled belief in the Babylonian god Bel. King Cyrus of Babylonia proposed a test by which they would know whether or not Bel was a living god. Food offerings were prepared and placed on the altar by King Cyrus himself, and at the request of Daniel, the floor around the offerings was sprinkled with ashes. The temple door was then sealed with the king's signet. The next day, although the food had been eaten, Daniel proved that Bel was not a living god by pointing out the footprints in the ashes leading to the secret door which the priests of Bel had used to enter the temple and eat the food. Cyrus executed the priests and allowed Daniel to destroy the idol of Bel and its temple.

According to the second narrative, the Babylonians also worshipped a dragon. Daniel received permission from the king and slew the dragon by feeding it cake made of pitch, fat, and hair. The dragon's death outraged the people, who, in turn, cast Daniel into a den of lions where he remained for six days. The lions did not harm Daniel, and he was fed by the prophet Habakkuk. On the seventh day, the king delivered Daniel from the den and threw his adversaries into it.

(3) Song of the Three Holy Children: In the third chapter of Daniel, three young Jewish friends of Daniel were thrown into a fiery furnace because they refused to worship Nebuchadnezzar's idol. This addition to Daniel is the only addition which is an integral part of the book, continuing, as it were, the canonical story. The addition is divided into three sections: the prayer of one of the young men, the description of the fiery furnace, and the song of the three children.

The song is an excellent example of Jewish liturgical devotion and has held a prominent place in liturgy of Christian churches for centuries. God is declared the only lord of heaven and earth, Israel's calamities are viewed as due to her sins, and penitence with humility takes the place of animal sacrifices. This apocryphal hymn is also referred to as "The Prayer of Azariah."

b. Additions to Esther

(1) These six insertions into the Esther narrative were made about 100 when the Hebrew Esther was translated into Greek. In Jerome's Vulgate, these additions were removed from the midst of the narrative and placed together at the end of the book. Explanatory notes were lost and later translators viewed this collection of fragments as a direct continuation of the canonical Esther.

(2) Scholars believe that these additions were clearly an attempt to make the book of Esther a religious work, the canonical book itself being renowned for its absence of the mention of God's name or any other religious element. In five of the six apocryphal additions, the name of God appears quite conspicuously and the additions even include prayers of Mordecai and Esther.

B. *Romantic Narratives*

1. The Book of Tobit and the Book of Judith are two apocryphal romantic tales which contain all the attributes of enchanting stories of any age. Both of these fictional stories convey to the reader examples of true Jewish piety as well as the spirit of God's interest in His people. Scholars believe that the Book of Tobit dates from late in the third century B.C.E. and that the Book of Judith dates from late in the second century B.C.E.

2. Contents

   a. Tobit: This is the story of Tobit, a Jew taken captive out of Galilee during the reign of Shalmaneser IV (c. 727-722) and Tobit's son, Tobias. The pious father and son were helped by the angel Raphael, who spared Tobias from death at the hands of the demon Asmodeus (Hebrew: *Ashmedai*) and restored Tobit's lost eyesight. The story closes with a psalm of thanksgiving by Tobit.

   b. Judith: The Jews of Bethulia offered resistance to Holofernes, one of Nebuchadnezzar's generals, in his effort to punish the Jews of Palestine for disobeying him. The Assyrians besieged the city, and when it was on the verge of surrender, Judith, a beautiful widow of the city, announced that she had a plan to defeat the enemy. Making her way to Holofernes' tent, she beguiled and allured him. Fascinated with her beauty, the general drank too much wine and fell fast asleep. Judith seized his sword, beheaded him, and escaped from the camp with Holofernes' head. The next morning, finding their leader dead, the Assyrians panicked and fled, and the city was thus saved. The book closes with a psalm composed by Judith to celebrate and to thank God for her victory.

3. Significance

   a. Both narratives are good examples of short stories of ancient times, and characters from both have served as favorite subjects for artists throughout the ages.

   b. In Tobit, God is a personal redeemer, whereas in Judith He intervenes as a national redeemer.

   c. Both stress the value of prayer. In addition, Tobit stresses almsgiving, fasting, and honoring the dead as requisites for pious living, while in Judith, piety is dependent on the observance of cleanliness, dietary laws, and temple offerings.

d. Both reflect the ideal religious attitudes of the early Pharisees and their immediate precursors.

e. Tobit manifests the religious virtues of gentleness and kindness, while Judith is an example of courage, steadfast devotion to God, and religious duty.

C. Historical Books

1. The apocryphal books of I Maccabees and II Maccabees were probably written during the first half of the first century B.C.E. Both are important historical sources for the period surrounding the Maccabean Revolt. Some scholars contend that I Maccabees, reflecting a conservative religious attitude, was composed by a Sadducee in the Hebrew tongue (though only the Greek translation has survived), while II Maccabees (composed in Greek), in its treatment of spirits, angels, and resurrection, is likely to have been written by a Pharisee. I Esdras is unique among apocryphal books in that it contains variations to historical data included in some canonical books.

2. Contents

   a. I Maccabees opens with a brief summary of the history of the Greek Empire from Alexander the Great to the accession to the Syrian throne of Antiochus Epiphanes. The remainder of the book covers the period from the outbreak of the Maccabean Revolt to the death of Simon (c. 168-135), last of the five sons of Mattathias, the Hasmonean. Each part of the book deals with a particular member of the family.

   b. II Maccabees is largely made up of glorious accounts of the victories of Judah the Maccabee. Unlike I Maccabees, it includes supernatural elements; refers to angels, miracles, and resurrection of the dead; and contains legendary accounts of the martyrdom of Eleazar the scribe and of the Jewish mother Hanna and her seven sons who were condemned to death for refusing to eat pork.

   c. I Esdras (Esdras is the Latinized spelling of Ezra) is largely based on the canonical books of Chronicles, Ezra, and Nehemiah. It appears to be an account of history from Josiah's celebration of the

Passover (621) to the reading of the Law in the time of Ezra after the Exile (444). In the Septuagint this book is called I Esdras, whereas in the Vulgate it is referred to as III Esdras (I and II referring to the Biblical books of Ezra and Nehemiah).

3. Significance

    a. I Maccabees serves as the chief source of historical data from the accession to the throne of Antiochus Epiphanes in 175 to the death of Simon in 135. It is a highly sober and accurate historical account of the Maccabean Revolt.

    b. II Maccabees was apparently written with the purpose of arousing a spirit of devotion to the Torah rather than the narrating of history, and is valuable for the light it sheds on the Jewish beliefs of the day. For the first time, resurrection is explicitly described in this book (7:9-11).

    c. Rabbinic tradition records an account of the rededication of the Temple and altar which came as a result of the victory of the Maccabees over Antiochus Epiphanes. This serves as the basis for the Jewish feast of Hanukkah (dedication), an eight-day period of praise and thanksgiving allegedly assigned by Judah and his brothers. (See Chapter XVIII, "Jewish Liturgy".)

    d. I Esdras is unique among apocryphal books in that it is the only one which relates merely a divergent account of a Jewish history already given by several canonical books. Scholars speculate that both I Esdras and Ezra and Nehemiah came from a common source, rather than one being derived from the other.

    e. Because of the stress on worship, ritual, priesthood, the rebuilding of the Temple, and the presentation of Ezra as the one important person in postexilic Jewish history, it appears that the purpose for the writing of I Esdras was religious.

D. *Wisdom Literature*

1. Traditionally, the wise man in Judaism has held a position almost as important as that of prophet or priest. Following the return from the Babylonian Exile, a definite school of wise men collected the edited wise sayings which had been passed down through the ages. Thus, probably, Wisdom Literature (Proverbs, Job, Ecclesiastes, etc.) came

to be incorporated into the Hebrew Bible. These postexilic sages also composed Wisdom Literature of their own—books which were not included in the Bible but which were held in high esteem by Jews of the Second Temple period. These are contained in apocryphal and pseudepigraphical writings. The apocryphal books of Wisdom Literature are Wisdom of Solomon, Ecclesiasticus, Baruch, Prayer of Manasseh, and II Esdras.

2. Content and Significance

   a. Wisdom of Solomon

      (1) This book begins with an exposition of the fate that will be the lot of the wicked as compared to that of the righteous. This is followed by a section praising wisdom as man's means of attaining immortality. The final section introduces a new subject, which has led some scholars to believe that it was appended to the two original sections. This section deals with the past history of the Jews and shows how wisdom has guided the fate of the Jews and other nations.

      (2) The book is pseudepigraphical in that an attempt is made to ascribe its authorship to King Solomon.

      (3) Written originally in Greek, the book has been dated at about 100.

      (4) The purpose of the author was threefold: to strengthen the faith of his fellow Jews, to warn renegade Jews, and to combat the worship of idols.

      (5) One of the finest examples of Wisdom Literature, which was regarded by the early Church as one of the most important apocryphal books.

      (6) This was the first attempt at a synthesis between the insights of Greek philosophy and Jewish truths.

      (7) The style and contents are on a high level. The book showed a marked Hellenistic influence and, in turn, exerted much influence on the Epistles of Paul, John, James, Hebrews, and the Book of Revelation.

(8) The book deviates from the ideas of traditional Judaism as God is pictured as performing His work not directly, but through an intermediary, namely wisdom. This is the forerunner of the *Logos* concept of Philo. In addition, the book introduced the concept of immortality, which is not a clear-cut Biblical belief.

b. Ecclesiasticus (The Wisdom of Ben Sira)

(1) In Hebrew the book is named for its author, Joshua ben Sira, and in Latin it is known as the Wisdom of Jesus, Son of Sirach.

(2) The book dates from c. 180 and was translated into Greek by the author's grandson in 132.

(3) Discoveries of Ben Sira fragments in the Cairo Genizah and among the Masada scrolls have made studies of the Hebrew original possible.

(4) The content of the book represents the more practical side of wisdom, in contrast to the religious side, presented in the Wisdom of Solomon.

(5) Unlike other apocryphal books, Ecclesiasticus influenced later Jewish literature. It was widely read and quoted by the rabbis and in the Midrashim.

c. Baruch

(1) This work consists of both poetic and prose sections. Baruch, secretary of Jeremiah, wrote to Jehoiachin and other Jews carried off to Babylon in the first deportation (597). The narrative relates that, in response to Baruch's letter, the exiles repented for their sins which had brought calamity upon them. The poetic section of the book is a hymn to the wisdom of the Law, lamentations, and words of consolation.

(2) Internal indications show that the book probably dates from a period later than the Exile, possibly during the persecution under Antiochus Epiphanes or after the destruction of the Temple by the Romans.

(3) Originally a separate book in the Septuagint, the so-called Epistle of Jeremy came to be attached to the Book of Baruch

because of the historical fact that Baruch and the prophet Jeremiah were close associates.

d. Epistle of Jeremy (Letter of Jeremiah)

    (1) This work, often attached to the end of the Book of Baruch, is really a separate composition. It is a letter which was supposed to have been written to the exiles in Babylon by Jeremiah the prophet. In it, he explains that Jews are in exile because of their sins. He then warns the Jews against idolatry and assimilation into the paganism of their masters.

    (2) The composition date of this work is not agreed upon by scholars. Some suggest a late fourth century B.C.E. date, while others affix the date of composition to about 70. It is likely that the work was written in Greek in Alexandria during the first century B.C.E.

e. Prayer of Manasseh

    (1) In II Chronicles 33:10-13 it is related that Manasseh, the most wicked of kings of Judah, was taken captive by the Assyrians and underwent a profound change while in prison. This short apocryphal book professes to be the prayer of repentance which he uttered there.

    (2) The author is unknown but the book is believed to date from about the beginning of the Christian Era.

    (3) It is of interest chiefly as a dignified example of an ancient Jewish penitential prayer.

f. II Esdras

    (1) In the Vulgate, this book, dating from the late first or early second century C.E., is called IV Esdras. Other sources refer to it as The Apocalypse of Ezra.

    (2) The book answered the problem of the tragedy suffered by Judaism in the fall of the Temple with the reply, revealed to Ezra, that Israel, though indeed chosen, must undergo this period of repentance for its sins.

(3) The book is eschatological in character, consoling its readers with speculations about the messianic age when Israel will be triumphant over the wicked.

(4) This book and the prayer of Manasseh were never included in the Septuagint but were appended to the Latin Vulgate.

IX

JEWISH SECTS DURING THE SECOND TEMPLE PERIOD

During the period from the rebuilding of the Second Temple (550-515 B.C.E.*) to its destruction in 70 C.E., a number of sects arose in Judaism. This fragmentation was due to important religious changes which had taken place during the Babylonian Exile and to the political atmosphere of the time. During the Exile, Judaism had turned from its origins as a sacrificial cult to the Law; prayer and study had therefore become more important. With the advent of Hellenism (see Chapter IV, "Hellenism"), especially during the second century under Antiochus IV (Epiphanes), life became extremely difficult for the Jews. This period culminated in the Maccabean Revolt. It was during the period of the Second Commonwealth (from the successful Maccabean Revolt in the second century, through the Roman period to the fall of Jerusalem in 70 C.E.) that distinctions and divisions among the sects became most pronounced. (See Chapter IV, "Rome and Jerusalem.")

Jews reacted in a variety of ways to changes in their religious and political situations. The Sadducees felt it most advantageous to befriend the Hellenists and the Romans, while the Pharisees were cooperative with them but were careful not to compromise their Jewish identity. The Zealots strongly objected to foreign rule. It is no small wonder that the Essenes sought an ascetic solution to the life of such a chaotic world. The Hasidim, or Pious Ones, were the forerunners of several Second Temple sects. They formed the nucleus of the Maccabean Revolt. They strictly observed Jewish Law, rejecting any compromise with the forces of Hellenism. Often known as the Assideans, they should not be confused with the eighteenth-century Hasidic movement in central Europe.

A. *Pharisees*

1. Origin and Development

   a. The Pharisees probably originated from the Hasidim, and certainly shared their devotion to the Law. They emerged as a distinct group in the middle of the second century.

---

*All dates given in this chapter are B.C.E. (Before the Common Era), often referred to as B.C., unless they are denoted C.E. (Common Era), often referred to as A.D.

b. The word *Pharisee* may come from the Hebrew word *parash* meaning "to separate," since their scrupulous observance of the Law led them to a separatist attitude toward all of life. Another meaning of *parash* is "those who expound" the Torah.

c. The Pharisees came to represent the religious beliefs, practices, and social outlooks of the majority of Jewish people of their day. They were largely responsible for the preservation and transmission of normative Judaism.

2. Beliefs and Doctrines

a. The Pharisees taught that the Torah which God gave to Moses was twofold, consisting of the Written (the Torah) and the Oral Law. They viewed the Law, its teachings, and commandments as having to be interpreted in conformity with the standard of the teachers of each generation. Accordingly, when in the course of time they had outgrown a certain law, they endeavored to give it a new and more acceptable meaning.

b. Certain Pharisaic beliefs reflected apocalyptic trends of the day. These included resurrection of the body, life after death, reward and retribution on the Day of Judgment, the advent of the Messiah, and the existence of angels. (See Chapter XVI, "Oral Law.")

c. Pharisaic doctrines admitted divine knowledge and predestination but maintained man's free choice between good and evil and therefore man's responsibility for his deeds.

d. In regard to the political affairs of the day, the Pharisees were ready to submit to foreign domination if it did not interfere with their religious way of life.

e. The Pharisees believed that there was no place where God could not be found and reached in prayer. They fostered the synagogue as a unique institution of religious worship—outside of and separate from the Temple. They felt that worship consisted not only of sacrifices but also of prayer and the study of God's Law. It is to this period that we trace the origins of the synagogue.

3. Pharisaic Influence on Later Judaism

   a. The active period of Pharisaism extended into the second and third centuries C.E.

   b. Pharisees were the most influential sect in the development of normative Judaism. They rejected the Zealot's appeal to force and violence, relying instead on God for the redemption of Israel.

   c. The Pharisees devoted much time to education. Their synagogues and schools became the mainstay of Judaism after the destruction of the Temple.

   d. The adaptability of the Pharisees enabled their form of Judaism alone to survive the turmoil of the change of the era. It was the synagogue and the schools of the Pharisees that continued to function and promote Judaism.

4. Pharisees and the New Testament

   a. The Talmud mentions certain types of Pharisees who, by not living up to the Pharisees' high ethical standards, were condemned as hypocrites. The New Testament's references to the Pharisees as "hypocrites" and the "offspring of vipers" were probably directed at this same minority of insincere members who were also condemned by the Pharisaic leaders. Therefore, the opinion that New Testament references are aimed at the Pharisaic group as a whole is probably wrong.

B. *Sadducees*

1. Origin and Development

   a. The most probable explanation for the uncertain name Sadducee is that it is derived from Zadok, the High Priest in the days of David. Solomon selected this family as worthy of being entrusted with the control of the Temple. In fact, descendants of this family formed the Temple hierarchy down to the second century. However, not all priests were Sadducees. Hence the name Sadducee may best be taken to mean anyone who is a sympathizer with the Zadokites, the priestly descendants of Zadok.

b. This religious sect was formed c. 200 as the party of the High Priests and aristocratic families.

c. Because the Sadducees were composed of the wealthier elements of the population, they were influential in political and economic life. In addition, they dominated in Temple matters and in the Sanhedrin (the supreme Jewish council and tribunal of the Second Temple period).

d. Historically, the Sadducees came under the influence of Hellenism and later were in good standing with the Roman rulers. They were unpopular with the common people, from whom they kept aloof.

e. Since the existence and power of the Sadducees depended on the Temple cult, the sect disappeared after the destruction of the Temple in 70 C.E.

2. Beliefs and Doctrines

a. The Sadducees were the conservative priestly group. They held to the Mosaic doctrines and possessed the highest regard for the sacrificial cult of the Temple. They were strongly opposed to any reform in the sacrificial functions of the Temple. They accepted the authority of only the Pentateuch .

b. While paying great attention to the letter of the Law, the Sadducees rejected the Pharisaic supernatural beliefs (e.g., resurrection of the body, immortality of the soul, existence of angels, etc.). They claimed that these beliefs had no basis in the Mosaic Law.

c. Unfortunately, we possess no statement from the Sadducean side of their beliefs and principles. There are controversial references in rabbinic literature to the Sadducees' interpretation of the Law. The Sadducees have been represented as lax and worldly-minded aristocrats, primarily interested in maintaining their own privileged position, and favoring Graeco-Roman culture.

3. Pharisees and Sadducees

a. For two centuries (from c. 200 B. C. E.), the religious and political affairs of Palestinian Jewry were controlled by the Sadducees, the representative of the priestly aristocracy, and by the Hasmonean rulers who were supported by the Sadducees. Pharisaic leaders (who usually rose from the ranks of the masses) waged a long and bitter struggle against the Sadducees in an effort to democratize the Jewish religion and remove it from the rigid control of the Temple priest. By the beginning of the second century, the Sanhedrin was composed of both priests and lay leaders.

b. While the Sadducean priesthood exhausted itself in the ritual of the Temple, the Pharisees found their main function in teaching, preaching, and constantly interpreting the Torah. (See Chapter XVII, "The Midrash.")

c. Generally, the Pharisees admitted the principles of evolution of the Torah in their legal decisions. The Sadducees, on the other hand, were incapable of adapting to the changing environment and hence clung to the letter of the Written Law. The Pharisees insisted on the binding nature of the Oral Law as well as the Torah. The Sadducees did not accept the Oral Torah.

C. *Zealots*

1. The Zealots' main characteristic was extreme opposition to any foreign rule. They were most active from the time of Herod (37-4 B.C.E.) to 70 C.E. In the period prior to the First Jewish Revolt against Rome (early 60s C.E.), the Zealots acquired their greatest following.

2. Their extreme tactics during the final Roman siege of Jerusalem brought about Jerusalem's destruction. Some of the Zealots were fanatics who carried concealed daggers or *sicae* and felt free to murder their opponents. They were known as Sicarii, or Assassins.

3. A small band of Zealots fled to the fortress of Masada after the destruction of Jerusalem in 70 C.E. and managed to hold their own against the Roman legions until 73 C.E., when they committed mass suicide rather than surrender. (See Chapter XIV, "Masada.")

D. *Essenes*

1. Organization

a. Members of this sect, which flourished during the Second Commonwealth, lived an ascetic and sometimes mystic life in monastic communities.

b. The main group of this sect was composed of men. Apparently this was true of the majority of branches, although Josephus mentioned an Essenic group which included women.

c. The initiate went through a one-year probation period before he received the symbol of the group: a hatchet, a belt, and a white garment. A further probationary year was necessary before being admitted to full membership.

d. The Essenes were very strictly disciplined.

   (1) The group was strictly ranked on the basis of age and learning. Members were absolutely subservient to their superiors. The authority of the superiors was never questioned.

   (2) Although disobedience was apparently rare, its cure was simple: Since the members believed in the necessity of fellowship and ritually pure food, a delinquent could be readily banished or starved into submission.

e. Emphasis on ritual purity conditioned some of the cultic life of the Essenes.

   (1) Great importance was attached to ritual cleanliness.

   (2) The Sabbath and Levitical laws of holiness were strictly kept.

   (3) Although the Essenes were adamant about the necessity of their isolation, they did visit the Temple periodically, bringing offerings of flour and oil, though never meat.

f. Each member performed some manual labor, usually in agriculture or handicrafts.

g. The common meal was apparently of some importance, since it was only after attaining full membership that new members were admitted to it.

2. Beliefs

a. The Essenes believed in the necessity of personal piety and ritual purity.

  b. They believed in immortality, but not in bodily resurrection.

  c. The sect attributed all things to fate.

  d. Their theology was dualistic, dividing the world into good and evil, or spirit and flesh.

3. Most scholars agree that the sect of the Dead Sea Scrolls were the Essenes. (See Chapter X, "The Dead Sea Scrolls.") However, there are some differences between the Essenes described by Pliny the Elder, Josephus Flavius and Philo of Alexandria, and the sect of Qumran, where the scrolls were found.

E. *Therapeutae*

1. The Therapeutae were an ascetic sect which in some ways resembled the Essenes. The sect existed during the first century C.E. near Alexandria, Egypt. The only source of information about this sect is Philo. We have no knowledge of the sect's origin or end.

2. The sect included both men and women, and was highly contemplative. As far as we know, prayer and study were the only activities of the members. Each member lived in an individual dwelling and remained in it six days a week, praying and studying the Scriptures (which they interpreted allegorically).

3. The needs of the body—eating, sleeping, etc.—were performed entirely at night.

4. On the Sabbath the sect gathered together for a common assembly, at which time they listened to discourses by the most learned member. On each fiftieth day the group gathered for a festival which consisted of a banquet (of bread, flavored with salt or hyssop, and spring water) during which the sect leader discussed a philosophical question. Following this, the members engaged in hymn singing and choral dancing until dawn, when they again withdrew to their individual sanctuaries.

5. Like the Essenes, the Therapeutae had a dualistic view of life, were ascetic, and believed in a secret doctrine hidden behind the literal words of Scripture. It is generally thought that the Therapeutae were a variety of Essenes.

X

THE DEAD SEA SCROLLS

The Intertestamental period is certainly one of the most exciting in the history of the Near Eastern world. Even though Rome replaced Greece as the major power, Greek culture remained and was adopted by the Romans. In Palestine, as in the Diaspora, the Jews attempted to deal with this foreign rule without sacrificing their own identity. The resulting cultural and religious tensions are seen in the development of various Jewish sects (and perhaps even the rise of Christianity); the need for Greek and Aramaic translations of the Hebrew Scriptures; and the pervasive apocalyptic thought in Jewish, and later, the Christian literature of the era. Political tension precipitated the Maccabean Revolt (concluding in 165 B.C.E.[*]), the Jewish war against Rome (66-73 C.E.), and finally the Bar Kokhba revolt (132-135 C.E.).

The above is sufficient background to appreciate the magnitude of the 1947 discovery of a Jewish sectarian (probably Essene) monastery and its library, the documents of which probably date from the second century B.C.E. to the first century C.E. Excavations at Khirbet Qumran (the ruins of the ancient monastery) and the discovery of sectarian literature in nearby caves have enabled archaeologists to reconstruct to some degree the life of the ascetic monks. The subsequent discovery of materials pertaining to the Bar Kokhba revolt, though at first somewhat overshadowed by the popularity of the Dead Sea Scrolls, has also revealed much about life and events of the Intertestamental period. All of this has much significance for students of ancient history, the text of the Hebrew Bible, Judaism, and early Christianity.

A. *Discovery*

1. In the spring of 1947, while searching for a stray goat in the vicinity of Qumran in the northwestern region of the Dead Sea in Palestine, two Bedouin shepherds stumbled upon a cave. Several earthenware jars were found in the cave, one of which contained decaying bundles of leather scrolls. The Bedouins brought the leather bundles to the marketplace in Bethlehem where they were bought by an antique dealer.

---

[*]All dates given in this chapter are B.C.E. (Before the Common Era), often referred to as B.C., unless they are denoted C.E. (Common Era), often referred to as A.D.

2. Upon closer inspection, the bundles were found to comprise seven large scrolls and several fragments, all wrapped in linen and written in Hebrew and Aramaic. (See C. 1. a., below.)

3. All seven of the original scrolls are now owned by the Hebrew University.

4. After the discovery of the first cave in 1947, Bedouins and archaeologists excavated about three hundred caves in the Dead Sea region. Eleven caves yielded material. The finds range from several more or less complete scrolls to tens of thousands of fragments.

B. *Dating of the Scrolls*

1. The question of the authenticity of the scrolls and the date of their composition has caused much controversy among scholars. A few scholars led by Solomon Zeitlin, an authority on Rabbinics, suggested that the scrolls were a forgery and a hoax, and others felt that they were authentic but not very old. A whole series of dates was offered— from the third century B.C.E. to the Middle Ages and even to the twentieth century. Most scholars now generally agree and date the manuscripts between the second century B.C.E. and the first century C.E.

2. The evidence provided by the scholars who studied the orthography and language of the scrolls showed that the language, based solidly on Biblical Hebrew, is strongly flavored with pre-Christian Aramaic, late Hebrew, and to some extent, Samaritan. The orthography and other linguistic features support a date between 200 B.C.E. and 100 C.E.

3. Archaeologists studied the context in which the manuscripts were found—the pottery, coins, and linens that were found with the scrolls.

   a. The pottery was clearly Roman, dating approximately from the second century B.C.E. to the first century C.E.

   b. The coins dated from the same period.

4. Nobel prize winner W. F. Libby used the radiocarbon method (which he developed) to date a fragment of the linen textiles in which the scrolls were wrapped. He reported a date of 33 C.E. with a two hundred-year margin of possible error either way. This would place the date of the linen wrapping roughly between 200 B.C.E. and 200

C.E. Thus, the conclusions of those Bible scholars and archaeologists who dated the Dead Sea manuscripts between the second century B.C.E. and the first century C.E. were confirmed by the radiocarbon method.

5. It is generally agreed that the scrolls were written before 68 C.E.; the caves in which they were found showed no signs of habitation after that date. Josephus, the Jewish historian of the time, wrote that 68 C.E. was the year the Roman legions swept down on Jerusalem, having passed through the Qumran area. It appears that the inhabitants of Qumran fled from the Romans. They temporarily stored away their documents, some with great care and others in haste, in earthenware jars in the caves. Apparently they were never able to return to reclaim them.

C. *The Qumran Library*

1. General Contents

   a. The Qumran library contains parts of some four hundred manuscripts. About ten scrolls have been relatively well preserved. Some texts are represented by only one fragment.

   b. The scrolls were written in Hebrew and Aramaic, and some are in ancient Hebrew (Phoenician) script. A few fragments are in Greek.

   c. The following are the seven scrolls originally discovered in the first cave:

      (1) A complete scroll of Isaiah, 24 feet long, written in Hebrew. This scroll is sometimes called the *St. Mark's Monastery Isaiah Scroll*, as it was previously owned by the monastery.

      (2) *The Manual of Discipline*, which contains rules by which members of the sect of the Dead Sea were governed.

      (3) *The Commentary on the Book of Habakkuk*, which gives the text of the first two chapters of Habakkuk, with a running commentary. It also contains some interesting historical allusions to figures believed to have lived at the time the scroll was written.

(4) *The Genesis Apocryphon*, which contains apocryphal accounts of some patriarchs in Genesis—Lamech, Enoch, Noah, Abraham, and Sarah. It is written in Aramaic.

(5) An incomplete scroll of Isaiah, also known as the *Hebrew University Isaiah Scroll.*

(6) *The Scroll of the War of the Sons of Light Against the Sons of Darkness (War Scroll)*, which gives directions for the conduct of an actual eschatological war between members of the sect and their enemies.

(7) *The Scroll of Thanksgiving Hymns*, which contains about thirty hymns resembling the psalms of the Old Testament.

2. Biblical Scrolls

a. About one fourth of the total manuscripts and fragments found in the Qumran caves consists of copies of books of the Bible, every book of the Hebrew Bible being represented except the Book of Esther. Parts of books such as Deuteronomy, Isaiah, the Minor Prophets, and the Psalms are represented by more than ten copies.

b. In general, the Biblical texts from Qumran indicate that the standard text of the Hebrew Bible, the Masoretic text, was prevalent in the first century C.E. Some of the Biblical texts were in circulation at the same time, at least up to 68 C.E.

c. Different textual traditions from the same book have helped clarify certain Biblical passages that were until now obscure. The 1952 Revised Standard Version of the Bible in its newest edition has followed the *St. Mark's Monastery Isaiah Scroll* in thirteen variant readings.

3. Apocryphal and Pseudepigraphical Literature

The popularity of apocryphal and pseudepigraphical works during the Intertestamental period is evidenced by the significant amount of this literature found at Qumran. (See Chapter VIII, "Apocrypha and Pseudepigrapha.")

a. Apocryphal works (religious literature which is not included in the Hebrew Canon) in the Dead Sea material include *Tobit*, *Ecclesiasticus (Ben Sira)*, and the *Epistle of Jeremy*.

b. Pseudepigraphical works (noncanonical writings ascribed to a famous historical personage in order to enhance the book's spiritual status) found at Qumran include fragments from the *Book of Jubilees*, the *Book of Enoch*, the *Testaments of the Twelve Patriarchs*, the *Prayer of Nabonidus*, and others.

c. The *Genesis Apocryphon* is a collection of stories written in the first person about Biblical patriarchs. It contains many parallels to the apocryphal *Book of Jubilees* and the *Book of Enoch*. It was written in Aramaic and has preserved contemporary Aramaic texts which increase our understanding of the language. It also sheds light on Talmudic and Midrashic lore.

4. Biblical Commentaries—*Pesharim*

a. The books of the Bible were the most important sources of study for the Qumran community, for like other teachers in Israel, the teachers of the sect believed that the words of the Scriptures could be applied to the events of their own lives.

b. The commentaries generally quote the Biblical text, a verse, or a few words of a verse. Immediately after the quotation the author adds his commentary, explaining the Biblical text in the perspective of his own day. This type of commentary is known as *Pesher* (Hebrew for "commentary").

c. The most complete of the Qumran commentaries is the *Habakkuk Commentary*.

d. The *Nahum Commentary*, like other Qumran commentaries, speaks of conflict and the sect's enemies, naming actual historical persons. It has been especially helpful in determining the date of the scrolls and in illuminating the identity of the sect, its history, and the history of the period in which its members lived.

e. The *Psalms Commentary* contains fragments from Psalms 37, 45, 57, and 68. The commentary on Psalm 37 is important for its biographical data on the "Teacher of Righteousness," the leader of the sect.

f. In addition, fragments have been found of commentaries on Genesis 49, Isaiah, Hosea, Micah, and Zephaniah. The *War Scroll* contains a commentary on a passage from Ezekiel.

5. Sectarian Literature

a. Some of the most interesting non-Biblical scrolls found at Qumran are the hitherto unknown writings of a religious sect that occupied the Qumran region.

b. *The Scroll of the Thanksgiving Hymns (Hodayot)* is a collection of hymns which vividly reflect the experiences and feelings of their author. This scroll has been of utmost importance for research on the comparative study of the doctrines of the Qumran sect and the background of Christianity.

c. The *Manual of Discipline* describes the doctrines of the sect and the regulations by which its daily life was governed.

(1) The scroll discusses the three-stage probationary period through which each initiate had to pass, the initiation ceremony, the daily life of the members, and the disciplinary code for the members of the sect.

(2) It explains that the members of the sect believed that they were volunteers who had pledged themselves to do what was good and right before God, according to the laws of Moses and the Prophets.

(3) We learn that the members sought to separate themselves from the society of wicked men, to love all sons of light and to hate all sons of darkness, to practice truth and modesty in the community, to act righteously and justly, to love mercy, and walk humble in all their ways.

(4) The scroll implies that the members were celibate, although there must have been women and children in the community, since the skeletons of females and children were found in the cemetery next to Khirbet Qumran. We may therefore assume that some of the members did marry. It is also possible that the members who volunteered to join in the community brought their wives and children with them.

d. The *War Scroll*, with its description of an actual or eschatological war between the members of the sect and their enemies, provides us with comprehensive data on military regulations of the Jewish armies during the late period of the Second Temple. It contains military and technical terms hitherto unknown, and it is the oldest record of Hebrew military craft extant.

6. The *Temple Scroll*

   a. Another Qumran scroll—the *Temple Scroll*—is the longest scroll found thus far near the Dead Sea. It is over 28 feet long.

   b. The *Temple Scroll* is unique in its content, being concerned with *halakhot* (religious rules on various subjects), sacrifices and offerings according to the festivals, statutes of the king and of the army, and a detailed description of the Temple.

7. The *Copper Scroll*

   a. Two copper scrolls which form a single scroll contain a long list of hidden treasures to the amount of some six thousand gold and silver talents. Many of the hidden items described in the *Copper Scroll* had been collected as "tithes" for the Temple and its priests.

   b. The *Copper Scroll* was probably intended to tell the Jewish survivors of the war then raging where this sacred material lay buried, so that if any should be found, it would never be desecrated by profane use. The scroll would also act as a guide to the recovery of the treasure, should it be needed to carry on the war.

D. *The Sect of the Scrolls*

1. There has been considerable controversy as to the identity of the sect that produced the Dead Sea Scrolls.

2. The sect of Qumran was part of the Jewish apocalyptic movement of the day. Its basic doctrine, institutions, and practices were in anticipation of the end of days when God would raise this sect to the position of the ruling class. They therefore dedicated themselves to a strict way of life in preparation for the time when they would triumph over their enemies.

3. The members of the Qumran sect led an austere, presumably celibate, life of shared goods, spending their time in study and writing, in crafts, and in agricultural works which helped support the community.

4. The sectarian literature of Qumran reflects the important position of the community's spiritual leader, the Teacher of Righteousness. He was the prime example of one who had been given a secret and profound knowledge, shared to a certain extent by, and confided only to, other members of the sect. A basic attitude of thankfulness for this gift is expressed in the Thanksgiving hymns.

5. The Qumran sect stressed the priesthood. Members often refer to themselves in their sectarian literature as sons of Zadok. They upheld rigid rules of Levitical purity, and though they recognized Temple service as obligatory, they dissociated themselves from the Jerusalem Temple. In their opinion, its priests were defiled and its liturgical calendar was incorrect.

6. Influenced by a description of contemporary Jewish sects in the writings of Josephus, many scholars have identified the Qumran sect with the Essenes, a group which flourished mainly in Palestine during the Second Jewish Commonwealth. (See Chapter IX, "Jewish Sects.")

E. *The Qumran Sect and Christianity*

1. Points of contact have been found between the way of life, practices, and doctrines of the Qumran sect and those of the early Christians.

   a. Both the Qumran community and the early Christian community held eschatological beliefs and both practiced a policy of shared goods.

   b. Many verbal parallels between the Qumran scrolls and the New Testament, especially the Gospel of John, have been noted by scholars.

   c. Parallels have been drawn between the leader of the Qumran sect—the Teacher of Righteousness—and Jesus of Nazareth. Closer inspection of their ways of life and doctrines clearly shows the two to be distinct from one another.

2. The differences between Qumran and the teachings of Jesus and early Christianity are most significant:

a. Jesus' objective was not to form a community of solitaries as the Qumran community seems to have been.

b. The universality of the Christian message stands in sharp contrast to the exclusiveness of Qumran.

c. The Qumran sect was ritualistic and legalistic, whereas Jesus stressed concern of one's fellowman.

d. The Qumran doctrines can be understood without their leader; Christianity is unthinkable without its leader.

F. *Significance of the Scrolls*

1. The Dead Sea Scrolls have shed light on the history of the Jewish religion and Jewish religious life and thought in Palestine during the period of the Second Temple.

2. They have given us a more precise insight into the life and faith of one of the dissident Jewish sects of brotherhood which existed during the Intertestamental period.

3. They have increased our knowledge of the history of the development of the text of the Hebrew Bible and of the Hebrew language and script.

4. The paramount importance of the scrolls to New Testament studies is their contribution toward knowledge of the immediate pre-Christian Era. They bring greater clarity to our understanding of the setting in which Christianity was born, the roots of some of its ideas, and its unique and distinct character.

XI

THE RISE OF CHRISTIANITY

Rome was at its height and enjoyed a unique and strong position in the ancient world; its empire extended from Britain to the Middle East. Rome, however, made few efforts to Romanize its subjects. The Romans favored the promotion of Greek culture instead. Eager to maintain law and order, the Romans left local populaces to their own affairs, provided they paid the tribute tax. However, the Jews in Palestine were hostile to Rome, both for taking away their independence and for instances of misrule on the part of proconsuls and procurators. Tension led to the outbreak of the war against Rome in 66 C.E.,* usually known as the First Jewish Revolt, with the resultant devastation of Jerusalem and Palestinian Judaism.

In the face of political tension and hardship, various responses are seen in the Jewish sects of the day. (See Chapter IX, "Jewish Sects.") The priestly Sadducees disappeared with the destruction of the Temple. The Zealots, their rebellion having failed, became almost nonexistent. The Essenes reflected widespread apocalyptic trends of the day—preparing for the end of the present era and the beginning of the Messianic Age which they believed to be imminent. After 70 the Pharisees emerged as the main sect and became responsible for transmitting the Jewish tradition. Greek philosophy and mystery religions also attempted to satisfy the ultimate questions and yearnings of the people of the day.

The many traces of Graeco-Roman thought and culture which abound even to this day in the Western world remind us of the greatness of this era in human history. But most significant of all, perhaps, is the influence which derived from the life and message of Jesus. It was he who drastically altered the course of human history and human life.

A. *Jesus*

1. Life

   a. Jesus was a Jew, born in Bethlehem in Judea about 4 B.C.E. His early life was spent in Nazareth in the Galilee with his mother Mary and her husband Joseph, a carpenter.

---

*All dates given in this chapter are C.E. (Common Era), often referred to as A.D., unless they are denoted as B.C.E. (Before the Common Era), often referred to as B.C.

b. At the age of about thirty, Jesus emerged from his humble surroundings. He was baptized in the Jordan by his cousin John. With this, his public life began.

c. Jesus' preaching, teaching, and healing ministry is believed to have lasted for about three years and to have taken place, for the most part, in Galilee. Like the rabbis of his day, Jesus spoke in the synagogues and debated with the scribes. Unlike the rabbis, he also taught in the open—in the streets, on the hillsides, and by the Sea of Galilee. In addition, he associated freely with all classes of people—with women, children, tax-collectors, sinners, and the poor who had no knowledge of the Law.

d. Because of his concern for the suffering and his healing activity, he was well received in many places. During his ministry he was accompanied by a small band of followers.

e. Having made a pilgrimage to Jerusalem for the celebration of Passover, Jesus was arrested by the Romans as a potential revolutionary, condemned as a false prophet, and executed in about 29 by order of the Roman procurator Pontius Pilate.

2. Teachings

a. The teachings of Jesus bear more resemblance to those of his contemporaries, the Pharisees, than to any other Jewish sect of his day. (See Chapter IX, "Jewish Sects.") He taught of the resurrection of the dead, life after death, reward and punishment on the Day of Judgment, the advent of the Kingdom of God, and the existence of angels and demons. In some cases, parallels exist between the sayings of Jesus and those of the rabbis. Like the rabbis, he often spoke in parables.

b. Though the gospels show that he was an observant Jew, Jesus differed with the Pharisees on the matter of scrupulous observance of the Law. His teaching emphasized purity of intention rather than external performance.

c. Like John the Baptist, Jesus preached of baptism and repentance in preparation for the Kingdom of God which, he taught, had begun.

3. Christian beliefs about Jesus include the following:

   a. That Jesus was the Messiah, the Christ, and that he was equal to God and yet fully man.

   b. That Jesus rose from the dead, ascended into heaven, and will return one day in glory to judge all men.

   c. That, though all are sinful, Jesus has won salvation for men by his life, death, and resurrection.

   d. That, through his life, death, and resurrection, Jesus gave men a foundation on which to hope for immortality, for life after death, for the triumph of good over evil.

   e. That Jesus was miraculously conceived by the Holy Spirit and born of the Virgin Mary.

   f. That Jesus is the Son of God, and with the Father and the Spirit, is one God in three divine persons.

   g. That Jesus is the Word (*Logos*) Incarnate and in him all of God's revelation to man is brought to completion.

   h. That Jesus sent God's Holy Spirit to be an abiding witness in his Church.

B. *Paul (Saul of Tarsus)*

1. Life

   a. Saul was born in the Hellenistic center of Tarsus in Asia Minor in one of the first years of the Common Era. Though he was knowledgeable of Greek culture, he was trained in the strictest Pharisaic manner and is believed to have studied in Jerusalem under Gamaliel I.

   b. Saul, a learned and zealous Pharisee, probably never met Jesus during his lifetime. Rather, he was initially a persecutor of the followers of Jesus.

   c. Having had a vision of the Risen Lord, Saul converted to Christianity and, after a period of solitude, became a zealous exponent of his new faith. Under the name of Paul, he undertook missionary journeys to Asia Minor and eastern Europe (Macedonia and Greece), and near the end of his life, he preached in Rome. On his journeys, Paul founded several Christian communities and later nurtured their development by return visits and/or by letters.

d. After his third journey, Paul was arrested in Jerusalem and tried before the Roman procurator. He appealed to Caesar and was taken as a prisoner to Rome, where he remained for several years. The Acts of the Apostles gives no account of Paul's death, but according to tradition, he was martyred, along with the apostle Peter, in Rome during the persecution of Nero (about 64).

e. Paul is called the Apostle of the Gentiles. Though he preached to his fellow Jews, he was the one largely responsible for the spreading of the gospel to the pagans. Most of his missionary activity and success was among Gentiles.

f. The life and teachings of Paul are found in the Acts of the Apostles and in the Pauline epistles of the New Testament.

2. Teachings of Paul

a. To the Jews, Paul proclaimed freedom from the Law and taught union with the Risen Lord as the new guiding principle.

b. In protest against the lax morals of the Hellenistic world, Paul taught a strong Jewish morality.

c. Paul's central teaching was that of *koinonia* ("fellowship"). He taught that the Christian was not alone with Christ, but, bound with his fellow believers, made up the body of the Risen Lord, the Church. Paul strove to weld this unity by directing his hearers to foster a closer relationship to their source of unity, Christ.

d. Paul taught that through faith and the acceptance of the gospel one could enter into the redemption accomplished by the death and resurrection of Jesus.

C. *The Early Church*

1. In the New Testament it is recorded that Jesus rose from the dead, appeared to his disciples, and commissioned them to spread the

message of the redemptive power provided by his death and resurrection. He then returned to the Father, but sent his Holy Spirit which enabled the disciples to become zealous teachers and witnesses to their faith in Jesus.

2. The Early Church had two main components—the Jerusalem Church and the Gentile Church.

   a. The Jerusalem Church centered around the apostles, who were Jewish and who had been with Jesus during his ministry. They were witnesses to his resurrection and had received his spirit. Their understanding of themselves as followers of Jesus was not contradicted by the keeping of the Law and Temple observance. They understood that their mission was to announce to the Jews that Jesus was the Messiah, the fulfillment of Old Testament promises. Initially, Gentiles were allowed baptism, but only after they were circumcised and agreed to follow the Mosaic Law.

   b. The Gentile Church had its center in Antioch in Syria. It consisted of believers who had been baptized but who were not previously circumcised and who did not feel bound by the Mosaic Law. It understood itself as related to Judaism but independent of it.

   c. The Council of Jerusalem (held c. 49 or 50) resolved the question of the observance of the Mosaic Law. There, the Jerusalem Church endorsed the policy of the Gentile Church and the mission of Paul to the Gentiles. At this point the Church destined itself to be a separate universal religion instead of a sect of Judaism.

3. The Jerusalem Church suffered intermittent troubles with the Romans and Jews. In general, they were disliked but tolerated. As Jewish-Christian differences mounted, the two became exclusive of one another and eventually their association deteriorated so that, in the following centuries, their main communication was through channels of polemical literature.

4. Having refused to join in the Jewish revolt against Rome (66-70), Christians in Jerusalem fled to Transjordan and to Gentile Christian centers. Thus, the center of Christianity was transferred to the Diaspora and, by the fourth century, was in Rome.

D. *Jewish Attitude Toward Jesus*

1. A passage about the life and death of Jesus appears in Josephus's *Antiquities*. However, the passage is thought to be a Christian revision of a statement by Josephus.

2. Some writings of the *amoraim* (see Appendix D, "Glossary") of the third and fourth centuries are directed against the Christian beliefs that Jesus was the Messiah, the Son of God, and, in fact, God. Some of these writings are polemics against specific Scriptural interpretations by Church Fathers.

3. References to Jesus and his teachings in early rabbinic literature are few. It is thought that the followers of Jesus were regarded much the same as the many other Jewish sects that existed near the end of the Second Temple Period.

4. The few references to Jesus in the Babylonian Talmud portray him as a rabbinical student who had strayed into evil ways. Conflicting references about Jesus' life and activities suggest that an accurate account of Jesus had not been transmitted in Jewish circles.

E. *Jewish-Christian Sects*

1. Though information about Jewish-Christian sects is scarce, it appears that there were a variety of groups in the early Christian centuries which consisted of persons born as Jews who continued to live by the laws of Judaism even though they accepted Jesus as teacher, prophet, and a messianic figure.

2. There is some confusion over the names of Jewish-Christian sects. Some sources speak of Ebionites (from the Hebrew *ebion*, "poor"). In the New Testament (Acts 24:5), they are referred to as Nazarenes. Other sources mention Elchasaites, named for a reputed founder, Elxai or Elchasai, who lived in the time of Trajan.

3. It appears that these groups varied in belief and practice. However, they were similar in that they adhered to Jewish practices and shared a common understanding of the nature and mission of Jesus.

   a. Some sources suggest that Jewish-Christian sects continued to observe the Sabbath in addition to keeping Sunday as the Lord's day (in memory of the resurrection of Jesus).

b. It is thought that although Christian baptism was practiced, some groups also attended Jewish ritual baths regularly. Other references suggest practices such as refraining from eating pork, etc.

c. The sects' understanding of the nature of Jesus and his mission differed from the view reflected in the canonical Gospels and accepted by the Church. They viewed Jesus as the prophetic lawgiver who renewed the Torah. Thus, they equated conversion to Jesus with conversion to Jewish Law. When the Church abandoned Jewish Law, it was considered a grave mistake by the Jewish-Christian sects.

4. Jewish-Christian beliefs often reflect Gnostic (see Appendix D, "Glossary") beliefs and thus were considered heretical by Jews and Christians alike. They were finally rejected by the Jews in the latter part of the first century. By 150 they were officially expelled from the Christian community by the Church of Rome.

F. New Testament Literature

1. The New Testament consists of twenty-seven canonical books which, according to Christian belief, complement the Old Testament and complete the written record of God's revelation to man.

2. All books of the New Testament, with the possible exception of the Gospel of Matthew, were originally written in the spoken Greek of the day, known as Koiné Greek. Frequent quotations from the Old Testament are, for the most part, taken from the Septuagint.

3. Most of the New Testament is believed to have been written after about 48 and before 150. The earliest works are believed to be those of Paul. The gospels were written between 65 and 95, and the Book of Revelation was probably written c. 96.

4. The complete list of the canonical books was recorded in a letter dated c. 367, so it is believed that these twenty-seven books were commonly accepted as canonical by that time. The New Testament books were officially canonized in one of the final years of the fourth century.

5. The New Testament canonical writings consist of:

a. Gospels: Accounts of the life and teachings of Jesus. Those of Matthew, Mark, and Luke bear a resemblance to one another in content, form, and language, and thus are called synoptic (taking a common view). The Gospel of John deviates from the others by inclusion or omission of portions of Jesus' life and teachings recorded by the synoptics or by the different arrangement of the contents. In general, the style of John is more mystical and poetic that that of the synoptics.

b. Acts of Apostles: Written by the gospel author Luke about 90, this is a record of the events of the early Church, centering chiefly on the activities of Peter and Paul.

c. Epistles: Letters by Christian leaders addressed, for the most part, to particular churches and presumably intended for public reading. In general, they concern problems facing the particular community. Others were pastoral in that they were directed to officials of various Christian communities. Romans, I and II Corinthians, and Galatians, the most important epistles for the elucidation of Paul's thought, were written by him, as were Philippians, Philemon, and I Thessalonians. Colossians and II Thessalonians are also often ascribed to Paul. Ephesians is thought by many to be the work of one of Paul's disciples. The Pastoral Epistles, I and II Timothy, and Titus, appear to be letters from Paul but are thought to have been post-Pauline, though they may contain genuine fragments from some of Paul's writings. The authorship of the Epistle to the Hebrews has been the topic of controversy since early Christian times. The "Catholic Epistles" are James, I and II Peter, I, II, and III John, and Jude. These epistles, more like tracts or instructions than letters, are called catholic because they are directed toward the Church at large rather than to an individual person or community. Authorship of these is not agreed upon by scholars.

d. Book of Revelation: Like other apocalyptic writings, it is likely that this work arose from the experience of persecution and difficulty, probably during the reign of Nero or Domitian. It contains usual apocalyptic elements such as symbolic forces of evil, visions, and clashing forces of good and evil in which God intervenes in a dramatic fashion and vindicates the persecuted. Unlike other apocalyptic works of the day, this work bears the name of its author, John (assumed to be the author of the fourth gospel), rather than a pseudonym.

New Testament Books*

Name of Book	Probable Date of Composition
1. Gospel According to Matthew	c. 75
2. Gospel According to Mark	c. 65
3. Gospel According to Luke	c. 80-90
4. Gospel According to John	c. 90-100
5. Acts of the Apostles	c. 80-90
6. Epistle to the Romans	c. 56-58
7. First Epistle to the Corinthians	c. 54 or 55
8. Second Epistle to the Corinthians	c. 55 or 56
9. Epistle to the Galatians	c. 49-54
10. Epistle to the Ephesians	c. 61 or 62 (or 65)
11. Epistle to the Philippians	c. 61 or 62
12. Epistle to the Colossians	c. 62 or 63
13. First Epistle to the Thessalonians	c. 50
14. Second Epistle to the Thessalonians	c. 50
15. First Epistle to Timothy	c. 100
16. Second Epistle to Timothy	c. 100
17. Epistle to Titus	c. 100
18. Epistle to Philemon	c. 62
19. Epistle to the Hebrews	either c. 68 or c. 96
20. Epistle of James	possibly 55-95
21. First Epistle of Peter	either c. 64 or c. 95
22. Second Epistle of Peter	possibly as late as 100-150
23. First Epistle of John	c. 70-100
24. Second Epistle of John	possibly 100
25. Third Epistle of John	possibly 100
26. Epistle of Jude	c. 90-125
27. Book of Revelation	c. 96 (?)

---

*All dates given are C.E. (Common Era), often referred to as A.D.

XII

PHILO (c. 30 B.C.E.-45 C.E.)

When Alexander the Great established Greek rule in the fourth century B.C.E., he built a metropolitan capital—Alexandria—on the northern shores of Egypt. The first population of this new capital was brought in from areas conquered by Alexander. However, the economic opportunities of the port city attracted others and Alexandria quickly became a commercial center. The famous Alexandrine Library and its academics also soon established that city as a great intellectual center. By the beginning of the Christian Era, Alexandria was second only to Rome as a focal point of the Western world.

Jews were among the builders of Alexandria. By Ptolemaic times, the city had become the most important center of Jewish life in Egypt. It is said that during the Roman period Jews composed two-fifths of the city's population. Alexandrian Jews enjoyed the rights of full citizens and participated in commerce, administrative affairs, and military service. In every aspect of life except religion, Alexandria's Jews assimilated into their Hellenistic environment. In addition, they enjoyed a certain autonomy. Their community affairs were handled by an ethnarch (i.e., head of the community), and the court system was in accord with Jewish tradition. Many Greeks objected to the fact that many Jews were recognized as citizens of the capital with the same rights as "natives." As a result, jealous competition between Jews and non-Jews entered nearly every aspect of life—shipping, crafts, governmental and military service, and the intellectual sphere.

The Jewish community in Alexandria maintained close ties with Jerusalem. Jews sent an annual contribution to the Temple and looked to Palestinian rabbinical centers for religious guidance. At the same time, they spoke Greek and participated fully in the intellectual and cultural life of Alexandria. Their aims were to familiarize Hellenistic Jews with their own national culture and to persuade their critics of the rationality of Judaism. Philo, a Jew of Alexandria, was the first Jewish philosopher to confront an alien culture and try to restructure Jewish thought accordingly. A product of Hellenism, he tried to reconcile Judaism with the Greek rational thought of the day.

Under the Romans the Jews in Alexandria were unique in being excused from the duty to worship Roman gods. Because this forced worship was meant to indicate loyalty to the Roman Empire, non-Jews of Alexandria accused the Jews of lack of patriotism. Greeks and Egyptians in Alexandria envied the self-government of the Jews, since they had been denied similar privileges. Thus, they were even more inclined to attack the

Jews, calling them a separate nation of foreigners in their midst. Tensions rose to the point of hostility. When Jews of Alexandria were forced to keep statues of emperors in their houses of worship, a delegation led by Philo was sent to the emperor concerning this violation of religious rights. At the same time, an anti-Jewish delegation was sent to Rome to represent the non-Jews of Alexandria. This group was headed by an Alexandrian anti-Semitic writer, Apion. The delegations finally met with Emperor Gaius Caligula in 37 C.E., but the emperor did not pay attention to the dispute and the delegations returned to Egypt with nothing changed. Soon after, however, Caligula was assassinated and the new emperor, Claudius (41-54 C.E.), ordered the restoration of rights to the Jews in the Diaspora. Thus the Jews in Alexandria regained, for a short time at least, their autonomy and their religious freedom.

A. *Life*

1. Little is actually known about the life of Philo, or Philo Judaeus (as he was called by the Christian Fathers), the most famous philosopher and writer of Hellenistic Jewry.

2. He was born probably between 30 and 20 B.C.E. in Alexandria, a descendant of a highly aristocratic family.

3. He devoted himself to Greek philosophy and to the Jewish life of the time.

4. He was an old man when he headed the delegation of Egyptian Jews to appeal to Emperor Caligula against the actions of anti-Semites in Alexandria.

B. *Major Philosophical Ideas*

1. Philo sees a basic dualism between a perfect God who is the foundation of being and the primal force, and an imperfect world (matter being the primal essence).

   a. He fails to define God clearly; basically, he states that God *is* (i.e., exists) and that He acts, but does not go further than that.

   b. He carries the idea of dualism to the individual, stating that the soul (which is of God) is imprisoned in the fleshly body (which is evil).

2. Philo merely states that man has an inclination to evil. He does not expound the concept of original sin but has probably influenced its development.

3. Philo relates the concept of a perfect God to the imperfect world by means of intermediaries which he refers to as angels. The chief intermediary is the *Logos*, or Word, which is the main agent of God's creative activity.

4. Philo sees philosophy or contemplation as the highest virtue. Philo's contemplation is not a strict rational philosophy, but more of a mystic union of God and man.

C. *Major Writings*

1. *Against Flaccus and Embassy to Gaius*: The former describes in detail the persecution of the Jews in Alexandria, while the latter is description of the mission to Rome that Philo headed.

2. *Allegorical Commentary on Genesis*: This is Philo's chief work. It is a commentary on the text of Genesis, with allegorical interpretations and philosophical teachings.

3. *Questions and Answers to Genesis and Exodus*: Although only fragments of this work remain in its original form, it was a short, verse-by-verse commentary.

4. *Outline of Mosaic Law*: A systematic presentation of the Torah with an attempt to arrange all Mosaic Law under the headings of the Ten Commandments.

5. *Life of Moses*: A description of Moses as the classical lawgiver.

D. *Significance*

1. Philo, through his exegetical and allegorical interpretation, attempted to reach a synthesis of Judaism and Greek philosophy. He tried to show that all the wisdom of Greece had its origins in the teachings of Moses.

2. He explained God's relation to this imperfect world by means of *Logos*, a concept which profoundly influenced early Christian theology.

3. His thought did not influence Judaism greatly, except, perhaps indirectly during the Middle Ages, when his influence is traceable in the Kabbalah (the mystic Jewish literature).

4. There are a few dubious references to Philo in rabbinic literature.

XIII

JOSEPHUS (c. 38-100 C.E.)

Josephus is important both as an historical figure and as an historian. His was a prominent, if somewhat notorious, role in the First Jewish Revolt against Rome. He was well educated in Jewish lore and in the Greek disciplines, and his writings are attempts to present himself and the Jewish people in the best possible light to the Roman world.

A. *Life*

Josephus was born c. 38 C.E.* as Joseph ben Mattityahu ha-Cohen, a descendant of a priestly family. After a youthful attachment to the Essenes, he associated himself with the the Pharisees. A visit to Rome at the age of twenty-six and contacts with the Roman imperial household convinced him of Rome's invincibility.

In 64 Josephus was appointed commander of Galilee. He was responsible for establishing a provincial government and for raising and commanding troops for the northern province. His indifferent efforts at waging war and his feelings toward Rome made his loyalty suspect. The patriotic Zealot faction led by Johanan of Gush Halav attempted several times, though unsuccessfully, to have Josephus deposed and assassinated.

Under the attack of Vespasian and Titus, Josephus's untrained troops fled to the fortifications at Jotapata, where, failing to defend themselves, they were massacred by the Romans. Only forty defenders remained, and they agreed to avoid surrender by committing suicide. They all did so, except Josephus, who surrendered to the Romans.

Installed at the Imperial palace in Rome, Josephus Flavius devoted his time to writing history. The surname Flavius—the family name of Emperor Vespasian—was added to honor his Roman patron.

B. *Works*

1. *History of the Jewish Wars*

   a. This, Josephus's most famous work, was originally written in Aramaic and then translated into Greek for the purpose of

---

*All dates given in this chapter are C.E. (Common Era), often referred to as A.D., unless otherwise indicated.

providing an officially Roman-sanctioned history of the Jewish Wars.

b. It is composed of seven books. The first two are devoted to a survey of Jewish history from the persecution of Antiochus Epiphanes in 168 B.C.E. to the war with Rome in 67, and the last five deal in great detail with the story of the Jewish rebellion against the Romans.

2. *The Antiquities of the Jews*

a. Josephus's magnum opus of twenty books was written in order to extol the Jewish people by recording their ancient and glorious history. He records the complete history of the Jews from the Creation to the Wars with Rome.

b. The first ten books are based mainly on Biblical records, with some condensation and embellishment. Postexilic history is the subject of the last ten books.

3. *Autobiography*

Written in 95, possibly as an appendix to his *Antiquities*, this book, although supposedly autobiographical, gives a detailed account of the war in Galilee. It is an attempt to justify his behavior, and as a consequence, there are many distortions of fact. There are many discrepancies between the account of his command as told in the *History of the Jewish Wars* and as told in the *Autobiography*.

4. *Against Apion*

a. The title to this book is misleading in that it deals not only with Apion, but with all slanderers of the Jews and Judaism. Apion has been described as the exponent and forerunner of classical anti-Semitism. Playing the role of the champion of the Jews, his book is permeated with an apologetic spirit.

b. Almost all of Josephus's writings served the purpose of defending the Jewish people and their religion before Graeco-Roman public opinion. He exposes the charges of the slanderers, extols the excellence of the Jewish character and the Jewish religion, and exalts Jewish social and ethical laws.

c. He also describes the Jewish concept of God and exalts Moses as the oldest legislator.

C. *Evaluation*

1. Josephus's accounts are colored to suit the desires of the Roman emperor.

2. There is evidence of many inaccuracies, discrepancies, and omissions in Josephus's writings. (He does not refer, for instance, to the great Jewish scholars of his day, such as Rabbi Hillel).

3. Josephus's works are the only historical accounts written by a Jew from this period.

4. They are valuable as documents of cosmopolitan ideas of the Diaspora.

5. Josephus served his people by giving his contemporary world the elements and ideas of Jewish history and faith.

6. Josephus's works record some aspects of Egyptian, Syrian, and Roman history.

7. The works of Josephus were rescued and preserved by the Church, undoubtedly because of an interpolated passage about Jesus (*Antiquities* XVIII, 3:3). He is highly extolled by Church historians.

XIV

MASADA

Masada is a fortress built on an isolated rock in the Judean desert near the southwestern shores of the Dead Sea. Until 1963 it was perhaps the best-known unexcavated site of antiquity in Israel. It was known to classical archaeologists as the site on which Herod the Great built his famous fortifications, palaces, and storerooms. And it is known to the youth of modern Israel as a regular place of national pilgrimage—a place to commemorate the tragic and heroic deaths of its 960 Zealot Jewish defenders, who in 73 C.E.* preferred to end their lives at their own hands rather than become slaves—both physical and spiritual—to the Romans.

In 1963 an archaeological expedition under the leadership of Yigael Yadin, one of the best-known archaeologists in Israel, set out to determine what archaeological discovery could add to the prevailing myth and legend of Masada's history. The excavation substantiated, for the most part, the sole contemporary historical account of Masada, that of Josephus. (See Chapter XIII, "Josephus.") The ornate mosaics discovered side by side with the crude living quarters showed the sharp contrast between Herod's life at Masada in 30 B.C.E. and that of the Zealots in 66. Masada is also an historical catalogue of the nature of art and architecture from Herod's time down to the Byzantine period.

A. *History of Masada*

1. Herod

   a. Masada first came to prominence during Herod's reign (37-4 B.C.E.).

   b. Herod the Great, an Edomite, was appointed by the Romans as king over Judea. He was disliked by his Jewish subjects and consequently he feared the masses lest they overthrow him and restore their former Maccabean kings to the throne.

   c. An even greater threat to Herod was Cleopatra, Queen of Egypt, who coveted Herod's ruling position in Judea and, with the support of her lover Antony, openly sought Herod's removal.

---

*All dates given in this chapter are C.E. (Common Era), often referred to as A.D., unless otherwise indicated.

d. Thus between 36 and 30 B.C.E., Herod built for himself and his family a formidable and seemingly impregnable fortress at Masada.

    (1) The surface of Masada (about 600 by 200 meters) was ringed with a protective casement wall. (A casement wall is a double wall with the space between the walls partitioned into chambers which serve as storerooms, barracks, arsenals, etc.)

    (2) A watercourse was constructed to catch the winter rains and many cisterns were hewn out of the rock.

    (3) Herod's buildings at Masada included administrative buildings, huge storehouses, a Roman bathhouse, and even a large swimming pool. A western royal palace seems to have served for residential, ceremonial, and administrative functions. An elaborate and luxuriously equipped northern palace served as Herod's private quarters. In addition, several smaller palaces were constructed for Herod's family and high officials.

2. Zealots

a. After Herod's death (4 B.C.E.) a Roman garrison took control of Masada. The Romans held the fortress until the beginning of the Jewish Revolt in 66. At that time the Zealots (see Chapter IX, "Jewish Sects") destroyed the Roman garrison and held Masada throughout the war (66-73).

b. Masada was the last stronghold to stand after Jerusalem fell to the Romans (70). For over two years, the Zealots and others who had escaped to Masada from Jerusalem and elsewhere used it as an outpost from which to harass and attack Roman garrisons.

c. The Roman general Flavius Silva was determined to crush this outpost of resistance. With five thousand soldiers and over nine thousand slaves and prisoners of war carrying water, timber, and provisions, he stationed himself along the slopes of Masada. (The remains of at least nine Roman camps around the base of the rock are clearly visible today.) From the Western approach to Masada they constructed a ramp of beaten earth and stones. On this ramp they erected a siege tower, and under covering fire from its top, they moved a battering ram up the ramp and directed it against the fortress wall. In April of 73 they succeeded in making a breach in the Zealot's fortifications at the top of Masada. Assured of their imminent victory, they retreated to their camps to prepare for an all-out attack the next day.

d. Josephus relates that at this point Eleazar ben Ya'ir, the leader of the Jewish defenders, delivered a stirring speech to his fellow Jews. They all resolved to burn their public buildings and die by their own hands rather than to submit to Roman defeat. It is said that each man killed his own wife and children and then laid down beside them to be killed by one of ten men chosen by lot. When these ten had slain all the men, they cast lots among themselves and one was chosen to slay the rest, then take his own life.

e. The next morning, as the Romans launched their confident assault, they met smoldering ruins and silence. Only two women with several children emerged from their hiding place to tell the story of the 960 Jews who had died.

3. After the death of the Jewish defenders a Roman garrison was again stationed on Masada for some time.

4. During the fifth and sixth centuries, Masada was inhabited by a small group of Byzantine monks. They lived in humble cells and caves and built a small chapel. It is assumed that they were forced to leave at the time of the Persian or Moslem conquest in the early seventh century. Since then, Masada has been unoccupied.

B. *Archaeological Excavations at Masada*

1. In 1963 Yigael Yadin and a company of professional archaeologists and zealous volunteers set out to verify the events recorded by Josephus about Masada. The archaeological expedition worked eleven months through two archaeological seasons, 1963-1964 and 1964-1965.

2. Finds

a. Excavations confirmed Josephus's detailed description of Herod's northern palace. Triple-terraced, it was built on the very edge of the precipice 900 feet above the Dead Sea. It is the only spot on Masada that enjoys constant shade and shelter from desert winds. The living quarters on the upper terrace were adorned with white and black mosaics and wall paintings. Best preserved was the bottom terrace with its multicolored wall painting adorning the double colonnade surrounding a large balcony overlooking the sea.

b. One of the biggest Roman public baths ever discovered in this part of the world, and definitely the best preserved, was found complete with all its installations and lavish adornments. The walls of the rooms were covered with Roman frescoes and the floors with beautiful mosaics.

c. Storeroom and water canals built by Herod to catch winter rains were discovered. Seven storerooms yielded hundreds of jars containing remnants of food with labels clearly describing their contents in Aramaic and Hebrew.

d. Yadin discovered that the Zealots had used several of Herod's public buildings for administrative purposes. The palaces housed a few families, but for the most part, the Zealots used the chambers of the casement wall as living quarters. Excavations of those chambers yielded cupboards, ovens, domestic utensils, and cosmetic items which told of the daily life of the Jewish defenders.

e. Two of the most interesting buildings excavated reflect the religious life of Masada's inhabitants.

   (1) What is believed to have been a synagogue is a rectangular hall with two rows of columns and mud benches all around. It faces Jerusalem. If this was a synagogue, it is not only the earliest synagogue known, but the only one to survive from the time of the Second Temple.

   (2) One chamber of the casement wall was a ritual bath (*mikveh*), It contained three basins, or baths, constructed according to Jewish religious law and supplied by rainwater. This is the only ritual bath to survive from this period.

f. Portions of fourteen scrolls—Biblical, sectarian, and apocryphal— have been found at Masada.

   (1) Biblical scrolls included five chapters of the Book of Psalms, identical in text and spelling to the traditional Hebrew text. Fragments from Leviticus, Genesis, and Ezekiel were also found.

(2) Among the scroll fragments is one which is identical to a scroll found in Qumran Cave IV. This particular scroll, consisting of liturgies associated with the heavenly Sabbath sacrifices, is highly sectarian and belonged to the Dead Sea Sect. (See Chapter X, "The Dead Sea Scrolls.") Its terminology is also similar to that of the Dead Sea Scrolls. This find has been of utmost importance. It is the first Dead Sea scroll to have been found outside of Qumran. And, since its contents are identical with some of the Dead Sea materials, we now have clear evidence that the Dead Sea Scrolls belong to the first century or before.

(3) Excavators found fragments of a copy of the Hebrew text of the apocryphal Book of Ecclesiasticus (Wisdom of Jesus the Son of Sirach, or, in Hebrew, Ben Sira) composed c. 180 B.C.E. This find was most exciting because the Hebrew original of the book had been lost and it existed only in translation. In 1896 a few chapters had been found in the famous geniza (hiding place for sacred manuscripts) in an old Cairo synagogue—known as the Cairo Geniza—and now more chapters were discovered at Masada. The scroll found at Masada verified that the Hebrew text from the Cairo Geniza was the authentic Hebrew text of the book, a point long disputed by scholars.

(4) Another scroll fragment discovered belonged to the pseudepigraphical Book of Jubilees.

g. Excavators also found a number of Latin papyri which were military documents left behind by the Roman garrisons.

h. Ostraca

(1) Numerous inscriptions were found on ostraca (inscribed pieces of pottery). Most of the inscriptions were names of owners, and most of these were familiar Hebrew names. Eleven potsherds inscribed with Jewish names (one with the name of Ben Ya'ir, who was the leader of the Zealots at Masada), found near the Zealots' public buildings, have been described by Yadin as his most exciting discovery. Could these possibly have been the lots cast by those last few defenders, as described by Josephus?

(2) The ostraca from Masada have been important for the study of the history of the Hebrew script.

(3) Some wine jars were inscribed with exact dates according to the standard Roman system of date recording, and included the name of the Roman consul of that particular year. Most of the jars bore the name of Sentius Saturnius, Roman consul for the year 19 B.C.E. Some were inscribed with Herod's name.

i. Potsherds from the Herodian period are of special significance, since they enable us to observe with ease the changes in shapes and makes of pottery vessels that occurred from the time of Herod to that of the Zealots—a period of about seventy years.

j. The thousands of coins found at Masada compose one of the largest collections of Jewish and Roman coins ever to have been catalogued. Most of the coins were Roman. However, some are stamped with the insignia and dates of the Jewish Revolt.

k. Excavators unearthed a simple Byzantine chapel of the fifth or sixth century, complete with its mosaic floor. A few coins from that period were also found.

C. Issues

1. The sectarian scroll, a duplicate of one found at Qumran, has caused considerable scholarly debate. The Dead Sea Sect is believed to have been the Essenes, who were pacifists. The Masada defenders were militant Zealots. How did an Essene scroll reach a Zealot stronghold? Some have used the discovery of this scroll to defend their view that Qumran was a Zealot stronghold and not an Essene monastery. On the other hand, Yadin suggested that the Essenes of the Judean wilderness joined the Zealots on Masada after the destruction of Qumran.

2. Some have claimed that the final heroic action of Masada's defenders was not heroism at all, since self-annihilation is contrary to basic Jewish doctrine. The only incident in Jewish tradition where precedent is found for condoning the taking of one's life in order to avoid dishonor at the hands of foes is the example of the Maccabees, two hundred years before the Zealots of Masada.

XV

DISCOVERIES PERTAINING TO
THE BAR KOKHBA REVOLT

The destruction of Jerusalem in 70 C.E.* put an end to Jewish hopes of rebelling against Roman control and oppression. The events at Masada (see Chapter XIV, "Masada") quelled the activities of the leaders of the revolt, the militant Zealots, and marked the end of the unsuccessful war against the Romans (66-73). After the war, the Jewish community in Palestine slowly revived. Under the leadership of the Sanhedrin, the Patriarch (Hebrew *nasi* or President of the Sanhedrin, this Patriarch was recognized by Rome as a political leader of the Jewish people), and local rabbis, the Jewish populace concentrated on deepening its religious and intellectual life. There was still a tribute to be paid, and Judea's postwar poverty made the Roman tax unendurable at times.

In protest against the policies of Trajan (97-117), the Jews of the Diaspora in Egypt, Cyrene, and Cyprus, with support from the Armenians and Parthians, rose in revolt in 115, but they were soon put down amidst much bloodshed. Meanwhile, the Jews in Palestine had been issued a vague promise, possibly by Trajan, that the Temple would be rebuilt. Hadrian (117-138) decided not to fulfill this promise and caused further consternation when he prohibited circumcision and other fundamental practices of Judaism. Relations between Jews and Romans reached the breaking point with news of Hadrian's decision to rebuild Jerusalem as a heathen city. The city was to be called *Aelia Capitolina* after the emperor Publius Aelius Hadrianus (Hadrian) and the god Jupiter Capitolinus, in whose honor a temple was constructed. The situation needed only a spark and a capable leader to bring about the inevitable explosion. The Jews' unshakable faith in a speedy, miraculous deliverance and the belief in a life hereafter had robbed war of its terrors. Hadrian provided the spark and a zealous leader appeared in Simeon Bar Kokhba.

The Second Jewish Revolt against Rome was not recorded by any second-century historian. Until 1951 the only information about it was that given in the Talmud, Midrash, and references in Roman and early Christian writings.

---

*All dates given in this chapter are C.E. (Common Era), often referred to as A.D., unless otherwise indicated.

A. *The Revolt*

1. Simeon Bar Kokhba

   a. Archaeological discoveries have revealed that the real name of the leader of the Second Revolt was Simeon Ben Kosiba.

   b. Simeon was declared messianic king by Rabbi Akiva and was henceforth called Bar Kokhba ("Son of a Star"), no doubt with reference to Numbers 24:17: "There shall step forth a star out of Jacob."

   c. It is known that not all the rabbis of the day shared Rabbi Akiva's enthusiasm for Bar Kokhba.

   d. Rabbi Akiva's role in the revolt remains obscure.

2. In its early stages (132), the uprising against the Romans was completely successful. The Romans were driven out of Judea, Jerusalem was captured, the sacrificial cult was apparently restored, the "Freedom of Israel" was officially proclaimed, and Jewish coins were once again struck.

3. In 133 the Romans counterattacked with an army of thirty-five thousand men under the command of Julius Severus. Talmudic extracts suggest that they first entered Galilee, then fought for the Valley of Jezreel, Ephraim, and the Judean hills, eventually retaking Jerusalem. In 134-135 the Romans invaded Bar Kokhba's stronghold, Betar, and gradually reduced the remaining hill and cave strongholds.

4. Betar fell to the Romans soon after, either through Samaritan treachery or through the failure of the water supply. The latter is the theory which archaeological evidence tends to support. Bar Kokhba was killed, reportedly by a poisonous snake, though a Samaritan claimed to have slain him. Virtually the whole population of Betar was slaughtered, including schoolchildren who, according to an eyewitness account, were wrapped in their study scrolls and burned to death.

5. Records tell of the destruction of 50 fortresses and 985 villages during the war, and of 580,000 Jewish casualties in addition to those who died of hunger and disease.

6. As a result of the revolt, Judea fell into desolation, its population was decimated, and Jerusalem was turned into a heathen city barred to Jews. (See Chapter IV, "Rome and Jerusalem.")

B. *Early Archaeological Discoveries Pertaining to Bar Kokhba (1950-1953)*

1. Discovery and Location

   a. The first documents dating from the period of the revolt were found in 1950 by Bedouin of the Ta'amireh tribe. In 1951 they brought to Jerusalem a group of manuscripts which they had found the preceding summer in caves at Wadi Murabbaat.

   b. The Wadi Murabbaat caves are situated 25 kilometers (about 15 miles) southeast of Jerusalem and 18 kilometers (about 10 miles) south of Qumran. The location of the caves makes access difficult.

   c. On the basis of the information given by the Bedouin, Father R. de Vaux and G. L. Harding, two archaeologists who had been working with the Dead Sea Scrolls from the very beginning, excavated the Wadi Murabbaat area in 1952.

2. Archaeological Finds

   a. In 1952 two letters, addressed by Simeon Bar Kokhba to Yehoshua ben Galgola, were found.

   b. In 1953 a letter was found that was written to Bar Kokhba from two officials of a Jewish community.

   c. Another letter addressed to ben Galgola was found. It was written by several leaders of the community in a village called Beth Mashko, and ben Galgola is addressed as the Head of the Camp, that is, commander of the army.

   d. Other fragments were found dating from the period of the revolt—documents dealing with real estate transactions, a bill of divorce, and contracts concerning the renting of fields guaranteed by the authority of Bar Kokhba.

3. Significance of Early Discoveries

a. The letter from Simeon to Yehoshua, son of Galgola, was probably written or dictated by Simeon himself. Signed "Simeon son of Kosiba," it acquaints us with the original form of the name of the revolt's leader. It also confirms the fact that Simeon was indeed the first name of Bar Kokhba. Until now this had only been inferred from the name of Simeon on certain coins.

b. The same letter shows that Hebrew was used, at least for official letters, and demonstrates the influence of Aramaic on this Hebrew.

c. The letter attests to the use of papyrus for letter writing in the second century and gives us an initial formula: "from X to Y," a greeting used at the time. It provides a specimen of a private (i.e., nonscribal) handwriting of that date.

d. The early finds were the first direct pieces of contemporary evidence in connection with the revolt of 132.

C. *Expedition of 1960*

1. Background

a. In 1953, additional caves located 1000 feet above sea level in the vicinity of Wadi Murabbaat were discovered by Y. Aharoni of the Hebrew University and a unit of paratroopers. Cigarettes, shreds of Bedouin clothing, and firearms were found in these caves (along with some documents), confirming suspicions that the Wadi Murabbaat caves were being rifled by Bedouins in search of documents for which Western scholars in Jerusalem would pay fantastic sums.

b. In 1955 Aharoni led a new expedition to the Hever Valley near Nahal Hever and slightly south of Wadi Murabbaat. There the Cave of Fears was discovered.

(1) The expedition found dozens of well preserved skeletons of adults and children. Other finds in this and nearby caves made it clear that this was one of the hideouts of the Bar Kokhba rebels after they had been driven into the mountains by the Roman legions.

(2) The tools, inscriptions, and documents found in 1955 showed that rather than surrender to the legionnaires who were besieging them, the rebels slowly starved to death in the caves after their supplies had given out. The Romans, on the other hand, were unable to storm the caves on the forbidding mountain slopes. The remains of several Roman siege camps were found in the area surrounding the mountain.

2. In 1960 archaeologists Y. Yadin, N. Avigad, Y. Aharoni, and P. Bar-Adon of the Hebrew University led a follow-up of the 1955 expedition. One large cave with three chambers in the Nahal Hever area yielded several important finds.

a. Burial Niche: Along the right-hand wall of the third chamber, which was several yards long and two yards wide, there was a collection of baskets overflowing with skulls. In the far corner were layer upon layer of large mats covering human bones. Between the mats and the bones were a great many fragments of colored cloth. In the center of the niche was another burial basket covered by large pieces of colored cloth. These were probably the remains of some of Bar Kokhba's warriors and their families who died of starvation and whose bones were later gathered up and placed in the niche.

b. Coin: A small coin was found on the ground in front of the cave. One side had a palm tree and the inscription *Shimon* ("Simeon"), and the other had a bunch of grapes and the words *Leherut Yerushalayim* ("for the freedom of Jerusalem"). It is likely that this coin had rolled to the foot of the cave when it fell from the hand of one of Bar Kokhba's men as he climbed into the cave.

c. Roman Cult Vessels: In the first chamber of the cave a woven basket with Roman cult vessels was unearthed. Some of the figures of deities had been rubbed out and their faces marred. These vessels were probably booty taken by Bar Kokhba's fighters from a Roman camp before they were forced to flee to the caves, since it is known that the Roman legions went into battle carrying all the equipment needed for ritual purposes.

d. Letters

(1) At the farthest end of the cave, in a bag containing women's treasures, was found a small package with fifteen Bar Kokhba

letters, nine in Aramaic, four in Hebrew, and two in Greek. The letters contained orders from Bar Kokhba to his fellow soldiers. One of them was signed "Shimon Ben Kosiba, ha-Nasi al Yisrael" (Simeon Bar Kokhba, prince or president of Israel).

(2) The letters confirm rabbinic stories that Bar Kokhba was a stern and ruthless commander who gave orders in a clear, concise style. He was undoubtedly a pious man concerned with religious observance. He might also have been a supreme egotist—he described himself as "prince over all Israel." In the Greek letters we have his name for the first time in Greek, the spelling now known to be Kosiba or Koziba.

Through the letters we learn the names of several people and villages involved in the revolt and a little about life in Judea at the time. One of the letters confirms Yadin's belief that the letters belong to the period before the rebels took refuge in the caves, since it deals with such matters as crops, fields, and houses. This letter also establishes the fact that rebel headquarters were at Ein Gedi, less than four miles north of Nahal Hever, where the letters were found. (Ein Gedi is the oasis of the entire region of the Dead Sea.) Another letter, giving instructions to two men in regard to the loading and unloading of supplies from a boat "at your port," also establishes the importance of Ein Gedi at the time.

One letter deals with the *lulav* and *etrog*, ritual articles needed for the holiday of *Sukkot*, which occurs in September. This letter strongly suggests that all the letters were written in the year before the defeat of the Jewish rebels, i.e., 134. Since, according to tradition the war ended on the Ninth of Av in 135, and since *Sukkot* falls two months later, it would seem that this was the last *Sukkot* festival to be celebrated in freedom by the rebels.

D. *Expedition of 1961*

1. In 1961 an expedition organized by the same archaeologists who had led the 1960 expedition set out to further explore the same area.

2. Finds included a cache of ancient objects—wooden tools, a lacquered jewelry box, household utensils of wood and copper, kitchen knives,

women's sandals, a scythe, and a hand mirror. Also found were five door keys, one of them particularly large, which are believed to have been the keys to the Ein Gedi fortress which the rebels were forced to abandon.

3. A hollowed-out reed containing a rolled-up scroll, a leather pouch containing several papyri, a goatskin bag containing skeins of yarn, pieces of cloth, and, at the very bottom, a bundle of thirty-five papyrus scrolls were found.

    a. Three documents from the leather pouch, written in elegant Mishnaic Hebrew, are contracts covering the lease of land in Ein Gedi. These documents are dated in the third year of Simeon Bar Kokhba, Prince of Israel. Another deals with the sale of a vegetable garden in Ein Gedi.

    b. The bundle of papyri found in the goatskin bag belonged to a woman named Babata and pertained to her legal affairs—which were extensive and complicated since she had two husbands and was involved in several disputes over property and the guardianship of her fatherless son Yeshua. Most of the thirty-five documents were in Greek, with some in Aramaic and Nabatean. These documents clarify much about the legal system of the times and explain many heretofore obscure references in the Talmud.

4. Skeletons, some in wooden coffins, were found in all the caves. In one cave as many as forty were discovered, most of them women and children, indicating that the majority of the men were killed in battle outside the caves. On one skeleton, found covered with canvas, the face was still clearly defined and even had some hairs left on the head. The way in which this skeleton was covered and preserved has led archaeologists to assume that he was one of Bar Kokhba's senior commanders and therefore was given a special burial.

E. *Summary of the Bar Kokhba Finds*

1. It is now known definitely that the Emperor Hadrian's troops, under the leadership of Julius Severus, crushed the Jewish rebels after the rebels had successfully captured about fifty towns from the Roman legions. Severus pushed the rebels into the last refuge among the caves of the Judean wilderness by the Dead Sea.

2. The caves were well stocked with food and contained natural cisterns. The Romans, knowing this, encamped at either end of the valleys leading into and out of the cave areas and waited. Rather than surrender, the rebels remained and died of starvation.

3. In addition to discoveries pertaining to the Jewish revolt of 132, Wadi Murabbaat and the surrounding areas have also produced significant finds from the Chalcolithic period (4000-3000 B.C.E.).

F. *Significance of Bar Kokhba Finds*

1. We learn from the letters that Bar Kokhba's authority might have been a little weak in the provinces, and that he probably had his headquarters in the vicinity of Bethlehem. We also learn of the importance of Ein Gedi as a port. Supplies must have come from the southern end of the Dead Sea or from the eastern bank of Ein Gedi on the western bank, then have been transferred inland to troops fighting the Romans.

2. We learn of the religious fervor of the rebels from their preparation for the holiday of *Sukkot*, and from the fact that the garments found were made entirely of wool. (Strict Jewish observance forbids mixing animal and vegetable fibers in a garment.) We learn of a new and unknown figure in Jewish history—Botniyz Bar Miasa, who is given the name Rabenu, a name given in other sources only to Moses and Judah. Bar Miasa must have been a great spiritual leader (probably head of the Sanhedrin) about whom all records have been lost.

3. Yadin feels that the letters were written before the flight to the caves because some of them deal with the village of Tekoah which, at the time of the last stand in the caves, was already in Roman hands. Also, the fact that some of the letters concern grain harvest indicates that the Jews still possessed some land. The collector of the letters must have prized them highly, since he or she took the trouble of carrying them along on the flight to the caves and depositing them among the women's belongings where they were not likely to be found by Roman captors.

4. The many documents and household, personal, and war items give us much new and valuable information as to how the people lived in Palestine during the Bar Kokhba revolt, some eighteen hundred years ago. This was a period of Jewish history which, until now, contained many gaps.

XVI

JEWS IN PALESTINE AND BABYLONIA:
THE GREAT RABBINICAL SCHOOLS

The spiritual vacuum created by the destruction of the first Temple and its sacrificial rites resulted in an emphasis on the Torah and a devotion to history. But intellectual activity seems to thrive among those who are not besieged by overwhelming obstacles, as is seen in the decline of Palestine and development of Babylonian intellectual centers.

Judaism's emphasis on the Torah and on learning was born in the Babylonian Exile. It developed in Palestine in the setting of Persian, Greek, and Roman rule, nurtured by Ezra, the Sopherim, and the Great Assembly, the authoritative group which carried out the reforms of Ezra. Under Roman rule the treatment of Jews in Palestine alternated between persecution and tolerance.

On the other hand, the Babylonian Jews, under Parthian and later under Persian rule, enjoyed a degree of liberty and prosperity which allowed them to devote themselves to intellectual growth and to establish the great Talmudic academies. It was here that the Talmud and numerous works of the Midrash were compiled. For the most part, the Jews here were autonomous. Their numbers grew as Jews from Palestine sought refuge in the aftermaths of the Hasmonean revolt, the destruction of the second Temple, and Bar Kokhba's revolt. Under Moslem rule (beginning in the seventh century), Jews enjoyed more peace than they had under the previous Persian rule and they thrived in the Moslem cultural revival. It was not until near the end of the tenth century that difficulties in trade relations between Eastern and Western Moslem people brought economic troubles and thus heavy taxes in the East. The academies suffered amidst a general cultural decline, and by about 1000 C.E.*, deteriorating conditions forced Jewish scholars in Babylonia to seek more favorable ground in Spain.

A. *Palestinian Center*

1. Pre-Mishnaic Period

   a. Five pairs (*Zugot*) of scholars representing five generations of leaders guided the Jews from about the time of the Maccabean

---

*All dates given in this chapter are C.E. (Common Era), often referred to as A.D., unless otherwise indicated.

Revolt to the time of Herod (i.e., second and first centuries B.C.E.).

(1) The pairs consisted of the *Nasi* (prince), president of the school, and the *Av-Bet-Din*, the dean of the Sanhedrin, the highest religious council and court.

(2) These scholars were concerned, for the most part, with *halakhah*—legal portions of the Oral Law which were interpretations of the Written Law of the Torah.

(3) The most renowned of the scholars of this time were Hillel and Shammai, noted for their respective schools and opposing opinions on many points of Jewish law.

b. The generations of scholars which followed the Zugot were called *Tannaim* (an Aramaic word for "those who study and teach"). The Tannaim flourished between the first century B.C.E. and the third century C.E.

(1) An important intellectual center was founded at Jabneh by Johanan ben Zakkai, the first Tanna after the destruction of the Temple.

(2) Subsequent Tannaitic scholars included Rabban Gamaliel, Rabbi Akiva ben Joseph, and Simon the Second, son of Gamaliel.

(3) The scholars of this period attempted to compile the vast collections of *halakhot* that had come down to them. They also served as guides in the application of these laws to daily life. Their legal decisions and opinions are contained in the Mishnah. (See Chapter XVII, "The Talmud.")

2. Mishnaic Period

a. By the middle of the second century, Roman hostility had lessened and schools were reopened; the Jewish community in Palestine regained some of its former strength.

b. During the last half of the second century, the Mishnah, which became the standard codification of Oral Law, was compiled and arranged by subject matter under the leadership of Judah ha-Nasi, the last of the Tannaitic scholars.

3. Post-Mishnaic Period

    a. The five generations of post-Mishnaic scholars in Palestine, called *Amoraim* ("commentators"), were concerned with expounding on the Mishnah. They flourished from the third to the sixth centuries. When Judean schools were forced to close, schools in Galilee—at Sepphoris and Tiberias—assumed leadership in scholarly activity.

    b. During the fourth century, the Gemara—scholarly discussions and elaborations on the Mishnah—resulted in the Jerusalem Talmud.

    c. Political, economic, and religious difficulties caused weariness in Palestinian intellectual life and the compilation of the Palestinian Talmud was never completed. As intellectual energy in Palestine lessened, the gradual shift of spiritual leadership to Babylon became apparent.

B. *Babylonian Center*

1. Pre-Talmudic Period

    a. Since the Babylonian Exile a Jewish community flourished in Babylonia though, like other groups in the Diaspora, it looked to Palestinian leadership. The scholarly centers were, for the most part, located in Palestine, and Babylonia's promising young students were sent there to study. Among them was Hillel, who became quite prominent in Palestinian Jewish circles during the first century B.C.E.

    b. A new era in Jewish intellectual history began about 220, when a certain Abba Arikha (later called Rav) returned to Babylonia after having studied in Palestine with Judah ha-Nasi. Rav established a school at Sura, which became a leading center for Babylonian Amoraim. Babylonian post-Mishnaic scholarly activity was transferred to nearby Pumbedita.

2. Talmudic Period

    a. Near the end of the fourth century, the head of the school at Sura, Rav Ashi, began to collect and arrange the Gemara as had been done in Palestine. His work was continued by others of the school at Sura. The result was the Babylonian Talmud, probably compiled about 500, though it reached its present state only during the eighth century.

b. The Babylonian Talmud is a massive work dealing with the conduct of the life of man in all its phases and relationships. Next to the Bible, it has been *the* book of the Jews. It consists of the text of the Mishnah with commentary and supplements (Gemara). (See Chapter XVII, "The Talmud.")

c. The scholars who followed the Amoraim, the *Sevoraim* ("men who reflect or reason") flourished between about 500 and 700. They clarified the Babylonian Talmud by setting it in order and by adding explanatory words and phrases where they felt them necessary. As a result, the Babylonian Talmud became more prominent than the Jerusalem Talmud with its abbreviated and sometimes abrupt style.

d. The Babylonian Talmud was written mainly in an Eastern-Aramaic dialect with some Hebrew passages, while the Jerusalem Talmud was written in Hebrew mixed with a Western-Aramaic dialect.

3. Post-Talmudic Times

a. The Gaonic period lasted approximately five hundred years (sixth through tenth centuries). The leadership of the *Geonim* ("eminent ones") united Jews scattered throughout what is now France, Germany, Spain, North Africa, Italy, and southern Russia.

b. Under Moslem rule (seventh century) study was revived in Palestine, especially in Tiberias, though Babylonia remained the center of scholarly activity. The schools of Palestine tended to concern themselves with the poetic and imaginative, while those of Babylonia concentrated on legalities in Jewish tradition. The Palestinian schools developed acrostics and poetic forms which were incorporated into the synagogue service, while the Babylonian schools offered guidance for daily life. Both schools laid the foundations for Hebrew grammar by linguistic studies which accompanied the development of their systems of vowels and diacritical marks. (See Chapter V, "The Making of the Bible.")

c. Internal rebellion by the Karaites forced the Jews to reassert the authenticity of Jewish oral tradition, while contact with the cultural renaissance in the Moslem world found Jews writing poetic and philosophical works in Arabic. Their foremost representative was Saadyah, Gaon of Sura. (See Chapter XXII, "Saadyah Gaon.")

d. General cultural decline, as well as political and economic circumstance, brought insurmountable difficulties to Jewish intellectual life in Babylonia, so that by the end of the first millenium, Jewish centers of learning were shifting toward the West, mainly Spain. Though Jews in Moslem Spain and Christian Europe built on the foundations laid by Babylonian scholars, they no longer looked to these scholars for leadership.

C. Other Rabbinic Literature

1. Tosephta (Aramaic: "Addition")

The Tosephta is a supplement to the Mishnah consisting of variant material on the same topics as those contained in the Mishnah. Like the Mishnah, the Tosephta dates from the Tannaitic period, though its final compilation is believed to date from the Amoraic period.

2. Aggadah (Haggadah)

a. The Aggadah is that part of Oral Law which is concerned with non-legal matters. Legends preserved among the people through parable, allegory, song, or prayer were included in significant amounts in the Gemara. A very small amount of Aggadah is included in the Mishnah.

b. From the time of the Tannaim to the tenth century, rabbinic scholars worked to collect Aggadah in written form and to arrange and edit it. The result was a great bulk of Midrashic literature. One of the most renowned is Midrash Rabbah on the Pentateuch and Five Scrolls. (See Chapter XVII, "The Midrash.")

ORAL LAW

The Torah is the authoritative guide after which the followers of Judaism have sought to fashion the conduct of their lives. However, with varied and changing circumstances in the lives of the Jewish people, problems of interpreting the Torah began to arise. Various methods were used in attempts to apply the meaning of the Torah to situations in which later generations found themselves. Eventually, there grew up a substantial body of "oral law"—traditions which were parallel and supplementary to the written Torah. The Oral Law provided a new interpretation of old laws and added new laws, rituals, and customs which would be consonant with changing social and cultural conditions. These practices had been handed down orally from generation to generation and were accepted as standard. Though these customs and traditions were eventually written down, they are referred to as Oral Law, since their roots were in an oral tradition.

A. *Development of Oral Law*

1. It is difficult to define the beginnings of Oral Law. Its development took place in the way of life and practices of the Jewish people from the time they received the Torah.

2. It might be said that the systematic development of Oral Law dates to the time of the establishment of the synagogue, the main purpose of which was to teach and interpret the written word of God.

3. Philo, writing in the first century, referred to "myriads of unwritten customs and usages" which then prevailed. Some of these old and well-established "customs and usages" not found in the Hebrew Bible are spoken of in Talmudic literature as "laws orally given to Moses at Sinai" and then transmitted from generation to generation (hence *Oral Law*).

4. Josephus wrote of ordinances made by the Pharisees according to the traditions of their fathers and mentions that there was nothing written in the Law of Moses concerning such ordinances.

5. The authorities whose opinions and interpretations became standard and recorded in the Oral Law were the rabbis.

   a. In the pre-Christian era and in Jesus' day, the term *Rabbi* ("my master") was merely an expression of respect used in addressing an older or more learned person.

   b. Later, the term *Rabbi* became a title indicating that its bearer had been duly recognized by Jewish leaders as a competent authority on Jewish law.

6. The work of the rabbis was carried on , for the most part, in rabbinical schools or academies. The academies developed Oral Law according to two methods.

   a. Some *halakhot* (Jewish religious laws) were developed and set forth according to a systematic topical arrangement; i.e., the rabbis interpreted the meaning of the Torah according to subject matter. This procedure is reflected in the Talmud where halakhot are topically arranged.

   b. The rabbis also derived rules from Scripture in the form of commentary.

      (1) Rabbi Hillel crystallized seven exegetical principles by which halakhot were derived from Scripture.

      (2) These principles were expanded to thirteen by Rabbi Ishmael, and later to thirty-two by Rabbi Eliezer ben Yose-ha-Galili.

      (3) This procedure for the derivation of Oral Law is reflected in Midrashic commentary.

7. The majority view became the practiced custom, even though divergent opinions continued to be taught theoretically in the academies.

8. Traditionally, it was forbidden for Oral Law to be written down. However, as individuals feared the loss of halakhot and the discussions through which these were developed they began to record them privately.

9. An outline of halakhot, apparently a synthesis of previous collections, was compiled by Rabbi Judah ha-Nasi during the latter half of the second century. This compilation is known as the Mishnah. (See Chapter XVII, "The Talmud.")

10. The laws of the Mishnah continued to be discussed orally in the academies. These discussions (Gemara) were eventually recorded. The collection of the halakhot of the Mishnah, together with their discussions by the rabbis, is known as the Talmud.

B. *Contents of Oral Law*

1. Oral Law attempts to interpret and clarify the precepts of the Written Law. For example, the Torah forbids work on the Sabbath. However, only four tasks are specifically prohibited in Scripture. The Oral Law specifies other areas implied in the Torah commandment about Sabbath observance.

2. Oral Law extends the Written Law to cases not specifically mentioned in the Torah. Thus, when the Torah forbids plowing with an ox and ass yoked together, Oral Law, concerned with the prevention of cruelty, extends this to all animals of different species and of unequal size (e.g., a mule and a cow).

3. Oral Law sets forth popular customs and traditions which are not mentioned in the Torah. Examples include the numerous religious laws connected with burial and mourning.

4. Oral Law contains legislation traditional in Israel and molded by the rabbis on matters not dealt with in the Torah. For instance, the Biblical law concerning divorce provides that the husband must give the wife a bill of divorcement. But it does not state plainly what grounds justify divorce or on what terms it is to be arranged. Oral Law supplies this information.

5. Oral Law modifies Biblical laws in accordance with changing standards of ethics and culture. The best-known instance is the *lex talionis* law: "an eye for and eye, a tooth for a tooth." There were some who took the phrase literally: One who physically injures another must have the same injury inflicted on him. However, because such practice seemed barbaric to the rabbis, they argued that the phrase must have another meaning. They explained that it required monetary payment for injury inflicted.

6. When necessity demanded, the rabbis allowed the violation of a Biblical law. Such action was rare but not unparalleled. Examples: Sabbath observances can be violated to save lives in case of dangers or emergencies.

7. Oral Law contains regulations and decrees advanced by the rabbis on their own authority on specific occasions. Such ordinances (Hebrew: *takkanot*) were not necessarily based on any Biblical warrant but represented the purely legislative activity of the rabbinical teachers.

Many such regulations were incorporated into current Jewish Law, such as the reading of the Torah on Sabbaths, the institution of the marriage contract (Hebrew: *Ketubah*), and the practice of monogamy.

C. *Response to Oral Law*

1. The authority of the Oral Law was enhanced by the tradition that it was handed down by God to Moses on Sinai together with the Written Law. According to this view, Moses received the Torah and an explanation of its precepts as well as methods for interpreting and developing what was written. This view was held and promoted by the Pharisees and became standard in rabbinic and later Jewish circles.

2. The Sadducees rejected the Pharisaic view. They believed that only the Written Law was binding. They rejected ordinances based on the traditions of the rabbis in favor of their own interpretations of Scripture. However, the Sadducees virtually disappeared after the First Jewish Revolt (66-73). As a result, Pharisaism was no longer a sect but became *the* Judaism of the people, with the rabbis as its spokesmen and interpreters.

3. During the Gaonic Period (sixth through tenth centuries), another group, the Karaites (see Chapter XXII, "Saadyah Gaon") rejected the authority of Oral Law, denied the validity of the Talmud, and instead emphasized a return to pure Scriptural Judaism.

4. Since the period of the Geonim, inquiries dealing with cases which have no parallel in the Talmud have been directed to qualified Jewish authorities. Their responses are known as *Responsa*. (see Appendix D, "Glossary").

•

XVII

THE TALMUD

The name Talmud comes from the Hebrew word *limmed* ("to teach"). It refers to each of two great compilations of records of academic discussions and judicial judgments by generations of Jewish rabbinic scholars during the centuries after 200 C.E.* (the approximate date of the completion of the Mishnah). One of the Talmuds originated in Palestine and the other in the Babylonian rabbinical schools. The Babylonian Talmud overshadowed the Jerusalem version in influence and importance. The Talmud is second only to the Bible itself in Jewish life and literature. It is the central document of post-Biblical Hebrew literature and the chief source book in Jewish law. It contains the Mishnah (Oral Law), i.e., the body of traditions which interpreted and applied the meaning of the Torah (Written Law) to changing times, plus Gemara (rabbinic discussions) on the *halakhot* (religious laws) of the Mishnah. In addition, it contains numerous folkloristic tales and stories. Encyclopedic in scope, the Talmud amasses a wealth of general information, law, and commentary collected over a period of eight centuries.

A. *Background of the Talmud*

1. Scholarly interpretations and commentaries dating from the time of Ezra and the Palestinian Sopherim were orally handed on from generation to generation.

2. About 200, under the leadership of Judah ha-Nasi, these traditions were compiled and systematically arranged. This collection of Oral Law is known as the Mishnah. There were many Tannaim (Mishnaic scholars) whose views were included in this compilation. These included Akiva, Meir, Hillel, and Shammai.

3. The Jews of Babylonia, unlike those of Palestine, enjoyed liberty and prosperity, and thus were able to devote themselves to intellectual growth. The academies established in Babylonia were renowned for their scholarship, particularly during the fourth and fifth centuries.

---

*All dates given in this chapter are C.E. (Common Era), often referred to as A.D., unless otherwise inidicated.

a. Upon his return to Babylonia in the third century, Abba Arikha (Rav), who had been a pupil of Judah ha-Nasi in Palestine, founded the academy at Sura.

b. Through the efforts of Rav and his contemporary, Mar Samuel, head of the academy at Nehardea, the reputation and scholastic achievement of these academies grew. Although the Sanhedrin in Palestine still remained the supreme legal authority, the interpretations of Babylonian scholars were followed in many instances.

c. After the death of Rav and Samuel, the academies continued under their successors. Using the Mishnah as the basis for all discussions, the rabbis and students (Amoraim) studied the law, added new opinions and interpretations, and tried to apply the law to the situation of daily living in Babylonia. All of this material was orally transmitted and memorized. This process of study and interpretation continued for a century and a half.

d. Gatherings of scholars, called *Kallot*, were convened twice a year for the purpose of studying and discussing a previously selected Mishnaic tractate. The record of these discussions constitutes the Gemara.

e. Toward the end of the fourth century, Rav Ashi, who was then head of the Sura Academy, collected the accumulated literature and learning of the post-Mishnaic period. He clarified and systematized this material into an authentic code. This work was completed, edited, and codified by his successor, Rabina, about 500.

B. *Contents*

The Talmud consists of the Mishnah and the Gemara.

1. Mishnah ("Study")

a. The Mishnah is a systematic collection of religious and legal decisions containing the accepted tradition of interpretation of the Written Law (Torah).

b. Traditionally, the Oral Law which constitutes the Mishnah was handed to Moses on Mount Sinai with the Written Law (Torah) and was transmitted by generations of sages to the Sopherim ("Scribes") and finally to the Tannaim ("Teachers"). (See Chapter XVI, "Oral Law.")

c. The Mishnah contains the sayings and teachings of the Tannaim. It was not intended to be a formulation of the binding law, for it contains many conflicting laws and traditions, but rather, was to give an orderly presentation of legal decisions without necessarily deciding which version of a particular law was binding.

d. About 200 Rabbi Judah ha-Nasi (Judah the Prince) collected and edited these laws and traditions. His collection of the core of Oral Law, based on earlier collections, is called the Mishnah.

e. The Mishnah is divided into six Orders (*Sedarim*):

(1) *Zeraim* ("Seeds") deals with laws of agriculture.

(2) *Moed* ("Holydays") is devoted to Shabbat, festivals, and fasts.

(3) *Nashim* ("Women") pertains to matrimonial law, women's rights and responsibilities, and divorce.

(4) *Nezikin* ("Damages") takes up the question of civil and criminal law. It also contains the popular tractate, *Pirke Avot* ("Chapters of the Fathers"), which has been an important ethical guide to the Jewish conscience through the ages. This tractate is also known as "Sayings or Ethics of the Fathers."

(5) *Kodashim* ("Holiness" or "Holy Matters") discusses sacrifices and the Temple.

(6) *Tohorot* ("Purification") treats the laws of purity and cleanliness.

f. Each order is subdivided into tractates (*masekhtot*), each of which deals with a specific topic. The Talmud consists of sixty-three tractates. The tractates are subdivided into chapters (*perakim*). The chapters contain smaller paragraph divisions.

2. Gemara ("Completion" or "Learning")

a. The Gemara is a commentary on and a supplement to the Mishnah.

b. It was developed by the Amoraim ("speakers" or "interpreters" of the Mishnah) who flourished both in Palestinian and Babylonian academies between c. 200 and 500. (See Chapter XVI, "Jews in Palestine and Babylonia.") These scholarly rabbis sought to determine which religious laws set forth in the Mishnah were binding. They also elaborated upon and explained the legal decision of the Mishnah.

3. Whereas the external form of the Talmud is divided into Mishnah and Gemara, internally, two types of subject matter can be distinguished.

    a. *Halakhah*, from the Hebrew root meaning "to walk," deals with legal matters—religious, civil, and criminal. It is an elucidation of laws and ethics and a discussion of their application. The English expression, "Judaism is a WAY of life," may be related to the Hebrew Halakhah.

    b. *Aggadah*, from the Hebrew root meaning "to tell," includes nonlegal explanatory matter in the form of narratives, parables, allegories, legends, songs, prayers, laments, and satires. Through folklore it illustrates the religious principles under discussion in Halakhic portions of the Mishnah. This portion composes about one third of the Babylonian Talmud.

    c. Halakhah and Aggadah are often intermingled in the text of the Talmud.

C. *Forms of the Talmud*

1. The Jerusalem Talmud represents the efforts of Palestinian Amoraim who reviewed and discussed the Mishnah.

    a. The Jerusalem Talmud is about one third the size of the Babylonian Talmud. It has survived only in part. Today, the Jerusalem Talmud contains only the first four Mishnaic Orders in their entirety and a part of the sixth Order.

    b. It is arranged as follows: The opening words of a sentence or paragraph from the Mishnah are cited and followed by relevant Gemara. It is more concise than the Babylonian Talmud, since little attempt appears to have been made to combine various paragraphs of Gemara into a continuous discourse.

c. The compilation of the Jerusalem Talmud is traditionally credited to Rabbi Johanan bar Nappaha (d. 279), founder of the academy at Tiberias. However, the origin and history of the Jerusalem Talmud is disputed by scholars.

2. The Babylonian Talmud is a record of Babylonian rabbinic discussions and decisions on the Mishnah.

a. It is written in Aramaic with Hebrew passages.

b. The Babylonian Talmud contains much more Aggadic material that the Jerusalem Talmud. Often it is not strictly relevant to the Mishnah or its commentary but is valuable for its historical, scientific, and medical information; anecdotes; proverbs; religious and moral sermons; essays in biblical exegesis; and general folklore.

c. The Babylonian Talmud is arranged like the Jerusalem Talmud with a section from the Mishnah followed by the Gemara.

d. Editorship of the Babylonian Talmud is attributed to Rav Ashi (d. 427), head of the Talmudic academy at Sura, and to his immediate successors. The history of the development of the Babylonian Talmud is incomplete, but it is known to have substantially reached its present form by the middle of the eighth century.

e. Mishnaic passages are in post-Biblical Hebrew while the Gemara is a mixture of Hebrew and Eastern Aramaic.

f. Both because of its greater length and its greater influence on Jewish life, the Babylonian Talmud is considered more significant than the Jerusalem Talmud. Numerous commentaries on it exist, the most famous being that of Rashi.

D. Talmudic Learning and Influence

1. The Talmud was important for the intellectual activity it stimulated among the Jews. Until the advent of the *Haskalah* ("Age of Enlightenment") it, along with the Bible, was the chief subject of Jewish secular and religious learning.

2. Talmudic study played a vital role in shaping Jewish ethics and folkways.

3. The Talmud preserved for the world the history, folklore, and wisdom of the Jews.

4. During the Middle Ages, the Talmud served as the basis for commentaries and discussions, called *Responsa*.

5. To the non-Jewish world, the Talmud remained largely a closed book and was viewed with suspicion. It was publicly burned in Paris in 1242, in Italy in 1553, and in Poland as late as 1757.

6. The first printed edition of the Talmud, the *Editio Princeps*, was published in Vienna in 1520-1523.

THE MIDRASH

The word *Midrash* comes from the Hebrew word *darash*, "to search" or "to investigate." Midrashic literature contains the works of rabbis, Sopherim, Tannaim, and Amoraim who searched and probed the Scriptures in an effort to continually interpret and reinterpret the Torah so that it conformed to and could be understood in relation to the growing complexity of the times. The aim of the Midrashic works was to enrich and illuminate the *spirit* (as opposed to the literal sense) of the Bible and thus to derive interpretations which were not immediately obvious. This was sought by means of a broad, homiletic interpretation of details in the text. The language of the Midrash is, for the most part, fluent, almost poetic Hebrew, although Aramaic is used occasionally. Midrashic literature was very popular in Jewish circles, works being compiled and redacted at various times from the Tannaitic period to the twelfth century.

A. *Development of Midrashic Literature*

1. When the Jews returned from the Babylonian Exile (sixth and fifth centuries B.C.E.), the Torah, through the efforts of Ezra the Scribe, became the law and the constitution of those Jews who were attempting to restore Jewish life in Palestine.

2. When the Torah was accepted as the guide for life, the study of the Scriptures became obligatory for the pious Jews. No word or letter of the Torah was overlooked or considered superfluous as teachers sought to extract the full implication and meaning of the text.

3. Thus began the Midrash, orally at first and later in writing. Early Midrashim originated with the same teachers whose sayings are preserved in the Mishnah. These early Midrashic works, for the most part, are Halakhic, i.e., they deal with legal matters.

4. After the compilation of the Mishnah, Aggadic Midrash in the forms of legends, exhortations, allegories, fables, etc., overshadowed the popularity of Halakhic works.

5. Midrashim flourished during the third and fourth centuries, when academies were on the decline and spiritual life centered around the synagogue. In Babylon, Midrashim predominated after the compilation of the Talmud until the Middle Ages.

B. *Kinds of Midrashim*

1. Halakhic Midrashim sought to elucidate details and meanings of Biblical texts which were concerned with legal commands or prohibitions.

2. Aggadic Midrashim are homiletical interpretations of nonlegal sections of the Bible. Vivid and imaginary details not mentioned in the Bible were appended to the text in an effort to appeal to and influence the masses of the people.

3. In early times, Halakhic and Aggadic Midrashim were harmonious components of exegetical works, Halakhah dwelling on rules for practical life and Aggadah on the philosophy of the generation. During the development of the Talmud, a distinction arose. In later periods, Halakhic Midrashim were largely overshadowed be the popularity of Aggadic Midrashim.

C. *Midrashic Works*

1. Many Midrashic works are arranged according to the consecutive Biblical passages on which they are based.

   a. *Midrash Rabbah* is a popular collection of Aggadic Midrashim on the books of the Pentateuch (Genesis Rabbah, Exodus Rabbah, etc.) and the Five Scrolls (Ruth Rabbah, Esther Rabbah, etc.). Originally, these were independent works, dating from different periods and different in general character.

   b. Midrashim on various individual Biblical books exist. Examples include those on Psalms, Proverbs, Samuel, etc.

   c. *Yalkut Shimoni*, a very popular thirteenth-century collection of Midrashic works, is arranged according to Biblical verses.

2. Other Midrashim are arranged according to the cycle of synagogue readings for festivals and special sabbaths. These are called *Pesiktot*. Examples include *Pesikta de-Rav Kahana* and *Pesikta Rabbati*, both of which are series of homilies for special occasions in the Jewish liturgical year.

3. Halakhic Midrashic works include the *Mekhilta* on Exodus, *Siphra* on Leviticus, and *Siphre* on both Numbers and Deuteronomy.

4. Other Midrashic works on various subjects exist.

   a. *Avot de-Rabbi Nathan* is an expansion of the Mishnaic tractate *Avot*.

   b. *Derekh Eretz Rabbah* contains ethical teachings on social conduct.

   c. *Seder Olam* contains historical Aggadah.

   d. *Pirke de Rabbi Eliezer* contains stories about events from the creation of the world until the wanderings of the Israelites in the wilderness.

5. In addition, much Midrashic literature occurs in the Gemara of the Babylonian Talmud.

D. *Importance of the Midrash*

1. Midrashic literature contributed many thoughts, ideas, and expressions to Jewish history which would have been lost without it. From the time of Ezra to the Middle Ages, along with the Talmud, it was a very important vehicle for Jewish thought and teaching.

2. The Midrash was very popular down through the centuries. Its influence is seen in the Renaissance and in the works of various writers. Milton's *Paradise Lost* and *Paradise Regained*, for example are based on material supplied by Midrashic sources.

3. The Midrash, to some extent, has influenced Christianity and Islam. The New Testament contains many Midrashic elements and Mohammed incorporated into the Koran a great deal of legendary Midrashic material.

STRUCTURE OF THE TALMUD—RABBINIC TRADITION

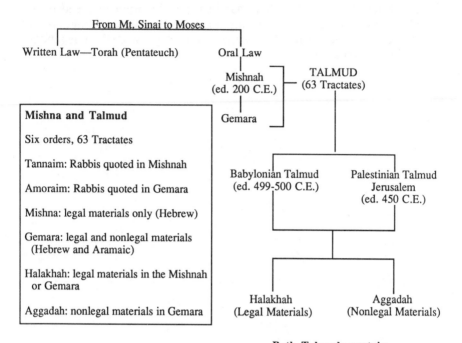

From Mt. Sinai to Moses

Written Law—Torah (Pentateuch)   Oral Law

Mishnah   TALMUD
(ed. 200 C.E.)   (63 Tractates)

Mishna and Talmud

Six orders, 63 Tractates   Gemara

Tannaim: Rabbis quoted in Mishnah

Amoraim: Rabbis quoted in Gemara   Babylonian Talmud   Palestinian Talmud
                                          (ed. 499-500 C.E.)   Jerusalem
Mishna: legal materials only (Hebrew)   (ed. 450 C.E.)

Gemara: legal and nonlegal materials
  (Hebrew and Aramaic)

Halakhah: legal materials in the Mishnah
  or Gemara

Aggadah: nonlegal materials in Gemara   Halakhah   Aggadah
                                          (Legal Materials)   (Nonlegal Materials)

**Both Talmuds contain
Halakhah and Aggadah**

XVIII

JEWISH LITURGY:
BACKGROUND OF THE PRAYERBOOK

Motivated by the love of God and belief in His concern for His people, Jews approach liturgical worship as an opportunity for praise and petition. It is an occasion for self-examination (the Hebrew word for "to pray" is *hitpallel*, "to judge oneself"), but is at the same time a turn outward in concern for universal needs in congregational prayer.

Very little is known about early Jewish liturgical worship. Prayer in Biblical times seems to have been largely an individual activity. Sacrifices were offered in the Temple by the priests and some of the psalms of the Hebrew Scriptures are thought to have been part of those sacrificial services. During the Babylonian Exile the Jews keenly felt the absence of the Temple, the symbol of their religious and national unity. It became customary for the exiles to assemble and remember the Temple and the "songs of Zion," to study the Law, and to hear its explanation. These gatherings served a threefold purpose: becoming a place of assembly (*Bet Knesset*), a place of prayer (*Bet Tefillah*), and a place of study (*Bet Midrash*). With the return from Exile, Jews continued the custom of local assemblies, usually on Sabbaths and festivals.

During the time of the Second Temple the earliest forms of Jewish liturgy were standardized by the Men of the Great Synagogue or the Great Assembly, the institution which embodied the spiritual leadership of the Jewish people at the beginning of the Second Temple period. When the Second Temple was destroyed in 70 C.E.*, local assemblies and prayers came to be regarded as substitutes for daily Temple sacrifices. Religious fervor gradually inspired additions to the basic structure of the synagogue service which was in use by the end of the second century. Some changes and additions were made later, but the basic structure of the service was not altered.

Though the main text of the worship service is uniform, details of style and order, as well as variant hymns, today reflect different traditional rites and countries. The main rites or actions (*minhagim*) include the Ashkenazic (originating among the Jews from Central and Eastern Europe), the Sephardic (from Spanish and Portuguese origins), and those of Oriental origins (North Africans, Yemenites, etc.).

---

*All dates given in this chapter are C.E. (Common Era), often referred to as A.D., unless otherwise indicated.

A. *Times of Prayer*

1. Jewish liturgy contains three daily services corresponding to the three daily sacrifices offered during the days of the Temple: *Shaharit*—in the morning, anytime from dawn to noon; *Minhah*—afternoon, from about a half hour after noon to a few minutes after sunset; and *Maariv*—evening, usually after sunset until midnight.

2. The custom of praying three times a day is reflected in Daniel 6:11: "And he kneeled upon his knees three times a day, and prayed, and gave thanks before his God." Also, the belief that men should pray at every main change of day was prevalent in ancient times. (Psalm 55 refers to prayer "evening, and morning, and at noonday.")

B. *The Traditional Basic Order of Daily Service*

1. *Barekhu* ("Bless ye")

   Praise ye the Lord to whom all praise is due. Praise ye the Lord to whom all praise is due forever and ever.

   The *Barekhu*, like most Hebrew prayers, is named for its opening word in Hebrew. It is a call to prayer which introduces every formal morning and evening service.

2. *Shema Israel* ("Hear, O Israel")

   Excerpt from the reading of the *Shema* (Deuteronomy 6:4-7):

   Hear, O Israel: The Lord, our God, the Lord is One. Blessed be His Name whose glorious kingdom is forever and ever.

   Thou shalt love the Lord, thy God, with all thy heart, with all thy soul, and with all thy might. And these words which I command thee this day, shall be upon thy heart. Thou shalt teach them diligently unto thy children, and shalt speak of them when thou sittest in thy house, when thou walkest by the way, when thou liest down, and when thou risest up.

   The *Shema* consists of three passages from the Pentateuch (Deuteronomy 6:4-9, 11:13-21, and Numbers 15:37-41), and the verse of *Barekhu Shem Kevod...* ("Blessed be His Name...") a non-Biblical expression used in the Temple in Jerusalem whenever the true name of

God was uttered. It is recited during both the morning and evening daily services and, traditionally, is recited as a night prayer before going to sleep. The *Shema* is considered the Jewish "confession of faith." It is commonly recited by a pious Jew on his deathbed. Thousands of Jewish martyrs throughout history have recited the *Shema* as they died.

3. The *Amidah* (prayers recited while standing)

   a. This part of the service is sometimes called the *Shemoneh Esre* (eighteen benedictions or blessings, although a nineteenth was added in the late first or early second century).

   b. Like the *Barekhu* and the *Shema*, the *Amidah* is read three times every day. It is recited silently by each member of the congregation and then is repeated aloud by the reader.

   c. The *Amidah* has three subdivisions. Benedictions 1-3 are praises. In public worship, when the reader repeats the *Amidah*, the *Kedushah* (a sanctification of God's holiness, glory, and kingdom) is inserted between the second and third benedictions. Benedictions 4-9 are personal petitions and benedictions 10-15 deal with national religious aspirations. The last three benedictions (17-19) are expressions of thanksgiving.

   d. The first (benedictions 1-3) and last (benedictions 17-19) subdivisions (expressions of praise and of thanksgiving) remain the same for every worship service while the middle part changes according to the festival which is being observed.

   e. A section of petitions, *Tahanun* ("Supplication"), follows the *Amidah* in weekday services.

   f. Certain prayers, the *Barekhu*, *Kaddish*, and *Kedushah*, cannot be recited in public unless there is at least a *minyan* (ten males above thirteen years of age) gathered in prayer.

4. Sections from the Torah (Pentateuch) are read on Mondays and Thursdays. These readings compose the first section of the Torah reading for the following Sabbath service. Members of the congregations are called upon to recite blessings pertaining to the law before and after the reading. A Cohen (descendant of the ancient priests) recites the first blessing. He is followed by a Levi (descendant

of the tribe of Levi), and by an Israelite (a Jew who is neither a Cohen
nor a Levi).

5. *Alenu* (for *Alenu le-Shabbeah*, "It is our duty to praise")

> It is our duty to praise the ever-living God, and ascribe greatness
> unto Him who spread out the heavens and established the earth,
> whose glory is revealed in the heavens above and whose greatness
> is manifest throughout the world. He is our God; there is none else.
>
> We bow the head in reverence, and worship the King of Kings, the
> Holy One, praised be He.

The *Alenu* is a prayer proclaiming the sovereignty and unity of God,
probably composed in Babylon in the third century. In many
Orthodox synagogues on *Yom Kippur* ("Day of Atonement"),
members of the congregation actually prostrate themselves during the
recitation of the *Alenu*. In the Middle Ages, it was the martyrs'
prayer, together with the *Shema*.

6. *Kaddish* ("Sanctification")

> *Mourner*: Magnified and sanctified be His great name in the
> world which He hath created according to His will. May He
> establish His kingdom during your life and during your days,
> and during the life of all the house of Israel, even speedily and
> at a near time, and say ye Amen.
>
> *Congregation and Mourner*: Let His great name be blessed
> forever and to all eternity.

a. The *Kaddish* is the most famous Jewish liturgical doxology. It is
   written in Aramaic and was known during Second Temple times.

b. Originally, the *Kaddish* was a formula recited by a preacher or
   teacher at the end of his discourse. As the synagogue became the
   center for preaching and teaching, the formula came to be
   incorporated into its worship and was recited by the congregation
   at the conclusion of his prayers.

c. The *Kaddish* is recited for eleven months after the burial of parent
   or child and each year on the anniversary of the death. In some
   circles, however, the simple faith and superstitious belief of the

people began to assign this prayer some sort of redeeming quality for the dead.

d. Thus, the *Kaddish* is essentially an expression of belief in God's kingdom. When a mourner recites the *Kaddish*, it is simply a reaffirmation, in the midst of grief, of his faith in God.

C. The Traditional Order of the Sabbath Service

1. The Friday night service begins with six psalms. These are followed by the daily evening service. The *Amidah* of the Friday evening service consists of the first and last three benedictions with a blessing for the day inserted in between. After the *Amidah* comes an abbreviation of the *Amidah* and a reader's *Kaddish*. The *Alenu* and the Mourner's *Kaddish* follow. The service ends with a closing hymn. *Kiddush* (the sanctification over wine) is sometimes said during the service and sometimes after the service.

2. The Saturday morning Sabbath service has the same basic order as the daily morning service.

   a. The *Amidah* for the morning service consists of the first and last three benedictions of the weekday *Amidah*, as it does on Friday evening.

   b. A special *Kedushah* is recited for public worship.

   c. The Torah reading follows. For Sabbath Torah reading, the Pentateuch was divided into small portions. Orthodox Judaism follows the Babylonian custom of reading fifty-four portions in one year. The portions are subdivided into seven small sections on the Sabbath.

   d. The Torah reading is followed by a reading from the Prophets. This is called the *Haftarah* ("Conclusion"). Prayers for the welfare of scholars and academies, as well as for the welfare of the country and the Jewish communities, are recited after the reading of the *Haftarah*.

3. The Sabbath morning service is followed by an additional service, the *Musaph* ("Additional"). This service consists of the first and last three benedictions of the *Amidah*, with a benediction inserted between them for the sanctification of the day.

4. *Minhah* is the Sabbath afternoon service. It consists of a Torah reading, an *Amidah* of seven benedictions, a full *Kaddish*, and *Alenu*.

5. The final Sabbath service is *Maariv*, the evening service. It begins near sundown of the Sabbath and is similar in form to the weekday evening service. Following *Maariv* comes a short ceremony which marks the end of the Sabbath. This is called *Havdalah* ("Separation"). It consists of benedictions over wine, the kindling of fire, spice, and a benediction on the separation between the Sabbath and the coming week.

D. *Siddur and Mahzor*

1. *Siddur* ("Order")

   a. As was the custom with the Oral Law, the earliest prayers of the Jews were not written down. However, in response to inquiries about the structure of synagogue worship, Rabbi Amram, Gaon of Sura in Babylonia, compiled the first complete Order of Prayers. He entitled his work the *Seder* or *Siddur* ("Order") of Amram and since that time any compilation of standard liturgical prayers has been called a *Siddur*.

   b. Early Orders of Prayers were also written by Saadyah, Maimonides, Rashi, and others.

   c. Today's *Siddur* is an anthology of Jewish pious thought spanning nearly four thousand years. It contains passages from the Bible, the Mishnah, and the Talmud, in addition to prayers from widespread Jewish centers. The *Shema* traditionally dates to the time of Moses, the *Amidah* to postexilic times, various prayers to the Middle Ages, and the prayer for the State of Israel to 1948.

   d. Different movements in Judaism have different *Siddurim*. In Reform congregations, every Hebrew text is rendered in a free translation or paraphrase in English. Paragraphs for unison and responsive reading are usually recited in English. The Reform prayers are much shorter than the traditional Orthodox ones.

2. *Mahzor* ("Cycle")

    a. The name *Mahzor* refers to a standard collection of liturgical poems (*piyyutim*) and regulations of the rituals for holiday services throughout the year.

    b. These special festival prayers originated, for the most part, in the Middle Ages. Jewish scholars devoted themselves to writing individual prayers which they recited daily before beginning their study. It was the custom of these scholars to embellish their prayers (often excerpted or paraphrased from Biblical passages) with acrostics and rhyme; thus, they were literary productions. These soon became the property of the nation and some were incorporated into the official liturgy.

RELIGIOUS FESTIVALS

The Torah lists five festivals in the Jewish liturgical year: the three pilgrimage festivals, *Rosh ha-Shanah* ("New Year"), and *Yom Kippur* ("Day of Atonement"). Since the Sabbath is also a special day in the Jewish year, it too is discussed in this unit. (See "Notable Days in the Jewish Calendar" at the end of this Chapter.)

The three pilgrim festivals—*Pesah* ("Passover"), *Shavuot* ("Weeks" or "Pentecost"), and *Sukkot* ("Tabernacles")—were originally historical or agricultural feasts which the Israelites adapted and embellished with deep religious significance. The other two main festivals are days of atonement and reconciliation with God and thus have always been strictly religious.

The Jewish New Year is celebrated for two consecutive days by all Jews except Reform Jews, who observe the first day only. The Day of Atonement is observed only one day. Two of the pilgrimage festivals, Passover and Tabernacles, are eight-day holidays (seven days in Israel), with the first and last two days being of particular religious importance. The Feast of Weeks is a two-day festival. Whereas special liturgical celebrations in the synagogue and abstention from work mark the solemnity of the festivals, the intermediate days of the feast are nonfestive and work is permitted. The last day of Tabernacles has become a special feast, *Simhat Torah*. Additional feasts, *Hannukah* and *Purim*, later came to be observed by Jews and are celebrated in the synagogue and at home with special rites.

A. *Festival Services*

1. Basically, the content and order of synagogue liturgy for the Sabbath, festivals, and *Rosh Hodesh* ("New Moon") is that of the weekday service. However, for these special occasions a service called *Musaf* is added to the morning service. These additional prayers correspond to the additional Temple sacrifices prescribed for these days.

2. On festivals, additional psalms and poetical liturgical compositions (*piyyutim*) reflecting themes of creation, joy, and future redemption are inserted into the structure of the regular daily service.

3. The liturgy of all festivals contains a reading from the Torah and a reading from the Prophets during the morning service. On the Day of Atonement readings from the Torah and from the Prophets are also recited during the afternoon.

4. *Megillot* ("The Five Scrolls"), books from the Hagiographa, are read during the festivals: Song of Songs is read on the Sabbath of Passover week, the Book of Ruth on the Feast of Weeks, the Book of Ecclesiastes on the Sabbath of the week of the Feast of Tabernacles, the Book of Esther on *Purim*, and Lamentations on the Ninth of Av, the traditional day of mourning major disasters in Jewish history (such as the destruction of the First and Second Temples and the collapse of the last Bar Kokhba stronghold).

B. *Sabbath*

1. The weekly Sabbath, named for the Hebrew word for rest, is the most important day in the Jewish year after the Day of Atonement, and lasts from sunset on Friday until nightfall on Saturday.

2. The hallowing of the Sabbath and the refraining from work on that day (in imitation of God's having rested after His work of Creation) constitutes one of the Ten Commandments.

3. Friday before sunset, the Jewish woman kindles a Sabbath lamp, usually consisting of two candles. While kindling the Sabbath lights, a blessing is recited. Festive meals in the home mark the day as one of joy, while in the synagogue services readings from the Torah and Prophets mark the day as one of spiritual and intellectual improvement. Sabbath afternoons are often occasions for the study of the Law, either individually or in groups.

4. Prohibitions against any contact with work on the Sabbath have been transmitted in tradition.

C. *Three Pilgrimage Festivals*

1. General Background

   a. The Hebrew people in the land of Israel commemorated three religious feasts of the Jewish year by pilgrimage to the Temple at Jerusalem (Deuteronomy 16:16-18; Leviticus 23:4-44; Exodus 23:14-19). The feasts were in celebration of important occasions in the agricultural year.

   b. The liturgical celebrations of these pilgrim feasts in the synagogues are very similar to one another. One element they share is that of *Hallel*. This is a group of psalms (Psalms 113-118) first recited in the Temple while the pilgrims' sacrifices were being offered. The *Hallel* is also recited on the Feast of *Hanukkah*.

2. *Pesah* ("Passover")

   a. Originally the pilgrimage festival of the barley harvest, Passover later became a celebration of freedom because it was linked with the Exodus from Egypt.

   b. The Passover meal, or *Seder*, is characterized by the eating of unleavened bread (*matzot*) and by a series of ritual questions and answers through which the various symbols of the service are explained. The main portions of the *Seder* consist of detailed and homiletic accounts of the Exodus, several psalms and songs. The special book used for this purpose is called the *Haggadah*. Unleavened bread is eaten during Passover.

3. *Shavuot* ("Weeks")

   a. The second pilgrimage festival is called the Feast of Weeks because it is celebrated on the fiftieth day after Passover, i.e., at the completion of a seven-week period during which the *omer* (barley harvest sheaves) are counted. It is also called Pentecost, the Greek term meaning *fiftieth*.

   b. Sometimes referred to in the Bible as the Feast of Harvest, this feast originally commemorated the grain harvest and only later came to include the ideas of the offering of first fruits in the Temple and the giving of the Law on Mount Sinai. In commemoration of the latter, it is customary that Jews spend many hours during the night of *Shavuot* reading passages from the Bible, rabbinic literature, and other texts on sacred topics.

c. The feast is observed in the synagogue by special Scriptural readings, among them the Book of Ruth, which mentions the barley and wheat harvests. The main character of the Book of Ruth was a Moabite woman who willingly accepted the God of Israel for herself.

4. *Sukkot* ("Tabernacles")

a. This festival, essentially a thanksgiving for the fruit harvest, is referred to as *Hag ha-Sukkot* ("The Feast of Tabernacles") or *Hag ha-Asif* ("The Feast of Ingathering").

b. Though *Sukkot* is an agricultural festival, it has taken on religious significance. The *sukkah* ("hut") commemorates the special protection given the Israelites during their forty-year wandering in the desert. Jews observe this by erecting such booths and dwelling and eating in them for seven days.

c. During the celebration of this festival, the *lulav* ("palm branch"), *etrog* ("citron"), myrtles, and willows are carried in procession around the synagogue each morning (except Sabbath). These are known as *Arbaah ha-Minim* ("The Four Kinds"). Because the rains were so important to the harvest of the coming year, water libations were offered in the Temple during this feast. Orthodox Jews have a special prayer for rain on the eighth day of *Sukkot*.

d. On the last day of *Sukkot*, *Simhat Torah* is celebrated. This feast was not observed in the very early days when the Torah was read according to a triennial cycle, i.e., the reading of the entire five Books of Moses once every three years. When the service was adapted and the Torah was read according to an annual cycle (a complete reading of the Torah every year), *Simhat Torah* commemorated the yearly completion of the last portion of Deuteronomy and the beginning anew of the first portion of Genesis.

e. In Israel, the last day of *Sukkot*, is celebrated both as *Shemini Atzeret* (literally "Eighth day of Solemn Assembly") and *Simhat Torah* ("Rejoicing of the Law"). In the Diaspora, these are celebrated as two separate days.

D. *Rosh ha-Shanah ("New Year")*

1. The Jewish New Year is celebrated on the first day of *Tishri*, the first calendar month of the Jewish year. The preceding thirty days of the month of *Elul* are traditionally regarded as days of self-examination, and special penitential prayers called *Selikhot* ("Forgiveness") are recited at dawn prior to the morning services. *Rosh ha-Shanah* commences ten days of repentance, the tenth day being the Day of Atonement.

2. The theme of judgment and repentance is prominent in the *Rosh ha-Shanah* liturgy, since according to legend, on that day God sits in judgment on mankind and on the universe. The *shofar* ("ram's horn") is sounded on this day. Throughout Jewish history it has been a symbol of approaching judgment, a call to spiritual reawakening and repentance.

3. *Rosh ha-Shanah* also commemorates God's creation of the world; thus, praise of His dominion is another main theme of the liturgy for the feast.

E. *Yom Kippur ("Day of Atonement")*

1. The Day of Atonement is the conclusion of the ten days of penitence which were begun on *Rosh ha-Shanah*. This day is also called *Shabbat Shabbaton* ("Sabbath of Sabbaths") indicating that the regulations of Sabbath observances are certainly to be strictly upheld on this day.

2. Jews observe *Yom Kippur* by complete abstention from work, food, and drink beginning the evening before *Yom Kippur* until darkness of the following day.

3. The liturgy of the evening service for *Yom Kippur* is preceded by a special prayer called *Kol Nidre* ("All Vows"). It is a formula, written in Aramaic, for the annulment of vows, usually interpreted as vows made by man to God during the preceding year. It was probably composed before the ninth century. In the afternoon service the Book of Jonah, a reflection on God's concern for all mankind as well as the

salvation of the repentant people of Nineveh, is read. A special additional service (*Musaph*) is observed. The afternoon service continues the theme of repentance. A fifth concluding service, *Neilah* ("Closing"), is unique for this day. Its origin was the special blessing given by the priests of Biblical times just prior to the closing of the Temple at the end of the day. The liturgy of the *Neilah* is now interpreted as referring to the closing of the heavenly gates as judgment is sealed. *Yom Kippur* ends with the sounding of the *shofar*.

F. *Minor Feasts*

1. The feast of *Hannukah* ("Dedication") is a celebration of the victory of the Maccabees and the rededication of the Second Temple in 165 B.C.E The lighting of an eight-branched *menorah* (candelabrum) is the main feature of the celebration. One candle is lighted each night until there are eight candles. The festival is linked with the miracle of the small cruse of pure oil which burned for eight days in the rededicated Temple.

2. *Purim* ("Lots") commemorates the rescue of the Jews from extermination at the hand of Haman, a Persian official, in the fifth century B.C.E., as described in the Book of Esther. The name *Purim* comes from the Biblical account which says that Haman, King Ahasuerus' chief officer, decided on the day of the destruction of the Jews by casting a lot. Queen Esther interceded, however, and on that chosen day the Jews defeated their enemies and on the following day celebrated *Purim*. The Book of Esther is read both at the evening and morning service of the feast. At mention of the name Haman, noises and rattles are sounded. Often the day is further celebrated by masquerades, plays, banquets, and the exchanging of gifts.

NOTABLE DAYS IN THE JEWISH CALENDAR

Rosh Hashanah (New Year)	2 days	1 Tishri	August-October
Fast of Gedaliah	1 day	3 Tishri	September-October
Yom Kippur (Day of Atonement)	1 day	10 Tishri	September-October
Sukkot (Tabernacles)	8 days†	15 Tishri	September-October
*Sh'mini Atzeret (Eighth Day of Solemn Assembly)	1 day	22 Tishri	September-October
*Simhat Torah (Rejoicing of the Law)	1 day	23 Tishri	September-October
Hanukkah (Feast of Dedication)	8 days	25 Kislev	December
Asarah B'Tevet (a fast day)	1 day	10 Tevet	December-January
Tu B'Shvat (New Year for Trees)	1 day	15 Shevat	January-February
Fast of Esther	1 day	13 Adar	February-March
Purim	1 day	14 Adar	February-March
Pesach (Passover)	8 days†	15 Nissan	March-April
Yom Hashoah (Holocaust Memorial Day)	1 day	27 Nissan	April
Lag B'Omer (The Thirty- third Day of Omer)	1 day	18 Iyyar	April-May
Yom Haatzmaut (Israel Independence Day)	1 day	5 Iyyar	April-May
Shavuot (Feast of Weeks)	2 days†	6 Sivan	May-June
Shiva Asar B'Tammuz (a fast day)	1 day	17 Tammuz	June-July
Tishaa B'Av (Fast of Av)	1 day	9 Av	August

---

*In Israel, these two festivals are observed on one day, 22 Tishri.
†In Israel, this festival is observed one day less.

XIX

JEWS UNDER CHRISTIAN RULE: FOURTH TO TENTH CENTURIES

In the fourth century, Christianity rose from being a tolerated religion—Constantine's Edict of Milan (313 C.E.*)—to the official religion of the Roman Empire under Emperor Theodosius I (392). Also during this century, the Roman Empire became weaker. Barbarian tribes invaded Roman territory and established themselves as rulers in several former Roman provinces. The Empire fell, but the Church survived and flourished. Although recognized by the early Empire, the Church retained a certain amount of autonomy, thus escaping the unpopularity of the Roman state. Later, the Church increased its power, Roman officials no longer being present to challenge its authority. The Roman Empire was divided geographically under Diocletian (c. 303; the Eastern part being known as the Byzantine Empire).

A. *Ruling Political Powers (300-700)*

1. The Franks occupied part of Gaul by about 450. Other germanic tribes, such as the Vandals, Burgundians, Saxons, and Angles, had previously invaded the rest of Gaul and other Roman provinces which are part of France today. The Frankish leader Clovis (481-511) extended his territory until he had himself crowned king. His sons completed the conquest of Gaul. The Merovingian Empire (led by Clovis's descendants) was split by a struggle for royal power which led to half a century of civil war. The Frankish kings Clotaire and Dagobert united Gaul and restored royal authority in the early seventh century. The monarch's authority ceased soon after Dagobert's death in 639.

2. The Visigoths were the first migrant Germanic people to challenge Roman authority. They first settled in Spain in 378. In 410 they conquered Italy. However, at the death of their leader, Alaric, they were forced back to southern Gaul. In 507 the Franks defeated the Visigoths, who returned to Spain. The Visigoths were defeated again in 711 by the Moslems.

---

*All dates given in this chapter are C.E. (Common Era), often referred to as A.D.

3. In the fifth century, Rome was sacked twice, and the Western Empire ended in 475. The germanic Ostrogoths ruled the Italian kingdom from 489-555. Although the generals of the Byzantine Emperor Justinian captured Italy in 555, they were only able to hold the territory for a few years. The germanic Lombard rule of Italy lasted from 566-774. However, large areas of Italian countryside were not under Lombard control.

B. *Arianism and Roman Catholicism in Europe*

1. Two opposing schools in Christianity vied for official status in the fourth century. Roman Catholicism was challenged by Arianism. Arianism differed with Roman Catholicism on the basic doctrine of the Trinity: Arian adherents claimed that the Father alone was truly divine, and thus Jesus and the Holy Spirit were not divine. Arian beliefs were declared to be heretical in the fourth century by the Roman Church councils and eventually Arianism was abolished in the Roman Empire.

2. Arianism continued to flourish among some Gothic tribes who had been converted in the fourth century by Arian missionaries. The Vandals, who conquered Spain in 412, and the Ostrogoths, who conquered Italy in 489, were both Arian tribes. The Vandals remained Arians until they converted to Roman Catholicism in 589. The Ostrogoths were destroyed by Justinian's forces in 555, ceasing to be a force against Roman Catholicism. In Gaul, the situation was different. The Franks had never converted to Arian Christianity, so they only had to convert from paganism to Roman Catholicism. The Franks' leader, Clovis, converted to Catholicism at the end of the fifth century.

C. *Jews in Europe (300-700)*

1. Jews were living in Gaul by the third century.

   a. In the beginning, the Franks treated Jews as they treated the pagan Romans. Jews lost their rights as full Roman citizens only after the Franks converted to Catholicism. The Church made certain that legislative restrictions against Jews were enforced.

   b. Except for restrictive measures of Christian councils under Clovis (481-511) and his immediate successors, the Jews were unharmed.

c. Their situation changed under Chilperic, a sixth-century king who was eager to convert the Jews.

d. Later Merovingian kings did not try to restrain anti-Jewish regulations and discrimination. Dagobert I, in 629, ordered all the Jews of France to convert or be banished. His efforts must have succeeded: No records of Jews in Frankish domains are found until almost the end of the Merovingian dynasty (789).

e. Only in Narbonne, under Visigoth rule, were the Jews able to preserve their status until they were expelled in 673. Some Jews remained even as late as 689.

2. By 300, the Jews were established in Spain.

a. They suffered little discrimination in Spain and enjoyed full rights of Roman citizenship.

b. After the Visigothic conquests of Spain in 412, the situation for the Jews was not changed.

c. During the sixth century the Jews were an especially favored group. However, this situation changed soon after the adoption of Roman Catholicism by the Arian rulers in 589.

d. Roman Catholic rulers were eager to prove their loyalty to Catholicism.

(1) They put all current clerical legislation into effect and zealously followed the Roman attitude towards the Jews.

(2) The enactments of King Sisebut in 616 outlawed the open practice of Judaism. His policy was strictly followed until the end of the century. Children were seized from their parents and raised as Christians.

(3) The majority of Jews became Marranos, pretending to be Christians while they secretly observed Jewish rites and customs. Marranos became particularly numerous at the time of the Spanish Inquisition (which began in the fifteenth century).

(4) Jews who openly observed their faith were exiled.

(5) Spanish imperial policy reached its height at the end of the seventh century.

(6) By the repression of their religion, the Jews had been changed from law-abiding citizens to a discontented group. They were enslaved and uprooted from their home.

3. Little is known about the Italian Jews during this time.

a. They were under various authorities and it is likely that their conditions varied according to the area.

b. Italian Jews were under the Theodoric Code during the fifth and sixth centuries, and under the Justinian Code after 555.

D. *Religious Developments in Judaism and Christianity*

1. During this period important developments were taking place in Jewish centers in Palestine and Babylonia.

a. While the Jews in Europe were developing settlements, Jews in Palestine and Babylonia were finishing the literary work of several centuries. The Palestinian Talmud was codified near the end of the fourth century, and the Babylonian Talmud in about the year 500.

b. Palestine eventually declined as a center of Jewish life and learning and Jews in Babylonia, enjoying a certain degree of peace and prosperity, assumed the role of leadership within Judaism.

2. The Christian Church spread in many directions during these centuries.

a. In the fourth century, Roman Catholicism became the official religion of the Empire and abolished the Arian heresy within the Empire. In following centuries it abolished Arianism among the Gothic tribes in Europe.

b. The Church regained the territory the Roman Empire had held and, in addition, conquered new territory.

c. The Church began missionary activities among the pagan tribes in Europe.

E. *National and Religious Legislation Regarding Jews*

1. Jews and Christians were fellow monotheistic minorities for two centuries during the later years of the Roman Empire.

2. With the linkage of Christianity to the Roman Empire in the fourth century the state began to legislate against Jews and other religions divergent from Christianity.

   a. When Arianism was abolished in the sixth century, the European states in France and Spain incorporated Roman legislation with Roman Catholicism.

   b. Roman legislation consisted of two divergent attitudes.

      (1) One attitude is shown in the Roman Emperor Theodosius II's Code of 438. It gave legal sanction to anti-Jewish discrimination and inferior civil status to Jews.

      (2) Justinian, a sixth-century Byzantine emperor (527-565), put forth a code which attempted to mold the beliefs of the Jews so they would eventually be converted.

   c. These political authorities were joined by Pope Gregory the Great (590-604), who saw Judaism as a depraved religion and thought Jews should be converted to Christianity by reason and not by force.

      (1) Under the rule of Gregory, the Jews could practice their religion but could not aggrandize or spread it by building new synagogues or proselytizing.

      (2) Gregorian legislation was soon put to use by Roman Catholic Spanish rulers and by the ever more powerful French clergy. Gregory's attitudes prevailed during the Middle Ages.

F. *Jews in Europe (700-1096)*

1. France

   a. Jews shared in the benefits of the firm regimes of Charlemagne (c. 768-814) and the early Carolingian kings (seventh to eighth centuries).

(1) Because of Christian law and the new feudal system, the Jews had been forced out of farming and landowning. The Jews flourished as merchants. Much of the commerce of the country, especially the import and export goods, came to be in Jewish hands.

(2) Charlemagne overrode theological prejudices of the eighth century in his fair treatment of the Jews. He realized the important contributions Jews could make to economic life and he patronized the Jews. He offered them protection and privileges and encouraged their immigration.

(3) Charlemagne's son Louis had a just and compassionate attitude toward the Jews. Louis was the first Christian monarch to place Jews under his direct tutelage.

b. Church councils regularly reenacted the old restrictions against Jews and urged the monarchs to put them into effect. As the Jews grew more influential, some important churchmen demanded that the civil rights and internal autonomy of the Jews be restricted. These restrictions were ignored by the monarchy.

c. After Louis the Pious's death (c. 860) the kingdom was divided.

(1) Royal power decayed and two institutions rose to take its place. On the one hand, the clergy became more powerful. They attempted to renew anti-Jewish agitation and were somewhat successful. The new feudal system also became important. The Jews were exposed to the nobles who arbitrarily treated them like serfs.

(2) The rise of the new Capetian dynasty in France in 987 did not bring the Jews any immediate security.

d. During this whole period, the Jews generally had good relations with their Christian neighbors.

(1) Jews could not have been merchants if Christians had not permitted them to travel freely.

(2) Jews got along well with Christians in their frequent business dealings. They mingled socially and were often close friends. The main difference between them was religious.

2. Germany

   a. Germany was a part of the Carolingian Empire until its disintegration in the ninth century.

      (1) Germany's first Jewish communities, located along the Rhine River, tended to be offshoots of the French colonies.

      (2) The feudal system prevented Jews in Germany from owning land.

      (3) The Jews had to be merchants; as in France, they flourished financially.

   b. The Jewish population found itself under the bishops' authority.

      (1) The bishops treated the Jews well because the Church gained from the Jewish trade.

      (2) The emperors of the Saxon dynasty treated the Jews kindly.

      (3) The Jews were forced to leave only one community in Germany in the eleventh century. In that community, they were allowed to return the following year.

      (4) During this time, many German Jews move to Poland and Bohemia.

3. Italy

   a. The Jews in Italy were under divided rule during this period.

      (1) The Jews in the north were governed by Rome.

      (2) The Byzantine Empire controlled the Jews living in southern Italy.

   b. The Italian Jews made considerable cultural contributions to medieval life.

XX

ENCOUNTER WITH ISLAM

An event which radically changed the course of Jewish history—and which was to have far-reaching effects in nearly every aspect of Jewish life and thought—was the birth of Islam. Islam, which derived much from Judeo-Christian tradition, became a major world religion in a phenomenally short time, and was to rule over half the known world. Its effect on Jewish intellectual and cultural life was profound; several of the greatest medieval Jewish philosophers, persons like Maimonides and Saadyah Gaon, were directly indebted to Moslem influence.

A. *The Nature of Islam*

1. Beginnings

   a. Islam was founded by Mohammed (570-632 C.E.*), a shepherd and camel driver who rose to the position of a religious leader. His travels brought him into contact with Christianity and Judaism. He was greatly impressed with monotheism. Islam means "submitting oneself" to God.

   b. In 610, following a time of asceticism and prayer, he was told in a vision that he was the prophet of the one God, *Allah.*

   c. Mohammed considered himself last and chief among the prophets of Allah. The prophets of Allah included Moses and Jesus.

2. Basic Beliefs

   a. The basic tenets of Islam are contained in the Koran (also Quran), the holy scripture of Islam. It contains the visions of Mohammed, Talmudic legends, and parts of the Old Testament and the Gospels.

   b. Islam is based on *Iman* (set of beliefs) and *Din* (religious practice or worship).

---

*All dates given in this chapter are C.E. (Common Era), often referred to as A.D.

    c. *Iman* includes five major beliefs:

        (1) The unity of God without saints. God is one and undivided. (This is the most important article in Moslem theology.)

        (2) His angels, through whom Allah makes known His will.

        (3) His scriptures—the Koran. Jewish and Christian scriptures have been superseded by the Koran.

        (4) The Prophets. Only six are recognized: Adam, Noah, Abraham, Moses, Jesus, and Mohammed—the last of the prophets.

        (5) Belief in the Day of Judgment.

    d. *Din* includes five religious duties ("pillars"):

        (1) Affirmation that there is no God but Allah and Mohammed is His messenger. This must be recited in Arabic.

        (2) Prayer five times daily. Prayer at the Mosque on Friday noon is obligatory for males only. Mosques contain no images of God.

        (3) Giving alms.

        (4) Pilgrimage to Mecca at least once in a lifetime (which applies to Moslem women also).

        (5) Fasting from sunrise to sunset during the Islamic month of *Ramadan.*

3. Theological Relationship to Christianity and Judaism

    a. Islam draws heavily on both Christianity and especially, Judaism.

    b. The Koran is filled with laws and stories taken from the Bible and with legends and injunctions taken from Oral Law.

    c. Mohammed thought of himself as the last in a long line of prophets (the "seal" of the prophets), the rest of whom were already venerated by the Jews and/or the Christians.

4. Among the principal tenets of Islam are:

    a. Circumcision of all male children is to be performed by the child's fifteenth year.

    b. Dietary laws include the Koranic precept concerning meat that one should "accept all flesh over which Allah has been named," but pork is expressly forbidden.

    c. Alcoholic drinks are forbidden.

    d. Up to four wives are allowed at one time.

B. *The Rise of Islam as a Militant Religion*

1. Historical Survey

    a. When Islam began, there were many Jews living in Arabia. They lived as the Arabs did, only practicing a different religion. Initially, Mohammed retained a number of Jewish practices, such as directing prayers toward Jerusalem and keeping the fast on the Day of Atonement.

    b. Mohammed failed to attract followers in his hometown. In fact, he was forced to flee for his life in 622 to Medina. He was able to win over part of Medina, and the Moslem Empire began to come about. The Islamic calendar begins with this date (622), known as the *al-Hijra*, or the migration.

    c. By 624, he had conquered Mecca, and by the end of the seventh century Moslem rule extended from Mesopotamia to the north coast of Africa. Early in the eighth century the Moslem Empire spread throughout Spain as far as the border of France.

2. Result of the Conquest

    a. Jews and Christians were considered "people of the Book" and were therefore not to be exterminated like the pagans. They were allowed, by and large, to live among Moslems with certain restrictions.

    b. The best-known compendium of laws pertaining to Jews and Christians is the Pact of Omar. This was a set of rules promulgated by Omar, caliph (spiritual ruler in the Moslem Empire) from 634-644. This required that Jews and Christians wear distinctive clothing, not ride horses, and not build their buildings higher than Moslem buildings.

c. Succeeding caliphs did not enforce these regulations strictly, and the Jews lived more freely under Moslem than under Christian rule. Under Moslem rule Jews were heavily taxed but were given the freedom to worship, to operate schools, etc.

d. As a result of the Arab conquests, Islam has become a world religion.

e. One of the most important results of the Moslem conquest was the profound and pervasive influence of Moslem thought on medieval Jewish thought. The influence of Moslem mystics is undoubtedly reflected in medieval Jewish philosophy and ascetic piety. Extensive polemical works written in Arabic also resulted from Jewish-Moslem interchange.

f. Arabic greatly influenced Medieval Hebrew. Some of the greatest Jewish classics by Saadyah, Ibn Pakudah, Maimonides, and Halevi were written in Arabic.

XXI

THE GOLDEN AGE IN SPAIN (c. 900-1200)

The Golden Age in Spain marks the Jewish Renaissance in poetry, linguistic study, philosophy, science, and statesmanship. It is one of the cultural and intellectual high points of Diaspora Jewry and has been a source of inspiration in Jewish life since the end of the twelfth century.

A. *Historical Background*

1. The Arab conquest of Spain in 711 removed many barriers for the Jews. Many Jews who had previously fled returned to Spain to enjoy the comparatively mild Moorish rule.

2. Due to the peaceful surroundings, the two centuries after 711 showed a slow but steady accumulation of knowledge.

3. The Moslems of Spain took over the interest in science, poetry, and philosophy of the Moslems in Persia and other lands of the Near East. The Jews were influenced by the intellectual pursuits of their rulers. They too became students in these fields.

4. Slowly, Jewish influence rose in the courts of the caliphs.

5. In about 1010, when the Berbers captured Cordova, the caliphate (area of the caliph's rule) was broken up and the Jews scattered into the principalities, where they rose to high rank.

6. Soon the independent principalities broke off and vied for cultural supremacy. Their rulers encouraged cultural independence among non-Moslems as well as Moslems. This breakup also led to greater Christian encroachment.

7. The Jews were normally well treated and free to manage their own communal institutions. To a large degree they were autonomous in judicial and fiscal matters. They recognized leadership in the *Nagid* who was appointed by the king and had authority similar to that of the exilarch in Babylonia. (Both the *Nagid* and the exilarch served as the recognized leaders of the Jewish community to the government.)

8. At the end of the eleventh century (c. 1086), the Almoravides from North Africa came to Spain to help the Moslems handle the Christian encroachment. At first, their policy against non-Moslems was harsh. As time passed, the Jews not only lived in peace, but some of them received posts of honor at the court. This was a time when knowledge of science and poetry was the qualification for high dignitaries.

9. In 1146 African Berbers, called Almohades, in the name of the "true faith," defeated the Almoravides, who had become lax and tolerant. They united all of Moslem Spain under their rule. They offered the Jews the alternatives of conversion or exile.

10. Many Jews fled to Christian Spain which had adopted a more tolerant policy. Here the Jews became diplomats, financiers, and agricultural colonists. Henceforth, the great centers of Jewish life were in the areas under Christian rule. In the thirteenth century, anti-Jewish propaganda and massacres put an end to peace and refuge for the Jews in the Iberian peninsula. During the fourteenth century, conditions became worse for the Jews and many converted to Christianity. In 1492 the final decree of exile came.

B. *Economic and Political Status*

1. Most of the Jews during this period possessed all the material symbols of success and had friendly relations with their non-Jewish neighbors.

2. In Spain the Jews participated in most areas of economic activity. Their right to engage freely in work, trade, and commerce was confirmed by a series of royal charters. Merchants had an opportunity to trade over the whole area of the Moslem world—stretching from the shores of the Atlantic to the eastern boundaries of Persia.

3. Jews held key positions as ministers, royal counselors, officials of state revenue, financiers of military enterprises and administrators in the estates of the crown and the higher nobility.

4. Many served as interpreters and intermediaries in the negotiations between Christians and Moors.

5. The Jews particularly excelled in medicine and other scientific endeavors. It was these skills which, in many cases, opened positions of importance for them in royal courts.

C. *Culture*

1. In no other period of Jewish history were life and literature so closely harmonious as in the Golden Age of Spain. Most of the great men had professions and at the same time were adept in Jewish Law as well as poetry, philosophy, exegesis, and grammar.

2. The culture of the Jews in Spain unfolded, to a large extent, through the efforts of the men in prominent positions. These leaders were able to protect and further literary efforts while they pursued other careers.

   a. The first of a long line of these men was Hasdai Ibn Shaprut.* Physician and adviser of state, Ibn Shaprut gathered around him men of learning whom he encouraged and supported. He befriended Moses ben Hanoch (a ransomed Talmudic scholar from Babylonia whose ship was pirated at sea) and laid the foundation of Talmudic study in Spain. As a patron of literature, his liberal encouragement of poetry and learning opened up a new era for Hebrew letters. He made contact with the Khazars, a kingdom in southern Russia that converted to Judaism in 740. This group was the subject for Judah Halevi's book *The Kuzari.*

   b. Samuel Ibn Nagdela was vizier to the king of Granada and was appointed *Nagid* of the Jews. He himself was a learned man—a poet, the head of a Talmudical academy, author of an introduction to the Talmud, and the editor of a dictionary of Biblical Hebrew. In addition, he was a patron of learning in Spain and also supported scholars in nearby lands. He accumulated a magnificent library and even imported copies of the Talmud from the then defunct academy at Sura in Babylonia.

3. Transmission of culture

   a. Important works originally written in Greek were translated into Arabic in the Moslem countries. The Jews later translated many of these works into Hebrew and they eventually made their way to the Christian Provence region of France. (This was accomplished by itinerant scholars such as Abraham Ibn Ezra.) In Europe these

---

*For additional information on prominent Jewish scholars and statesmen mentioned in this chapter, see the chapters that follow.

works were translated into Latin and were thus made available to the rest of the continent.

D. *Education*

1. Jewish religious education included reading and translating the Bible, Hebrew grammar, and intensive Talmudical study.

   a. The first important Talmudic academy was founded by Moses ben Hanoch in Cordova c. 950. It was supported mainly by Hasdai Ibn Shaprut.

   b. Isaac Alfasi (1013-1103) fled from Fez in North Africa at the age of 75 and opened an academy in Lucena which attracted many great scholars, including the poet Judah Halevi. Alfasi, while in Spain, wrote a compendium of the Talmud.

   c. Joseph Ibn Abitur, a disciple of Moses ben Hanoch, translated the entire Talmud into Arabic.

   d. Samuel Ibn Nagdela was a great Talmudic scholar and wrote explanations of many difficult passages.

   e. Moses Maimonides, the great Talmudic scholar, started his *Commentary on the Mishnah* while still in Spain and was very much influenced by the Spanish schools.

2. Secular education. In the education of cultured Spanish Jews, mathematics, philosophy, and science went hand in hand with the study of Hebrew and Talmud.

   a. While the Jewish community in Spain did not officially support or promote secular education, it generally approved of its cultivation as long as it was subordinate to the program of religious instruction and did not undermine faith.

   b. The typical curriculum of secular studies in the twelfth century included arithmetic; mathematical works of Nicomachus, Theodosius, Menelaus, Archimedes, etc.; elements of Euclid; poetry forms; logic of Aristotle; metaphysics; the relationship between philosophy and religion; mechanics; music; natural science; medicine; optics; and astronomy.

E. *Studies in Grammar and Language*

1. Influence of the Arabic language

   a. There was a great emphasis on the study of the Arabic language among the Moslems. This led the Jews to examine the Hebrew language more intensively in both its style and grammar.

   b. Because the Arabic language was the vernacular in Moslem Spain, it was used by many Jews in their scientific and philosophical treatises and in treatises on the Hebrew language itself. In addition, Arabic was rich in scientific terminology which Hebrew lacked.

2. Grammarians and Linguists

   a. The first work on the Hebrew language in Spain was written by Menahem ben Saruk (910-970). His great work in the field of grammar and lexicography distinguished him as a master of the Hebrew tongue.

   b. Dunash ben Labrat (920-970) was the first to distinguish between transitive and intransitive verbs. He also created the artistic form of Hebrew poetry.

   c. Joseph Ibn Jannah (990-1050) devoted himself to the structure of the Hebrew language as it related to an explanation of the Biblical text. He also created the science of Hebrew syntax.

   d. Judah Hayyuj (late tenth century-beginning of the eleventh century) was the first to assert that every Biblical Hebrew root must have three letters. He made it possible to know the different forms and their changes and led the way to applying this to poetry.

   e. Abraham Ibn Ezra (1092-1167) wrote many works on grammar, including *Moznaim* ("The Scales") and *Safah Berurah* ("The Pure Language"). Through his travels he brought the accumulated philological knowledge of the Spanish Jews to the Jews of Western Europe.

3. General Status of the Hebrew Language

   a. Despite the revived interest in Hebrew grammar and style, the masses of the people had only a superficial knowledge of the language.

   b. Hebrew poets and grammarians, as well as exegetes, were not satisfied with the neglect in formal instruction of Hebrew linguistics. They wanted Hebrew to be the spoken tongue and wanted to see its grammar and philology studied more intensively.

F. Science

1. With the beginning of the Arabic period, the Jews began to participate freely in the culture of the age, which included writing literature of a scientific nature.

2. Many of the sciences were directly related to Jewish religious life. In order to calculate the Jewish calendar one needed a knowledge of astronomical calculations; in order to understand some Talmudical treatises on weights and measures of distance, a knowledge of mathematics or geometry was needed. Works on calendar intercalation (insertion of days into the calendar to make it in accord with the solar system) included *Sod Ha-Ibur* ("Secret of Intercalation") by Abraham bar Hiyya and *Sefer ha-Ibur* ("The Book of Intercalation") by Abraham Ibn Ezra. Also, in his *Mishneh Torah*, Maimonides includes a treatise on intercalation.

3. Abraham Ibn Ezra wrote many books on astronomy and astrology including *Kli ha-Nechoshet* ("The Copper Instrument"), a treatise on the astrolabe.

4. In the Middle Ages, medicine formed part of the curriculum of a liberal education, equivalent to the study of natural sciences today. Maimonides, a great physician as well as a Talmudic scholar, wrote many treatises on medicine including "On Poisons," "On Hygiene," etc. He was an advocate of mental therapy as well as medicinal therapy.

G. *Conclusion*

1. The Golden Age in Spain was filled with great luminaries in poetry, Talmudic lore, philosophy (see Chapter XXII, "Medieval Jewish Philosophy"), grammar, science, and diplomacy.

2. In this time of relative security, the Jews had an opportunity to benefit from their own culture and from that of their neighbors.

3. The Jews were the great scientific, commercial, and philosophical intermediaries of the Middle Ages. They were also cultural intermediaries, for they played a large part in the transmission of Graeco-Arabic culture from Islam to Christianity, and thus helped Europe to come into contact with Moslem treasures of civilization.

HEBREW POETRY IN SPAIN

The period of Hebrew literature in Spain stretches over five hundred years, from about 950 to the expulsion of the Jews from Spain in 1492. The "golden" or classic era, during which the most beautiful of the fruits of Medieval Hebrew poetry were produced, lasted from 1020 to 1150.

A. *Historical Background*

In 711, with the conquest of Spain by the Arabs, the Jews were no longer oppressed in Spain. Many Jews who had been exiled by the Visigoths returned to Spain, while new immigrants from Judaism, which had previously shifted from Palestine to Babylonia, now moved westward to Spain. Jews became merchants and businessmen, trading throughout the area controlled by the Moslems. This area stretched from the shores of the Atlantic to the eastern boundary of Persia. The Jews of many countries in the Diaspora were now more closely linked together, since they lived under the same authority. This elimination of dividing boundaries for the Jews soon became important in international trade. Cultural activities were not neglected. Spain became not only the richest country in Europe, but also the most cultured. Its cities became centers of cultural life, and with this came the advancement of scientific and philosophical studies. Schools were established and scholars were exchanged with other countries. Books were translated into other languages of the cultured world. Thus, the East was joined to the European world through trade, and the culture of the East was transmitted to Christian Europe through its scholars.

B. *Language of the Poetry*

1. The Spanish period of Hebrew literature marks a revival of pure Biblical Hebrew.

2. Instead of inventing new, cryptic words as the *paytanim* (composers of liturgical poetry) had done in the pre-Spanish period, the poets in Spain used unchanged Biblical words and idioms. They inserted into their poems whole verses from the Bible, often investing them with new and richer meaning.

3. This renaissance of Biblical language in poetry was paralleled and strengthened in Spain by linguistic studies of the Bible, by the exploration of basic questions of Hebrew grammar, and also by Bible exegesis. All of these were important strides toward our contemporary understanding of the Bible.

C. *Rhythm and Music of the Poetry*

1. The Spanish period brings one more innovation to Hebrew poetry: the introduction of the quantitative meter, which is based on the alternation of long and short syllables (and not of stressed and unstressed syllables as in the tonic meter).

2. The poems were not only read in the rhythms of this meter, but were also sung or hummed to the accompaniment of an instrument. (Only the names, but not the nature, of these poem-melodies and instruments are known to us today.)

D. *Poets of the Period*

1. Solomon Ibn Gabirol (c. 1021-c. 1056) (see Chapter XXIV, "Solomon Ibn Gabirol") was the first famous Spanish Jewish poet. Although a spirit of gloom pervades his works, his spirit soars when he speaks of God. One of his best known works is "Royal Crown."

2. Moses Ibn Ezra (1055-1135) was one of the most prolific poets of the age. He is best known for his *Selihot* ("Penitential Prayers").

3. Judah Halevi (c. 1075-1141) is considered by many to be one of the greatest Hebrew poets who ever lived. His songs of Zion express a spirit of longing, yearning, and grief for desolate Zion. In spite of

great physical dangers, Halevi himself set out for Israel near the end of his life. His best known poem is "Ode to Zion."

4. Abraham Ibn Ezra, although mainly a Bible commentator, an astronomer, and a grammarian, also wrote some poetry. Many of his satirical pieces are gems of wit and irony.

E. *Religious Poetry*

1. Before the Spanish period, religious poets gave voice more to the collective feelings of their nation than to their purely personal sentiments.

2. Liturgical and moralistic verse of the Spanish period dwells on themes of man's utter insignificance in the face of God's omnipotence and the necessity of a profound personal faith and confidence in God. Many of the poems are indirect pleas to call the reader to account for his conduct and to entreat him to remain steadfast in his faith.

F. *Secular Poetry*

1. The emergence of Hebrew secular poetry is to be attributed to several factors.

   a. Arabic literature flourished in Spain, with many important and prolific writers. We know of Jews who were prominent as Arabic writers before, and also after, Hebrew secular literature came into being in Spain.

   (1) The Arabic custom of writing letters of friendship in verse was adopted by the Spanish Jews and necessitated a knowledge of prosody.

   (2) Hebrew poets were partial to Arabic verse forms such as *makama* (rhyme prose, see section G below), *ghazel* (short lyric), and *tajanis* (in which every couplet ends with the same word, which has a different meaning in each line).

   (3) Because of the Arabic modes of poetry, the Hebrew poets felt no need to apologize for writing on nonreligious themes.

b. Many nations lived on the Iberian peninsula and each cultivated its own national literature, writing in its own national language though using Arabic in daily life.

c. Jewish patrons of poetry (mostly doctors, merchants, and high government officials) began to offer support to the poets.

    (1) Poets who composed poems in honor of their patrons thereby perpetuated their names and memories.

    (2) This praise was often exaggerated and was usually written for a family event, i.e., birth, wedding, etc.

    (3) Competition sometimes arose between poets for the protection and support of a certain patron.

    (4) If the hoped-for help was not forthcoming, the poets often retaliated by lashing out at the stingy patron in a thinly veiled, satirical poem.

    (5) Some poets were independent of patrons and made their living as doctors, judges, or rabbis.

2. Themes of Secular Poetry

a. The secular poetry of the age ranged from praises of the beauty of nature, to wine songs, love songs, songs for weddings, death, etc.

    (1) Most of these poems were undoubtedly based on actual experiences.

    (2) In order to preserve a semblance of objectivity in these poems, writers often conformed to certain poetic conventions, for example in the description of love. In these somewhat idealized poems, the affection of the lover for the beloved is never returned; he therefore endures difficult days and nights while trying to conceal his suffering, but the beloved inevitably knows of the lover's suffering and enjoys watching it.

b. The poets constantly eulogized and praised each other.

    (1) The laudatory poems had introductions in which the poets expressed purely personal thoughts and feelings.

(2) It is actually in these prefaces, which are more important than the "body" of the poems, that Hebrew secular poetry came into being in Spain.

(3) Those preambles constitute the main novelty of Hebrew literature in Spain for they mark the emergence of lyric poetry in which the poets expressed personal impressions and experiences.

c. Other kinds of secular poetry were reflective, didactic, and philosophical in character.

(1) They dealt with universal questions of life and death and often conveyed an elegiac mood. In such cases, both growth and decay in nature were ascribed to the might of God.

(2) The poets supplemented pictures of death and burial with exhortations to the sinful to reform, for they believed that only the sinful needed to fear death and God's judgment.

d. The national poems form another part of the secular poetry in Spain.

(1) Jewish national poems express attachment and longing for Zion.

(2) They bewail the suffering of the Jews at the hands of their enemies and also pray for the coming of the Messiah.

3. Negative Responses to Hebrew Secular Poetry in Spain

a. The two major groups among the Jews who disliked and tried to impede the growth of Hebrew secular poetry were

(1) The assimilationists, who preferred the alien and then flourishing Arabic culture.

(2) The ardent conservatives, who did not approve of the use of the holy language for secular poetry.

b. The poets themselves also had doubts about the appropriateness and purposefulness of writing lyrical poetry.

(1) These scruples stemmed not only from the Jewish but also from the general medieval pattern of thinking.

(2) According to this thinking, only arts (crafts) and sciences which had a definite purpose were accepted and justified.

(3) The arts (crafts) had a clear practical value and the sciences— mathematics and medicine—and philosophy were sanctioned because they increased the knowledge of God's universe.

(4) Poetry was regarded as a "beautiful lie" because it was a fruit of the imagination.

(5) On the other hand, in the Middle Ages it would have been unthinkable for a poet to justify poetry on purely aesthetic grounds.

(6) These doubts and hesitations left their marks on the poets, and with advancing age some of them gave up lyric poetry and expressed deep repentance for their sin of having written secular poetry.

G. *The Makama*

1. A unique form of poetry in Spanish Hebrew literature is the *Makama* which corresponds to our fiction.

2. If most poetry had an edifying and didactic purpose, the *Makama* was intended mainly for amusement.

   a. It consists of stories written in rhymed prose and interspersed with scanned poems.

   b. It contains both accounts of travels and adventures undertaken by the author and witty parables and riddles.

   c. Like Hebrew secular poetry, it is of Arabic origin.

H. *Universal Quality of Poetry*

1. The Spanish poets contemplated the macrocosmos with its wonders which were inaccessible to the human intellect. They viewed this against the human microcosmos, which also had its insoluble riddles.

2. With these general philosophical speculations—influenced by Graeco-Arabic philosophy—the poets fused their Jewish heritage and religious belief, thereby imparting to the poems a particular and recognizable Jewish flavor.

3. By token of these qualities, Spanish Hebrew poetry assumed a singularly universal interest and appeal.

I. *Decline of the Golden Age of Spanish Poetry*

1. The great age of Hebrew poetry in Spain began to decline during the thirteenth century.

2. However, there were some poets of distinction who continued to exemplify what came to be called a Silver Age.

   a. Judah al-Harizi (early thirteenth century) established irony and satire as characteristic features of Hebrew poetry. His irony and satire were didactic as well as moralizing.

   b. Judah Ibn Sabbatai was also a clever satirist who, in the spirit of the times, began to mock women. One of his most famous poems in this vein is "The Gift of Judah the Woman-Hater."

XXII

MEDIEVAL JEWISH PHILOSOPHY

It has often been suggested that all philosophy begins with doubt, and that this is especially true of religious philosophy which, given a setting that is free and open to learning, will inevitably arise from the contact of cultures and the exchange of ideas. Indeed, Jewish philosophy was born in the midst of the Hellenic culture in Egypt, thrived in the Islamic cultural revival of North Africa and Spain, and flourished in the Christian culture of Spain, southern France, and Italy.

Jewish philosophy is essentially religious philosophy: Its central theme is God. Early Jewish philosophical effort was an attempt to reconcile religious beliefs with the principles of the prevailing culture. Therefore, Jewish philosophers, until the latter part of the Middle Ages, wrote in the language of the general culture in which they found themselves. After that time Jewish philosophers wrote their works in Hebrew and did not limit their work to religious subjects.

A. *Background and Underlying Concepts*

1. A central concept in Jewish philosophy was the nature of God Himself. Philosophers treated questions of God's existence, His essence, His unity, and His attributes.

2. The Law was seen as the expression of God's will and therefore obedience to the Torah was central to Judaism.

3. The concept of God in relation to the world gave rise to questions about creation, providence, and human freedom of action.

4. Another significant problem was the concept of the soul, its nature, its divisions, and its immortality.

5. The concept that occupied the most important place in Jewish philosophy was that of ethics, since Judaism, in practice, is a way of life.

B. *Main Philosophical Periods*

1. Hellenic Period

   a. Contact with Greek culture gave rise to Jewish religious philosophy which sought to harmonize Jewish teachings with Greek philosophy.

   b. It is best exemplified by Philo of Alexandria (see Chapter XII, "Philo") who, through his Biblical commentaries and exegesis, tried to reconcile the sacred text with current philosophical thought.

   c. Jewish philosophical works of this period were written in Greek.

2. Islamic Period

   a. This was a revival in Jewish philosophy which here sought to harmonize Judaic beliefs with Islamic principles of reason as well as to defend Judaism against contemporary external heresies.

   b. The need for a proper, systematic expression of Jewish philosophy came in part from the dissident Jewish sect, the Karaites, who flourished from the ninth to the twelfth centuries.

      (1) Karaites adhered exclusively to the Hebrew Bible and rejected all subsequent rabbinic teachings.

      (2) They boasted of the superiority of their methods of interpreting the Bible in a rational way, so as to remove all anthropomorphic expression.

      (3) They accused the rabbis of holding gross misconceptions of God.

      (4) In order to refute the claim of the Karaites, Jewish scholars resorted to philosophy in attempting to show the rationality of rabbinic orthodox theology.

   c. Certain Islamic philosophical schools, many of which had inherited much from ancient Greek philosophy, left an indelible mark on all Jewish philosophical work of the period.

(1) Mu'tazilite Kalam, the eighth-century rationalists who dealt with the problems of the unity of God (the fact that He had many attributes and yet is One) and the justice of God. (If God is omnipotent then is man responsible?)

(2) Neoplatonists, who were characterized by the doctrine of emanation, the belief that the world and its parts emanated from a first principle.

(3) Aristotelians, who taught that the world must be known through observation by means of either the speculative sciences (physics, mathematics, metaphysics) or the practical sciences (ethics, economics, and politics).

(4) Critics of Aristotelianism, who accepted Aristotelian logic as the prerequisite of all sciences but rejected truths held by Aristotelian physics and metaphysics.

d. Main Jewish philosophers of this period include

(1) Saadyah Gaon (882-942), called the father of Jewish philosophy because he was the first to present a systematic Jewish philosophy. He spent his life combating the Karaites and, in his many religious and philosophical works, succeeded in reconciling religious faith with reason.

(2) Maimonides (1135-1204), whose extreme rationalism started bitter controversies and whose *Guide for the Perplexed* became the most influential exposition of Judaism for medieval times.

(3) Solomon Ibn Gabirol (Latin: Avicebron) (c. 1021-c. 1056), the Neoplatonic philosopher writing in Spain whose works influenced Christian scholastics and Kabbalistic thought. (See Chapter XXIVb, "Solomon Ibn Gabirol.")

(4) Judah Halevi (1086-c. 1141), a critic of Aristotelian rationalism, who thought that truth sprang from historical experience rather than from physical and metaphysical speculations.

e. Jewish philosophical works of this period were written in Arabic.

3. Christian Period (c. thirteenth through fifteenth centuries)

    a. Moslem persecution sent Jews to Christian Spain, southern France, and Italy.

    b. Jewish philosophers, unlike those of the Greek and Islamic periods, sought to vindicate Judaism on its own grounds rather than to try to create a harmony with the philosophical climate in which the Jews found themselves.

    c. Jewish philosophy was largely based on the Islamic philosophical tradition.

    d. Jewish philosophers of the period produced vast literature on purely philosophic—not necessarily Jewish—topics, as well as works relating Judaism and philosophy. They are best represented by

        (1) Don Isaac Abravanel (1437-1508), most noted for his *Pinnacle of Faith* as well as for several small treatises.

        (2) Hasdai ben Abraham Crescas (c. 1340-1410), noted for his *The Light of the Lord.*

    e. Jewish philosophical works of this period were written in Hebrew.

SAADYAH GAON (882-942)

Saadyah was the first Jewish scholar whose mind embraced all the branches of learning known in his time. Though he has been called the father of Jewish philosophy, he also made extensive contributions in the fields of grammar, lexicography, poetry, exegesis, liturgy, calendar regulation, and polemics in defense of Judaism. He dedicated his life to strengthening Judaism by reconciling it to the rational philosophy of his day.

A. *Life*

Saadyah ben Joseph was born in 882 C.E. in the district of Fayyum, Upper Egypt. As a young man he left his wife and family behind and started a pilgrimage through the centers of Jewish learning in Syria, Palestine, and

Mesopotamia. He spent time in Aleppo and Baghdad. About the year 922, he settled permanently in Babylonia as a member of the Academy of Sura. At the age of 36, Saadyah was appointed head of the academy and thus became one of the spiritual officials of Babylonian Jewry. When he declined to endorse an unethical document for the Exilarch David ben Zakkai, Saadyah retired to Baghdad to study and write. He recorded his stormy experiences as Gaon in *Sepher ha-Galui* ("The Open Book"). About 939 a reconciliation took place between Saadyah and the Exilarch and Saadyah again took the office of Gaon until his death in 942.

B. *Works in Language and Grammar*

1. Saadyah was the founder of Hebrew philology. He was the first to lay down the scientific rules for a systematic treatment of the Hebrew language.

2. *Egron* (912)

   a. Written when Saadyah was still a young man, the *Egron* is a Hebrew dictionary in two parts. It was intended to teach the art of versification.

   b. In the first part all the words (nouns and verbs) are arranged in alphabetical order to help the writers of poetry make acrostics. In the second part, the final letters of words are alphabetically arranged to facilitate the making of rhymes.

   c. In the introduction Saadyah gives a brief summary of the Hebrew language in pure Biblical Hebrew, deploring its woeful neglect by the Jews of his time.

   d. Later he enlarged this work and translated each word into Arabic and inserted parts dealing with various subjects and forms of poetry. He also changed the title to *The Book on Hebrew Poetics*.

3. *Kutub al-Lugha* ("Books on Language")

   a. This is a grammatical work in twelve parts which established the principles of Hebrew grammar.

   b. It was later quoted by Dunash ben Labrat and Abraham Ibn Ezra.

4. Evaluation

    a. The Arabic influence on these works is considerable. Saadyah expressed his indebtedness to Arabic authors whose works served as models for his task.

    b. Although his efforts at lexicography and grammar were eclipsed by succeeding scholars, many built their works on foundations Saadyah had built.

C. *Exegesis*

1. Hebrew philology was considered an auxiliary science to Biblical exegesis. Exegesis was one of the chief occupations of Saadyah's life.

2. "Explanation of the Ninety Isolated Words," written in Arabic.

    a. Actually this work contains ninety of the so-called *hapax legomena* ("isolated words") in the Bible.

    b. He interprets these words by analogy, quoting for each word a passage from post-Biblical literature.

3. *Tafsir* (Arabic translation and commentary of the Bible)

    a. Saadyah felt that the Jews needed a translation of the entire Bible into Arabic as well as commentary in the same language. He was the first to translate the Bible into Arabic from the original Masoretic text.

    b. Besides clarifying philological difficulties, his translation dealt with the historical, religious, and philosophical implications of the text. His primary purpose was to make the Bible accessible to all. Saadyah does not hesitate to insert words or phrases or to divide and connect verses and sentences in his own way.

4. Influence of *Tafsir*

    a. This translation was the standard Bible for all Arabic-speaking Jews, and Christian scholars made use of it, too.

    b. It paved the way for the glorious Spanish-Arabic period, when the Jews were the mediators between the Orient and the Occident.

c. Saadyah's elimination of anthropomorphisms and his philosophic handling of the Biblical text had a great influence on Maimonides.

D. *Liturgical Works*

1. Liturgical Pieces

   a. Saadyah wrote synagogue poetry in every form which was in vogue in his time, including acrostics of names and alphabets as well as catchwords from Biblical passages.

   b. His liturgical pieces include *selihot* ("penitential hymns"), *tokhehot* ("admonitions"), *azharot* ("exhortations"), *avodot* ("part of the *Yom Kippur* service"), *hoshanot* ("praises"), and *bakkashot* ("supplications").

2. The Collection of Prayers and Hymns

   a. Saadyah compiled a complete *Siddur* ("order of prayers") for the whole year, including many liturgical pieces written by some of the famous synagogue poets as well as some of his own compositions. He used his own judgment in selecting the prayers; Saadyah criticized and omitted what he felt was unnecessary.

   b. In the introduction to this collection, he wrote a small treatise, the "Obligation of Prayer," in which he discussed the necessity of prayer on the basis of the Bible, reason, and tradition. He also enumerated the various categories of prayers which occur in the Bible.

3. Evaluation

   a. The verses of Saadyah's liturgical pieces are artificial, and in the manner of the times, he used obscure words which make the pieces difficult to comprehend. His prayers in plain Hebrew prose, such as his *bakkashot*, are graceful and stylistically pure.

   b. In his collection of prayers, Saadyah was a logical systematizer; his goal was to bring the scattered material under some general heading.

E. *Halakhah ("Rabbinic Law")*

1. Saadyah wrote commentaries on parts of the Talmud.

2. He wrote small codes about specific groups of laws, e.g., "On Inheritance," "On Pledges," "On Testimony and Contracts." These are the first codes of Jewish Law written in a language other than Hebrew or Aramaic.

3. His method of codification was first to lay down general principles and then to deduce the laws which follow these principles. His method served as a model for subsequent Halakhic codifiers.

F. *Polemics*

1. Polemics are a natural result of intellectual life and activity. Polemics against what he viewed as heresies, in general, and Karaism, in particular, are a very conspicuous feature in most of Saadyah's writings.

2. Hivi al-Balkhi lived in the middle of the ninth century and wrote a book which included two hundred arguments against the teaching of the Pentateuch. Saadyah refuted all of those arguments in a Hebrew book in rhymed prose called *A Refutation of Hivi al-Balkhi.*

3. Controversy with Ben Meir

   a. About 922 the Geonim of Babylonia and Rabbi Ben Meir, an eminent Palestinian Talmudist, participated in a controversy over the Jewish calendar.

   b. At the request of the Exilarch and the Geonim, Saadyah wrote *Sepher ha-Zikkaron* ("Book of Rememberance") in which he was able to refute Ben Meir most effectively because of his superior knowledge of astronomy and mathematics. The book was intended for distribution among all the Jews of the Diaspora with the injunction that it be read annually in public to serve as a warning against possible upheavals of a similar nature in future generations.

   c. The effect of this book was great; it apparently put an end to the agitation which had lasted nearly two years.

d. After this controversy, Saadyah wrote *Sepher ha-Moadim* ("Book of the Holidays"), fixing the Jewish festivals in accordance with the accepted calendar.

G. *Saadyah and the Karaites*

1. Saadyah was the first to recognize Karaism's threat to rabbinic Judaism and was the first to challenge its theorists and proponents.

2. The Karaites

   a. The Karaites (from *kara*, meaning "a reader of Scripture") were an ascetic Jewish sect which originated in the eighth century in Persia under the leadership of Anan ben David.

   b. In 760, at the death of a certain childless Exilarch, the Geonim of Sura and Pumbedita accepted the task of appointing a successor from among the Exilarch's closest relatives. Though the Exilarch's nephew Anan was clearly well qualified, the Geonim doubted his devotion to Jewish tradition and feared he might not enforce Talmudic laws. They also feared his threat to impose his own authority over the academies. Thus, a younger and weaker nephew, Hananiah, was appointed.

   c. As a result, Anan spoke out against the Geonim, the academies, the Talmud, and Jewish tradition in general. Eventually he announced that he was founding a new religion.

   d. Principles of Karaism

      (1) The Karaites believed that the rabbis had distorted the original intentions of the Bible and that numerous laws which had grown up as a result of their interpretations were superfluous.

      (2) They also believed that each Jew had a right and a duty to study and interpret the Bible for himself. Thus, they felt that the interpretations offered by the Scribes or any of their followers were not binding.

      (3) Following their principle of literal interpretation of the Bible, the Karaites rejected the Oral Law as developed by the rabbis.

3. Saadyah's Role in the Dispute

    a. At the age of twenty-three Saadyah wrote the *Refutation of Anan*, a polemic against Anan ben David in which he accused Anan of low motives and selfish interests in starting the Karaite movement.

    b. In subsequent writings Saadyah sought to undermine the whole structure raised by the Karaites by attempting to prove that the Karaite legal constructions were based on a misinterpretation of the Biblical text and Hebrew language.

    c. As a reaction to Saadyah's refutation, the educated among the Karaites set out to systematize their beliefs. This work unified the group, which had been weak and divided until this time.

    d. This systematic statement of their beliefs set the Karaites apart from the Jewish community as a separate, schismatic group.

4. The Golden Age of Karaism was during the eleventh and twelfth centuries. Karaite centers were in Palestine and Egypt.

5. Jews and Crusaders finally suppressed the Karaites, so that after the twelfth century their strength declined.

H. *Philosophy*

1. One of Saadyah's fundamental theories was that philosophy and religion do not contradict one another; rather they are taken from the same divine force and from the start were destined to help supplement each other in the quest for truth.

2. *Book of Beliefs and Opinions*

    a. This book was a milestone in the history of Jewish philosophical literature.

    b. Saadyah wrote out of concern for the spiritual plight of many of his contemporaries.

c. Contents

(1) Saadyah upheld the traditional Jewish belief of *creatio ex nihilo*. From the act of creation Saadyah went on to prove the logical necessity of the existence of God.

(2) God is indefinable and man's limited intelligence cannot encompass the infinity and actual nature of God.

(3) As a believing Jew, Saadyah was convinced that God can do everything, but he also believed that it was impossible that God would act contrary to reason.

(4) The Torah is divinely revealed and all the laws of the Torah are rationally justified, even when limited human intelligence cannot discern the reasons for some of the commandments.

(5) Saadyah expresses a traditional belief in the "world to come" in discussing the rewards of the righteous and the punishment of the wicked.

(6) The last chapter deals with what is the best conduct for man in this world.

d. Evaluation and influence

(1) Saadyah's was the first attempt to show that the principles of Judaism are compatible with reason and are not to be doubted. Also, he interpreted them in such a way that their rationality was evident. This very same method was employed by succeeding Jewish philosophers.

(2) Even if Saadyah had written nothing else, this book would have been sufficient to entitle him to a place of honor in medieval Jewish thought.

I. *Conclusions*

1. Saadyah's activity shaped diverse subjects of study into a coherent religious system and opened up new perspectives to the thinking minds of the generations that followed him. Maimonides, especially, was able to build upon the foundation that Saadyah had laid and to follow Saadyah's rationalistic approach to religion.

2. It was Saadyah's philosophical approach to Judaism that governed his writings and helped to shape his works.

3. Many of Saadyah's works were discovered in the Cairo Geniza in 1896, while others remain lost.

XXIII

MEDIEVAL JEWISH TRAVELOGUES AND CHRONICLES

In the Middle Ages, Jewish histories took the form of uncritical chronicles which include legends and traditions as well as historical facts. A large number of these histories contain merely the list of generations of scholars and other leaders of the era. There are some histories that deal mainly with communal aspects of Jewish life. Their interest and importance thus lie in the personal and communal details with which they abound. These Jewish "histories" throw light on Jewish life, and inasmuch as that life was interwoven with their non-Jewish contemporaries, glimpses of non-Jewish life can also be seen. Why this limited value of medieval Jewish histories? Without a united national life the Jewish people could not produce an actual history. Jewish history clustered around the memories of the lives of its outstanding personalities, who for a long time were either the scholars or the chiefs of exile. Only in such cases where the historian turned to the earlier period of Jewish life, namely the one before the destruction of the Second Temple, do we get a more or less consecutive history. The Jewish "histories" shared their unscientific character and other shortcomings with the non-Jewish "histories" of the time. These histories, too, are merely chronicles of events or lists of kings and other outstanding characters interspersed with stories of miracles and curious happenings. There is seldom an attempt to sift the facts or doubt the narratives.

A. *Beginnings*

1. The medieval "historian" relies on the reader's credulity. He uncritically incorporates in his histories all that the narrators of former generations related.

2. Many other medieval Jewish books are accounts of travels and supply important geographical data.

   a. These travelogues describe in detail the life of the people in the Jewish communities which the traveler visited.

   b. Thus they are excellent sources for Jewish history of the periods in which they were written and they can be classed as historical as well as geographical.

c. The tales of travel suffer from the same defects as the chronicles; they are also mixed with legends and fantastic stories. However, they do contain a good deal of genuine historical material. It is left to the modern historian to sift out the truth.

B. *Josippon*

1. The most important of the early medieval Jewish histories is the one known as *Josippon*

   a. This book purports to be a condensed account of Josephus's historical works written by Josephus himself. It is strange, however, that Josephus is not called here the son of Mattathias, as in his own books, but the son of Gorion, the name of one of the Jewish generals and governors of Jerusalem in the early stage of the war against the Romans.

   b. The book is thus an historical pseudepigraphic work. It is culled from many sources including Josephus, Titus Livius, Strabo, and other Roman historians.

2. Internal evidence (e.g., the author mentions such European nationalities as Danes and Irish, which could only be known by one who lived in the last century of the first millenium of the Common Era) determines the date of the composition as approximately 960.

3. It is not a chronicle, but a regular, well connected history.

   a. It begins with Adam, gives a brief genealogy of the children of Noah, and then deals extensively with the table of nations in Chapter Ten of the Book of Genesis.

   b. It covers many aspects of ancient history in general; it describes in great detail the life of Alexander, and also gives a short chronicle of Roman history up to Augustus.

4. Its main content and purpose is the narration of Jewish history.

   a. It supplies genuine historical material with a mixture of tales common to the period.

b. The author identifies Biblical personages with the heroes of Roman history; thus, he makes Zepho, a grandson of Esau, one of the founders of Rome.

5. The language and style of the book are pure Hebrew.

6. It was well received and became very popular.

7. It was quoted and referred to by many important authors, such as Rashi and Abraham Ibn Ezra.

C. *The Daud's Book of Tradition*

1. Another historical book which exerted a strong influence in the Middle Ages was the *Sefer ha-Kabbalah* ("Book of Tradition") also called *Seder ha-Kabbalah* ("Order of Tradition").

2. It is not anonymous, like *Josippon*, but is known to have been written by Abraham Ibn Daud (c. 1110-1180?).

   a. Ibn Daud was a well-known philosopher.

   b. He is the first Jewish philosopher who can be called a close follower of Aristotle.

3. The "Book of Tradition," written in 1161, was designed to present, in opposition to the Karaites (see Chapter XXII, "Saadyah Gaon"), the chain of Jewish tradition as a series of unbroken links from the age of Abraham to Moses to Daud's own times.

   a. The history starts with the creation and ends with a virulent attack on the Karaites.

   b. Ibn Daud says the Karaites never composed a single important book on any subject and did not contribute to science and poetry.

   c. Ibn Daud shows considerable critical power, though his book is not free of the shortcomings which are due to the general conception of history which prevailed in the Middle Ages.

4. Ibn Daud is the only authority for the famous story of the four captives who founded spiritual centers in Spain, North Africa, and Egypt.

   a. The story of the four captives.

      (1) In 960, four great men—Rabbi Hushiel, Rabbi Shemaryah, Rabbi Moses, and one whose name is unknown—were sent by the Academy of Sura in Babylon as emissaries to the Jews of Europe to raise money for the support of the school.

      (2) On the way their vessel was captured by the admiral of the Caliph of Cordova, who sold Rabbi Moses to Cordova; Rabbi Hushiel to Kairouan, North Africa; and Rabbi Shemaryah to Alexandria, Egypt.

      (3) These men established academies at the respective places and thus put an end to the spiritual dependence of these Jewish communities upon Babylon.

   b. Modern historians hold that these scholars were Italians, not emissaries from the academy of Sura as Ibn Daud assumed. This is proved by the fact that immediately upon the arrival of the scholars, the Palestinian Talmud became known in these new centers of learning. Italian academies derived from Palestinian influences and had studied the Palestinian Talmud for centuries, whereas in Babylon the Palestinian Talmud was almost unknown.

5. Whatever the authenticity or validity of many of the Daud's accounts, it is a fact that the influence of his "Book of Tradition" was great. For generations it was considered an authentic source book on Jewish history.

D. Eldad the Danite

1. The community of Kairouan was greatly puzzled during the ninth century by a visit from a strange character who called himself Eldad the Danite.

   a. He claimed to be a representative of the Ten Lost Tribes and told fantastic tales of his people.

b. The men of Kairouan thereupon wrote to Zemah Gaon, the leader of the Babylonian community of Sura, giving a full account of Eldad's story and inquiring how much credence should be given to it.

c. It is in this account that the stories of Eldad were preserved.

d. The Gaon replied that, on the whole, he believed the stories to be correct.

2. Content of Eldad's Stories

   a. Eldad, who originally came from either Arabia or East Africa, where in those times there were some independent Jewish tribes, left his country and went on a journey by boat.

   b. On the way he was shipwrecked, but he and another Jew from the tribe of Asher were saved by clinging to a board of the ship.

   c. They were seized by an African cannibal tribe that devoured his companion, but Eldad managed to escape.

   d. He was then taken prisoner by another African tribe that took him with them to their country.

   e. There he was ransomed by a Jew from the tribe of Issachar and taken to his country.

   f. Eldad then began his travels.

   g. Eldad's story distributes the Ten Lost Tribes over the whole of the known globe: East Africa, Persia, Arabia, and Khazaria.

      (1) It is likely that he heard about the conversion of the Khazars and mistook them to be of Jewish origin.

      (2) His work could have been one source for Judah Halevi's work *The Kuzari*.

   h. Since he is of the tribe of Dan, he is very explicit about that tribe. He tells that the tribe of Dan left Palestine prior to the exile by the

Assyrians (721 B.C.E.) and passed through Egypt on their way to eastern Africa.

   i. He gives a detailed description of the children of Moses, who live, he says, on the other side of a wonderful river, Sambatyon.

      (1) This river is mentioned in the *Aggadah* as one which is very stormy the whole week, casting forth stones, but is quiet on the Sabbath.

      (2) These children of Moses were carried across the Sambatyon by a cloud at the time of the destruction of the Temple and presently are protected by the River Sambatyon.

      (3) They are all virtuous, happy, and long-lived.

   j. The kernel of truth in Eldad's tales is that he probably came from among the Jews who inhabited the shores of the Gulf of Aden and who lived an independent tribal life.

   k. When he began his travels, he found it necessary to tell the dispersed Jews the stories about the ten tribes with the purpose of encouraging them, and indeed, he did give them encouragement.

3. Eldad's stories made a great impression on the Jews of his time and on the succeeding generations. They rejoiced to hear of the existence of Jewish kingdoms elsewhere in the world.

4. Eldad's mythical narratives seemed to them a corroboration of the Aggadic tales (e.g., about the River Sambatyon), as he imparted to them the strength of the testimony of an eyewitness.

5. The style of Eldad's Hebrew is peculiar, containing many Arabisms and strange words.

E. *Travels of Benjamin of Tudela*

1. A more important historical-geographical document is the itinerary of Benjamin of Tudela, which possesses great value for Jewish and general history, geographical knowledge, and the history of commerce.

2. Little is known about the life of the author except his name and birthplace—the city of Tudela in northern Spain—and the date of his travels, 1160-1173.

   a. Though he is often called Rabbi Benjamin, it is doubtful whether he was a professional scholar.

   b. Since he dwells on matters of commercial interest in considerable detail, it is often assumed that he was a merchant.

3. His journey was no doubt partly prompted by commercial motives.

   a. He was probably even more motivated by the desire to communicate with his fellow Jews scattered to the four corners of the earth.

   b. It is only natural to assume that this desire was stronger at the time of the Crusades, when the most prosperous Jewish communities in Germany had been exterminated or dispersed.

   c. It is likely that Benjamin undertook his journey with the additional object of finding out where his expatriated brethren might find asylum.

   d. Benjamin's wish to make a pilgrimage to Israel was probably an additional motive.

4. As to general history, the itinerary of Benjamin throws light upon a very important part of medieval history. This is the time of a struggle between Christianity and Islam, i.e., the period between the Second and Third Crusades and an important revival of Islam.

5. Benjamin began his travels from Saragossa in 1160. He traveled through Italy, Greece, and Constantinople to Syria and Palestine. From Palestine he went again to Syria and Baghdad. He visited Egypt, Arabia, Persia, and Ceylon, and reached the frontiers of China about two decades before Marco Polo.

   a. To the description of Palestine, Benjamin devotes a number of chapters.

b. He visited every important city on his way and states the number of Jews, their occupations, leaders, and scholars.

c. In his itinerary, Benjamin not only gives remarkable historical and geographical facts, but also some equally remarkable fables and legends.

   (1) In his description of Persia he tells the legend of the glass coffin of Daniel which hung suspended in midriver at Susa, Babylonia (called Shushan in the Bible).

   (2) Benjamin also tells the story of the false Messiah, David Alroy, who became the hero of one of Benjamin Disraeli's novels.

   (3) In his description of Ceylon he tells of the remarkable Sea of Nikpa between that island and China. At times, severe storms rage in this sea and wreck all vessels, but the passengers manage to save themselves in a miraculous way. They wrap themselves up in the skins of cattle and throw themselves into the ocean. A griffin, an animal represented in ancient mythology as a cross between lion and eagle, comes and picks them up and carries them to the land with the intention of devouring them, but there the men kill the bird with knives prepared beforehand and thus escape. This strange tale is repeated in the stories of Marco Polo.

d. All that Benjamin tells about distant places, such as the coast of Malabar and the island of Kish in the Indian Ocean, is corroborated by later travelers.

6. The style of the *Travels of Benjamin of Tudela* is rabbinic Hebrew, a plain and prosaic narrative.

   a. We have clear indicators that the record of Benjamin's travels which we possess has been abridged by editors.

   b. The book was held in great esteem by later historians and geographers, both Jewish and Gentile.

   c. It was translated into many European languages, beginning with Latin in the sixteenth century. It was a real contribution to history and geography. Its exaggerations and fantastic fables are ascribed to the spirit of Benjamin's time.

F. *Judah Ibn Verga and Obadiah of Bertinoro*

1. The productivity in the field of historical and geographical literature continued throughout the Middle Ages. The quality of this literature gradually improved, though it did not yet rise to the level of real history. Legends and folktales were still recorded as facts.

2. What is noted is an improvement in the method of treatment of the historical material. Whereas most early chronicles related events in a confused manner, later books follow a systematic division into periods and epochs and treat their material in an orderly sequence.

3. Another distinctive feature of the later histories is their special attention to the suffering of the Jews in the Middle Ages. Some of the Jewish histories undertook to chronicle all the principal persecutions through the ages and to describe their origins and results.

4. One of these histories of persecutions is *Shevet Yehudah* ("Rod of Judah"), a work which was begun by Judah Ibn Verga of Seville, Spain, who lived around 1480.

    a. Judah Ibn Verga was a mathematician and astronomer as well as the representative of the Jews at court.

    b. The *Shevet Yehudah* was continued by Judah's son and completed by his grandson.

    (1) It tells, in detail, the persecutions which befell the Jews of Spain and Portugal.

    (2) A special feature of the book is the inclusion of numerous debates or dialogues between Jews and Christians that took place in the presence of kings and popes.

    (3) One of these dialogues contains an early version of Lessing's story of the three rings told in his famous drama "Nathan the Wise." It is not known whether Lessing used the *Shevet Yehudah* as the source for his parable.

5. Obadiah of Bertinoro

  a. The greater part of the travel literature in the later Middle Ages consists of Palestinian itineraries.

  b. In almost every century there were a few scholars who visited the country and considered it their duty to impart information to their brethren in exile concerning Israel.

  c. Most itineraries of Palestine concentrate on matters of religious interest, such as the location of holy places and the graves of the sages, as well as legends about the lives of the holy men and their wondrous deeds.

  d. Some of the itineraries, however, contain valuable descriptions of the life and customs of the Jews in Palestine.

  e. To the latter belongs the itinerary of Obadiah of Bertinoro, Italy (c. 1470-1520).

    (1) Obadiah tells us that in his time (he arrived in Jerusalem in 1488), there were only seventy Jewish families in Jerusalem, all poor and ignorant.

    (2) In general he has a very low opinion of the Palestinian Jews of his time.

    (3) This itinerary also contains valuable data and interesting descriptions of the Jewish communities which he visited on his way from Naples to Palestine.

    (4) He visited several communities in Sicily, on the island of Rhodes, and in Egypt.

    (5) Obadiah of Bertinoro settled in Jerusalem and there wrote his famous commentary on the Mishnah. The commentary is written with the hope of explaining the Mishnah to those who make a special study of it apart from the Gemara. Bertinoro explains every word and expression which needs explanation, but his primary purpose is that of clarifying the meaning of entire passages. For this purpose, he interprets every Mishnah in accordance with the results arrived at in the discussions of

the Gemara. Moreover, he also supplies all necessary details regarding the subjects treated in the various Mishnayoth. As his sole purpose is to comment upon the text, he does not give any pilpulistic discussions (i.e., debates on small points).

(6) His stay in Palestine was of great assistance to him in his Mishnaic commentary, for many conditions of life there in his time resembled the life reflected in the Mishnah.

(7) His acquaintance with this life and the Arabic language enabled him to explain many words and customs mentioned in the text.

(8) All these qualities make the work of Obadiah of Bertinoro the standard commentary on the Mishnah which is printed in all editions of the Mishnah.

G. *David Reuveni*

1. Obadiah of Bertinoro's travelogue was an exception because it dealt with countries other than Palestine. Another exception is David Reuveni's *Book of Travel*.

2. David Reuveni (c. 1490-1537?) appeared suddenly in Rome and declared himself an ambassador from the Jewish king in Arabia on a political mission to some of the Christian kings in Europe.

   a. His appearance aroused hope in the hearts of Jews and wonder and astonishment on the part of the Christians.

   b. Reuveni's deeds and exploits during the eight years that passed from his appearance (1524) until his arrest by King Charles V in 1532 certainly testify to his remarkable personality.

   c. History has not as yet succeeded in solving the riddle which this peculiar personality presents.

      (1) We cannot know whether Reuveni was a shrewd adventurer who relied upon the credulity of the people of the time or a dreamer and visionary who deluded himself and involuntarily misled others.

    (2) His itinerary, therefore, which is quite an extensive work and describes not only his travels but many of his deeds and visits in royal courts, is of great interest.

    (3) It sheds much light upon his character, though it does not solve the riddle of his personality.

  d. The travel narrative begins with a short statement of Reuveni's genealogy and the purpose of his trip.

    (1) He calls himself David, son of King Solomon and brother of King Joseph who ruled over thirty thousand men belonging to the tribes of Gad, Reuben, and half of the tribe of Manasseh in the desert of Habur, Arabia.

    (2) He informs us that the king and council of seventy elders sent him on a mission to the Pope in Rome.

    (3) He does not entirely disclose the nature of this mission, but it is evident from numerous places in the book that he was sent to form an alliance between the Christian powers and his brother Joseph in order to drive the Turks from the Holy Land.

    (4) After this introduction, Reuveni begins to describe his routes and adventures. From the coast of the Red Sea he crossed to Africa and went to Nubia in Egypt and to Palestine. In the Islamic countries he posed, for reasons of safety, as a Muslim. Only after he had arrived in Italy did he disclose his identity and mission.

  e. The Pope and cardinals received him with great honor and took his propositions seriously.

    (1) He apparently had some authentic documents.

    (2) This honor heightened his importance in the eyes of the Italian Jews and his fame spread to other countries.

  f. The Pope gave him a letter of recommendation to the king of Portugal, who also treated him, at first, with exceptional honor and promised to supply warships and arms to King Joseph.

(1) But the Portuguese king's nobles and counselors raised objections and made protests against this support and royal treatment.

(2) Finally, the king dismissed Reuveni from his presence, disregarding his former promises and had him arrested and put in jail.

(3) Reuveni died in prison.

3. Reading the last part of Reuveni's book, one is surprised that his complete confidence in himself was not shaken even after the disappointment in the promises of the Portuguese king.

4. The source of the self-confidence which marked his ties with the Pope and the king, and the nature of the documents which Reuveni presented to the Pope and the kings which caused them to receive him as an ambassador will forever remain a mystery.

5. Another factor in the undoing of Reuveni was his carelessness in fraternizing with the Marranos.

   a. Among those he attracted was a noble youth—a Portuguese Marrano, Solomon Molcho—who at the risk of his life returned to Judaism.

   b. Deeply impressed by Reuveni's personality, Molcho was filled with religious enthusiasm and had strange visions.

   c. Though he never announced publicly that he was the Messiah, Molcho entertained the idea secretly.

   d. For a time, Molcho, too, gained the ear of great men; finally, he was arrested.

   e. Molcho was condemned by the Inquisition and went to the stake, at Mantua, triumphantly announcing that he was giving his body as a "burnt offering" to God.

   f. Molcho and his deeds are not mentioned by Reuveni, but by a contemporary Jewish historian, Joseph ha-Cohen.

XXIV

SAMUEL IBN NAGDELA: HA-NAGID (993-1056)

Samuel Ibn Nagdela, also called ha-Nagid, was the first great poet of the Spanish Golden Age. Although Dunash ben Labrat (who introduced the quantitative meter borrowed from Arabic poetry into Hebrew) and Menahem ben Saruk preceded Nagdela, their influence as poets was not as great for the period which was to follow. Quantitative meter pertains to a metrical system, as that of classical verse, based on the alternation of long and short—rather than on accented or unaccented—syllables.

A. *Life*

Samuel Ibn Nagdela was born in Cordova where, in his youth, he acquired an extensive Hebrew and Arabic education. After North African Berbers ransacked and demolished Cordova he settled in Malaga, a city in the kingdom of Granada. There he quickly grew rich and won a reputation as a man of outstanding talent and assiduity. In 1027 he became the head of the Jewish community in Granada with the title of Prince (*Nagid*). His talents came to the notice of the local king, who appointed him to an important post. Eventually he rose to the rank of grand vizier (roughly equivalent to the rank of prime minister in our day), an exceptional position for a Jew in a Moslem kingdom. As such, he was not only a competent administrator but also a successful general. He was exposed not only to the hazards of his war campaigns, but also to the intrigues which were incessantly hatched at the court of his king. The heavy strain of his administrative and military obligations left its mark on him. It gradually weakened his health until his death in 1056. His son Joseph inherited his post as grand vizier, but he and most of his Jewish brethren in Granada were killed in anti-Jewish riots in 1066.

B. *Work*

1. Engrossed though he was in his administrative and diplomatic activities, Samuel ha-Nagid was able to produce outstanding scholarly and literary works. He also was known as a generous patron of learning.

a. Poetry

(1) Most of Ibn Nagdela's poetry—friendship poems, elegies, love and wine poems, and sacred poetry—has been preserved.

(2) Unlike the other Hebrew poets in Spain, most of his poems are of a predominantly narrative character, though in each individual poem the narrative is set in a lyrical framework.

(3) The poems mostly describe the poet's life experiences, e.g., adventures like the assault of a whale on a ship in which he was traveling and which was miraculously saved.

(4) His realistic war songs, though strongly influenced by Arabic style, revived the tradition of the prophetess Deborah and King David. These battle poems repeatedly express the belief that, on the battlefield, it is always God who in the end brings victory to the deserving righteous.

(5) Ha-Nagid's wine poems are among the best of their kind in Spanish Hebrew poetry. They again reflect his personal experience. Drawing on Greek, Persian, and Arabic traditions, they describe the drinking feasts in their natural outdoor scenery. They praise the pleasure of wine which drowns a poet's anxieties and makes him oblivious to the flight of time.

(6) Ha-Nagid's love poems remind us of the troubadour tradition. They describe the suffering brought about by his burning, but always unrequited, love for his beloved. It is a hopeless love because it always remains concealed in the lover's heart. The beloved is addressed, not by name, but as a gazelle. Other Hebrew poets in Spain compared their beloved to a dove (*Halevi*) or fawn (*al-Harizi*). But as with the troubadours, we do not have to believe that ha-Nagid expressed his genuine feelings in these poems. These love poems were probably no more than exercises or amusements intended to show the poet's stylistic artistry and rhythmic mastery.

b. Ha-Nagid wrote three works imitating three Biblical books, Psalms, Proverbs, and Ecclesiastes, under the names of *Ben Tehilim* ("Son of Psalms"), *Ben Mishle* ("Son of Proverbs"), and *Ben Koheleth* ("Son of Ecclesiastes"). Here we find variations on the themes of the three Biblical books.

c. He also wrote an introduction to the Talmud, a Biblical commentary, and treatises on Hebrew grammar.

C. *Conclusion*

Owing to the individuality, depth, and originality of his poetic themes; the richness of his style; and his skillful use of language; Samuel ha-Nagid takes his place in Hebrew literature as the first great poet of the Golden Age in Spain.

SOLOMON IBN GABIROL (c. 1021-1056)

The unusual blending of philosophic and poetic talents in Solomon Ibn Gabirol led the German poet Heinrich Heine (1797-1856) to describe him as "the poet among philosophers and the philosopher among poets." Ibn Gabirol was a key figure in the shift of the center of Jewish learning from Babylonia to the West. Not only was Solomon Ibn Gabirol the first Jewish philosopher in Spain, but he was the first Spanish philosopher and the first exponent of Neoplatonism in Europe.

A. *Life*

Ibn Gabirol was born in Malaga, Spain, in about 1021, and his early years were spent at Saragossa, where he came under the protection of his friend (and Jewish minister) Samuel Ibn Nagdela, also known as Samuel ha-Nagid, the well-known patron of learning (see Chapter XXIVa, "Samuel Ibn Nagdela.") He also became the friend and protégé of the Jewish statesman Jekuthiel Ibn Hasan (d. 1039). Ibn Gabirol was orphaned very early in his life. Having no family, he wandered about Spain recording what he heard and what he saw in the various communities that he visited. The most important result of his wanderings was the record he made, a collection of notes on how these Jews lived. Ibn Gabirol was a poet, philosopher, and moralist whose writings had great depth, subtlety, seriousness, and sadness. Like Philo of Alexandria (see Chapter XII, "Philo"), Ibn Gabirol was a teacher of the Neoplatonic school, holding to the belief of creation by emanation. Solomon Ibn Gabirol died in Valencia about 1056. Legend relates that an Arab poet slew him out of envy for his masterly powers of song and buried his body beneath a fig tree. The tree produced such extraordinary blossoms that attention was drawn to it and suspicion was aroused. The body was exhumed and the culprit was punished by being hanged on that marvelous fig tree.

B. *Works*

1. Poetry

   a. Ibn Gabirol's poetry reflects circumstances of his life and times.

      (1) Traces of loneliness and depression in some of his works may be the result of sufferings from physical illness as well as disillusionment with the world.

      (2) Influence of earlier Spanish poetry, mystic literature, and Muslim Sufism can be recognized in Ibn Gabirol's poetic works.

      (3) Ibn Gabirol's secular poetry ranges from gaiety in concerns of nature, life, love, friends, drinking, etc., to deep depression, loneliness, and bitterness.

      (4) In his sacred poetry, the personal joys and sorrows of Ibn Gabirol often were transformed into the joys and sorrows of the Jewish people. He expressed, on the one hand, the deep longing for Israel and for redemption and, on the other hand, the anguish of the human soul defiled by the sinfulness of the body and the yearning for reunion with its Maker.

   b. The language of the Scriptures became fluid at Ibn Gabirol's touch. Integral passages from the Bible were woven into his verse to round off a stanza, adding piquancy by the very suitable use to which they were put.

   c. At the age of sixteen Ibn Gabirol gave poetic form to the rules of Hebrew grammar. The work was made up of four hundred verses and entitled *Anak* ("Necklace").

   d. Several of Ibn Gabirol's poems became included in the liturgy.

      (1) One of his earliest efforts was the *Azharoth*, a versification of the 613 commandments. This is recited in Sephardic synagogues on the Feast of Weeks.

      (2) Ibn Gabirol's best-known liturgical poem is his poetical philosophical work, *Keter Malkhut* ("Royal Crown"). The poem is logically divided into five parts with a prologue and

an epilogue. It is not bound by meter, but has rhyme and each strophe ends with a Biblical verse. It is a hymn in praise of the splendor of God's creation and His wisdom ruling the world. It bears traces of the philosophy of *Fons Vitae* ("The Fountain of Life"). It is an appeal to God for mercy and forgiveness, based upon the contrast of the greatness of God and the insignificance of man. It is recited during the services of the Day of Atonement.

2. Philosophical works

   a. Ibn Gabirol's chief philosophical work, which was written in Arabic and later translated into Latin was entitled *Fons Vitae* (*Mekor Hayyim*, or "The Fountain of Life").

      (1) Background

      Until the last century this work was assumed to have been written by an Arab scholastic philosopher, Avicebron. The original work was translated from Arabic into Latin in 1150 under the patronage of Archbishop Raymond of Toledo. In the nineteenth century Solomon Munk discovered that Ibn Gabirol was the author. Munk uncovered selections of the *Fons Vitae*, which had been translated into Hebrew by Falaquera in the middle of the thirteenth century. The entire work was then completely translated into Hebrew for the first time.

      (2) Content

      The work is written in Arabic as a philosophic dialogue between a master and his disciple. Philosophical problems are treated without any pronounced theological preconceptions. There are three categories of being: (1) God—the primary substance, (2) World—composed of matter and form, and (3) Divine Will—intermediary between God and the world.

      Matter underlying spirit is derived from God. Creation is the product of a series of emanations, the lowest of which is the sensible world. Mystic knowledge beyond understanding is required to make contact with the realm of the "universal." The purpose of life is the soul's reunion with the upper world from which it derives. This is brought about by knowledge and practice.

(3) Evaluation

The style is vague and tedious. Ibn Gabirol's view differs from the Neoplatonic view on two important points. First, he introduces the will of God as the cornerstone of all these emanations, while in the Neoplatonic system the gradual emanations are performed in a mechanical way. Ibn Gabirol has thus preserved the Jewish idea of creation. The second point is Ibn Gabirol's acceptance of the Aristotelian doctrine of the dualism of matter and form. Ibn Gabirol raises matter above form. It emanates from the essence of the creator, forming the basis of all subsequent emanations.

It is a peculiar combination of logical formalism with mystic profundity. The profundity did not appeal to the rationalists, and, since Neoplatonism was giving way to Aristotelianism, the mystic elements were employed in a lost cause. Resting on such a basis, the system was given a death blow by the Aristotelian approach of Maimonides.

(4) Influence of Jewish Thought

The work was sharply criticized by Abraham Ibn Daud in the twelfth century; it was ignored by later Jewish thinkers. There is little specifically Jewish content in the work. This and the Neoplatonic basis made it of little Jewish interest. In later periods some of its formulas were borrowed by the Kabbalists, especially its theory of emanations.

(5) Influence of Christian Thought

The work exerted strong influence upon the Platonist Franciscans, principally John Duns Scotus (c. 1265-1308). There was opposition from the Aristotelian Dominicans, among them Albert Magnus (c. 1200-1280) and Thomas Aquinas (1225-1274).

b. Ibn Gabirol wrote two other works:

(1) *Mibhar ha-Peninim* ("The Choice of Pearls"): A collection in sixty-four chapters of maxims, proverbs, and moral reflections. Many of these wise sayings are Arabic in origin.

(It should be noted that there is disagreement as to whether Ibn Gabirol is the author of this work.)

(2) *Tikkun Middot ha-Nephesh* ("The Improvement of Moral Qualities"): This work on ethics and morals was written in Arabic at Saragossa in 1045. Ibn Gabirol systematizes all man's ethical principles on a psychological and physiological basis. Spiritual qualities are linked to the individual physical senses. It is difficult to understand on what basis the groupings are made. Man's animal nature must be controlled by his rational nature. This involves the use of intelligence and the avoidance of things which appeal to the senses. Humility is to be cultivated as an essential virtue.

This work enjoyed great popularity in the Jewish community. Although it does not have the depth of some of his other works, it is remarkable for the peculiar spirit which pervades it. The work shows an intimate acquaintance with the Bible, various Arabic writers, and the masters of philosophy. It was translated into Hebrew by Judah Ibn Tibbon (c. 1120-c. 1190) and in recent years into English by S. S. Wise.

C. *Importance*

1. Although Ibn Gabirol's *philosophy* has not had too great an influence on Jewish thought, it was influential in shaping the church's philosophy of the thirteenth century and helped toward the incorporation of Greek philosophy into Christian thought.

2. Ibn Gabirol's influence was in part responsible for the ascendance of Jewish cultural creativity in Spain.

3. His magnificent religious poetry plays a major part in synagogue liturgy to the present day.

4. Ibn Gabirol's contributions to literature and philosophy were made within a life-span of less than forty years.

XXV

RASHI (1040-1105)

Rabbi Solomon Yitzhaki, better known by his acronym, Rashi, has become one of the mainstays of Judaic tradition. It was largely through his efforts as a commentator of the Bible and the Talmud that these works were brought to the general populace. His commentaries are so inextricably bound up with the texts that the study of the text itself almost presupposes that it will be studied "with Rashi."

A. *Historical Background*

1. At the time of Rashi's birth, France was divided into a dozen principalities, one of the most important ones being Champagne in the northeast.

   a. Troyes, a great commercial center and the city of Rashi's birth, was the capital of Champagne.

   b. This city was the scene of many fairs and rabbinical synods.

2. The Jews had a close relationship with their French Christian neighbors; they used the French language and many of them had French names. The French Christians, however, did not possess the breadth of knowledge that distinguished the Moslems of Spain during that period.

3. The Jews in France did not indulge in poetry or philosophy, but gave their attention to the study of the Bible and the Talmud, and many were engaged in biblical exegesis.

   a. Southern France seemed to have had exegetes who specialized in *aggadic* or homiletic exegesis.

   b. Scholars in northern France inclined toward the *peshat* method, which concentrated on the simple, literal meaning of the scriptures and the grammatical and linguistical problems pertaining to the Hebrew language.

4. During the period there were many travelling scholars in western
   Europe (France and Germany) who helped transmit the oral exegetic
   tradition in northwest Europe.

5. France was comparatively peaceful until the advent of the Crusades in
   1096 when lawlessness and persecution gave rise to much chaos and
   bitterness (see Chapter XXX, "Jewish Communities"). In many
   instances, Rashi's commentaries show the imprint of this period.

   a. In his first commentary on the Bible (Genesis 1:1), Rashi argues
      that the Holy Land does not belong to either Christians or Moslems
      (who were then engaged in a struggle over it), but to the Lord,
      who had already given it to the Jewish people.

   b. In his *Responsa* he deemed it necessary to make allowances for
      many forced conversions which resulted from persecutions.

B. *Life*

Rashi was born in 1040 in Troyes, France, to a wealthy, scholarly family.
As a student, Rashi left his family for long periods of time to study in the
greater centers of Jewish learning in France and Germany. After eight
years of study in Germany, he returned to Troyes at the age of twenty-five
and began a lifelong career of teaching and writing. He married at a young
age and had three daughters. Two of these daughters later married noted
scholars and in turn gave birth to sons who also became noted scholars. In
France, Rashi, who became the accepted authority on Jewish law and
practices, had occasion to write *Responsa* (see Chapter XXIX, "Responsa
Literature"). In 1070, Rashi established an academy that became the center
of rabbinical studies for the entire region. The academy flourished and
attracted many students and scholars. As was the custom of the time, Rashi
drew no salary from either the community or the academy. He earned his
livelihood by growing grapes in his family's vineyards near Troyes. After
Rashi's death on July 13, 1105, his work was continued by his famous sons-
in-law, Rabbi Meir and Rabbi Judah ben Nathan (Riban), as well as his
famous grandsons, Rabbi Shmuel ben Meir (Rashbam) and Rabbi Jacob
Moses Tam (Ribam). These descendants of Rashi, along with some of his
other disciples, became the founders of a school of talmudic commentators
known as the Tosaphists (Annotators).

C. *Commentaries*

1. Introduction

   a. With his commentaries on the Bible and Talmud, Rashi helped link European Jewry to the chain of tradition of the Palestinian and Babylonian schools.

   b. In Rashi's commentaries there is a blend of the *peshat* (literal exegesis) and the *derash* (free interpretation and homiletic comment).

   c. His style of writing is clear and precise. Where it was necessary to clarify a text further, Rashi translated some words into Old French, the vernacular. These French words were transcribed into Hebrew characters and formed an integral part of the text. Today they serve as an important source for the study of Medieval French.

2. Commentary on the Bible

   a. Rashi wrote commentaries on all the books of the Bible except Ezra, Nehemiah, Chronicles, and parts of Ezekiel and Job.

   b. His biblical commentaries often cite and follow Targum Onkelos (see Chapter VI, "Ancient Versions of the Bible"), the *Masorah*, the body of traditions regarding the text of the Hebrew Bible, and earlier commentaries, including some grammatical contributions.

3. Commentary on the Babylonian Talmud

   a. Rashi's interest in the Talmud was a practical one. He attempted to apply its teachings to the solution of religious, social, economic, and personal problems which arose in everyday affairs.

   b. Rashi's work on the Talmud is a running commentary on the text and was designed to facilitate the study of its contents.

   c. Simple, concise, and lucid, his commentary made the Babylonian Talmud popular among students of the Torah. The Babylonian Talmud thus escaped the neglect that the Jerusalem Talmud suffered.

4. Influence of Rashi's Commentaries

    a. Rashi and his commentaries became a part of Jewish religious life. Generations of Jewish scholars were trained in Rashi's commentaries and quotations from Rashi were frequently used.

    b. Rashi's first commentary on the Pentateuch was the first dated Hebrew book to be printed in 1475, in Reggio. This edition was printed without the Bible text accompanying it.

    c. Nicholas de Lyra (c. 1270-1349) in his book, *Postillae*, so slavishly copied Rashi that he was nicknamed *Simia Solomonis* ("The Ape of Solomon"). Since de Lyra had a great influence on Martin Luther, it follows that Luther's translation of the Bible was influenced by Rashi's interpretations.

5. Evaluation

    a. Rashi had an extraordinary mastery of the Bible, the Talmud, the whole range of biblical exegesis, and other Jewish literature.

    b. His commentaries illuminate many obscurities in the Biblical text.

    c. Rashi adhered to traditional exegesis; however, his work was not mere exegesis, but rather was amalgamated with the Torah itself, becoming part of its soul and spirit.

    d. Rashi recognized pedagogic value in similes and examples and used them often to help clarify meanings.

    e. Through his interpretation of Hebrew he systematized a considerable amount of Hebrew grammar.

    f. To this day Rashi remains the most widely read commentator by students of the Bible and the Talmud.

ABRAHAM IBN EZRA (1089-1164)

Abraham Ibn Ezra carried the rich treasures of Spanish-Jewish learning into the non-Arabic communities of France, Italy, and England. These communities would probably have remained ignorant of much of the culture and accomplishments of the Jews of Spain had it not been for him.

He not only translated some important works from Arabic into Hebrew and wrote many original works himself, but he also helped to establish new centers of learning and literary activity, especially in southern France (the Provence region). He was a wanderer who brought his poetic gift, his varied learning, and his striking ideas into many lands as he mediated between the cultures of the East and the West.

A. *Life*

Abraham Ibn Ezra was born in 1089 in Tudela, Spain. He had a tendency to embrace and to attempt to master all existing sciences, particularly mathematics, astronomy, biblical exegesis, and philosophy. He had already gained the reputation of being a great poet and thinker when he left Spain for North Africa, England, France, and Italy. His creative work of this period included biblical commentaries, works on philology and philosophy, as well as poetry and works dealing with science and mathematics. Wherever he went, Abraham Ibn Ezra stimulated scholarship and produced a profound impression on those he visited. He always regarded himself as an "exile," signing his name as Ibn Ezra the Spaniard (*ha-Sephardi*). As he grew old, he longed to return to his native Spain. He began his return journey, but died on the borders of Navarre and Aragon in Calahorra in 1164.

B. *Character and Personality*

1. Abraham Ibn Ezra was devoted to his God; nonetheless, he also believed in the influence of the stars, attributing his disappointments in life to a conspiracy of ill-omened planets at his birth.

2. He lacked the concentration and continuity of thought necessary for exhaustive treatises; hence, his writings are often unsystematic.

3. As a result of his many wanderings, many of his works have been lost, unfortunately.

C. *Poetry*

1. Types

a. His poems are remarkable for their peculiar and unique construction.

(1) "The Tree," written in honor of Jacob Tam (1100-1171) who was Rashi's grandson, is arranged according to the following construction: The center line of the poem represents the trunk on a tree and out of the trunk run branch lines to the right and left, each beginning with a word of the trunk line.

(2) "The Song of the Chess" begins with the words, "I will sing a song of battle/planned in days long past and over." Most ingeniously, practically all the moves in the game are described in this poem by employment of quotations drawn from the Bible (a poetic device typical of medieval Jewish poets).

b. Besides a number of satirical poems, Ibn Ezra's works include poems of friendship, wine ditties, and poems of love (e.g., "Far Sweeter Than Honey").

c. Ibn Ezra's didactic poems deal with topics of nature, astronomy, the seasons, and the calendar.

d. His sacred poetry reflects a longing for God despite the infinite distance between Him and man. Examples include "The Living God," "The Law," and "God Everywhere."

e. In national poems Ibn Ezra feels deep pain because of the suffering of his people and at times breaks out in vehement protest, arguing with God on behalf of the people.

f. His philosophical poems are modeled after Ibn Gabirol's "Royal Crown" (see Chapter XXIVb, "Solomon Ibn Gabirol").

2. Evaluation

a. Abraham Ibn Ezra's wit is inimitable and his satire is superb.

b. He brings to his poetry a feeling heart and a keen, penetrating mind. However, he lacks Halevi's and Ibn Gabirol's spirit of sublime joyousness, which expresses itself in hymns.

D. *Biblical Exegesis*

1. Method

    a. Ibn Ezra intended first to explain single words, elucidating their derivations and grammatical structures, and then give the meaning of the entire verse.

    b. This plan was not carried out fully by Ibn Ezra. In some cases he lapses into lengthy digressions and at times even into allegorical and symbolic interpretations.

    c. He uses astrology and numerology to interpret biblical verses.

2. Commentaries

    Ibn Ezra wrote a commentary on all the books of the Bible. Unfortunately, we have only his commentary on the Pentateuch, Isaiah, the Minor Prophets, Psalms, Job, Daniel, and the Five Scrolls.

3. Critical Views

    a. Ibn Ezra thought that the Book of Job was not originally written in Hebrew.

    b. He intimated that chapters 40-66 of Isaiah were written during the Babylonian Exile.

    c. He considered some psalms to be of later origin than traditional dating and also hinted at a later origin of some chapters of the Pentateuch.

4. Evaluation

    a. Though composed far from Spain, Ibn Ezra's exegetical works represent the height of Spanish exegesis. Not only did he make use of earlier Spanish commentators, but he also brought to the task the accumulated knowledge of the Jews in Spain in the fields of grammar and language study.

    b. He raised biblical exegesis to the level of a science with fixed principles.

c. His style is scintillating and witty, but sometimes cryptic. He often uses the formula, "There is a mystery involved here."

d. His commentary deals more with individual, detached questions, rather than trying to connect biblical passages into an organic whole.

e. His commentaries were seen as second only to Rashi's and were studied by many. The prying into his "secrets" and "mysteries" was a favorite diversion of Jewish scholars for centuries.

E. *Philosophy*

1. Works

a. In *Sepher ha-Shem* ("The Book of the Name of God") Ibn Ezra expounds theories regarding the concepts of God conveyed by His different names.

b. In *Yesod Mora* ("Foundation of Reverence") Ibn Ezra discusses the knowledge of God and attempts to state his philosophy of religion.

c. *Shaar ha-Shamayyim* ("The Gate of Heaven") was intended as an introduction to the Book of Genesis. Only the first chapter has been preserved.

d. *Arugot ha-Hokhmah u-Pardes ha-Mezimah* ("Flower Beds of Wisdom and the Garden of Thought") is a short pamphlet, written in rhymed prose, on the proof of the existence of God and His attributes.

e. Bearing remarkable similarity to Dante's *Divine Comedy, The Letter of Hai ben Mekiz* is an allegorical work. The title speaks of a person who is living and awake, i.e., the active "reason" which penetrates all of creation and endeavors to conceive of the Creator.

f. Ibn Ezra's *Sabbath Epistle* is a defense of the Sabbath.

2. Survey of Ibn Ezra's Philosophical Ideas

a. The highest level of knowledge is the understanding of God and his goodness.

b. There are two ways of knowing God: through a study of nature and from His revelation in the Law.

c. Ibn Ezra attempted to reconcile astrological fatalism with the ethical purpose of Divine Providence. The rational soul of man, he concluded, has the power to counteract, in part, the indications of the stars, but cannot annul them entirely.

d. Ibn Ezra believed that nothing exists that is solely material in nature. Everything contains spirituality, though it is more evident in some things than in others.

F. *Grammar*

1. Works

a. *Moznaim* ("The Scales"), a complete grammar in brief form, is primarily an explanation of grammatical terminology.

b. In his *Sefat Yeter* ("The Preferred Language") Ibn Ezra defends Saadyah Gaon against the strictures of Dunash ben Labrat, Hebrew poet and grammarian. The work also contains some of Ibn Ezra's own grammatical views.

c. *Yesod Dikduk* ("The Elements of Grammar") is a complete set of rules of Hebrew grammar.

d. *Tzahut* ("Purity," or "Clarity") is an exposition of the niceties of Hebrew style. It also contains several chapters on prosody and theory of Hebrew meter.

e. In one of his last books, *Safah Berurah* ("The Pure Language"), Ibn Ezra discusses certain problems of Hebrew grammar, though his manner of discussion is not always clear. This language study surveys relationships between Hebrew, Arabic, and Aramaic.

f. Ibn Ezra also translated the grammatical works of Judah ben David Hayyuj (c. 940-c. 1010) from Arabic into Hebrew.

2. Evaluation of Grammatical Works

a. None of Ibn Ezra's grammatical works exhaustively treats Hebrew grammar. Rather, these works were written for individuals or particular occasions and treated only the section of philology which interested the author or those who commissioned him.

b. Nevertheless, Ibn Ezra's writings were the first systematic grammatical works written in Hebrew which embodied the fruits of the labor of the great Spanish grammarians and lexicographers.

c. His concise, vivacious, and witty style imparts a peculiar charm even to rules of grammar.

d. Ibn Ezra gave impetus to other scholars to continue work in this field.

G. *Other Works*

1. Ibn Ezra's mathematical works include *Sepher ha-Mispar* ("The Book of Numbers") and *Hokhmat ha-Tishboret* ("Treatise on the Science of Fractions").

2. Ibn Ezra wrote a book on the astrolabe, *Kli ha-Nehoshet* ("The Copper Instrument"), and also translated the commentary of the Arabic astronomer Al-Matani on the astronomical tables of Muhammed al-Khwarizmi (780-850) into Hebrew.

3. *Sepher ha-Ibur* ("The Book of Intercalation") contains the calendar rules for calculation of various festival dates.

4. Both *Sepher ha-Moladot* ("The Book of Nativity") and *Sepher ha-Goralot* ("The Book of Destiny") contain rules for forecasting events that will happen to men by coursing the stars.

H. *Conclusion*

1. Ibn Ezra is said to have written 108 books covering all the fields of knowledge known in his day. In the Jewish world, his fame rests primarily on his work as a biblical commentator.

2. Ibn Ezra was distinguished from his Spanish contemporaries in that he never wrote a book or a poem in Arabic, but was a most accomplished and gifted Hebrew stylist.

3. Despite the inconsistencies and extremities of his ideas as well as his inability to create a systematic whole, he contributed a great deal to Jewish thought.

4. Ibn Ezra was a man of remarkable ability, energy, genius, and wit, who was able to enlighten the non-Arabic speaking Jews of England, France, and Italy. In a language they understood, he brought them the grammar of Judah Hayyuj, the mathematics and astronomy of the Greeks and Arabs, and the scientific and rationalistic way of thinking which had developed in Spain.

XXVI

MOSES IBN EZRA (c. 1055-1138)

Moses Ibn Ezra was a poet, linguist, philosopher, and author of many works. He not only was a prolific composer of *selihot* ("penitential hymns"), but he also wrote more Hebrew poems on secular themes than any other Jewish poet in the Middle Ages.

A. *Life*

Moses Ibn Ezra was born in Granada circa 1055 to a learned and wealthy family. His father, Jacob, occupied an office under the vizier, Samuel Ibn Nagdela (see Chapter XXIVa, "Samuel Ibn Nagdela"). He had three brothers, Isaac, Judah, and Joseph. He and his niece, the daughter of his eldest brother Isaac, fell in love. Isaac refused, however, to let his daughter marry Moses and instead forced her to marry Joseph, the youngest brother. After that unhappy incident, Moses fled from his father's house and wandered to Portugal and Castile. Estranged from both his brother and his beloved, he sought to drown his sorrow in earnest study. During this time he won the close friendship of Judah Halevi whose poetic gifts he encouraged (see following Chapter XXVIb). A reconciliation took place with his brother when Isaac's daughter, the love of his youth, died in childbirth. Ibn Ezra wrote an elegy so imbued with feeling and tenderness that, when Isaac read it, all was forgiven. When each of his brothers passed away, Moses wrote great elegies in their memory. When Moses Ibn Ezra died c. 1138, Judah Halevi wrote a beautiful tribute to his memory.

B. *Poetry*

1. General Characteristics

   a. Moses Ibn Ezra's poetry is dominated by a spirit of gloom. He complains much about deception, jealousy, and of the hardships and faithlessness of the times.

   b. Ibn Ezra was fond of using words of the same sound that had different and sometimes opposite meanings. He adopted this device from Arabic poets.

   c. His works reflect a brilliant command of the Hebrew language.

d. He employed a variety of meters in his poetry.

2. Secular Poetry

Ibn Ezra's secular poetry includes two major works, *Tarshish* and *Diwan*.

a. *Tarshish (Sepher he-Anak)* is so named because it is made up of 1210 verses (the letters of the word *Tarshish* being the numerical equivalent of 1210).

   (1) It is divided into ten chapters, each of which contains the twenty-two letters of the Hebrew alphabet in order.

   (2) It is written in the form of the Arabic *tajnis* ("punning rhyme"), each couplet ending with the same word but having a different meaning in each line.

   (3) The ten chapters deal with themes which to a large extent reflect the life of Moses Ibn Ezra: wine, love, and song; the charm of country life; lovesickness and the separation of lovers; unfaithful friends; old age; the vicissitudes of fortune and death; confidence in God; and the glory of poetry.

b. *Diwan* is a collection of poetry consisting of about 300 secular poems whose major themes are the praise of friends and elegies on the death of scholars.

c. Ibn Ezra's love poems are especially touching. He wrote a poem in honor of the wedding of Solomon Ibn Matir and describes the betrothal of Solomon and his bride as being similar to the betrothal of the moon and the sun. He also wrote much about his own hopeless love.

3. Sacred or Liturgical Poetry

a. Ibn Ezra found refuge for his suffering soul in religion. He composed hundreds of hymns and songs of praise to God. Many of these were *selihot* (penitential poems), which are included in the *Mahzor*.

b. Through these poems run a note of humility before God, the consciousness of sin, and the longing for repentance.

c. The dim character of his poetry is intended to make man realize the emptiness of life, the vanity of worldly glory, the bitter disillusionment that comes at last to the seeker of pleasure, and the inevitability of divine judgment.

d. Ibn Ezra also wrote a poetic paraphrase of the Book of Jonah for the Yom Kippur service. It is a fine example of a biblical epic and was adopted in the Avignon *Mahzor*.

4. Evaluation of Ibn Ezra's Poetry

a. Despite the purity of language and elegance in form, the tone and sound of his verse occasionally bear the mark of artificiality.

b. There is a certain earnestness in his poetry so that even when he sings of wine and love, he seems preoccupied with the graver problems of life.

c. His poetry appealed especially to scholars and those who were able to appreciate his command of the technical devices of the art. According to al-Harizi (Hebrew poet, 1170-1235), his poetry was preferred by poets over the poems of Judah Halevi and Solomon Ibn Gabirol.

C. *Arugat ha-Bosem ("Bed of Spices")*

1. This is Moses Ibn Ezra's only philosophical work. For the most part, it is a collection of quotations on the transcendence of God, the meaning of philosophy, the position of man in the universe, motion, nature, and intellect.

2. There is little originality in the book. He does, however, show profound knowledge of Graeco-Arabic thinkers as well as the philosophy of Saadyah Gaon and Solomon Ibn Gabirol. He compiles the sayings of Pythagoras, Empedocles, Socrates, Plato, Aristotle, Saadyah, and Ibn Gabirol in order to stress his own views. There seems to be little attempt on his part to contribute original thoughts.

D. *Kitab al-Muhadara w' al-Mudhakara*
(*"Conversations and Recollections"*)

1. This work discusses the rules of poetic art. It was written in Arabic by Ibn Ezra at the request of a friend who addresses eight questions on Hebrew poetry to him.

2. The first four chapters deal with prose poetry and the respective prose writers and poets. These chapters also concern themselves with the natural gifts of the Arabs on these art forms.

3. The fifth chapter begins with the history of the settlement of the Jews in Spain. It continues with a full description of the literary activity of the Spanish Jews. Also described are the general intellectual conditions of the time. The last chapter deals with poetic forms.

4. This account of the Jews in Spain and their literary contribution has been a valuable source of information as a history of Spanish-Jewish poetry from its beginnings.

E. *Conclusion*

1. Moses Ibn Ezra was one of the most prolific poets of the Middle Ages.

2. His religious expressions were of such a universal nature that his poems (especially the *selihot*) came to be used by all Jews.

3. His Arabic treatise on prose and poetry was a great contribution to the literary history of Spain as well as to Jewish literary history.

4. He was highly honored by his contemporaries and was praised by many in both prose and poetry.

JUDAH HALEVI (1075-1141)

Judah Halevi has been called the greatest Hebrew poet of the Middle Ages. Even today, many of his poems still retain their original brilliance, power, and popularity. In addition, he is remembered as the author of *The Kuzari*, which established him as one of the greatest Jewish philosophers of Muslim Spain.

A. *Life*

Judah Halevi was born in Toledo, Spain in 1075. He began to write poetry early in life and mastered Hebrew, Arabic, biblical and rabbinic literature, Greek philosophy, and medicine. His life and the lives of his fellow Jews were affected by the tumultuous times in which they lived, for they were caught between the Christians and Muslims who were fighting desperately for control of the Iberian peninsula. Halevi either studied under, or came under the influence of, Isaac Alfasi, author of the digest of the Babylonian Talmud. Moses Ibn Ezra, an influential figure, respected Halevi, aided him financially, and helped him to move to Granada. Due to the troubled political situation, Halevi appears to have wandered a great deal and then finally to have settled in Cordova, Spain, where he practiced medicine. After the completion of his philosophical work, *Sepher ha-Kuzari* ("The Kuzari") in 1140, he left on a pilgrimage to the Holy Land via Egypt. Nothing was heard from him after his departure from Egypt, where he spent more than two years. Legend has it that an Arab horseman rode him down before the Western Wall in Jerusalem.

B. *Writings*

1. Poetry

   a. Style

   (1) Judah Halevi was a master of the poetic style of the times. He wrote Hebrew poetry in accordance with the rules of Arabic verse. He was able to convey a simplicity and tenderness in his poetry which most poets could not find in the forced framework of earlier Hebrew poetry.

   (2) In his later poetry he began to use the *piyyut* (a Hebrew religious hymn or liturgical form), the structure of which does not adhere to the Arabic forms.

   (3) He wrote more than 800 poems, among which are many acrostics and epigrams. (An acrostic is a composition, usually in verse, in which successive letters, taken in order, spell out a word, a name, a phrase, or the whole alphabet.)

b. Content

    (1) Halevi's secular poetry, like that of his contemporaries, deals with the theme of life and its pleasures. Examples include "The Roses of Spring" and "Storm at Sea."

    (2) Individual and secular motifs are replaced by religious and national poetry. These are powerful expressions of the value of Judaism and the contrast between the destiny and actual plight of the Jewish people. Among his many liturgical writings and hymns are "Oh Lord, Where Shall I Find Thee?" and "The Word of God."

    (3) Halevi's nationalistic poetry centers on the search for a solution to the plight of his people. Examples include "My Heart Is in the East" and "Zion Wilt Thou Not Ask for the Welfare of Thy Exile?"

2. Philosophical Work

    a. *Kitab Al Khuzari*, or *Sepher ha-Kuzari*, is a philosophical work consisting of discourses among a Khazar king, a Jew, a Christian, a Muslim, and an Aristotelian philosopher. As a result of the debates, the king embraces Judaism.

    (1) This debate is based on the author's conception of the actual conversion of a Khazar king to Judaism.

        (a) The Khazars were a Turkish or Finnish tribe which controlled the Volga area of the Crimea from the eighth to the tenth centuries.

        (b) In the eighth century the Khazar king embraced Judaism; many of his nobles and subjects followed suit (see Chapter XVIIIb, "Four Medieval Jewish Writers").

    (2) This work takes the form of five essays.

        (a) Essay One relates how the Khazar king realizes that the roots of Christianity and Islam are in Judaism. He calls in a Jewish scholar who explains that just as man is higher than other forms of matter by virtue of his intellect, so the Jewish people are superior, since they alone have not only a written history of the human race, but also a history of revelation and tradition.

(b) Essay Two deals with the particular qualities of the Jewish people, the explanation of why Palestine is the land of revelation.

(c) Essay Three deals with the history of the Talmud and the development of the worship of God.

(d) Essay Four is an analysis of the different names of God as used in the Bible and discussion of prophecy and revelation.

(e) Essay Five is a criticism of contemporary philosophies, most notably Aristotelian philosophy, which is not criticized in Essay One. The problems of free will and providence are also discussed.

b. Religion, in the view of Halevi, has a secure foundation in the experiences of the Jewish people and in their history, in revelation, and in tradition. Religion is primary. Philosophy is serviceable only for those whose faith is not strong enough to escape doubt. Halevi's *Kitab Al Khuzari* is intended to show the insufficiency of philosophy and the superiority of the truths revealed by religion over those arrived at by mere reasoning.

(1) Halevi recognized an indissoluble union between Judaism and the Jewish people.

(a) He considered Israel to be the people of revelation and felt that the aptitude to receive the divine illumination distinguished the chosen individual, the Jew, from others.

(b) As intellect sets man apart from mineral and plant, so the still greater endowment of prophecy—receptivity to the divine influence—distinguishes some individuals from the rest of mankind.

(c) This is the prophetic gift whereby God makes himself known: If Israel is the people of revelation, so Palestine is the land of revelation.

(2) The connection of Judaism with the Jewish people gives it its distinguishing characteristic. In contrast to Christianity and Islam, which variously centered on the personalities of the founders, Judaism is the religious expression of the Jewish people.

C. *Importance of Halevi*

1. Halevi's "Ode to Zion" has been translated into German, Dutch, Italian, English, and Russian and is considered to be one of the great achievements of world literature.

2. Some of his works are recited in the synagogue service on Saturday and on other Holy Days throughout the Jewish calendar.

3. Traces of his writings have been found in the mystical works of the Middle Ages.

4. By means of his philosophical writings, he attempted to free religion from philosophy. His *Kitab Al Khuzari* is of first rank among the Jewish philosophical writings of the Middle Ages.

D. *Summary*

Halevi is generally acclaimed as the greatest Hebrew poet of the Middle Ages. He attained full mastery of the poetic style of his day (Hebrew poetry subject to the rules of Arabic versification). He forced cumbersome forms to express the tenderest emotions and sentiments; he made frequent use of the acrostic. In later years he came to regard the practice of forcing Hebrew poetry into the metrical schemes of the Arabs as perversity. He saw a way out of the corrupting influence in the *piyyutim*, which are free from strict Arabic forms and used rhymed verse of approximately an equal number of syllables. In addition, he is one of the great medieval Jewish thinkers as witnessed in his *Kitab Al Khuzari*.

XXVII

MAIMONIDES (1135-1204)

Moses ben Maimon, better known as the Rambam or Maimonides, was the foremost intellectual figure of medieval Jewry. He wrote important works on astronomy, medicine, logic, philosophy, and jurisprudence. He was one of the greatest Jewish halakhists (authorities on Jewish law) and wrote commentaries on both the oral and written law which are renowned for their systematic approach and erudition. Maimonides tried to be a mediator between two seemingly incompatible world views, the Greek and the rabbinic.

A. *Life*

Maimonides was born in Cordova, Spain, on the fourteenth day of Nisan (the day before Passover) in the year 1135 to a distinguished Spanish-Jewish family of scholars. His father was a learned talmudist and a member of the Rabbinical College at Cordova. Maimonides was thirteen when the Almohades (a fanatical North African Moslem sect) conquered Cordova, closed down all the churches and synagogues, and demanded conversion to Islam. Maimonides and his family fled, wandering from city to city in Spain. They then emigrated to Fez, Morocco, and stayed there from 1159 to 1165. In 1165 they went to Palestine, but remained there less than a year. Finally they settled in Old Cairo (Fostat), Egypt. Despite the upheavals of a transient life, Maimonides continued his studies and even did some writing. He was erudite in Jewish and secular studies. He practiced medicine as a profession and was involved in the family's trading firm. He did not approve of taking money for performing religious duties. By 1177 he was considered the religious and secular leader of Egyptian Jewry. In 1183, Maimonides married and his wife bore him a daughter who died at birth, and a son, Abraham, who inherited his father's position and later became the *nagid* (ruler) of Egyptian Jewry. The constant strain that characterized Maimonides's life—his medical practice, communal activities, and the constant writing and revisions of his literary works—gradually undermined his health. He died at the age of 69 on December 13, 1204. A three-day period of mourning was observed by Egyptian Jews and a fast was declared in Jerusalem. He is buried in Tiberias, Israel.

B. *Early Works*

1. Maimonides's early works were composed while he was in Spain. He composed a brief manual on logic, analyzing some seventy basic philosophic terms and helping to classify the science.

2. He wrote a treatise, *Intercalation* (*Maamar ha-Ibbur*), a review of the principles of the Jewish calendar.

3. While still in his early twenties he compiled commentaries on a few tractates of the Talmud.

4. At the age of twenty-three he began his *Commentary on the Mishnah*, which was completed ten years later.

C. *Commentary on the Mishnah*

1. Begun in 1158, the *Commentary* is written in Arabic with Hebrew characters. He gave it the title *Siraj* (Hebrew, *Ma'or*), which means "luminary."

2. In a general introduction he discusses the origin and plan of the Mishnah and gives an account of the development of the oral law.

3. Maimonides embodies in his *Commentary* a summary of debates of the ancient academies of Palestine and Babylonia and points out what he felt to be the prevailing law.

4. In his introduction to the *Avot* ("Sayings of the Fathers") section of the Mishnah, he wrote eight chapters which are outstanding for their understanding of secular Jewish ethics. This soon circulated as an independent treatise called *Shemonah Perakim* ("Eight Chapters").

5. In his introduction to the last chapter of *Sanhedrin* he elucidates the fundamental doctrines of Judaism. Here, his famous Thirteen Articles of Faith are stated. They are belief in (1) God's existence, (2) His unity, (3) His incorporeality, (4) His eternity, (5) His exclusive claim to worship, (6) prophecy, (7) the uniqueness of Moses among the prophets, (8) the Law of Moses as in its entirety given by God, (9) the Law's eternal immutability, (10) God's omniscience, (11) reward and punishment, (12) the coming of the Messiah, and (13) the resurrection of the dead. These principles are included in both the Ashkenazic and Sephardic prayerbooks.

6. Evaluation and Influence

   a. The *Commentary on the Mishnah* is considered valuable because it renders the decision of the Law which the reader might otherwise not be able to determine from the Mishnah alone.

   b. The *Commentary* was written for laymen rather than for the scholars of the period, and was read in the synagogue on the Sabbath by the Jews of Egypt.

   c. It is saturated with philosophical and theological principles of Judaism. Maimonides seized every opportunity in this and other tracts to expose abuses, superstitions, and errors.

   d. Some of the introductions were translated into Hebrew during his lifetime, but the entire *Commentary* was not translated into Hebrew until 1492.

D. *Mishneh Torah ("The Repetition of the Torah")*

1. Also known as the *Yad Hazakah* ("Strong Hand")—a code of Jewish laws—this work was written between 1166 and 1176. It is a clearly worded summary of the rabbinical halakhah, or law, and is divided into fourteen books (*yad* numerically equals 14).

2. Written in mishnaic Hebrew and intended for nonprofessional students of the Talmud, it is more than a vast compendium of laws; rather, it is a brilliant survey of theology, metaphysics, and ethics of Judaism in their relation to the faith and practice of the Jewish people.

3. Where several opinions are adduced in the Gemara, Maimonides gives only the one he accepts.

4. He drew no distinctions between regulations still valid in his own time and others which had been considered obsolete.

5. Effects

   a. There were objections made to:

      (1) the unprecedented method of arrangement.

      (2) the failure to supply sources.

(3) the fact that some of the declarations sounded presumptuous and arbitrary.

(4) the fact that Maimonides declared that he was summarizing the entire oral law and that no one would have to read any other work except the *Torah* and *Mishneh Torah*. It was felt that this would result in neglect of talmudic study.

b. Abraham ben David of Posquières wrote *Hassagot* ("Objections") to the *Mishneh Torah* which today are included as marginal notes in printed editions of *Mishneh Torah*. Because of the controversy, the study of Talmud was actually stimulated.

6. Evaluation

a. Maimonides was aware of the shortcomings of this work and he constantly revised it, hoping to supply references for the sources.

b. Despite the objections to it, it became the standard book on Jewish law and rules on how to study it were laid down by rabbinical scholars. Commentaries and books were written about it.

c. The *Turim* and *Shulhan Arukh*, later compendiums, used the *Mishneh Torah* as one of their main points of reference.

d. It fixed the reputation of Maimonides for all time, and this reputation is one of the reasons why his *Mishneh Torah* and *Moreh Nevukhim* ("Guide for the Perplexed") have been more widely read by Jews than any other philosophical works by Jewish scholars.

E. *Moreh Nevukhim ("Guide for the Perplexed")*

1. Completed in about 1190, this work grew out of a series of essays in Arabic in which Maimonides answered some incisive questions put to him by his pupil Joseph Ibn Shamun.

2. He addressed himself to persons attracted by reason who found it "difficult to accept as correct the teaching based on the literal interpretation of the Law (Torah)." Many Jews at the time searched for guidance in reconciling the truths of their religion with the philosophic and scientific teachings of the Greek scholars, then available in Arabic translation.

3. It was written in the style and spirit of Aristotelian philosophy, the tenets of which were universally accepted at the time in educated circles and which Maimonides accepted where they did not conflict with what he regarded as basic to Judaism.

4. Contents

   a. In the first part Maimonides discusses biblical expressions which are apt to be theological pitfalls. He insists that whenever reason is absolutely sure of its findings, the contradictory statements in the Bible must be explained in an allegorical way.

   b. He goes on to discuss the nature of God and presents his doctrine of the "negative attributes"—that is, anything attributed to God is intrinsically different from a similar attribute of man; we really know more what God is *not*, rather than what He *is*.

   c. He goes on to prove that the universe was created and hence created by God (against the view of Aristotle).

   d. He analyzes the nature of prophecy as an inspiration from God, which passes through the mediation of the "active intellect" of humans to the rational power and then to the faculty of the imagination. It is the highest state a person can reach. He grades eleven degrees of prophecy as recorded in the Bible; Moses was the greatest of all prophets, as he alone received his communication directly from God.

   e. In the third part, Maimonides offers rational explanations of the ceremonial and legislative details of the biblical laws, stressing above all their educational purpose.

   f. He concludes his work by elaborating on the steps a person must take to attain perfection, the highest degree being the development of intellectual and spiritual qualities, so that he may know God. Having acquired this knowledge, he will always seek righteousness and try to imitate the ways of God.

5. Impact

   a. The assumption of the supremacy of reason and the need to harmonize the revealed word with Aristotelian philosophy aroused sharp opposition from many quarters during Maimonides's life as well as after his death.

b. Particularly after Maimonides's death, *Moreh Nevukhim* ("Guide for the Perplexed") became the stimulus for a long and bitter fight between the Maimonists and anti-Maimonists. Polemics were issued from both camps. Finally, in 1234, the dispute was referred to the Christian authorities and all available copies were burned, because it was supposedly heretical for both Christianity and Judaism.

c. In the thirteenth century the controversy over the *Guide* came to an end and its influence was seen in the philosophical defenses of traditional Christianity by such leading Christian scholastics as Albertus Magnus and Thomas Aquinas.

d. Even modernists like Spinoza and Leibnitz, despite their criticism of the *Guide* in its details as well as its basic assumptions, used it as a reference.

e. It was translated into Hebrew by Samuel Ibn Tibbon during Maimonides's lifetime and later by Judah al-Harizi. Many commentaries have been written on it, the most famous and outstanding ones being by Moses Narboni, Profiat Duran, and Isaac Abravanel.

6. Evaluation

a. Although many of its scientific theories became obsolete with the discoveries of Newton, the *Guide* is significant for its role in the development of Jewish thought.

b. Set against the spirit of the time in which it was written—an age fraught with religious superstition—this work marks a milestone in human advancement by preaching a faith governed by reason.

c. Maimonides attempted to reconcile the outlooks of faith and philosophy, which hitherto were considered incompatible.

d. Because of the complex nature of *Moreh Nevukhim*, the rabbis permitted study of it only after years of studying *Talmud* and other simpler works.

e. Among its greatest achievements is its inspiration for other Jewish scholars in pursuing these same types of philosophic and scientific studies.

F. *Other Works*

1. Throughout his life Maimonides was involved in writing *Responsa* (authoritative responses to questions concerning Jewish law) and "letters" on theological subjects (see Chapter XXIXb, "Responsa Literature").

2. *Iggeret Ha-Shemad* ("Letter on Apostasy")

   a. In this, which is one of his earlier works, Maimonides absolves the Moroccan Jews from their feelings of guilt for practicing Judaism secretly due to persecution. At that time some fanatical rabbis had come out with the statement that they were no longer considered Jews. Maimonides states that a feigned transgression of the law cannot be regarded as willful departure from it.

   b. It is believed that he and his family also lived disguised as Moslems and this letter gives rationale for his own actions.

   c. Although Maimonides did not consider Islam idolatry, he believed one should leave his native country rather than embrace another faith.

3. *Epistle to Yemen*

   Written in about 1174, Maimonides advises the Jews of Yemen not to be discouraged by their persecution and to remain true to Judaism. Since there were a number of "false Messiahs" arising who promised redemption and amelioration of their misery, he goes into the doctrinal and historical aspects of the traditional messianic teaching in an effort to point out the falsehood of these messiahs.

4. *Ma'amar Tehiyat Ha-Metim* ("Treatise on Resurrection")

   In this treatise he defends himself against the suspicion that he had denied the basic creed of resurrection of the dead.

5. *Sepher Ha-Mitzvot* ("Book of Precepts")

Written in Arabic, this work is a summary of the entire body of Jewish law under the headings of the traditional 613 biblical commandments.

G. *Maimonides as a Physician*

1. Maimonides was taught medicine by his father and studied further during his family's stay in Fez, Morocco, where he mingled with well-known physicians. Maimonides classified medicine into three divisions: preventive medicine, healing of the sick, and care of the convalescent. He stressed preventive medicine and was opposed to the use of charms and amulets. Maimonides was familiar with the writings of various Greek physicians such as Hippocrates and Galen, and his beliefs were influenced by their teachings. Maimonides, who had many students and disciples, was highly regarded as a physician among the Moslems.

2. Works on Medicine

   Maimonides wrote several treatises and books on astronomy and medicine including the following:

   a. *Fusul Musa* ("The Aphorisms of Moses") is a collection of medical aphorisms and information, collected from the writings of Hippocrates, Galen, and various Arab authors.

   b. *Sharh Asma al-Aqqar* ("Glossary of Drug Names") is an alphabetical classification of over 300 remedies, mostly derived from plants. The names are given in Arabic, Greek, and Persian.

   c. *Fi Tadbir al-Sihha* ("Guide to Good Health") teaches that physical well-being is dependent on psychological stability and rest. This treatise stresses the importance of hygiene, physical exercise, work, sexual life, and diet, and suggests the beneficial qualities of music, poetry, painting, and a pleasant environment.

   d. Maimonides also wrote treatises on asthma (Fi al-Rabw), hemor-rhoids (Fi al-Bawasir), and sexual intercourse (Fi al-Jamaah).

H. *Conclusion*

1. Maimonides was essentially a rationalist and he placed human reason above all other human faculties.

2. His code of laws is still among the most authoritative guides for Jewish observance.

3. His writings have influenced the thoughts of theologians of Islam and Christianity, and of course had a profound impact on Jewish thinkers.

4. He exerted a great influence on the medieval world of thought and Jewish intellectualism and did much to help unify the Jewish community.

XXVIII

BAHYA IBN PAKUDA (c. 1050-1120)

While most of the Jewish philosophical endeavor of the Middle Ages was directed to a defense of the faith in terms of the current philosophical mood, Bahya Ibn Pakuda worked toward meeting another serious need. Contemporary Jewry was deteriorating through indifference to the faith and a mere observance of its outer formalities. Bahya prepared a systematic presentation of the inner moral responses essential to Judaism, eloquently exhorting their observance.

A. *Life*

Little is known of the life of Bahya ben Joseph Ibn Pakuda, the Jewish ethical writer and philosopher who lived in Moslem Spain. He was *dayyan* or rabbinical judge in a Spanish city (probably Saragossa). As well as being knowledgeable in the Law, he was interested in the human attitudes which are the foundation of law. Judaism, he argued, is a religion which imposes a great many duties upon a human being. The mind has a duty to absorb knowledge; the tongue has a duty to speak truth; the hands have a duty to do charity; and so on. But the heart also has duties, and these are more numerous and more important than those of any other part of the body. For unless the heart accompanies every act with the proper feeling and emotion, actions become merely mechanical and therefore religiously insufficient.

B. *Major Work —"Duties of the Heart"*

1. *Hovot ha-Levavot* ("Duties of the Heart") is a classic statement of the inner response required for the true observance of Judaism.*

2. It is written in a clear, often eloquent Arabic. This clarity was not captured in the Hebrew translation completed by Judah Ibn Tibbon in 1160, nor in the translations made from Hebrew into several European languages.†

---

*This work shows the influence of Aristotelean (Neoplatonic) philosophy and Moslem mysticism. Despite these non-Jewish influences, it is a Jewish philosophical treatise in contents and character.

†In 1973, Menahem Mansoor published an English translation of *Duties of the Heart* from the original Arabic.

3. This work was a great treasury of spiritual inspiration during the Middle Ages.

4. At least six complete commentaries in Hebrew have been written on the text.

5. Contents

    a. The work is essentially moralistic. Its tendency is to elevate spirituality and inner piety above formalism and to place the love of God and complete trust in Him above the actions performed by the parts of the body. There is a definite preference for asceticism and withdrawal from the world.

    b. In his introduction the author divides the precepts of the Torah into two parts:

        (1) The duties of the organs (such as the precept of wearing Tefillin) imply observance of outward ceremony.

        (2) The duties of the heart include those involving the human conscience. (Many books and codes had been written on the first, but few on the second of these parts).

    c. His book was written in ten sections. Each of the ten "gates" represents one of the principles of man's spiritual life, including love of God, worship of God, humility, and temperance of human conduct.

        (1) *Shaar ha-Yihud* ("The Gate of Divine Unity")

            (a) Here Ibn Pakuda gives proofs for the existence of God and defines His attributes.

            (b) In this discussion he follows the arguments of the Jewish philosopher Saadyah Gaon (see Chapter XXIIb, "Saadyah Gaon").

            (c) Ibn Pakuda is the first Jewish philosopher to employ the "Argument from Design," which states that the world in its complicated aspect and its harmonious arrangement testifies that it was created according to the design of a creator.

(d) God's essential attributes are existence, unity, and eternity.

(e) There are many gradations of unity of which God is the purest representation.

(2) *Shaar ha-Hokhma* ("The Gate of Wisdom")

(a) God can be known only through His works.

(b) In observance of the created universe and his own intricate existence, man is moved to reverence and thankfulness to God for His worldly creation.

(c) Bahya examines and describes Divine Wisdom, the various kinds of creation in the universe as a whole, and the different kinds of creatures.

(3) *Shaar ha-Tefillah* ("The Gate of Divine Worship")

(a) Man is richly endowed with blessings. It is proper that he offer prayers of thanksgiving to his benefactor, i.e., his God.

(b) Bahya differentiates between the thankfulness which we may feel toward human benefactors and the type we feel towards God.

(4) *Shaar ha-Bitahon* ("The Gate of Trust")

(a) Trust in God is the highest and most ennobling virtue.

(b) God provides for the needs of all creatures. However, this does not remove from man the responsibility of seeking his own livelihood and betterment. Real trust in God brings man to a happy state of mind, accepting all vicissitudes of life with a cheerful attitude.

(c) God's care is extended to man's spirit beyond the limits of this life.

(5) *Shaar Yihud ha-Avodah* ("The Gate of the Unification of Action")

   (a) Man is turned from the path of righteousness by the lure of worldly things and evil inclinations. He craves pleasure and power.

   (b) The Law directs man to the proper midground between abstinence and self-indulgence.

   (c) The worst sin is hypocrisy. Man is to worship God for no other reason than the desire to serve Him.

(6) *Shaar ha-Anavah* ("The Gate of Humility")

   (a) A comparison of man's modest endowments with the greatness of the Almighty leads the pious individual to an attitude of humility in relationship to God and others.

   (b) This most important character trait is not to be confused with weakness or servility.

(7) *Shaar ha-Teshuvah* ("The Gate of Repentance")

   (a) The truly penitent are ever acceptable in God's sight.

   (b) Repentance involves four elements: regret, discontinuing the wrong, confession and seeking of pardon, and a promise not to repeat the offense.

(8) *Shaar Heshbon ha-Nefesh* ("The Gate of Self-Examination")

   (a) Self-discipline, through contemplation of that which is good in the world, is a higher form of observance than blind obedience to the Law.

   (b) Man can only attain higher respect through examination of his own possession of Divine Wisdom.

(9) *Shaar ha-Perishut* ("The Gate of Asceticism")

   (a) Asceticism is essential to the religious life for the control of bodily passions.

(b) True total ascetic discipline is possible and desirable only for a select number of qualified persons.

(c) The highest form of asceticism is an inner detachment maintained while living in society.

(10) *Shaar ha-Ahavah* ("The Gate of the Love of God")

(a) The goal of all self-discipline is rising to the love of God and serving Him with one's whole being.

(b) This love must be unlimited and man must be ready to sacrifice everything for God's sake.

(c) True love of God implies the mystical concept of the union of the soul of man with the "Divine Light" of God.

(d) Having attained this level of love, the 613 commandments of the Torah become minimal in service to God.

C. *Minor Works*

1. Ibn Pakuda wrote a number of fervent religious poems. A few of these and portions of his philosophical writings were included in the Jewish liturgy.

2. *Torot ha-Nefesh* ("Reflections of the Soul"), a recently discovered philosophical work, is believed by some to have been written by Bahya. Neoplatonic in character, this work portrays the created universe, spiritual and material, in a descending series of emanations. However, since this is not in accord with views expressed in Bahya's other works, some scholars doubt his authorship of *Reflections of the Soul*.

D. *Importance*

1. Bahya Ibn Pakuda attempted to formulate an ethical system from Jewish teachings which would reconcile the inner feelings with the outward deeds and give the proper stress to this inner obligation of the heart.

2. The rabbinical concept of law was revered by Bahya, who made it part and parcel of the Jew's inner life.

3. His success was based on the fact that his ethical system was founded on the Talmud and on the Aristotelian philosophy of his time, as tempered by the Arabic *Kalam* (see Glossary).

4. The popular appeal of *Hovot ha-Levavot* ("Duties of the Heart") is enhanced by the anecdotes, stories, and fables that Bahya included to elucidate his concepts. He endeavors more to thrill the reader by his religious enthusiasm than to win him over by cogent argument.

E. *Conclusion*

1. *Duties of the Heart* was the first systematic work on Jewish ethics.

2. The *Duties* became the most popular work of Jewish devotional literature.

3. Bahya was the first Jewish philosopher to use the design of the universe as proof of the existence of God.

4. His arguments for the existence and unity of God influenced, to certain extent, Christian scholastic philosophy.

FOUR MEDIEVAL JEWISH WRITERS

Prior to the eighth century, the Jews of Spain lived under Christian rule and were subjected to the most severe restrictions and persecutions. After conquering Spain, the Moslems extended freedom to the Jews and encouraged the pursuit of learning. Thriving Jewish communities were established in Granada, Cordova, and Toledo. The career of Hasdai Ibn Shaprut (915-970) is indicative of the freedom and favor extended to the Jews, and of Jewish influence among other communities in other parts of the world.

Nahmanides (1194-c. 1270) shared characteristics with such outstanding Jews of this period as Maimonides and Abraham Ibn Ezra. Like them, he was a man of wide erudition. His philosophy differed from theirs in that it inclined away from emphasis on reason and philosophy and tended toward mysticism. The philosophical works of Maimonides and Abraham Ibn Ezra were intended for the learned and intellectuals among the Jews. Nahmanides was more interested in the religious attitude of the average Jew.

Little is known about the philosopher Joseph Albo (c. 1830-c. 1435). His major work, *Sepher ha-Ikkarim* ("Book of Principles"), invested the Jewish religion with philosophical foundations and endowed philosophy with a preeminently religious content. Through his work he sought to refute the fundamental claims of Christianity and bolster Jewish morale.

Isaac Abravanel (1437-1508) is an outstanding historical figure among the Jews in the closing period of the Middle Ages. Statesman, diplomat, courtier, and financier of international renown, he was, at the same time, an encyclopedic scholar, a philosophical thinker, a noted biblical commentator, and a brilliant writer. In Abravanel, two long lines of tradition meet and end, the lines of medieval Jewish statesmen and medieval Jewish philosophers.

A. *Hasdai Ibn Shaprut*

1. Life

Hasdai Ibn Shaprut was born in Cordova in 915. He studied Hebrew, Arabic, and Latin. Since Latin was usually known only to the higher Christian clergy, Ibn Shaprut was one of the few Jews able to have discourses with the clergy and to read the works of the Church. In

940, Ibn Shaprut was appointed interpreter and physician to the Caliph Abdul Rahman III from which post he rose to a position of great influence in the court: responsibility for finances and foreign affairs. As the recognized head of the Jewish community of Cordova, he used his influence to intercede on behalf of the well-being of the Jews of Spain and other lands. He lent his support to Jewish learning, importing texts from the East and lending financial support to poets, philosophers, and scholars, among whom were the grammarian Menahem ben Saruk and the poet Dunash ben Labrat. He was instrumental in gaining the freedom of Moses ben Hanoch, a captured emissary from the Babylonian academy of Sura, and in helping him to establish a great talmudic academy in Cordova. Hasdai Ibn Shaprut died in 970.

2. The Khazars

    a. Despite the favored position of the Jews in Spain, Hasdai Ibn Shaprut felt that a landless people would always be limited in strength. He pursued the rumors that somewhere there existed a state under Jewish rule.

    b. He learned of the Khazars, a warlike tribe of Turkish origin who lived in the Ural region of southern Russia and who were reported to be of the Jewish faith.

    c. In 960, a letter which Shaprut had written the Khazars reached Joseph, the Khazar king, who replied, telling of their state, the conversion to Judaism of Bulan, the first Khazar king, and of their desire for contact with Jews elsewhere.

    d. Shortly after this exchange of correspondence, the kingdom of the Khazars collapsed in a war with the Russians. It was never restored.

3. Influence

    a. Shaprut's position of influence in the government helped to win safety and freedom for the Jews of Spain.

b. Through his patronage he gave great impetus to Jewish culture. The center of Jewish creativity was shifted from Babylonia to Spain.

c. Judah Halevi's philosophic masterpiece *The Khuzari* (see Chapter XXVb, "Judah Halevi") was based upon the story, unearthed by Hasdai Ibn Shaprut, of King Bulan's search for faith and his ultimate conversion to Judaism.

B. *Nahmanides*

1. Life

Nahmanides (Ramban, Rabbi Moses ben Nahman) was born in Gerona (city in Aragon), Spain, in 1194. The greatest part of his life was spent in his native city where he practiced medicine and served as rabbi to the Jewish community. Through his teachers he became heir to the traditions and methods of Franco-German scholarship and transplanted its ideas in Spain. Through his efforts, the study of Talmud came to be of primary importance in Spain. At the age of twenty he began a series of commentaries on the Talmud. He refused to look upon philosophy as the key to religious truth, and regarded the teachings of the Bible and the Talmud as the ultimate authority, no matter what reason might say. Judaism, which to the rationalists was an open book, was to Nahmanides full of mysteries beyond the comprehension of human reason. Thus, his biblical commentary is a rational interpretation with an insistence on mystical implications. When conflicts about the teachings of Maimonides broke out in the middle of the thirteenth century, Nahmanides, being somewhat adverse to philosophy but a great admirer of Maimonides, tried to mediate between conflicting factions.

In 1263 Nahmanides had a public dispute with an apostate named Pablo Christiani. The topic of debate was the messiahship of Jesus. From talmudic and midrashic sources Nahmanides claimed victory in the debate and published a pamphlet entitled *Sepher ha-Vikkuah* ("Book of Debate"). Because of this he fled Spain in 1267 for fear of punishment by the Christian authorities. He settled in Palestine where he established a center for talmudic studies. While there, he spent his time immersed in the Scriptures rather than in the study of the Talmud. He died in Palestine in 1270.

2. Works

    a. Nahmanides's greatest work is his *Commentary on the Pentateuch.*

        (1) While writing this work, the author had in mind the layman who possessed both the requisite schooling and the interest to understand an exposition on the Word of God.

        (2) Nahmanides endeavored to present the Torah in the light of deep piety. At the same time, he tried to show the reason for every law and precept and to show how reason could be deduced from the meaning of the words.

    b. He had a strong inclination toward mysticism, but whether certain kabbalistic works are rightly attributed to him is not known.

3. Importance

Nahmanides's brief sojourn in Palestine reinforced the teaching of Torah among the Jewish communities there. In Spain, he was one of the foremost talmudists and his teachings took root in a circle of disciples. Apart from his mystical views, Nahmanides brought the Torah to a great number of Jews in Europe and in the Middle East. His commentary is still considered to be of great value.

C. *Joseph Albo*

1. Life

Joseph Albo was born c. 1380 in Spain. He was a student of Hasdai Crescas and took part in the Tortosa disputation (1413-1414). A physician by profession, he was well acquainted with the physical sciences and with the philosophical thought of his time. Albo did not possess the profundity of his teacher; as a thinker he was superficial, commonplace, and incapable of writing with logical sequence. On the advice of his friends he began to investigate how far freedom of inquiry in religious matters was possible within the limits of Judaism. As a preacher, he was one of the most clever and graceful.

2. Major Work—*Sepher ha-Ikkarim* ("Book of Principles")

   a. In this work for which Albo is best known, he sought to show that all religions grow out of the same ideas and that only after they grow out of these roots do various religions begin to differ from one another. He restated Maimonides's Thirteen Articles of Faith into six dogmas of faith.

   b. Albo attempted to prove that Judaism is superior to Christianity as a religion. The principles of Christianity, according to Albo, are less pure than the principles of Judaism; furthermore, Judaism is more in harmony with philosophy.

   c. According to Albo, one may still be considered a Jew even though he believes that creation was preceded by primeval matter.

   d. Similarly, he feels that belief in the Messiah, fundamental to Christians, is not central to Judaism.

   e. According to Albo, highest happiness consists not so much in the exaltation of the soul as in its salvation.

   f. Only after death does man attain the perfection for which he is destined by God.

3. Importance

   As a reaction against his anti-Jewish surroundings, Albo constantly took issue with Christianity, both directly and indirectly. His work quickly won great popularity and became one of the most widely read books on Jewish theology.

D. *Isaac Abravanel*

1. Life

Isaac Abravanel was born in 1437 to a wealthy family in Lisbon, Portugal. He received a thorough education in both Jewish and secular matters. His thought turned early to philosophical problems. Under the persecution of John II, Isaac was forced to flee to Toledo with his family. Soon he became the treasurer to Ferdinand and Isabella.

In 1490, edicts for the expulsion of the Jews from Spain were issued. Though he was a royal favorite, Isaac was unsuccessful in attempts to persuade Ferdinand and Isabella to allow the Jews to remain in Spain. Despite the willingness of the king and queen to make an exception for him and his family, Abravanel chose to leave with his fellow Jews. He went to Naples, where he came into the service of the Italian King, Ferdinand. A short time later when Naples was captured by Charles of France, Abravanel and his family were again forced to flee, finally arriving in Venice. Isaac continued his role as diplomat and negotiated a commercial treaty between the Venetian republic and Portugal. He turned to literary activity and began his commentary on the Bible. He also wrote works on philosophy and devoted considerable time to the messianic doctrines. He died in Venice in 1508 and was buried in Padua.

2. Works

    a. Abravanel wrote a treatise entitled *Rosh Emunah* ("Pinnacle of Faith")

        (1) The greatest part of this work forms a defense of Maimonides. In spite of this fact, Abravanel must not be considered a "Maimonist." Rather, it was a feeling of piety towards him that led Abravanel to defend Maimonides.

        (2) Abravanel's view was that it is a mistake to formulate dogmas of Judaism, since, he thought, every word in the Torah has a divine meaning in itself.

b. As a biblical commentator Abravanel was an innovator.

    (1) He was one of the first to view the books of the Bible as a whole and to write his commentaries from that point of view.

    (2) He was also one of the first to study the Bible systematically, examining biblical incidents and teaching in the light of their political and economic background.

    (3) He also wrote extensive introductions to the biblical books.

c. In defense of Jewish beliefs against Christian attacks, Abravanel wrote three works on the doctrine of the Messiah. These were *Maayene ha-Yeshuah* ("Sources of Salvation"), *Yeshuath Meshiho* ("The Salvation of His Anointed"), and *Mashmiah Yeshuah* ("Proclaiming Salvation"). These were written to bolster the people's faith in these times of desolation.

3. Importance

Abravanel's biblical commentaries were popular among both Jewish and Christian theologians as late as the nineteenth century. His three volumes of messianic tracts influenced the messianic movements of the sixteenth and seventeenth centuries.

XXIX

ETHICAL WILLS (Tsavaot)

While a last will and testament concerns itself with transfer of material property, the ethical will, a unique Jewish contribution to world literature, concerns itself with transfer of a moral and spiritual heritage from one generation to another. Dating from the Middle Ages into the early modern period, these written moral commandments to surviving children serve as historical documents reflecting changing customs, folk beliefs, and literary tastes of the time in which they were written. These wills were usually written years before the writer's death. Many were revised and therefore amount, in some cases, to formal ethical treatises.

A. *History of Ethical Wills*

1. Examples of deathbed commandments to children can be found in the Bible, the Apocrypha, and in rabbinic literature.

2. The earliest example of a written ethical will, existing as an independent document, comes from the Middle Ages when almost every scholar or educated layman felt it his duty to leave his children or disciples a spiritual legacy as well as a proportion of his material goods.

3. The practice of writing ethical wills persisted up to the eighteenth century, if not later. Examples of these writings can be found in Jewish communities throughout Europe.

4. Although these testaments were not originally intended for publication, in 1927 Israel Abrahams published a selection of ethical wills along with English translations.

B. *Ethical Wills—Eleventh Through Fifteenth Centuries*

1. The will of Eliezer of Worms (1050) contains elevated moral counsel. Some of his exhortations are:

   a. "Think not of evil, for evil thinking leads to evil doing."

b. "Be not a fly over thy fellowman's sore, leaving the healthy parts and pouncing on the plague spot. Cover up thy neighbor's disease and lay not his corruption bare to the world."

2. Judah Ibn Tibbon (c. 1120-after 1190), the great translator of many works of the Golden Age in Spain, gives some very good advice to his son on the care of books:

a. "Never refuse to lend books to anyone who has not the means to purchase books for himself, but act only thus to those who can be trusted to return the volumes."

b. "Avoid bad society; make books thy companions; let thy bookcases and shelves be thy gardens and pleasure grounds. Pluck the fruit that grows therein."

3. Nahmanides (1194-1270) who was banished from Europe in 1267 (see Chapter XXVIIIb, "Four Medieval Jewish Writers"), wrote letters to his son from his new home in Palestine.

a. In an epistle to his oldest son, Nahmanides eulogizes humility as the source of reverence and the state of being that is needed to receive Divine Spirit: "Every man should seem in thine eyes as one greater than thyself." If he be wise or wealthy, it is thy duty to show him respect. If he be poor and thou the richer, or if thou be the wiser than he, bethink thee in thy heart that thou art more guilty, he the more innocent. If he sin, it is from error; if thou sin it is from desire."

b. In a letter to his younger son, Solomon, who was in the court of Castille, he wrote a eulogy of chastity and warns him against the allurements of court life: "Keep thy father's image always before thine eyes."

4. Judah ben Asher (1270-1349) was a rabbi to Toledo. His will is divided into three parts.

a. In the first part he told of his own life. This has great historical significance because he gave an account of the personal relations between the rabbi and the congregation during a transitional period when the position of rabbi was changing from a volunteer status to a salaried office.

b. In the second part he gave ethical instructions and advocated the avoidance of what he considered to be the four cardinal vices: lying, scoffing, flattery, and slander.

c. In the third section he spoke of management of finances and the distribution of charity.

5. Asher ben-Jehiel (1250-1327), the father of Judah and Jacob ben-Asher, was a great talmudic scholar also known as the *Rosh*. He wrote a treatise known as "Paths of Life" or "Rules of Conduct for the Health of the Soul."

   a. "Do not obey the Law for reward, nor avoid sin from fear of punishment, but serve God from love."

   b. "Look not at him who is above these riches, but at him who is below."

6. Jacob ben-Asher (c. 1270-1343), author of the *Turim* and brother of Judah ben-Asher, shows in his testament a scrupulous regard for ceremonial minutiae, but also offers pietism with spirituality.

   a. "Study the Law for its true end—for thyself to know the right and avoid the wrong."

   b. "A man's toil in the concerns of his body is to preserve the soul."

   c. "Give thy whole heart to God. Trust not in dreams or omens."

7. Joseph Ibn Kaspi (1279-1340) was a philosopher and scientist. In a letter to his son he presents a way of life that is pious, rational, and ethical, and expounds a conception of Judaism which insists both on the observance of precepts and in a pure belief in its principles. He also sets up a course of study for his son which includes scientific and philosophical works as well as Jewish studies. He praises Maimonides highly and urges his son to study that scholar's works.

8. Eleazar ben Samuel Halevi (fourteenth century) of Mayence, Germany, wrote of his concern for the studies and occupations of his daughters. He also advised living in a large enough Jewish community so that children can receive a good Jewish education.

9. Solomon Alami (1391-1415), in the early part of the fifteenth century, wrote a "Letter of Advice" in beautiful rhymed prose. It is an important historical document because he shared the sufferings of the Jews of the Iberian peninsula in 1391. "Flee without hesitation when exile is the only means of securing religious freedom; have no regard for your worldly career or your property, but go at once."

10. Solomon ben Isaac (not to be confused with Rashi) was a Provençal Jew living in the late fourteenth century.

   a. The first part of his testament contains his own rules of self-taxation. "So long as I enjoy good health, am free from constraint (accident), and think of it, I shall not eat on any day before I have studied one page of Talmud or one of its commentaries. Should I transgress this rule intentionally, I must not drink wine on that day, or I shall pay half a ducat to charity."

   b. The second part contains fine moral counsels that he wants his children to read over once a week. All of his children are to study Torah, but one of them is to devote all of his time to it and he is to be supported by his brothers so that he and his family might be freed from worldly cares.

   c. He also quotes Nahmanides's letter on humility.

C. Ethical Wills of the Sixteenth and Seventeenth Centuries

1. Three generations of the Horowitz family—Abraham, Jacob, and Shabbtai—give in their testaments a composite picture of life in Bohemia over a span of a century. Their testimonies are permeated with a spirit of mysticism and asceticism, but are tempered with the sentiments of piety and ethics.

   a. Abraham wrote a testament entitled *Yesh Nohalin* ("Some Inherit") which contains eighteen chapters on all aspects of human life.

   b. Jacob, the son of Abraham, added fifty-two glosses to his father's will. He tells his children to read the will twice a year, on the eve of the Jewish New Year and on the eve of the Day of Atonement.

   c. Shabbtai Horowitz in his testament gives the family genealogy and urges the practice of virtues. His testament is a notable example of a combination of legalism and mysticism.

D. *Ethical Wills of the Eighteenth Century*

1. Jonah Landsofer, called the Scribe of Sacred Scrolls, wrote that "the purpose of man's creation is the service of God."

2. Moses Hasid, a kabbalist, spoke of ritual ablution and prayer and warns against a state of gloom.

3. Alexander Suesskind, nicknamed Ish Gamzu for his extreme optimism (*Gam-zu le tovah*—"This too is for the best") said that one should make confession if one utters words of prayer without devotion. He also includes benedictions for the slightest of events; e.g., when his snuff box fell and nothing spilled.

4. Elijah DeVeali was a rabbi in Alessandria, North Italy. His testament concerns the subject of death and repentance. He also is the author of the important maxim, "Do what you say, but say not what you do."

5. Elijah, the Gaon of Vilna (1720-1797), in a letter to his family and disciples while journeying in Palestine, urges his wife and his mother to get along well together. He also tells his disciples to devote themselves wholeheartedly to the study of the Torah.

6. Israel Baal Shem Tov (1700-1760), the founder of Hasidism, gives an urgent plea to his disciples to be in the service of God at all times; to the Baal Shem Tov, the end of life was not the Law; rather it was unity with God.

E. *Conclusion*

1. The ethical wills and testaments give a picture in miniature of the life and ideals of the time in which they were written. They reflect moral and spiritual aspirations, domestic and social relations, and even approved methods of doing business—all with the view of enhancing the operation of the moral law.

2. They show an absolute faith in God and devotion to His Law.

3. Although some were of poor literary quality, they possessed the revelation of innermost feelings; they displayed the high moral quality and ideals that kept the Jewish people together during those troubled times.

RESPONSA LITERATURE

A *responsum* is a written answer by an outstanding talmudic scholar to a question put to him concerning topics of either a religious or a legal nature. The Hebrew name for the genre is *she-elot u-teshuvot*—"questions and answers." There are two types of queries: academic and practical. Academic questions were predominant in the early period of Responsa, and practical ones in the later period, although either could be found in both periods. From the practical queries, the desire of the Jews to live in accordance with Jewish law is especially evident. Responsa literature is therefore the product of an active and creative Jewish life. The Responsa became the medium through which the labyrinth of laws in the Talmud was analyzed and interpreted to fit new conditions, thereby becoming a living force in Jewish life. Certain Responsa are famous because they contain cases which illustrate the development of the Law, or because they are vital in the way that they reflect the times in which they were written. Many rabbis considered it their duty to write a book of Responsa, although there were a large number who answered questions but left no recorded Responsa.

A. Development

1. As soon as the prohibition against writing down the Oral Law lapsed and the Mishnah was compiled (third century C.E.), there were no objections to writing new questions about the Law, with their appropriate answers issued by the rabbinic authorities.

2. From the sixth to the eleventh century, letters with questions about the Law came to Babylonia from all parts of the Jewish world. These letters constitute a great mass of legal material and are the chief components in the foundations of Responsa literature. Most of these letters have been lost.

3. The Geonim (heads of talmudic academies) encouraged the sending of questions because of their consciousness of their own authority in Jewish life and their desire to guide their respective communities.

4. It was not until the eleventh or twelfth century that the Responsa were widely preserved and considered a separate branch of rabbinic literature. The Responsa became not only decisions but full discussions of the Law. From that time on, the style and the structure remained basically the same:

a. The statement of the case—usually in the form of a question.

b. *Responsum*—what would at first seem to be the Law.

c. The discussion of the difficulties due to contradictory opinions, then back to a basic talmudic discussion.

d. Analysis of passages in the Talmud that might possibly yield a principle relevant to the case at hand.

e. The final decision of the case.

5. The earlier Responsa (eleventh-fifteenth centuries) show the wider, inner autonomy of the Jewish communities and deal with nonhalakhic inquiries which were historical, theological, philosophical, etc. The later period (sixteenth-nineteenth centuries) reflects the persecutions, exile, and restricted rights of the Jews. It is therefore more limited to cases of law and urgent practical matters.

6. The Responsa of the early Geonim are brief, with only a few references to the Talmud, while those of later scholars are elaborately written and contain detailed discussions of the pertinent talmudic passages.

B. *Eleventh-Twelfth Centuries*

1. This period is known as the first rabbinic epoch and comprises the Responsa of the teachers of the early French and Spanish schools.

2. With the decline of the gaonate in the first half of the eleventh century, the Jews began to send their inquiries to rabbinical authorities in their own or neighboring countries.

3. The questions were by no means restricted to practical problems. Many were theoretical in nature, including some interpretations of passages in the Talmud.

4. Writers of Responsa Literature

a. The chief representative of the French school in the eleventh century was Rashi (see Chapter XXVa, "Rashi"). His Responsa have been preserved in *Pardes* and *Mahzor Vitry*.

b. Isaac Alfasi (1013-1103) was the leader of the Spanish school during this period. Most of his Responsa are devoted to the interpretation of aggadic passages of the Talmud.

c. The chief representatives of the French-German school were Rabbenu Gershom Meor ha-Golah ("Light of the Diaspora"), 965-1028, Jacob ben Meir Tam ("The Perfect One"), 1100-1171, and Abraham ben David of Posquières, 1120-1198.

d. Maimonides was the chief representative of the Spanish school in the twelfth century (see Chapter XXVII). Among the Responsa of Maimonides is one concerning a Moslem proselyte to Judaism. It was here declared that Moslems were not to be regarded as heathens. Also famous is his "Letter to Yemen" regarding false messiahs.

C. *Thirteenth-Fourteenth Centuries*

1. The Responsa of this period reveal the independent, communal organization of the Jews, formed under medieval law and yet independent of it.

2. Fiscal burdens and persecutions are also revealed through these Responsa.

3. Writers of Responsa Literature

   a. One of the chief representatives of the Spanish Responsa in the thirteenth century was Solomon ben Adret (Rashba) (1235-1310). All aspects of law and communal affairs were referred to him.

      (1) His Responsa supply much information concerning Jewish life in Spain, including the regulation of statutes fixed by the elders and fixed-price commodities.

   b. The chief representative of the German schools in the thirteenth century was Meir of Rothenberg (1220-1293).

      (1) His Responsa deal mostly with financial matters. He also deals with the problem of forced conversions brought about by persecutions.

c. Isaac ben Sheshet Barfat (Ribash) (1326-1400) is a representative writer of fourteenth-century Responsa. He fled to Spain and went to Algiers during the persecutions of 1391.

    (1) His Responsa reflect the turbulent conditions of the times and depict the life of the Jews in Spain as well as North Africa.

    (2) The question of Marranos (forced converts) and their relationship to Jews is also discussed in his Responsa.

D. *Fifteenth-Eighteenth Centuries*

1. The Responsa of the previous epochs dealt with all aspects of knowledge. However, from the fifteenth century onward the Responsa were mainly restricted to legal regulations.

2. This period is one of the richest in Responsa literature in the depth of learning displayed.

    a. One of the most important respondents in fifteenth-century Germany was Israel Isserlein (1390-1460). His book, *Terumat ha-Deshen* ("The Fat Offering"), contains 354 Responsa.

        (1) Some of his Responsa show that life was not always gloomy in a medieval ghetto. There were times for dancing and merriment.

        (2) The poverty of the communities becomes apparent when we read that one *etrog* (citron) served a whole community during Sukkot.

    b. Joseph Colon (Maharik) (1420-1480) is representative of fifteenth-century Italian Responsa writers.

        (1) A strong personality, he wielded his rabbinical authority with great dignity.

        (2) His Responsa show respect for custom and strong resolution to maintain what he believed to be correct.

    c. The chief Polish representatives of the sixteenth century were Moses Isserles (1525-1572), Solomon Luria (1510-1573), and Meir Lublin (1558-1616). Their Responsa throw light on the conditions of the Jews in Poland, including their scholarly and military exploits.

d. During the seventeenth century, in Poland, Menahem Mendel Krochmal (1600-1661) decided in favor of universal (male) suffrage in the community, giving all an equal share in the choice of the rabbi, *dayyan* ("judge"), and president.

e. Poland also took the lead in Responsa literature in the eighteenth century, and the Responsa of Ezekiel Landau (1713-1793) are especially distinguished for their logical discussion and erudition.

(1) Some questions reflect the modernization of Jewish life.

(2) Infractions of marital chastity are also dealt with.

E. *Nineteenth-Twentieth Centuries*

1. The sweeping changes occasioned by new movements and new inventions are dealt with in the modern period of Responsa literature.

   a. Moses Sofer (Hatam Sofer) (1762-1839) was an opponent of Reform Judaism. His Responsa gave traditional Judaism a rebirth in Hungary.

   b. Isaac Elhanan Spector (1817-1896) was a rabbi in Kovno, Lithuania. Many of his Responsa deal with the *agunah* ("deserted wife") and reflect the sudden breakup of the old communities by the mass emigration overseas.

2. During the Holocaust, a number of religious and moral questions were posed: not fasting on Yom Kippur, working on the Sabbath, revolt, etc.

3. In Israel, the Chief Rabbinate has dealt with such questions as military service for women and who is a Jew.

4. There are contemporary Responsa which deal with the use of electricity, artificial insemination, abortion, and space flight.

F. *Conclusion*

1. Through the Responsa, Jewish life was shaped and molded into the pattern which the scholars of the day believed to be "the true" talmudic ideal.

2. Through the Responsa, the ancient legal system of Jewish law was made flexible and adjustable under new situations.

3. The Responsa have been a barometer of the needs and conditions of the Jewish people through the centuries.

XXX

JEWISH COMMUNITIES IN MEDIEVAL
FRANCE, GERMANY AND ITALY

The medieval period starts approximately at the beginning of the ninth century. During this period, the Church, secular rulers, and trade guilds enforced many laws which changed the Jewish way of life. This period was marked with a high frequency of anti-Jewish massacres, the introduction of the ghetto, and a restructuring of the economic and social structure of the Jewish community. The end of this period came in the sixteenth century with the advent of the Renaissance and the Protestant Revolution. By this time many of these individual legislations such as the ghetto had become an integral part of Jewish life in Europe.

A. *Historical Background*

1. The Crusades, lasting from the eleventh century to the thirteenth century, were organized to free Jerusalem from the "infidel" Muslims. In the course of these Crusades to the Holy Land, many Jewish communities in northern France and in the Rhineland were massacred (see Chapter XXVa, "Rashi").

2. The Crusades had a lasting effect on the Jewish communities of these areas and some were completely wiped out. Their martyrdom is recorded in elegies and prayers written during this period.

3. Gradually, Jews lost the right to practice trades and to participate in agriculture. Lack of choice forced them to become moneylenders and merchants of secondhand goods.

4. The Third Lateran Council (1179) and the Fourth Lateran Council (1215) forbade the practice of "usury" (any moneylending at interest) by Jews to Christians.

5. From the twelfth century onward, Jews were repeatedly expelled from France and then readmitted under royal and noble "protection," which allowed kings and nobles to use the services of Jewish moneylenders while extorting, and sometimes confiscating, their profit.

6. In Germany, despite statements by secular rulers and even by the papacy that such charges were false, trials against Jews on charges of

ritual murder (accusation that Jews murdered Christian children in order to use their blood for the preparation of matzoh for Passover) and of desecration of the Host (mutilation of the wafer representing the body of Jesus which is used in the mass) were frequent, as were riots and massacres of innocents which followed the trials.

7. When the Black Death (Bubonic Plague) came to Europe (1348-1349), a third of the population of Europe was destroyed. Jews were often accused of starting the plague by poisoning wells. From Jewish sources we learn that many Jews also lost their lives in the plague. Proportionately fewer Jews died in the plague because of the stricter hygienic and sanitary rules imposed on the communities by the local rabbis. Such rules included immediate burial of the dead and frequent bathing of the body.

8. The Fourth Lateran Council imposed the wearing of the red or yellow Badge of Shame by all non-Christians, an action which made individual Jews the target of contempt and violence throughout Europe.

9. The Third and Fourth Lateran Councils forbade close contact between Christians and Jews and directed that Jews live apart from the rest of the general community.

10. These rulings were by no means rigidly enforced, and despite the existence of *Judengassen* ("Jew Streets") in Germany, ("Jewries") in England and *carrés juifs* ("Jewish quarters") in France, the practice of enforced separation was not universal.

11. From the sixteenth century, however, the papacy began to insist upon segregation and full-scale ghettos were set up in Italy from 1517 to 1555. Soon afterwards similar quarters were set up in France and Germany.

B. *Jewish Economic and Social Life*

1. Moneylending

   a. In feudal society where tillage of the land was controlled by lord-serf relationships, Jews were often forbidden either to own or till the land.

b. Forced into the towns, Jews were forbidden to practice crafts and trades, and were excluded from the merchant and craft guilds.

c. Up to the eleventh and twelfth centuries, Jews had been traders, often invited into cities by bishops or city leaders to promote economic development, and farmers, with a few wealthy members of the community lending money at interest. In the early Middle Ages, most wealthy people—priests, town dwellers, merchants— were approached for loans. The Third Lateran Council now forbade this.

d. Large numbers of Jews, left without any means of making a living, turned to moneylending as a profession.

   (1) In many communities, Jewish lenders carefully regulated their rates of interest so that the rates of Gentile lenders who practiced in defiance of the Church were usually higher.

   (2) After the thirteenth century, the predominance of Jews in moneylending passed its peak, with many Gentiles flouting the will of the Church and practicing moneylending.

   (3) With the granting of full economic and political rights to Jews in the eighteenth and nineteenth centuries, moneylending was no longer a characteristic Jewish occupation.

2. Communal Isolation Before the Ghetto

   a. The ghetto as an official institution developed only at the very end of the Middle Ages.

   b. The force of circumstances and the nature of Jewish life made for a social solidarity and a physical closeness long before Jews were compelled to live in ghettos.

   (1) Common defense against physical attacks was often the motive for Jews living on the same street or in the same quarter of the city.

   (2) More than mutual defense was involved in the communal structure: the Jewish community had existed for a long time, held together by observance of the Torah, a system of education, and support of the community's impoverished.

(3) Homes would be grouped around the synagogue, with the public bathhouse, school, and other community services nearby. The home was the nucleus of the social order. Frequently women carried on the business affairs of the family, as well as caring for the home, in order to permit their husbands to study Torah.

3. Education

a. Mass literacy is generally considered a modern development, but within most European Jewish communities, education was widespread. Most Jews of this period were able to read Hebrew, which was used as a liturgical language as well as a language for communication with other Jewish businessmen.

b. In most communities, schools for the study of the Torah were established.

(1) These schools were designed for people of every economic station and were generally supported by the community, not by tuition or other special fees.

(2) The rabbi's role was as teacher, not necessarily priest or minister.

(3) Teaching and scholarship was performed without pay. Such work was considered an honor and enjoyed much social prestige.

4. Ghettos

a. The Third Lateran Council's injunction forbidding Jews and Christians to live together was seldom obeyed, even in Italy under watch of the popes.

b. In 1517, however, a secular power, the Venetian Republic, segregated the Jews in a quarter of the city known as the *Ghetto Nuovo*, the "new foundry" quarter.

c. This practice of segregating Jews in a separate quarter spread to the Papal states in the 1550s; the name "ghetto" adhered to the quarter as the practice spread to other Italian cities.

d. By the end of the century, the official ghetto had spread to cities in France, Germany, Poland, and Bohemia.

   (1) These quarters were usually walled off and were provided with a locked gate to keep Jews in and, as it sometimes turned out, the enemies of the Jews out.

   (2) It was considered a crime by Christian authorities for Jews to be found outside the gates at night.

e. Despite large families and growing population, ghettos were seldom allowed to expand in area.

   (1) The ghetto grew upward, in the form of tall, rickety houses, rather than outward.

   (2) As one would expect, the hazard of fire was great, and considerable loss of life due to fires was experienced.

f. Nevertheless, a vigorous Jewish community life grew in the ghetto.

   (1) Besides schooling, needy students were provided with food and clothing by the community.

   (2) There were organizations for religious and communal functions such as fasting, prayer, and burial of the dead; charitable objectives such as assistance to women in childbirth, obtaining dowries for the poor, visiting the sick, and redeeming Jews in captivity, adult education, and fraternal comfort.

   (3) A lively social life ensued from the many festivals and liturgical events on the Jewish calendar.

   (4) Artistic activities such as adornment of holy objects and illumination of texts were carried on, frequently showing the artistic influence of the outside community in the various lands where Jews lived.

g. The ghetto, while sustaining and strengthening Jewish life, was also influential in narrowing the scope of Jewish activity.

(1) The lack of occupations involving physical labor or outdoor work tended to reduce the height and health of Jews, institutionalized certain degrading occupations such as peddling old clothes, and spread Jewish pauperism.

(2) A community chauvinism developed which made fruitful intellectual contacts with Christians extremely difficult.

D. *Conclusion*

The Middle Ages, especially in northern Europe, was one of the great testing periods of Jewish history. Jewish communities survived without a homeland in the face of great pressures: government legislation, impoverishment, and massacres. The ordeal left its scars in its shaping of the Jews' physical and spiritual conditions. Despite all of these difficulties, Jews did survive and managed to preserve the traditions of their ancestors.

XXXI

THE EXPULSION FROM SPAIN

The final demise of the Jewish community in Spain occurred during the fourteenth and fifteenth centuries. The community had experienced persecutions from the end of the Golden Age in Muslim Spain (c. 1205); in other words, since the gradual reconquest of the Iberian Peninsula by the Christians. During this period there were many forced conversions and a new segment in the society arose, the Marranos (Christians). They were Jews who were forced to accept or willingly embrace Christianity, but secretly practiced their Judaism. It was only during the later part of the fifteenth century that the Christian powers made a conscious and concentrated effort to eliminate Jews and Judaism from Spain.

A. *Historical Background*

1. Although the persecution of Jews had been increasing in Spain during the past two centuries, the reigns of Henry IV of Castile (1454-1474) and John II of Aragon (1458-1479) provided something of a respite.

   a. The laws prohibiting contact between Jews and Christians were sporadically neglected.

   b. The monarchs, Henry IV and John II, employed Jewish physicians and had court favorites among the Jews.

   c. The death of Henry IV in 1474 brought Isabella to the throne of Castile; she was joined a few years later by her consort, Ferdinand of Aragon.

2. Because of her strong religious beliefs, Isabella allowed the Inquisition of the Catholic Church to operate in her realm, which was under her full control.

   a. Introduced in 1480, the function of the Inquisition was to root out heresy and unbelief (two headings that easily included the Marranos—Jews who had embraced Christianity but were secretly practicing Judaism) in order to enrich piety and achieve national unity. The court undertook this task with vigor.

b. Since Ferdinand had also ascended the throne in Aragon, the Inquisition, which had started in Seville, quickly spread throughout the peninsula, leaving a trail of burnings and tortures of Marranos in its wake.

c. Once Ferdinand and Isabella had forced the Moslems from Granada, their last stronghold in Christian Spain, the monarchs declared on March 30, 1492, that by July 30, 1492, all Jews were to be baptized or else expelled from Spain under penalty of death for noncompliance. Despite attempts to obtain lenience, the edict was enforced.

3. Many Jews fled to Portugal; however, in 1497 when Portugal was linked by royal marriage to Spain, Jews were then persecuted and expelled from this new nation also. Small communities of Jews who managed to survive the difficulties of the voyage settled in Italy, Greece, the Ottoman Empire, and North Africa, where they were welcomed. They also settled in northern centers such as Amsterdam and Hamburg and in the new colonies in America (see Chapter XXXIX, "Jews in America").

B. *After Persecution and Expulsion*

1. The Marranos

a. The term *marrano*, "swine," was applied to baptized Jews in Spain and Portugal, as well as to their descendants, who were suspected of secret adherence to Judaism. The term came into use when this group became numerous after the massacre of Jews in 1391.

b. The Inquisition was established, in part, to deal with these dubious Christians who by the beginning of the fifteenth century had gained wealth and social status. It must be noted that the Inquisition could deal only with Marranos because they were Christians, whereas the Jews who were non-Christians were out of their jurisdiction.

c. After the Edict of Expulsion in 1492, the Inquisition pitilessly pursued these "heretics" and gradually forced many of them to flee the Iberian peninsula.

d. Among the emigrant Marrano groups were many distinguished intellectuals, among whom, perhaps the most famous, were Manasseh ben Israel (1604-1657) and Baruch Spinoza (1632-1677).

e. Down to the late nineteenth century there remained a small Marrano community in Spain and Portugal, still maintaining their secret Jewish traditions.

2. Jews in Europe

a. Jews and Marranos made their way to Amsterdam, Hamburg, northern Italy, Constantinople, Algiers, Tunis, Damascus, Corfu, Cairo, and Curaçao.

b. Marranos were granted the right of residence in the Netherlands, but Charles V, the nominal Spanish sovereign over the Netherlands, later introduced the Inquisition and renewed persecution of the Jews in his territories. The revolt of the northern provinces of the Netherlands, culminating in the Union of Utrecht (1597), greatly eased conditions. Soon many Marrano communities were living openly as Jews, while the Dutch Jewish communities prospered.

c. In Italy, conditions were varied. Ferrara, at least until the end of the sixteenth century, provided a generally free environment for Jewish life and Jews remained relatively unscathed in the Papal States. In Ferrara, Jews became prominent in commerce and produced great works of scholarship.

d. On the other hand, after the first European ghetto had been established in Venice in 1516, Jewish residents of that city suffered a series of expulsions.

e. From 1513 onward, Spanish viceroys ruled Milan and Jews were henceforth banished.

f. The Ottoman Empire, as mentioned earlier, generally welcomed the Jews. Many Jews rose to prominence there; for example, the Hamon family, who provided several physicians to the sultan, and the Nasi family, who were rich and influential (see Chapter XXXII, "Joseph Nasi and Manasseh ben Israel").

g. Spanish Jews emigrated to England only in later years and eventually a large Sephardic community was established there. After the end of the Stuart monarchy, Oliver Cromwell (1653-1658) made overtures to the Dutch Jews to emigrate to England to help further the new West Indies trade. But there was much hesitation and temporizing in following up these overtures on the part of the English government.

3. Jews in the New World

    a. One of the most ambitious ventures of Spanish navigation, the voyage of Christopher Columbus (1492), was largely financed by Jews, even though this voyage took place at virtually the same time that the Jews were being expelled from Spain.

    b. A baptized Jew named Luis De Torres accompanied Columbus as interpreter.

    c. Marranos penetrated all of the Spanish and Portuguese colonies in the New World.

        (1) They settled in large numbers and made particular contributions in Mexico, Brazil, and Peru, providing leadership in all branches of economic life.

        (2) However, they continued to be pursued by the Inquisition, as were the Marranos in Europe.

        (3) Their lot improved when Holland conquered Brazil in 1624. For thirty years, the Marranos openly proclaimed themselves Jewish. Marrano immigration to Brazil increased and the number of prosperous Jewish settlements grew rapidly.

        (4) When the Portuguese reconquered Brazil in 1654, the Jews left Brazil. They settled in the Dutch and English colonies in the West Indies and in North America, setting up the first North American Jewish communities in New Amsterdam (New York) in 1654 and in Newport, Rhode Island, in 1658.

C. *Conclusion*

The expulsion from Spain brought about the end of an era of Jewish history—an era which saw the fruition of Jewish culture, literature, and learning. As a result of the expulsion, the center of Jewish life shifted to eastern Europe, while Jewish communities in Arab countries absorbed most of the refugees. Thus, terror in Spain resulted in major dispersion for a large portion of the Jewish people, a dispersion whose results are still apparent today.

XXXII

JOSEPH NASI AND MANASSEH BEN ISRAEL

Although the sixteenth and seventeenth centuries were extremely bleak for the Jewish people as a whole, certain Jews did achieve high status during this period. Two prominent figures are Joseph Nasi (c. 1520-1579) and Manasseh ben Israel (1604-1657). Joseph Nasi was significant in the political arena during the sixteenth century when his political finesse served to maintain the Turkish empire as a much-needed haven for the Jews of this period. Manasseh ben Israel was important both as a literary and as a political figure. He wrote many influential books and pamphlets during his lifetime and was also a renowned Jewish educator. Manasseh ben Israel became politically influential as a result of some of his books and pamphlets and was instrumental in gaining the eventual readmission of the Jews into England in the 1650s.

A. *Joseph Nasi*

1. Joseph Nasi (João Migues) was born in Portugal into a Marrano family that had become wealthy through banking interests. The family, with hopes of being able to practice Judaism openly, left Portugal and traveled to Antwerp, Venice, and Ferrara. The family's wealth, however, had made them so important and well-known that jealous parties now found an opportunity to harass them. The matriarch of the family, Doña Beatrice, was imprisoned for attempting to abandon Christianity. Pressure from Sultan Sulaiman II of Turkey led to her eventual release. In 1553 the family arrived in Turkey where they openly proclaimed their Judaism.

2. In Turkey, Joseph Nasi was allowed to pay a visit to the court of Sultan Sulaiman II. After his visit, Nasi became an important adviser to the Sultan on political affairs in Europe.

   a. When the Sultan's sons began quarreling over succession to the throne, Nasi supported the elder son, Selim.

   b. When Selim II succeeded to the throne (1566-1574), Joseph Nasi found himself in a very favorable position.

      (1) The Sultan named Nasi the Duke of Naxos and the Seven Islands, which are located in the Aegean Sea.

(2) As a gift, the Sultan gave to Nasi the district in which Tiberias (now in present-day Israel) was located. This district was to serve as an area which Jewish refugees could settle.

c. Nasi set up his own printing press for the purpose of publishing Hebrew works and introduced the manufacturing of silk to the region. He was also the financial patron of many scholars and supported the yeshivah in Constantinople.

d. Whenever possible he used his diplomatic influence to help his fellow Jews.

e. After the death of Selim in 1574, Joseph Nasi's power declined and the position of the Jews in Turkey deteriorated.

f. The decline of Joseph Nasi's power and influence also led to the eventual deterioration of the Jewish community in Tiberias.

3. At a time when Jews throughout the world were suffering severe persecution, Joseph Nasi's importance should not be discounted. Although his work did not produce anything of lasting value to Judaism, his influence with the Sultan did succeed in giving the Jews a much-needed haven in Turkey and also helped make the plight of the Jews in foreign lands a little easier.

B. *Manasseh ben Israel*

1. Manasseh ben Israel was born of Marrano parents. His father, a native of Lisbon, had fled persecution in Spain and Portugal, eventually finding his way to Amsterdam where Manasseh (then Manoel Dias Soeiro) grew up. At the age of seventeen, Manasseh wrote a Hebrew grammar called *Safah Brurah* ("Clear Language"); at eighteen he became rabbi of the Neveh Shalom congregation in Amsterdam. He became well-known as a preacher and a leader of his people. In 1626 he started a Hebrew printing press in Amsterdam, and in 1627 he published an edition of the Hebrew Prayer Book. In 1628 he published an index to *Midrash Rabbah*. In 1640 two of his friends established a yeshivah and Manasseh was appointed principal. He died in 1657.

2. Manasseh ben Israel produced many important literary works.

a. *The Conciliator*, written in Spanish, was an attempt to reconcile apparently contradictory parts of the Scriptures. This book, written in four parts, was begun in 1632 and completed in 1651. It established Manasseh as a representative of Jewish scholarship to the Christian world.

b. The best-known of Manasseh's literary efforts was *Vindiciae Judaeorum* ("Defense of the Jews"), published in 1656. This apologetic work was written to counter superstitious charges against the Jews made by opponents of their readmission into England. Regarded as one of the best defenses of Judaism ever written, Manasseh presented it to Oliver Cromwell, Lord Protector of England. The immediate response was trivial, but his defense had undoubtedly prepared the way for the eventual resettlement of Jews in England, an event which Manasseh did not live to experience.

c. His book *Tikvat Yisrael* ("The Hope of Israel"), written in 1650, expressed the belief that certain of the American Indians could be identified with the "Ten Lost Tribes of Israel." This book caused a flurry of interest in England, especially among English mystics, and elicited several favorable replies.

3. Manasseh ben Israel's work was crucial to the readmission of Jews to England.

a. Jews had been expelled from England by Edward I in 1290. Manasseh devoted himself to gaining their readmission and *Tikvat Yisrael* was intended to further this cause.

b. Around the middle of the seventeenth century, civil war had broken out in England between Charles I and his subjects. Although Manasseh's sentiments were with the Stuart dynasty, the rise of Puritanism was definitely helpful to his cause. The Puritans held the Old Testament in high regard and tried to live in accordance with its precepts. This produced a somewhat more favorable climate for Manasseh's attempts at readmission of the Jews.

c. At this time a movement toward religious toleration can be discerned. The Puritan victory resulted in the fall of the Established Church. Very soon a variety of Protestant sects emerged, some of which favored religious liberty.

d. Although there was much pressure for religious freedom, the post-war Parliament adopted a modified constitution in 1649 that guaranteed religious liberty to Protestants, but not to Jews.

e. Oliver Cromwell, who became Lord Protector of England in 1653, was kindly disposed toward the readmission of Jews, if only for the purpose of increasing trade, thereby bettering England's position in the rivalry with Holland and Spain.

   (1) Cromwell invited Manasseh to England for talks with the English Council of State; due to illness, Manasseh sent his son Samuel and a friend instead.

   (2) Although the two Jewish representatives received a favorable hearing, the committee originally appointed to consider the situation returned a negative verdict.

f. In October 1655, Manasseh himself came to England and promptly wrote a pamphlet to Cromwell setting forth the case for readmission of the Jews.

   (1) This created a stir and a multitude of replies were published.

   (2) Manasseh met with Oliver Cromwell who brought his petition for readmission before the Council of State in Whitehall.

g. In December 1655, a national conference was held to discuss the matter.

   (1) Cromwell told the conference to decide whether it was lawful to readmit the Jews to England and, if they were admitted, on what conditions this admission would be based.

   (2) Since the expulsion of 1290 had been by order of the king rather than by an act of Parliament, it was decided that it would be legal to countermand this order and readmit the Jews.

   (3) The conference was unable to decide on the conditions upon which the Jews would be readmitted, so Cromwell took this issue to the Council of State. A committee appointed to recommend a course of action suggested that the Jews be admitted, but under very restrictive conditions. This

recommendation was rejected and readmission was not officially sanctioned.

h. Manasseh died two years later in Holland (1657) thinking that he had failed in his mission.

4. Jews were eventually readmitted to England.

   a. A small colony of Spanish Marranos had fled the Inquisition and settled in England. By 1655 the Marrano community had grown to include about 200 people, all of whom practiced Judaism secretly.

   b. In 1656, the government proclaimed that all property belonging to Spanish citizens living in England be confiscated, in view of the war between England and Spain.

      (1) The Marranos, who were still considered Spanish nationals, petitioned Cromwell to let them live openly as members of the Jewish nation.

      (2) Permission was granted and for the first time since 1290 Jews were able to live in England, openly practicing their religion.

      (3) In December 1656, a synagogue was established in London.

C. Conclusion

Joseph Nasi and Manasseh ben Israel, through their political influence, were able to bring some relief to their troubled Jewish brethren. Although these two men lived in an extremely difficult period for the Jews, their work began a process that would lead to greater religious freedom. The reopening of the gates of England to Jews was an important turning point in the process of Jewish emancipation.

XXXIII

JOSEPH CARO (1488-1575)

Any discussion of Rabbi Joseph Caro and his work necessarily centers on the codification of Jewish law that has served as the standard law code of observant Jews since the sixteenth century. Caro's major work, *Bet Yoseph*, ("House of Joseph"), a laborious and extensive codification of halakhic law, established him as a recognized rabbinic scholar. However, it was his *Shulhan Arukh* ("Arranged Table"), a digest of the *Bet Yoseph*, which made Caro a figure of historic importance, for through the *Shulhan Arukh* the regulations of daily life for both Ashkenazic and Sephardic Jews were unified.

A. *Life*

1. Joseph Caro grew up among those Jews who had been expelled from Spain. The expulsion came in 1492 when Caro was four years old. His family first fled from Toledo to Constantinople and then to Adrianople, Turkey. Caro was descended from a line of rabbinical scholars and he too became a scholar.

2. In 1520, he wrote *Keseph Mishneh* ("A Double Silver"), a commentary on Maimonides's *Mishneh Torah* (see Chapter XXVII, "Maimonides"). In 1525 he moved to Safed in Palestine, where many scholars and mystics lived.

3. On his way to Palestine, he stopped in Salonica where he met the renowned kabbalists Solomon Molcho and Solomon Alkabetz, who had a great influence on Caro's later works.

4. For twenty years of his life (1522-1542) Caro labored over the *Bet Yoseph*. There had been codifications of the Law before: Isaac ben Jacob Alfasi's *Sepher ha-Halakhot* ("Book of Laws") in the eleventh century, Maimonides's works from the twelfth century, and those of Asher ben Jehiel (thirteenth-fourteenth centuries) and his son, Jacob ben Asher (fourteenth century). The *Bet Yoseph* was a commentary on ben Asher's codification. Caro's comments and judgments were supported by citations from various sources.

5. In 1565, the *Shulhan Arukh*, the abridgment of the *Bet Yoseph*, was completed. With the publication of this work, Caro became perhaps

the most famous teacher of his time, answering letters from all over the Jewish world (Responsa).

B. *Mystical Influences*

1. Caro was passionately fond of the study of mysticism and the Mishnah, whose contents became so identified with his own being that "they" shaped themselves into the form of an "angel" (*Maggid* or "Preacher") who became his advisor and teacher.

2. The angel "preacher" (or the Mishnah personified) descended upon Caro during the night. It continually whispered revelations to him, and carried on discussions with him for nearly half a century.

3. Caro wrote down his visions and, thirty years after his death, these diary notes were published in a book called *Maggid Mesharim* ("The Preacher of Righteousness").

4. In Caro's visions the Maggid imposed heavy penances on him.

   a. It forbade him to eat meat or drink wine.

   b. If prohibited excessive drinking of water.

   c. If Caro slept too long or did not study enough, he was reproved.

5. He was also reminded of the necessity of reading devotional books such as *Duties of the Heart* by Bahya Ibn Pakuda and of devoting himself to the study of the Kabbalah more diligently.

6. The Maggid gave hope to many of Caro's aspirations.

   a. Caro was told that he would be blessed with a son who would be a great mystic and who would write commentaries on his father's books.

   b. Caro was anxious to have the privilege of spreading the Torah in Israel. He was told that he would be recognized as a Jewish authority of the first rank and that his books would be accepted as standard references.

   c. Another of Caro's great aspirations was that he should die the death of a martyr. This may have been due to the influence of Solomon

Molcho, a friend and fellow kabbalist, who suffered a martyr's death. Caro died of natural causes, however, and so this great hope of his was not fulfilled.

C. *Works*

1. *Bet Yoseph* ("House of Joseph")

   a. Rabbi Joseph ben Asher (1280-1340) had collected all the material since Maimonides's *Mishneh Torah* and codified it. He divided his code into four parts, *Arbaah Turim* ("Four Rows"), later known simply as the *Tur*.

   b. Caro then undertook a commentary which was more thorough and extensive than the *Tur* itself. He went back to the Talmud and halakhic midrashim, discussed the arguments of the authorities cited in the *Tur*, and examined other authoritative opinions as well. He analyzed the different views and finally gave his own opinion.

   c. This then is the *Bet Yoseph*, a four-volume compilation which covers the spectrum of talmudic and rabbinic literature.

   d. Caro devoted twenty years to writing this work and twelve years (1542-1554) to its revision. It finally appeared in print in 1555.

   e. Evaluation

      (1) Caro wrote a commentary on the *Tur* rather than on Maimonides's *Mishneh Torah* because the *Tur* was more widely known among both Ashkenazim and Sephardim. Moreover, he did not favor Maimonides's codes because it tended to give decisions without tracing the reasons or sources for them.

      (2) Caro felt that a work like the *Bet Yoseph* was especially necessary ever since the expulsion from Spain, because the people needed a central authority to which they could turn with questions concerning religious observance.

      (3) The work shows Caro's remarkable powers of critical investigation and his ability to create order out of chaos.

2. The *Shulhan Arukh* ("Prepared Table")

   a. Why It Was Written

      (1) It appears that Caro intended the *Bet Yoseph* to be the authoritative code of law. *Shulhan Arukh*, on the other hand, was written to be a study manual for younger students. Once written, the use of the *Shulhan Arukh* surpassed the author's own intention.

      (2) The kabbalist mystic rabbis welcomed this abbreviated law code which allowed them more time for the study of divine mysteries. After Moses Isserles's annotations for the Ashkenazic community appeared in 1578, the *Shulhan Arukh* began to replace the *Bet Yoseph* as the standard reference.

   b. Organization

      (1) The *Shulhan Arukh* consists of four parts:

         (a) *Orah Hayim* ("Way of Life") dealing with the duties of prayer and benediction which a Jew must perform daily and on the Sabbath and festivals.

         (b) *Yoreh Deah* ("Teacher or Guide of Knowledge") concerning such matters as dietary laws, cleanliness, and uncleanliness, circumcision, vows, mourning laws, and laws against idolatry.

         (c) *Even ha-Ezer* ("Stone of Help", or "Rock of Assistance") dealing with all aspects of marriage and divorce.

         (d) *Hoshen Mishpat* ("Breastplate of Judgment") which contains civil and criminal law.

      (2) The sections are divided into chapters according to subtopics, and the chapters are divided into paragraphs, each dealing with a particular point of law.

      (3) The *Shulhan Arukh* not only quotes the many earlier rabbinic opinions concerning points of law but—and this is what distinguished Caro's codes from the earlier ones—makes decisions as to which opinion is the most valid, citing

authoritative reasons. It attempts to avoid the use of aggadic sources and metaphysical abstractions.

c. Historical Influence—Positive and Negative

(1) Although controversy over the authority of the *Shulhan Arukh* raged on for nearly one hundred years, the mere fact that the commentators who criticized it also made it the basis of their own works shows the pervasive influence of this work.

(2) With the acceptance of Isserles's annotation of the *Shulhan Arukh*, which dealt mainly with laws and customs concerning Ashkenazic communities of Europe whereas Caro dealt with the Sephardic community and culture, Jews dispersed throughout the world gained a unified, universally accepted law code.

(3) The *Shulhan Arukh* served as a unifying force among the Jews who, through persecutions and expulsions, were in constant danger of losing their identity, beliefs, and ways of life.

(4) The *Shulhan Arukh* is still consulted by traditional Jews.

(a) The title means "Arranged Table"; the *Shulhan Arukh* was supposed to set all the spiritual food of the Law on the table so that all one had to do was to sit down and digest it.

(b) The *Shulhan Arukh* was so skillful in doing its job that for centuries no scholars attempted to improve or change it.

(c) Many commentaries on the *Shulhan Arukh*, commentaries upon the commentaries, abridgments, and translations of the abridgments into foreign languages have been written.

(5) Because many of Caro's decisions were based on Sephardic customs, the Ashkenazic Jews resented the *Shulhan Arukh*. It was only after Rabbi Moses Isserles (c. 1525-1572) of Cracow, Poland, modified and added to Caro's decisions in his work *Ha-Mappah* ("The Tablecloth") that the code was considered complete and authoritative.

3. Other Works

a. *Keseph Mishneh* ("A Double Silver") is a commentary and a spirited defense of Maimonides's *Mishneh Torah.*

b. *Kelale ha-Talmud* ("Rules of the Talmud") contains numerous original observations of the various devices used by the Amoraim. It is a good example of Caro's passion for system, order, and logical thinking.

c. *Bedek ha-Bayit* ("Repairing the House") is a supplement which includes corrections to the *Bet Yoseph.*

d. *Avkath Rokhel* ("The Powder of the Spice Dealer") contains Responsa concerning religious law and civil law.

D. *Conclusion*

Rabbi Joseph Caro in his *Shulhan Arukh* provided an abridged code of law which was both concise and authoritative. It became a foundation stone of a continuing Jewish life, but also menaced the healthy growth of scholarship as time passed. Though Caro was a kabbalist, his scholarly gifts of clarity and accuracy are characteristic of his *Shulhan Arukh.*

XXXIV

KABBALAH

The word *Kabbalah*, meaning "tradition," comes from the Hebrew, but implies the "reception of tradition." Kabbalah has come to signify the mystical-religious trend in Judaism. Originally, the Kabbalah was concerned with the oral tradition which coincided with the Written Law, or Bible. However, in the late Middle Ages, the term was adopted by Jewish mystics and came to denote the continuous mystical "tradition" which developed through the ages.

As with most mystical movements, Kabbalah attempts to bring about a deep contact with the Divine on a personal level of communication. Philosophically, Kabbalah strives to unite the apparent inconsistencies of good and evil, to explain the relationship of God and His creation, and to direct a personal attainment of spiritual perfection. Although strongly influenced by other philosophies, such as Gnosticism, Neoplatonism and Islamic mysticism, Kabbalah has remained essentially Jewish in character.

In the beginning, Kabbalah had an esoteric tendency, appealing mainly to the intellectual segment of Jewish society. By the sixteenth century, however, the movement had reached the masses and later influenced Hasidim and other sectors of Jewish life (see Chapter XXXVII, "Hasidism").

A. *Historical Background*

1. Mystical movements in Judaism first existed within the Jewish sects of the second and first centuries B.C.E.

2. Through study of the Dead Sea Scrolls, scholars have found certain mystical traditions among those people who inhabited the Qumran caves.

3. The School of Simeon ben Yohai (second century C.E.)

   a. This school of thought was concerned with three basic issues:

      (1) The mysteries of Creation (*Maaseh Bereshit*) and the Divine Chariot (*Maaseh Merkavah*), and their relationship to the various manifestations of God and His attributes.

      (2) The eternalization of the Torah as God's laws.

(3) The assignment of powers and other attributes to the angels.

b. The dualist concept of Gnosticism was studied for possible clues to the creation of the world. This dualism was rejected, however, in the final system of kabbalistic beliefs.

c. The mystery of Creation and the mystery of the Divine Chariot were studied in terms of *Pardes*, the mnemonic acronym used to signify the four levels of biblical interpretation.

   (1) *Pehsat*—the literal meaning.

   (2) *Remez*—allegorical, or philosophical meaning, or allusion.

   (3) *Derash*—biblical exegesis, often in the form of *aggadah*.

   (4) *Sod*—mystical level.

B. *Maaseh Bereshit ("The Mystery of Creation") and Maaseh Merkavah ("The Mystery of the Divine Chariot")*

1. *Maaseh Bereshit*

   a. Refers to the concept of Creation as related in the first chapter of Genesis.

   b. It was considered by Maimonides to be a physical science, which was useful for the purpose of study.

2. *Maaseh Merkavah*

   a. Refers to the vision of a Divine Chariot, as related in the first chapter of Ezekiel.

   b. Maimonides considered the study of the secrets of the Divine Chariot as theology.

3. The soul of the individual receiving a vision of such events became aware of the various secrets not overtly known to man:

   a. The mysterious nature of creation.

b. The actions of angels.

c. The actual date of the Messiah's advent and the time of redemption.

4. The actual adherents had to prepare themselves for this visionary experience by rigorous physical discipline such as fasting, and mystical meditation.

C. *Kabbalistic Literature*

1. The literature dealing with the *Maaseh Bereshit* and the *Maaseh Merkavah* is called *hekhalot* ("Heavenly Palaces") literature.

   a. These are the records of the ecstatic experiences of the mystics.

   b. The divine majesty of God is expounded in these hymns of praise.

   c. Much of this literature has been incorporated into the Ashkenazic liturgy, especially for the High Holy Days.

   d. The literature enumerates the seven celestial palaces populated by angels. In the highest palace, the Divine Spirit resides.

      (1) All those individuals who experienced these mysteries recorded the dangers encountered as they ascended through the seven palaces, until they saw the radiance of the Divine Spirit.

      (2) God seldom lets His actual face be shown, except to a few biblical personalities. Thus, only His radiance can be seen.

   e. The *hekhalot* literature was transmitted to Europe in the ninth century by Aaron ben Samuel of Baghdad.

2. The *Sepher Yetzirah* ("The Book of Creation")

   a. This work, of Palestinian or Babylonian origin, deals with cosmology as it was understood at the time (third to sixth centuries C.E.).

   b. The structure of the universe is enumerated in terms of the Hebrew alphabet and the ten primary numbers.

   c. The numbers are called *sephirot.*

d. Knowledge of the mysteries surrounding the *sephirot* resulted in magical powers, such as the *golem.*

   (1) The word *golem* comes from the Hebrew for "shapeless mass."

   (2) The word came to mean a humanlike robot summoned by pronouncing the Holy Name.

   (3) References to the appearances of *golems* are found in Jewish literature from the twelfth through the sixteenth centuries.

   (4) In later literature, the *golem* was portrayed as a tangible being, capable of fulfilling seemingly impossible tasks such as protecting the Jewish populace from destruction. The most famous of these legendary *golems* is the *golem* of Prague created by Judah Löw ben Bezalel in the sixteenth century.

e. The Kabbalists considered the *Sepher Yetzirah* as important as other canonical literature.

f. Many commentaries were written on the work, notably by Saadyah Gaon.

3. *Sepher Hasidim* ("Book of the Devout")

   a. In the twelfth century, a group of pious German Jews, called *Haside Ashkenaz* ("the devout of Germany"), felt a strong affinity for the mystical and ascetic.

      (1) The followers called for extreme devotion and rejection of worldly actions, emotions, and hopes.

      (2) There was a distinction made between the incomprehensible, transcendent God and those manifestations of His glory.

      (3) The divine attributes include God's revelation to the prophets.

   b. Prominent leaders in this movement were Rabbi Judah He-Hasid (1150-1217) and Rabbi Eleazar of Worms (1160-1238).

4. Book of *Bahir* ("Shining")

   a. This is one of the oldest examples of kabbalistic literature.

      (1) It was available to Jews at the close of the twelfth century in southern France.

      (2) Its authorship and composition date are unknown.

   b. In the Book of *Bahir* a doctrine of *sephirot* is implied.

      (1) There are ten divine characteristics termed *sephirot*.

      (2) These *sephirot* are derived from the *Ein Soph*, or the "eternal, never-ending God."

   c. It also contains proverbs and homiletic sayings of the *tannaim* and the *amoraim*.

   d. Stylistically the work is written in a mixture of Hebrew and Aramaic. There is little apparent organization and the language is obscure at times.

5. The *Zohar*

   a. This work is considered the apex of literature from the Spanish kabbalistic movement (thirteenth century).

   b. All later developments in the Kabbalah issued from this major source book (see Chapter XXXIVb, "Zohar").

D. *Later Developments in Kabbalah*

1. Shabbetai Tzevi (1626-1676), influenced by the Safed School of Kabbalah, led a messianic movement which reached its climax in the mid-seventeenth century (see Chapter XXXVb, "False Messiahs").

2. The kabbalistic movement led by Isaac Luria (1534-1572) (see Chapter XXVa, "Great Kabbalists") was adopted into the doctrines of the Hasidim who popularized these teachings.

3. Rabbi Avraham Yitzhak Ha-Cohen Kook (1865-1935) developed a kabbalistic system relating the development of the Jewish nation to a mystical nationalism.

4. Gershom Scholem (1897-1982) was the leading contemporary scholar who had based his research on a scientific study of the philology and sources for the kabbalistic literature, especially as it related to outside historical and spiritual movements.

E. *Conclusion*

The growth and development of kabbalistic literature and tradition has had a profound influence upon popular religious movements throughout Jewish history. Kabbalistic thought is still studied and practiced by many today and a revived interest in Kabbalah has produced a vast quantity of new research on this subject.

ZOHAR

The Zohar, which first appeared in the thirteenth century, is a series of mystical works which can best be described as the Bible of the Kabbalah. It is a pseudepigraphic work supposedly written by Simeon ben Yohai in the second century, with the help of an assembly of sages initiated into the secrets of mysticism. Its fundamental view is that all wisdom is contained in the Bible, but that much of this wisdom is hidden. Thus the Zohar attempts to probe and solve these mysteries. It narrates stories and events in the Bible, such as the creation of the world, attempting to explain it in a symbolic and midrashic manner.

A. *Background of the Kabbalah*

1. Mystical teachings, although not mentioned in the Bible or Talmud, were handed down from generation to generation. The early phase of Jewish mysticism was called *Ha-Torah ha-Nisteret* ("The Hidden or Unrevealed Torah"). From the end of the twelfth century, however, Jewish mysticism is known as the Kabbalah.

2. There are three main elements in both phases of Jewish mysticism:

   a. Teachings about the *Merkavah* ("Divine Chariot" mentioned in the first chapter of Ezekiel), the manifestation of God, His attributes, and His relation to the world and creation.

   b. The hypostatization of the Torah, making it and its letters eternal and an instrument for creation in the world.

   c. The attribution of powers to the names of God and the angels.

B. *Authorship of the Zohar*

1. The classic period of the literature of the Kabbalah began in the last quarter of the twelfth century and terminated with the appearance of the Zohar. The authors of this period wanted to demonstrate that their new views of life and the world were actually very ancient ones, which had been hidden from humanity, and were now being revealed.

2. There were sound arguments against the view that Simeon ben Yohai was responsible for the authorship of the Zohar.

   a. If the Zohar was the work of Simeon ben Yohai, it would have been mentioned in the Talmud, as was the case with the *Sifre* and other works of the talmudic period.

   b. The Zohar contains names of talmudic scholars who lived much later than Simeon ben Yohai.

   c. If Simeon ben Yohai was the father of Kabbalah and knew by divine revelation the hidden meanings of the precepts, his halakhic decisions would have been adopted by the Talmud. This, however, was not the case.

   d. If the Kabbalah was a revealed doctrine, there would have been no divergence of opinion among the kabbalists concerning the mystical interpretation of the precepts.

3. Many modern scholars, including Gershom Scholem, an authority on Jewish mysticism, attribute the Zohar to Moses de Leon (1250-1305), a Spanish kabbalist.

a. According to de Leon's own story, the book was hidden in a cave in Palestine, the same cave in which Simeon ben Yohai and his son, Eliezer, hid for thirteen years during the persecutions of Hadrian in the second century C.E. Nahmanides, the great medieval Jewish scholar, discovered the book in Palestine (1194-1270) and eventually it fell into de Leon's hands in Spain.

b. There are a number of similarities between de Leon's other works and the Zohar.

(1) These include similar deviations from common usage, similar mistakes and wrong constructions, and similar verb inflections.

(2) In all of his quotes from the Zohar, de Leon shows a keen understanding of meanings and interpretations.

(3) De Leon's later writings are a genuine continuation and, in some cases, further development of the Zohar. It seems obvious that the subject matter of the Zohar was constantly on his mind. De Leon wrote about twenty kabbalistic works of which only six have been printed.

(4) According to Scholem, it is likely that Moses de Leon wrote the Zohar in order to stem the growth of the radical rationalistic mood that was prevalent among his educated contemporaries. He probably felt that a mystical Midrash which presented an impressive picture of profundity of the divine would be the best instrument for awakening a mystical, and thus a deeper, understanding of Judaism.

4. Despite all the controversy, there is still no conclusive evidence about the authorship of the Zohar. Its contents seem to indicate that the work is neither a production of a single author nor a single period, but of many authors, periods, and civilizations. Moses de Leon probably played an important part in shaping the literature to its present from.

C. *Language and Style*

1. The Zohar is written as a pseudepigraphon similar in form to a mystical Midrash.

2. The literary method is modeled after the Midrash and preference is given to homiletics.

3. Although it is written in Aramaic, the spirit of medieval Hebrew permeates the work.

4. According to Gershom Scholem, the artificial use of Aramaic, with its strangeness and solemnity, helped the literary success of the Zohar.

5. The language of the Zohar is strong, powerful, highly poetic, and makes use of an extensive vocabulary.

D. *Structure*

1. The Zohar comprises three kabbalistic works, which were printed at different times.

   a. The Zohar proper (*Sepher ha-Zohar*—"Book of the Zohar") was first printed in Mantua, Italy in 1560.

   b. *Tikkunei ha-Zohar* ("The Explanations or Additions to the Zohar") was printed in 1588-1590 in Mantua, Italy.

   c. *Zohar Hadash* ("The New Zohar") was printed in Salonica, Greece in 1597.

2. Several books are attached to the main portion, *Sepher ha-Zohar*.

   a. *Midrash ha-Zohar* is the largest work of the group. In it all of the teachings, including the theory of the *sephirot* ("Divine Emanations"), are developed. Also dealt with here are freedom of will, reward, and punishment.

   b. *Siphra di Tseniuta* ("The Book of Concealment, or Veiled Mystery") contains only five chapters. It deals with the mysteries of creation, human soul, and the relationship between spirit and matter.

   c. *Sitre Torah* ("Secrets of the Torah") includes a kabbalistic study of angels, the mysteries surrounding the divine name, and the divine unity.

d. *Raaya Mehemana* ("The Faithful Shepherd") presents a conversation between Moses, the prophet Elijah, and Simeon ben Yohai on the allegorical importance of the Mosaic commandments and prohibitions, as well as of the rabbinical injunctions.

e. *Midrash ha-Ne'elam* ("The Hidden Midrash") contains scriptural expositions by *gematria* (assignment of numerical values to the letters of the Hebrew alphabet in order to discover the "secret" meaning of words).

f. *Tosephta* ("Additions") contains fragmentary supplements to the main exegesis of the Zohar and has references to the *sephirot*.

g. *Sepher Hekhalot* ("Book of Palaces") pictures the abodes of paradise and hell, and the grades of angelic hosts and their dealings with men's souls are described.

h. The *Idra Rabba* ("The Great Synod") and *Idra Zuta* ("The Lesser Synod") are amplifications of the *Siphra di Tseniuta*. Supposedly these are teachings revealed at an assembly of initiates presided over by Simeon ben Yohai.

3. The *Zohar Hadash* consists of three different parts:

a. Additions to the Zohar or different sections of the *Humash* (Five Books of Moses) as well as the critical revisions of various passages contained in the old Zohar.

b. Large fragments of two mystical works, *Midrash ha-Ne'elam* and *Raze de-Razin*, dealing with the physiognomy of the Kabbalah and the connection of the soul with the body.

c. Three small Zohar midrashim to Song of Songs, Ruth, and Lamentations.

4. Tikkune ha-Zohar is a collection of seventy additions to the Zohar (printed separately) which are concerned with the first section of Genesis. It was probably composed after the Zohar.

5. There is considerable overlapping of both theme and treatment in many of these divisions. Like the old midrashim, the Zohar follows the division of the Torah into sections for use in synagogues. With each portion or *Sedra* there are introductions, systematic mystical

midrashim on certain verses, and—scattered among these homiletic explanations—various literary compositions in the form of anecdotes.

E. *Teachings*

1. *Sephirot* ("Divine Emanation")

   a. The theory of *sephirot* is very prominent in the Zohar. They are, in essence, abstractions of the divine powers manifested in the world. Though they are ten in number, they are all connected and form one unity consisting of *kether* ("crown"); *hokhmah* ("wisdom"); *binah* ("understanding"); *hesed* ("mercy"); *gevurah* ("strength"); *tipheret* ("beauty of glory"); *netzah* ("might or victory"); *hod* ("splendor"); *yesod* ("foundation"); and *malkhut* ("kingdom").

   b. An analogy is made between the order of the *sephirot* and the form of the human body; e.g., *kether* is the head as a whole; *hokhmah* is the right side of the head; *binah*, the left side.

   c. Each of the names of the *sephirot* is combined and permutated, resulting in the assignment of new meanings and significations.

2. The Soul

   a. The soul of man has three parts and each of these parts has its source in one of the ten *sephirot*.

      (1) *Neshamah* is the highest phase of the soul: It is the divine spark which is beyond sin.

      (2) *Ruah* is the seat of good and evil and the dwelling place of moral attitudes.

      (3) *Nephesh* is the grosser side of the spirit, is closest to the body, and is the cause of all the movements and instincts of the physical life.

   b. The soul seeks to enter consciously into the presence of God. Man's intimacy with God is described in sexual terminology.

   c. The Zohar is filled with references to the dominating part played by man's soul in the furtherance of his own good, as well as in the development of the workings of the universe with which man is so intensely and inextricably bound. Man is unique only because of his soul.

d. The transmigration of the soul is taught by the Zohar as a solution to the problem of the prosperity of the wicked.

3. Concept of God

   a. The Zohar's treatment of the divine nature is the attempt to combine the transcendent and immanent aspects of the Deity in a single concept.

   b. God is unknowable (He is referred to as *Setiman di Setimim*—"Hidden of all Hidden"), and yet the universe and man's heart reveal His infinite power.

   c. One of the main themes in the Zohar is that the revealed word of God, the Torah, was designed for no other purpose than to effect a union between the soul of man and the soul of God.

F. *Influence*

1. With the appearance of the Zohar, the Kabbalah began to spread to other countries outside Spain and Provence (the southeastern part of France).

2. During the thirteenth century, the mystic literature began to reach new heights, unlike the decline in other aspects of Jewish literature. The Zohar became the axis around which later kabbalistic literature turned. Moses Cordovero (1522-1570), who lived in Safed, wrote a long commentary on the entire group of works on the Zohar called *Or Yakar* ("Precious Light").

3. For some centuries after its first appearance, the Zohar, like the Talmud or the Midrash, was generally regarded by Jews as an integral part of the literature of the Torah. Thus, it was considered one of the subjects of religious study of Talmud Torah. It was often referred to as the Midrash of Rabbi Simeon ben Yohai. The study of the Zohar was especially popular in Sephardic communities.

4. The Zohar, as one of the most influential parts of the Kabbalah, had a great influence on the messianic stirrings of the Jews and the rise of

popular movements such as Hasidism which tried to introduce a new spirituality to Judaism (see Chapter XXXVII, "Hasidism").

5. The Zohar influenced many Jewish religious ceremonies.

   a. It introduced ecstasy into prayer.

   b. Many of its mystical fomulae, names, and symbols were introduced into the pages of the prayer book.

      (1) When blowing the *shophar* ("Ram's Horn") on the Jewish New Year (*Rosh Hashanah*), Zoharic prayers ask that "the angels emanating from the *Shophar* may bring the prayers of Israel to the Divine hearing."

      (2) The *Brikh Sh-meh*, recited before the reading of the Torah on Sabbaths, is introduced with a passage from the Zohar which states, "When the Scroll is taken out in the assembly to read therein, the gates of the Heavens of Mercy open and the celestial love awakens."

6. Christian scholars wrote treatises in which the teachings of the Zohar are made to reflect many of the cardinal doctrines of Christianity. Among them are Pico della Mirandola, Petrius Galatinus, and Knoor von Rosenroth, who published the *Kabbalah Denudata* in 1677.

G. *Conclusion*

The Zohar is the cornerstone of Jewish mysticism. For over six centuries this work has played a significant role in Jewish life. Since the Zohar is the standard work of the Kabbalah, it contains all elements of Jewish mystical thought, whether they be rational or irrational. Despite the disputations about the authorship of the Zohar, it must be admitted that behind this unusual work stands a genius who started out with philosophy and Talmud as his basis, but permitted himself to be drawn into the mystical and gnostic ideas of the Kabbalah. The Zohar was a book for the people. In times of crisis, they could find solace in its doctrines, particularly the belief in an inner, unseen spiritual universe and an eternal moral order.

XXXV

GREAT KABBALISTS—ISAAC LURIA AND HAYYIM VITAL

The sixteenth century witnessed great developments in kabbalistic thought. In this century the Zohar was first published and a number of great kabbalists became very influential. Included among these great mystics are Isaac Luria Ashkenazi (known as the *Ari*, or "Lion") and his foremost disciple, Hayyim Vital.

A. *Isaac Luria (1534-1572)*

1. Life

    a. Isaac Luria was born in Jerusalem to a family of German descent (the family name was Ashkenazi, which means "German" in Hebrew). After being orphaned at an early age, he was sent to Cairo where he was brought up by a rich uncle.

    b. Luria received a thorough training in the Talmud. This study, however, did not capture the young man's interest.

    c. After marrying his cousin at the age fifteen, Luria turned to the study of mysticism and began to immerse himself in the study of the Zohar.

        (1) From his study of the Zohar, Luria began seeking solitude for study and meditation.

        (2) In his early twenties he became a hermit. For the next thirteen years he lived alone, going out only to visit his family on the Sabbath.

        (3) During this period, with the aid of the Zohar and other mystical writings, he perceived visionary spirits.

        (4) Luria believed he could communicate with Elijah the prophet, who would at times explain to him difficult passages in the Zohar.

    d. In 1569 he received the "Divine Call," and travelled with his wife and child to Safed, the center of mysticism in Palestine.

e. In Safed many of the inhabitants and rabbis were kabbalists.

(1) At first Luria received little notice in Safed, but soon he was surrounded by a core of disciples and colleagues called *Gur Aryeh* ("Lion's Cubs"), which was derived from the acronym of Luria's name, *Ari* ("Lion"). One of those disciples who recognized Luria's great knowledge of the Kabbalah was Hayyim Vital.

(2) After becoming a disciple of Luria, Vital began to spread the fame of his master. Soon Luria's new revelations on kabbalistic thought attracted kabbalists from all parts of the world to hear his teachings.

f. The sudden death of Isaac Luria at the age of 38 glorified his name still more.

2. Works and Ideas

a. Most of what we know of Luria's revelations have come from the writings of Hayyim Vital rather than from Luria himself. The major presentation of Luria's ideas is *Etz ha-Hayyim* ("The Tree of Life"), a book written by Hayyim Vital.

b. Before traveling to Safed, Luria collaborated with two other talmudic scholars in the writing of a commentary on the mishnaic tractate *Zebahim* ("Sacrifices"), which has since been lost. This is one of the few works that Luria himself actually wrote.

c. A mystical explanation of religious ceremonies and rituals, as viewed by Luria, serves as the basis for the book *Shulhan Arukh Shel ha-Ari*. This work is drawn primarily from the writings of Jacob Zemah, one of Hayyim Vital's disciples.

d. The doctrine of the transmigration of souls is the gist of Luria's Kabbalah. According to this theory, even the souls of the pious have to suffer transmigration since not even they are free from the taint of evil. It follows, therefore, that there are no righteous people upon the earth.

3. Although Luria himself wrote little, his importance in the development of the Kabbalah was tremendous.

a. He preached the concept of *Tikkun* ("restoration").

    (1) At the time of creation the process of *Tzimtzum* ("contraction") occurred. God withdrew into Himself, leaving a vacuum which was filled with emanations from the *Ein Soph* ("eternal").

    (2) This act caused the *Shevirat he-Kelim* ("breaking of the vessels") in which light from the *Ein Soph* descended lower and lower; thus evil and darkness entered into the world at the time of creation.

    (3) The function of the *Tikkun* is to return the fallen sparks to their proper place.

    (4) The restoration of the *Tikkun* will lead to the redemption and the coming of the Messiah.

    (5) The *Tikkun* could be expedited by study and observance of the Torah, Talmud, and other mystical writings.

b. He developed a new school of thought, Practical Kabbalah. The study of mystical writings should not only be a form of pseudomagic (juggling numbers and letters, attempting to create *golems*, etc.). Instead, Kabbalah and mysticism should be used for practical purposes, such as redemption of Israel and the bringing of the Messiah.

B. *Hayyim Vital (1543-1620)*

1. Life

a. Hayyim Vital was born in Palestine (presumably in Safed) to parents of Italian origin.

b. He studied Talmud and later in life became a prolific writer on the subject, though few of these writings have been preserved.

c. In 1654 Vital began to study Kabbalah. At first after his arrival in Safed he studied under Moses Cordovero (1522-1570), but eventually became Luria's chief disciple.

d. From 1577 to 1585 Vital lived in Jerusalem where he was head of a yeshiva.

e. Early in 1586 he returned to Safed, where he remained until 1592.

f. In 1593 he returned once again to Jerusalem, staying several years until he moved to Damascus. He remained there the rest of his life.

2. Works

a. Vital's major work is entitled *Etz ha-Hayyim* ("Tree of Life"). It is a compilation of all of his writings that elaborate on the teachings of Isaac Luria.

(1) The work is divided into eight major sections, termed *gates*. The first gate contains everything that Luria himself had written.

(2) This massive work remained in Damascus with Vital's son, who did not allow it to be recopied for several years. When he did allow circulation of the work, it was only after he had reedited and rearranged it himself.

(3) A new edition of this work was recently published in Tel Aviv (1961-1964).

b. Vital is famous for his sermons. Many of these deal with his ideas on the Kabbalah. Such writings as *Sepher ha-Hezyonut* ("Book of Visions") have been preserved until the present day.

c. In addition to his works dealing with the Kabbalah, Vital also wrote a work on astronomy entitled *Sepher ha-Tekhunah*.

d. Hayyim Vital is important, first, for his transmission of the ideas of Isaac Luria (were it not for Vital, Luria's ideas may have been lost forever); second, for his own original works and the influence he exerted on future generations of kabbalists.

C. *Conclusion*

The development of the "practical" aspects of the mystical teachings as conceived by Isaac Luria and transmitted by his disciple, Hayyim Vital, paved the way for many trends in Jewish thought. Through the application of the Kabbalah and its teachings, the coming of the Messiah can be brought about and the suffering of the Jews alleviated. The ideas of redemption and salvation were the underlying reasons for the success of the two mystical movements that would later capture the minds and souls of the Jewish people: the false messianic movement of Shabbetai Tzevi and the Hasidic movement of the Baal Shem Tov.

FALSE MESSIAHS—SHABBETAI TZEVI AND JACOB FRANK

The Middle Ages were a time of great persecution for the Jews. Accusations of ritual murder, public burnings of the Talmud, and expulsion from homelands were frequent occurrences that Jews were forced to endure. Of all the horrors that plagued the Jews during this period, the most serious occurred between 1648 and 1655. During this seven-year span, Bogdan Chmielnicki (1593-1657), a Cossack leader, led the Cossacks and the Ukrainian peasants in attacks upon Jewish communities in Poland and the Ukraine in their revolt against the Polish overlords. According to Jewish sources, over 100,000 Jews were brutally tortured and killed and over 300 communities were completely annihilated. World Jewry was shocked by the Chmielnicki massacres. The question was raised as to why God had permitted His Chosen People to be slaughtered in this manner. One popular response was that these massacres were intended to herald the coming of the Messiah. The great popularity of the false messianic movements of this period is a result of this historical background.

A. *Shabbetai Tzevi (1626-1676)*

1. Shabbetai Tzevi was born in Smyrna, Turkey, on the ninth of Av, 1626. His father, Mordecai, was of Spanish descent

2. Receiving a thorough talmudic education, Shabbetai was more attracted to Kabbalah and study of the Zohar.

3. While still young, Shabbetai began to engage in rigid ascetic practices such as frequent bathing in the sea during both winter and summer.

4. By the age of 20, he already had a small group of followers.

   a. His height and handsome looks attracted people's confidence.

   b. His beautiful voice enchanted his followers when he sang the poems of Isaac Luria.

5. Kabbalists and mystics (includes some Christians) believed that the year 1648 was the year in which messianic redemption would occur. This coincided with the beginnings of the Chmielnicki massacres.

a. Shabbetai Tzevi was moved by a "messianic spirit" during this period.

   (1) He now pronounced the Ineffable Name of God (the *Tetragrammaton*) and announced the abolition of fasts.

   (2) The Smyrna rabbis opposed these actions and Shabbetai Tzevi was excommunicated.

b. Shabbetai travelled to Constantinople in 1658. However, he did not feel that this was the right place to continue his messianic practices.

6. In 1654, he travelled to Salonica where he enacted a marriage ceremony between himself and the Torah. Although this attracted large masses, the rabbis of Salonica were outraged and Shabbetai was banished from the city.

7. After travelling to Cairo in 1662, Shabbetai continued on to Jerusalem where he found the Jewish community in dire straits.

a. As a result of the Chmielnicki massacres, economic support of the Palestinian Jewish community by the Polish Jewish community had ceased.

b. The Jewish community of Jerusalem suffered severe economic difficulties.

c. Shabbetai left Jerusalem for Cairo in an attempt to raise funds for the impoverished Jewish community of the Holy City.

   (1) While on this mission, Shabbetai first heard about a girl named Sarah, a survivor of the Chmielnicki massacres, who proclaimed that she would marry the Messiah. Shabbetai sent for this girl and married her.

   (2) On his return journey to Jerusalem, Shabbetai met Nathan Benjamin Levi (1644) of Gaza. Nathan, who claimed to possess prophetic visions, proclaimed in 1665 that Shabbetai Tzevi was the Messiah.

d. Upon his return to Jerusalem, the masses rejoiced at the arrival of the Messiah. The Jerusalem rabbis were far less impressed, however, and they excommunicated Shabbetai.

8. In December 1665, Shabbetai returned to Turkey where he was greeted with shouts of exultation by masses of Jews.

9. Shabbetai's fame spread throughout the Jewish world.

   a. In Amsterdam, a number of important rabbis and theologians (including a fellow student of Baruch Spinoza) expressed their faith in the new Messiah.

   b. In Hamburg, many Jews sold all their belongings and prepared for the messianic return to the Holy Land.

10. Shabbetai travelled to Constantinople where he expected the Sultan to recognize him as the king of kings.

   a. Instead of the Sultan proclaiming Shabbetai to be the king of kings, he had the messianic figure arrested.

   b. Despite his imprisonment, Shabbetai was allowed to live a life of splendor. His followers looked upon this imprisonment as a necessary step towards the ultimate goal of the messianic age.

   c. While in prison, Shabbetai made a number of religious proclamations. He abolished the fast of the seventeenth of Tamuz and established the ninth of Av, the fast day on which the Jews mourn the destruction of both temples, as a day of feasting and celebration.

11. The downfall of Shabbetai Tzevi's messianic movement began with his meeting with Nehemiah Cohen, a Polish Jew who visited him in prison.

   a. After this visit Cohen did not believe Shabbetai Tzevi was the Messiah.

   b. After embracing Islam, Cohen reported to the Sultan that Shabbetai was intending to overthrow the Ottoman rule.

   c. The Sultan sent one of his physicians to go to Shabbetai and persuade him to become a Moslem.

d. Either out of fear for his own life or the lives of the Jews of the Ottoman Empire, Shabbetai agreed to the conversion.

e. On September 15, 1666, Shabbetai Tzevi appeared before the Sultan where he shed his Jewish headgear and replaced it with the white Turkish turban.

12. Shabbetai's conversion was a severe, but not fatal, blow to his messianic movement.

a. Shabbetai claimed that his conversion resulted from a commandment from God.

b. Other followers believed that it was not Shabbetai himself who had apostatized, but rather a phantom who had taken on his appearance.

c. Nathan of Gaza travelled to many parts of the world trying to prevent Shabbetai's followers from losing faith in the messianic mission.

d. Many people, including many rabbis, lost faith in Shabbetai Tzevi and were greatly disheartened.

13. Although outwardly professing to be a devoted Moslem, Shabbetai still studied and expounded the Zohar.

14. Some Jews who continued to believe in Shabbetai Tzevi converted to Islam while retaining their Jewish observance. This Judeo-Moslem sect became known as the Donmeh, a sect that still exists in Turkey.

15. Shabbetai Tzevi is reported to have died on Yom Kippur (the Day of Atonement) in 1676.

16. Even after Shabbetai Tzevi's false messianic movement died out, other smaller messianic movements arose, the most important being led by Jacob Frank.

B. *Jacob Frank*

1. Jacob Frank (born Jacob ben Judah Leib, or Leibovicz) was a Podolian (a region in Poland) Jew who was associated with the Donmeh sect.

2. Frank believed that he was the reincarnation of Shabbetai Tzevi.

   a. After travelling to Turkey, Frank returned to Poland where he announced that redemption would come only after people had fully satisfied the evil within themselves. Once this had happened, people would no longer be subject to temptation.

   b. Men and women who followed Frank's teachings began to engage in licentious orgies in an attempt to remove the evil from within themselves.

3. The Jewish population was shocked by the Frankists (the name given to Frank and his followers).

   a. The Frankists were chased from community to community by the outraged Jewish population.

   b. In 1756, a conference of Polish rabbis excommunicated Jacob Frank and his followers. This conference also declared that no one under the age of thirty should study the Kabbalah and that no one under the age of forty should study Isaac Luria's writings.

   c. The Frankists now presented their case to the Catholic bishop Dembowski of Kamieniec.

      (1) A large number of Frankist doctrines were similar to the doctrines of Christianity.

      (2) The Frankists declared their opposition to the Talmud.

      (3) The Catholic bishop organized a disputation in 1757 in which the rabbis were to come and answer the charges against the Talmud. The disputation concluded with a mass public burning of the Talmud.

4. After a second disputation in 1759 where it was argued that the Talmud commanded Jews to use Christian blood for ritual practices, the Frankists accepted baptism.

   a. The Christians themselves soon came to doubt the Frankist adherence to Christianity.

   b. Jacob Frank was arrested and imprisoned in a citadel for thirteen years.

   c. Frank's followers looked upon this imprisonment as a necessary part of his messianic career.

5. After his release from prison, Frank spent the last twenty years of his life as the head of his cult in Moravia and Germany.

6. Frank's daughter, Eve, continued the Frankist philosophy until her death in 1816.

C. *Conclusion*

The false messianic movements of Shabbetai Tzevi and Jacob Frank ended in mental anguish for the Jews. Shabbetai Tzevi's movement, which had originally heightened the depressed Jewish spirits to a level unknown in the later Middle Ages, only served as a tremendous disappointment to Jews throughout the world. The Frankist movement was a shocking experience for all Jewish communities. However, out of these disappointments did come some good. Some Jews began to look for new beliefs and ideas, developments that led to the rise of the Hasidic movement in eastern Europe and to the rise of the Haskalah (enlightenment) movement in western Europe.

XXXVI

BARUCH SPINOZA (1632-1677)

Baruch Spinoza was a brilliant Jewish philosopher whose ideas shook the very foundations of Judaism in the seventeenth century. His radical ideas on the authorship of the books of the Bible and on the relevance of observance of the Jewish ceremonial law posed serious threats to the authority of the rabbis, who excommunicated the philosopher in an attempt to smother his heretical views. This attempt was unsuccessful for, although the philosopher died at the young age of 45, his ideas lived on and were expanded upon by a number of well-known philosophers and biblical critics of the next three centuries.

A. *Life*

1. Baruch (Benedict) Spinoza was born in Amsterdam in 1632 to a Portuguese Marrano family who had settled in Holland a few years before his birth. He received a traditional education, one of his teachers being Manasseh ben Israel (see Chapter XXXII, "Joseph Nasi and Manasseh ben Israel"). The young Spinoza also received instruction in Latin, which enabled him to study the writings of non-Jewish philosophers such as the French philosopher Descartes (1596-1650). This exposure allowed Spinoza to associate with a number of free-thinking Christians, while at the same time, it served to estrange him from the synagogue. As a result of his belief that reason is the sole source of knowledge, he grew skeptical about, and questioned the truth of, *all* organized religion, going so far as to stop observing the Jewish ceremonial laws. The Jewish elders in Amsterdam who discovered Spinoza's laxity tried to persuade the young man to mend his ways. Spinoza, however, refused to put aside his beliefs. So great a clamor was raised against him that he was forced to flee the Jewish Quarter. This disdain for the Jewish ceremonial law culminated in Spinoza's formal excommunication from the Jewish community on the sixth of Av (July 27), 1656.

2. After his excommunication, Spinoza had very little to do with the Jewish community. Most of his time was spent with a group of young Christians with whom he studied. In order to sustain himself, Spinoza worked as a lens grinder.

3. Despite his excommunication and his radical ideas, Spinoza's popularity grew. He was invited to become a professor of philosophy at the University in Heidelberg. Spinoza, however, declined the offer.

4. Spinoza died, reportedly from tuberculosis, at the young age of 45.

B. *Writings and Beliefs*

1. Despite the great amount of time Spinoza spent immersed in study, he wrote surprisingly little. Even though the quantity of his work is limited, what Spinoza did write had a profound effect on later thinkers such as Kant, Goethe, Hegel, and Einstein.

2. Spinoza's excommunication served as the inspiration for a protest work which he later expanded into his *Theologico-Political Treatise*, published anonymously in 1670.

   a. This tractate attempted to shake the foundation of traditional Jewish authority.

   b. Spinoza claimed that the Mosaic law was only applicable while a Jewish state existed in Palestine. Once the Jewish state had fallen, the covenant no longer existed and it was unnecessary to observe Jewish ceremonial law.

   c. Spinoza felt that the Jewish ceremonial law was intended to serve as the basis for political solidarity.

   d. Observance of the commandments, some of which resulted in the separation of the Jewish people from their surrounding environment, accounted for universal hatred of the Jewish people.

   e. Spinoza's work is a defense of freedom of thought. It is a criticism of the narrow-mindedness of the Jewish community that had excommunicated him.

3. Spinoza also laid the foundation for methodical biblical criticism.

   a. He felt that many books of the Bible were not written by the authors to whom they were ascribed. In so doing, Spinoza questioned the Mosaic authorship of the Five Books of Moses (the Torah).

b. Spinoza believed that the historical books of the Bible were actually one large work that was written by Ezra the Scribe in the 400s B.C.E.

4. Spinoza never embraced Christianity, and was always cautious about his criticism of the dominant religion of the Netherlands.

   a. He showed deference for Jesus and the apostles.

   b. His *Theologico-Political Treatise* was condemned, however, not only by the Church authorities but also by the States General (the legislative body of the Netherlands).

   c. Spinoza worked closely with a number of young Christians, many of whom formed a group of disciples of the radical Jewish philosopher.

5. Spinoza's philosophical system was pantheistic.

   a. This system was presented in mathematical propositions.

   b. Spinoza's system is largely based on Jewish philosophy which adheres to the following concepts:

      (1) The unity of God as an absolute.

      (2) The entire universe as a manifestation of God's presence.

      (3) Man's attainment of freedom only by willing what God wills.

      (4) Worship and obedience to God through charity and justice.

      (5) Salvation by obeying God.

      (6) Forgiveness by God for those who repent.

6. Spinoza felt that philosophy and religion were two entirely different realms.

   a. Religion deals with the concept of revelation. Its dogmas, since they stem from a belief in God, do not need to have any philosophical basis. These dogmas are concerned with a person's conduct.

b. Philosophy deals with knowledge arrived at through a process of logical deduction. It remains divorced from any concept of divine revelation.

7. Spinoza's chief work entitled *Ethics* was not published until after his death.

   a. This work was written in the style of Euclidean geometry.

   b. This book translates the Jewish belief in God into the language of the mathematical age.

   c. One of the work's primary concepts is that of the unity of God and nature.

C. *Conclusion*

Baruch Spinoza's philosophy was centuries ahead of its time. In the seventeenth century he laid the foundation for modern biblical criticism, which did not reach its peak until well into the nineteenth century. His ideas concerning observance of the Jewish ceremonial law posed a tremendous threat to seventeenth-century Judaism. This threat was confronted in the following century by Moses Mendelssohn (see Chapter XXXVIII, "Haskalah") who argued that the ceremonial law was an integral part of Judaism. Thus, Baruch Spinoza's ideas continued to be the basis of much Jewish thought in the two centuries after his death and helped to develop Judaism into a modern religious force.

XXXVII

HASIDISM

Hasidism (not to be confused with earlier groups bearing the name in the second century, B.C.E, and twelfth and thirteenth centuries C.E.) is a religious and social movement based upon a school of Jewish mysticism. It was founded in the eighteenth century as a reaction to the scholastic oligarchy in Jewish communities and as a reaction to the disillusionment with the false Messiah, Shabbetai Tzevi, and as a general reaction to the economic and social conditions in eastern Europe. Hasidism, preaching the equality of all before God and the relationship of piety to scholarship, won millions of followers. Despite a great decline in its influence during the present century, Hasidism still exists as a way of life with adherents in parts of America, Europe, and Israel.

A. *Historical Background*

1. Both materially and spiritually, the Jews of Poland and the eastern Baltic region were in a lamentable state at the end of the seventeenth century. The Polish kings had assured Jewish communities of protection, but much of the kings' power was lost to the Diets, or administrative councils, who revoked this protection to the Jews.

2. The Jews of eastern Europe suffered severe persecution.

   a. In 1648, the Cossack chief, Bogdan Chmielnicki, led massacres which exterminated many Jewish communities and terrified the Jews.

   b. At the beginning of the eighteenth century, Jewish communities were vulnerable to pillaging, synagogue desecration, and massacre. No government protection was provided.

   c. The authorities restricted the Jews to petty trades, and their meager incomes were taxed for the "privilege" of living as Jews.

   d. Accusation of ritual murders which resulted in massacres were frequently made against Jews well into the nineteenth century.

3. Because of extreme persecutions and disappointment over unfulfilled expectations raised by the false Messiah Shabbetai Tzevi, the Jewish community was ready for a change.

   a. It is not surprising that schools of Jewish study were not productive and vibrant in this period of violence and impoverishment.

   b. There were few outstanding scholars at this time. Many who might have gone into study of the Law turned instead to mysticism in the hope of reaching direct communion with God.

4. This was the historical climate in which the Baal Shem Tov preached his doctrines of Hasidism.

B. *The Development of Hasidism*

1. Israel Baal Shem Tov (c. 1700-1760)

   a. The true founder of Hasidism was Israel ben Eliezer, who was later given the title *Baal Shem Tov*, or "Master of the Good Name" (often known by the abbreviation of the three Hebrew words, *Besht*, which is given to a person of good reputation who performs miracles and helps others in their hour of need).

   b. He came from a very poor family, and was not regarded as a great scholar. He was employed in such occupations as sexton, teacher's assistant, and innkeeper.

   c. After marriage, the Besht and his wife lived in solitude in the Carpathian mountains, but soon moved to the town of Medzibozh in Podolia. Here the Besht revealed himself and gathered followers who became his disciples.

      (1) He taught his doctrines by word of mouth; he wrote no books.

      (2) Ben Eliezer taught that persons should serve God in every thought and action. God is diffused through all creation and it is our task to unify all of creation with God. Prayer and study sustain the angels, but it is devotion which is the heart of our striving for union with God. This devotion must permeate all action and must be done with joy and ecstasy.

d. The Besht lived in Medzibozh from 1740 until his death, mixing with the people, and spreading his doctrines and way of life.

e. After the Besht's death in 1760, Dov Ber, the *Maggid* (preacher) of Mezhirich (c. 1710-1772), became leader of the Besht's followers, the Hasidim ("pious ones").

   (1) Dov Ber attracted scholars and kabbalists because he gave the Besht's religious teachings a firm foundation in traditional Jewish learning.

   (2) Dov Ber extended the movement into the Ukraine and Galicia.

2. Doctrines

   a. At the heart of Hasidic doctrine from its very inception is the statement, "There is no place empty of Him."

   (1) The Besht took this traditional proposition to its extreme.

   (2) Meditation on this doctrine would bring joy, for if God exists in everything, how can evil exist?

   (3) The doctrine steers clear of pure pantheism by its theory of the *kelipot* ("husks").

      (a) The "lower" or terrestrial world, both living and inanimate, contains sparks of the Divine within everything.

      (b) These sparks are enclosed in husks.

      (c) The husks also account for evil in this "lower" world.

      (d) Man's task is to liberate these sparks from their husks in order to achieve unity with God. Man must do this to usher in the time of *tikkun*, or "repair," when all will be unified with God, and when the Messiah will come (see Chapter XXXVa, "Great Kabbalists").

   b. This doctrine of the sparks comes from an older kabbalistic tradition.

(1) To separate the good from the evil, unifying all things with God, all thoughts and actions must be liberated from sensuality and must be invested with *devekut*—intense love of God—and ecstasy.

(2) Evil desire can only be overcome by ecstatic joy, and thus Hasidism exalts the melody, which overcomes melancholy and draws the heart of man to God.

c. The *tzaddik*, the "righteous man," was at the head of the Hasidic community.

(1) He was intermediary between man and God.

(2) It was believed that he could perform miracles.

(3) The concept of the *tzaddik* was an innovation, for Judaism had never conceived of an intermediary between God and man.

(4) This position was passed down from father to son.

(5) Eventually many dynasties were formed with thousands of Hasidim owing allegiance to their respective *tzaddiks*.

3. The Habad School

a. Habad is the contraction of the words *Hokhmah Binah va-Daat*, Hebrew for "Wisdom, Understanding, and Knowledge."

b. This was a more intellectualized variant of Hasidism which was founded by a disciple of Dov Ber, Shneour Zalman of Lyady (1747-1813).

(1) Zalman tried to guide Hasidism back into the ways of traditional Judaism.

(2) His work, *Likkutei Amarim* ("Collections of Sayings"), also known as the *Tanya*, forms the foundation of Habad teaching.

c. Habad shares the emphasis on *devekut* with the original form of Hasidism, as well as the doctrines of ecstasy and divine content of all things.

d. Habad differs from the original Hasidism in its emphasis upon intellectual striving in religious experience.

(1) The *sephirot* (see Chapter XXXIVa, "Kabbalah"), the powers of contemplation and analysis, which are the higher powers of the human being, must control the "lower" powers of the emotion.

(a) The emotional effects of prayer are intensified and concentrated.

(b) This control of the emotions by the intellect could be called a systematizing of prayer.

(2) The Habad school of Hasidism was also more institutionalized than other schools of Hasidism.

(a) Habad conducted missionary activity in the nineteenth century to combat the loosening of Jewish life.

(b) It founded schools, orphanages, and study groups.

(c) Many activities of Habad continue to this day. Although originating in Lithuania, Habad has dispersed over the globe, including New York, Canada, Australia, and North Africa, and has established agricultural settlements in Israel.

4. Mitnaggedim (Hebrew: "opponents")

a. This was a movement, with its center in Vilna, Lithuania, which opposed the Hasidic movement.

b. Elijah ben Solomon Zalman, more commonly known as the Vilna Gaon (1720-1797), was the spiritual leader of the Mitnaggedim.

c. The Mitnaggedim based their opposition to the Hasidim on the following reasons:

(1) The feeling that Hasidism would lead its adherents away from study.

(2) Hasidism would break up and weaken the community.

      (3) The Hasidic use of the Sephardic liturgy, with its emphasis on mysticism.

      (4) The belief in the *Tzaddik* as the intermediary between God and man.

   d. For a time, the Mitnaggedim were successful in quelling the Hasidic movement.

      (1) The Hasidim recognized the importance of study.

      (2) The Hasidic movement put a greater emphasis on scholasticism and intellectualization.

      (3) The Mitnaggedim became more tolerant in their view of Hasidism because of the "normalization" of Hasidism and the alliance of the two groups in combating the Haskalah movement (see Chapter XXXVIII, "Haskalah").

5. Neo-Hasidism

   a. The term "neo-Hasidism" has been applied to the thought and work of Martin Buber (1878-1965) and Abraham Joshua Heschel (1907-1972) (see Chapter XLV, "New Thinking"), two religious philosophers of our century.

   b. Martin Buber was descended from a family of rabbinic scholars.

      (1) He is noted for his work in rekindling interest in Hasidism among the non-Jewish and assimilated Jewish public.

         (a) His works retell Hasidic legends.

         (b) Other works enumerate his idea of the personal God-man relationship

      (2) For Buber, all human relationships in which we treat the other as more than an object, relationships in which the deeper meaning of existence is revealed, contain part of the essence of our relationship to God.

(3) While Buber's philosophy has points of contact with Hasidism, it is a philosophy rather than a way of life and prayer as Hasidism is.

(4) Buber was strongly influenced by Hasidim, as is seen in his emphasis on striving to be united with God. However, he did not emphasize many elements of Hasidism such as ecstasy, the *tzaddik*, and *kelipot*.

c. Abraham Joshua Heschel's philosophy is closer to Hasidism than is Buber's. Heschel refers to the *Baal Shem Tov* as the one who "banished melancholy from the soul and uncovered the ineffable delight of being a Jew."

d. Both Buber and Heschel saw Hasidism as an inspiration to modern secularized man, who had been alienated from God and from the meaning of existence.

C. *Conclusion*

Hasidism scandalized the traditional scholars of the eighteenth century, and in 1781, the Vilna Gaon excommunicated the new sect. Nevertheless, Hasidim and Mitnaggedim found common ground in combatting the Haskalah movement. Despite attacks from the Mitnaggedim and Maskilim, Hasidism managed to spread and extend its influence over communities in eastern Europe. Dynasties of *tzaddikim* arose; some were wealthy and lived in luxury from fees charged for performing miracles; however, many others were poor, refusing to accept money for their actions. After the Holocaust destroyed the European centers of Hasidism, many of these decimated communities relocated themselves in Israel and the United States. During times of trouble, Hasidic ideas that are found in its legends and melodies have helped strengthen and revitalize Judaism. Through the activity of various Hasidic communities and neo-Hasidic philosophers, Hasidism has remained an important force in modern Jewish theology.

XXXVIII

HASKALAH

Haskalah comes from the Hebrew word "enlightenment." The Haskalah movement connoted the idea of a humanism that aimed to free the Jews from the medieval asceticism and spiritualism that had continued with them into the eighteenth and nineteenth centuries. The movement began in Germany with the goal of broadening and reforming the Jewish way of life. It set out to cultivate in the Jew an understanding of the universe, via a systematic study of history, science, and philosophy. The Haskalah attempted to revitalize Jewish existence and expand the intellect of the Jews by broadening their scope of knowledge. The revival and use of the Hebrew language became a means for the achievement of this aim. The *Maskilim* (advocates of the Haskalah) purified the existing Hebrew language and modernized its biblical form.

A. *Historical Background*

1. The Haskalah had its roots in the westernized Jewish communities of seventeenth-century Holland and Italy.

2. As a popular movement, the Haskalah began in the later part of the eighteenth century in Berlin.

   a. Mercantilism had created a small Jewish capitalist class.

   b. In the secular atmosphere of the European Enlightenment of the seventeenth and eighteenth centuries, a more liberal view about Jews was taken.

3. The Haskalah had a more lasting impact outside of Germany, where trends toward assimilation were retarded.

   a. The Galician Haskalah flourished following the Edict of Tolerance (1782) of King Joseph II of Austria, a policy of secularization and Germanization of the Jewish community. The Maskilim Naftali Herz Homberg and Naftali Herz Wessely were influential in secularizing the Jewish educational system in Austria.

b. In Russia, emancipation had not been granted.

 (1) Czarina Catherine II (1762-1796), Czar Paul I (1796-1801), and Czar Alexander I (1801-1825) did not treat the Jews favorably. Because of the annexation of Poland in the eighteenth century, a large Jewish population was added to the Russian Empire.

 (2) From the beginning of the reign of Czar Nicholas I (1825-1855), a repressive policy toward the Jews was instituted.

  (a) The Cantonist system was imposed on the Jews: Jewish children were inducted into the Czarist army for 25 years of service, and these soldiers were usually baptized; many eventually forgot their Jewish heritage.

  (b) There was a new delineation of the Pale of Settlement, a specified area in the Russian Empire in which Jews were allowed to live.

  (c) The Pale of Settlement remained in effect until the Russian Revolution. These restrictions paved the way for the acceptance of the Zionist and revolutionary ideals among Russian Jewish communities.

B. *Literary Activities*

1. The Educational Haskalah

 a. Writers and advocates of the Haskalah, who were called Maskilim, composed and translated literary works.

 b. The initial literary production was a monthly publication called *HaMeassef* ("The Magazine") published from 1783 to 1829.

  (1) Moses Mendelssohn (1725-1786) inspired and patronized the movement.

  (2) Naftali Herz Wessely (1725-1805) was the master poet and ideologist of the German Haskalah.

  (3) Mendelssohn and Wessely contributed to *HaMeassef* and were instrumental in the composition of a new Hebrew commentary

to the Bible called *Biur* ("Commentary"). The intention of this work was to sweep aside all mystical and allegorical interpretations of the Scriptures.

c. Though the Maskilim wrote mainly works of utilitarian character, Hebrew literature branched out into many areas.

(1) Naftali Herz Wessely wrote a biblical epic based on the Book of Exodus called *Shirey Tiferet* ("Songs of Glory").

(2) Solomon Pappenheim (1740-1814) wrote a sentimental elegy called *Aggadat Arba Kosot* ("The Legend of the Four Cups"). In this work he shows how the rationalism of the Enlightenment will overcome the prevailing medieval beliefs which were found in the Jewish community.

d. By the first quarter of the nineteenth century the center of Hebrew literature moved to Galicia. The main subject matter of these writings was philosophy, history, literature, and science.

2. Romanticism

a. The literary genre of Romanticism which was popular in nineteenth century European literature penetrated into Hebrew literature around 1840.

b. The Romantic movement made its first appearance in Lithuania.

c. The works reflect a longing for the idyllic life of biblical times because during this period the Jews had a nation-state in Palestine and were not exiles in the Diaspora.

d. Micah Joseph Lebensohn (Mikhal) (1828-1852) expounds this romantic ideal in his poems, which use both biblical and historical themes.

(1) His lyrical poems deal with personal emotions and sentiments, such as love, appreciation of nature, and religious reflection.

(2) In *Shlomoh* ("Solomon") and *Kohelet* ("Ecclesiastes") he depicts different phases from the life of King Solomon; the former, his youth in which the young king is optimistic; the latter, an older, more cynical man.

(3) In *El ha-Kokhavim* ("To the Stars") he describes his own life, which was slowly fading away because of tuberculosis.

e. Novelists

(1) Abraham Mapu (1808-1867) wrote about his personal belief of the final victory of good over evil. He expresses an admiration for the idyllic life through his descriptive style of writing.

(a) *Ayit Zavua* ("The Hypocrite") expresses Mapu's feelings about the hypocrisy that he finds in contemporary Jewish society.

(b) *Ahavat Ziyyon* ("Love of Zion") is the first Hebrew novel to use the Bible as background for the story. In this novel, Mapu uses Israel in the time of Isaiah as the setting for the story.

3. The Militant Haskalah

a. With the realization that romantic Haskalah literature had concentrated in the mind of the Jew, there was a shift toward subjects dealing more with various aspects of Jewish life.

b. Especially in Russia, the Haskalah movement became a passionate advocate of the continuation of Jewish life.

c. This new trend was encouraged by the educational opportunities offered to the Jews.

d. The movement turned toward the Jewish religion and culture. Since the economic, political, and social life was being created for them by external forces, only an internal religious life remained of the Jews' own making (see Chapter XL, "Jewish Nightmares").

e. The Maskilim held that it was antiquated Jewish customs and religious beliefs which stood as a barrier between Jew and non-Jew, between the medieval world of the Jew and the modern world of contemporary society.

f. The Maskilim directed their zeal for religious reform through education via such media as the novel, the poem, and the newspaper.

g. Novelists of the Militant Haskalah.

   (1)   Isaac Erter (1791-1851) was a doctor who wrote *Ha-Zofeh le-Bet Yisrael* ("The Watchman for the House of Israel") consisting of five novels satirizing all phases of Jewish life that he considers irrational and primitive. He is especially critical of the Hasidic movement.

   (2)   Reuben Asher Braudes (1851-1902) describes the struggle between the Maskilim and Orthodox Judaism in his novel *Hadat Vehakhayim* ("Religion and Life"). He was active in the Zionist movement and advocated Jewish nationalism as the natural synthesis of tradition and Haskalah.

C. *Personalities*

1. Moses Mendelssohn (1729-1786)

   a. He wrote a translation of the Pentateuch into German and the *Biur* ("Explanation"), which is a Hebrew commentary on the Bible.

   b. He helped found the Hebrew magazine *HaMeassef* ("The Magazine"), published by the Friends of the Hebrew Language.

      (1)   The publication hoped to expose Jewish and non-Jewish thought and literature to the Jewish world.

      (2)   This journal had a great influence outside Germany.

2. Leopold Zunz (1794-1886)

   a. Zunz was a pioneer in the establishment of the *Wissenschaft des Judentums* ("The Science of Judaism"), a movement aimed at promoting Jewish historical research via modern methods, such as the examination of literary sources, utilization of recent archaeological discoveries, and study of comparative literature and linguistics.

   b. In 1819, Zunz and other young Jewish students formed the Association for Jewish Culture and Science.

    (1) The goal of the organization was to bring secular studies to Jewish youth by expanding their cultural level and reforming traditional lifestyles.

    (2) Two prominent members of the group, Eduard Ganz and Heinrich Heine, became converts to Christianity for the purpose of furthering their careers.

  c. In his major historical studies, Zunz resurrected early Jewish liturgical works.

    (1) He encouraged a reforming of Jewish worship, including the use of music, choral singing, new forms of recitation of prayers, and German vernacular in worship. These were innovations which Zunz felt would revive what he had considered fossilized and abused forms of worship.

    (2) Although Zunz believed Hebrew literature and many customs were stagnant and antiquated, he staunchly opposed breaking with the Talmud and the belief of the coming of the Messiah or the rejection of the Sabbath and the covenant made with Abraham.

  d. In general, Zunz extended and preserved Jewish tradition in the western Haskalah while planting the seeds for a reform Jewish movement.

3. Abraham Geiger (1810-1874)

  a. His major literary work is *Urschrift und Übersetzungen der Bibel* ("The Original and the Translation of the Bible") published in 1857.

    (1) The work is a study of the development of Jewish religious ideas as seen through the changes in the early versions and original text of the Bible.

    (2) Geiger's approach to Judaism was similar to Zunz's: Judaism was seen as a finite historical entity and as such, was considered capable of further change.

b. Geiger was an influential Reform rabbi.

   (1) He helped establish reform-oriented rabbinical seminaries, notably the Jewish Theological Seminary of Breslau.

   (2) He introduced many reforms in the worship services and in religious practices:

      (a) Use of German in prayer.

      (b) Elimination of references to the return to Zion in the daily prayers.

      (c) Abolition of circumcision.

   (3) Geiger was considered one of the most articulate spokesmen of the German Reform movement.

4. Zechariah Frankel (1801-1875)

   a. Frankel was a Bohemian rabbi who had received a secular education.

   b. Frankel was instrumental in securing abolition of anti-Jewish legislation in Saxony. This set the example for the repeal of anti-Jewish laws in other German states.

   c. In 1851, Frankel founded a scholarly periodical devoted to Jewish science, *Monatsschrift für Geschichte und Wissenschaft des Judentums* ("Monthly Periodical for the History and Science of Jews").

   d. Frankel was chosen to direct the rabbinical school at Breslau over Geiger.

      (1) Frankel opposed religious reforms such as prayer in the vernacular and the removal of references to sacrifices and the return to Zion.

      (2) Frankel had withdrawn from Geiger's 1845 Conference of Reform Rabbis at Frankfurt when the majority decided that Hebrew prayer was not required.

e. Frankel took a middle position in the conflict between those advocating traditional orthodoxy under the leadership of Samson Raphael Hirsch (1808-1888), and those advocating radical religious reform under the leadership of Geiger.

    (1) Frankel asserted Israel's separateness and mission to the world.

    (2) Frankel became the father of the Conservative movement in Judaism.

5. Nahman Krochmal (1785-1840)

a. He was a Galician scholar who devoted his time to the study of philosophy and history and was leader of the Polish Haskalah movement.

b. He expressed a vision of Judaism as an expression of the national history and destiny of the people.

c. Krochmal wrote *Moreh Nevukhei ha-Zeman* ("The Guide to the Perplexed of Modern Times"). Influenced by Hegel, the work is a systematic analysis of the philosophy of Jewish history.

6. Isaac Baer Levinsohn (1788-1860)

a. He has been called the father of the Russian Haskalah (see chapter XLII, "Yiddish Culture").

b. Like his predecessor Moses Mendelssohn, Levinsohn's essays advocate the broadening of Jewish intellectual and economic bases.

c. He was known for his satirical works about contemporary Jewish society, notably *Dis Hefker Welt* ("The Empty World").

d. He received financial support from the Russian government in his endeavors to "enlighten" the Jewish community.

e. His work made a considerable impact on the Jewish population; unfortunately, his defense of Judaism did little to alleviate the Czarist policies towards the Jews.

7. Judah Loeb Gordon (1830-1892)

    a. Called the champion of the Haskalah, he originally wrote about romantic themes; however, his writings evolved into realistic commentaries and criticisms of his environment.

    b. A nationalistic poet, Gordon was motivated by the idea of reform and enlightenment. He espoused his beliefs in his influential Hebrew newspaper *Hamelitz* ("The Adviser"). His slogan for Jewish emancipation was "be a Jew at home and a man on the street."

    c. Gordon was strongly opposed to the fanaticism of the rabbis, the anachronistic education given to the children, the social condition of the Jewish women, and the squalid economic state of the people.

    d. Such events inspired Gordon's famous historical and sentimental poems *Ben Shinne Arayot* ("In the Jaws of the Lions") and *Kotso Shel Yod* ("The Point of a Yod") in which he criticizes the people for being overly concerned with spiritualism and adherence to outdated laws and customs.

    e. In his poetry he tried to give a realistic depiction of ghetto life.

D. *Conclusion*

The Haskalah movement began in Berlin as a result of the efforts of Moses Mendelssohn. Mendelssohn's aim was to break down the intellectual and physical walls of the ghetto and lead the Jewish people into the world of secular European culture. The Haskalah's ultimate purpose was to mediate between ghetto Judaism and total assimilation. Yet, in Germany, the country of its birth, cultural assimilation rapidly surpassed the efforts of the Maskilim.

Later, the Haskalah found a new home in Russia where it took the form of the introduction of secular literature to the Jewish masses through the media of the Hebrew and Yiddish languages. After a short romantic period in which authors described an idealized biblical period, a new literary generation was born. This group saw in the liberating tendencies of Alexander II an opportunity to advocate a complete transformation of Jewish life through education. These Maskilim encouraged the Jews to abandon their traditional social and economic ways of life, to reject their religious heritage and practices, and to seek equality by mingling with the native population and adopting its culture.

With the resurgence of anti-semitism in the latter part of the nineteenth century, there was a realization that a program of internal Jewish reform could not bring about Jewish emancipation. An example of the general disillusionment is the reaction of Leo Pinsker (1821-1891) (see Chapter XLIa, "The Zionist Dream"), who, following the pogroms of 1881, published *Auto-Emancipation*. Here, Pinsker observed that Jewish equality could only be realized in a Jewish state.

The Haskalah must be given credit for paving the way for "modernism" in Jewish thought and lifestyles by creating an urbanized and secularized stratum among the Jews, which would later express its needs and desires via such movements as Liberalism, Zionism, Socialism, and Communism.

XXXIX

JEWS IN AMERICA

The European atmosphere of the suppression of religious, economic, and personal freedom helped shape the idea that America was the "land of milk and honey." The immigrants looked to the "New World" for the chance of attaining those freedoms that were never possible in the "old country." In America, immigrants thought they could begin a new life; the past was forgotten and they could look forward to a future of prosperity and happiness.

A. Major Waves of Immigration

1. The Beginnings

   a. America attracted Jewish settlement from the time of its discovery in 1492.

      (1) Many Marranos (see Chapter XXXI, "Expulsion from Spain") came to the Spanish and Portuguese colonies to escape the Inquisition.

      (2) Marranos settled in Mexico, Brazil, Chile, and Peru.

      (3) The Dutch set up colonies in Recife and Curuçao which attracted many Jews who practiced their religion openly.

   b. The first Jews came to North America in 1654 after the Portuguese conquered the Dutch colonies in Brazil. These Jews settled in New Amsterdam (New York). Other Jews began settling in some of the other New England colonies.

   c. In the early part of the seventeenth and eighteenth centuries, Jews did not find established settlements particularly receptive to their arrival. Most of the original colonies had been established by Protestant sects who were often intolerant to immigrants of other Protestant beliefs, let alone the immigration of Jews.

   d. In the beginning of the eighteenth century, Jews began settling in the Middle Atlantic colonies where a large Jewish community was established in Philadelphia.

e. Jewish settlement in the southern coastal colonies did not gain momentum until the middle half of the eighteenth century with the establishment of Jewish communities in Charleston and Savannah.

f. Jewish settlers contributed to the building of the nation. At first they had to vie with their Christian neighbors for the right to trade with the Indians.

   (1) Many chose to go into manual trades, such as tailoring, watchmaking, saddlemaking, or distilling.

   (2) Others became itinerant peddlers trading with Indians and settlers.

g. After the American Revolution religious freedom did not come automatically.

   (1) Long debates ensued over the question of the state's religious authority over its inhabitants.

   (2) Three of the constitutions of the original colonies limited officeholding to Christians only.

   (3) Eventually all of the states allowed Jewish men full equality as citizens. (Jewish women, as well as other American women, could not vote until 1920.)

2. 1800-1900

   a. In the beginning, a large proportion of the American Jewish settlers were of Spanish-Portuguese origin.

      (1) They brought with them their own rituals and customs.

      (2) Sephardic rituals and practices were accepted in conducting prayer services.

      (3) The first Jewish synagogue, Shearith Israel ("Remnant of Israel"), was established in New York in 1730.

      (4) In 1740, Congregation Mikveh Israel was established in Philadelphia.

b. In the early part of the nineteenth century there was a migration of approximately 35,000-40,000 German Jews.

   (1) The failure of the German revolution of 1848 actualized the realization that there would never be political or complete religious freedom in Germany.

   (2) Because of the reaction after the failure of the revolution, immigrants of many political and religious persuasions came to America to make a new and better life for themselves.

c. As immigration continued, the community tried to transplant itself in America. The German Jewish community introduced many of the reforms of the Haskalah to America.

   (1) One of the first efforts of the community was to build a place of worship.

   (2) Because of divergent backgrounds, the communities were not united on such traditional issues as *kashrut* (observance of dietary laws), language of prayer, and Jewish burial.

   (3) As communities split on various issues, temples advocating various reforms were set up by dissident members.

d. With the discovery of gold in California, many Jews joined the move toward the Pacific coast, some of them becoming itinerant peddlers.

   (1) Later, it became evident that a peddler's material earnings would increase if he established himself in a business center. Thus, small Jewish settlements cropped up all over the country.

   (2) As interaction with Gentile neighbors increased, the younger generation rejected those outward religious traditions that separated them from their fellow citizens.

e. Through the efforts and reforms of the German-Jewish rabbi Isaac Leeser (1806-1868), these new immigrants were able to retain their identities as Jews without the hardships that Orthodox Judaism imposed upon them.

(1) He felt that Jews should come together and identify themselves as American Jews with an American Jewish ritual.

(2) Leeser himself did much to promote his views. In his own congregation, he gave the sermon in English rather than in German; he translated both the Ashkenazic and Sephardic prayerbooks into English; and he eliminated those aspects of Christian interpretation found in the King James translation of the Bible.

(3) Leeser's aims were not realized for a generation; however, his work laid the basis for American Reform Judaism.

f. Another leader of American Jewry was Isaac Mayer Wise (1819-1900)

(1) Upon his arrival in America from Germany in 1846, he aligned himself with Leeser and his movement.

(2) Wise felt that the growing disunity among American Jews could only prove detrimental.

(3) Isaac Wise wrote extensively on the subject of reforms in Jewish ritual and his hopes for Jewish unity in America.

(4) In 1873, Wise established the first organization of Jewish congregations, composed of communities mainly in the South and Midwest.

   (a) This organization, which had its headquarters in Cincinnati, was to become the Union of American Hebrew Congregations (UAHC).

   (b) From UAHC, Wise established a reform rabbinic training school. This institution, Hebrew Union College (HUC), was led by Wise for the next twenty-five years. Wise was also instrumental in establishing the Central Conference of American Rabbis (CCAR).

(5) In 1885 at a meeting in Pittsburgh, Wise and other rabbis adopted the Pittsburgh Platform which served as the basis for American Reform Judaism until the Columbus Platform of

1937. Among the resolutions of the Pittsburgh Platform were the following:

(a) A declaration that the role of the Jews was to spread "godliness" among the peoples of the world.

(b) A declaration that some of the rabbinic legislation no longer applied.

(c) A rejection of a return to Zion.

3. 1880-1910

a. The end of the nineteenth century saw radical changes in the American Jewish community. The United States again became a haven for Jewish immigrants.

(1) Because of oppression in Russia, millions of Jews left and settled in the United States, Argentina, and western Europe (see Chapter XL, "Jewish Nightmares").

(2) Between 1881 and 1914, over 1,300,000 Jews entered America, bringing the total Jewish population to almost three million.

(3) Approximately 70 percent of the new arrivals remained in New York City, another 15 percent preferred to make the Atlantic seacoast cities their home.

(4) If the new Jewish immigrants met with any opposition in America, it originated from members of their own religion. The longer-established Jews looked down upon the new settlers who clung to their European-Jewish traditions.

(a) The older settlers had forgotten their own experiences, not recalling that they too had once felt ill at ease with the new language, customs, and thinking. Nevertheless, organizations sprang up to help the immigrants adjust to the new lifestyle.

(b) Many of the older immigrants were very patronizing to the new immigrants, which created some tension between the two groups.

(c)   Incentives were given to Jews to move westward and southward to develop lesser populated areas.

b. The immigrants were compelled to find immediate gainful employment.

(1)   They usually sent money back to their relatives in Europe for support and boat passage to the United States.

(2)   Many immigrants, in addition to becoming peddlers, worked in factories producing cigars, leather, metal goods, and most importantly, clothing.

c. The rise in manpower was exploited by some of the established Jews who quickly realized the market potentiality.

(1)   Wages were low, hours long, and working conditions unsafe.

(2)   These small shops in which they labored were called sweatshops.

(3)   The majority of those employed were women, which brought the wage scales even lower.

d. Little time was available for religious prayer and study so greatly valued in the past.

(1)   Older children were often compelled by their parents to leave school at an early age in order to help support the family.

(2)   Religious education became the haphazard occupation of a few old, often unqualified immigrants.

(3)   The anguish of these workers was expressed in their activism in labor organizations and the influence of various socialist-oriented groups among the new immigrants.

(4)   Despite the oppression experienced by these newcomers, they managed to create a literature both personal and universalistic in its scope.

(a)   Among the more prominent American Jewish writers of the time were Morris Rosenfeld, Solomon Bloomgarden (better known as Yehoash), Abraham Goldfaden, Jacob Gordin, David Pinski, and Perez Hirschbein (see Chapter XLII, "Yiddish Culture").

(b) Yiddish newspapers such as *The Forward* were established in order to cater to the needs of the Jewish immigrants.

e. The Jews saw a need for reforming their religious beliefs in order to comply with the American way of life.

(1) Some saw the answer in the Reform movement.

(2) Others felt that the Pittsburgh Platform, adopted by UAHC, was too radical in its scope.

(3) With this as an impetus, the Conservative movement was begun. The Jewish Theological Seminary (JTS) was formed in New York in 1886 as the seminary for the training of Conservative rabbis. JTS did not flourish until Solomon Schechter (1850-1915), a noted scholar, became its president in 1902. The seminary's position was that changes were necessary; however, a thorough knowledge of past tradition was deemed necessary in order that this change would correspond to recognized rabbinic authority.

(4) In 1896, the Rabbi Isaac Elchanan Theological Seminary was founded in New York. This was a seminary for the training of Orthodox rabbis. It later was expanded to include a liberal arts college and graduate schools, and is now a division of Yeshivah University.

B. *Conclusion*

Because of the relatively "free" nature of American society, the Jews found themselves in a new and perplexing situation. Whereas in Europe restrictions were placed on all aspects of economic, religious, and political life, America, in contrast, was conceived as "the land of milk and honey," with the "Horatio Alger" myth of "rags to riches" being the norm. Despite the initial setbacks and culture shocks that new immigrants faced, the Jews were able to adapt slowly to the new language and customs and integrate themselves into "American" society. The problem of retaining a Jewish identity confronted Jewish leaders, thus initiating the development of

American Reform Judaism, the establishment of Conservative Judaism, and a reorientation of Orthodoxy. Their task was to create a vibrant Judaism which could survive and flourish in America.

XL

JEWISH NIGHTMARES IN FRANCE AND RUSSIA

In the nineteenth century, Jews discovered to their dismay that their emancipation from the ghetto into the Christian world only meant that they as a group became the convenient scapegoat in the new wave of mass politics. There was nothing new about the libels and persecutions endured by the Jews; accusations of ritual murder and revolutionary conspiracy were no more than a continuation of medieval anti-Semitism. What is significant for all concerned is that this was occurring in a "modern" and "enlightened" Europe, where freedom and emancipation were supposed to be highly valued.

A. *Historical Background: France*

1. Political and economic rights were first granted to the Jews during the French Revolution.

   a. By 1791 citizenship was granted to the Jews of France.

   b. Countries such as Holland and the Hamburg city-state had already granted limited liberties in practice, but France was the first European country to recognize Jewish civil rights by law.

2. During the nineteenth century, Jews took full advantage of their citizenship rights and many prospered.

   a. The Foulds and the Pereires were bankers and confidantes of Napoleon III. Their massive industrial expansion and public works helped to finance the regime of the Second Empire.

   b. The Rothschilds had a branch of their banking empire in Paris. Originally from Frankfort, they eventually established banking branches in the major cities of Europe.

   c. Giacomo Meyerbeer was one of the most popular musicians of nineteenth-century France.

3. Anti-Semitism persisted in France among political parties of the Right.

    a. The Rightists detested all that the Republic stood for: liberalism, republicanism, anticlericalism, antimonarchism, secularism, and Jewish civil liberties.

    b. The word *Jew* connoted images of such people as Baron de Rothschild and Karl Marx.

    c. In France, an influential statement on racial thought, "Essay on the Inequality of the Races," was published by Count Joseph deGobineau.

    d. The collapse in 1888 of the Union Générale, a large bank owned by Catholic interests, was attributed by some writers of the French press to a Jewish conspiracy.

    e. Matters were made worse by the revelation in the anti-Semitic press that two of the masterminds of the huge Panama Canal stock swindle (1891-1892), Jacques Reinach and Cornelius Herz, were Jewish.

    f. These events created an atmosphere of anti-Semitism and panic. This mood, in conjunction with the political climate of jingoism which had been growing since France lost Alsace and Lorraine to Germany in the Franco-Prussian War of 1870-1871, precipitated the rioting and slander of the Dreyfus affair.

B. *The Dreyfus Affair*

1. This famous scandal, which centered around Captain Alfred Dreyfus and involved many important political and military officials, had serious repercussions for the French and the Jewish people.

    a. Late in 1894, a member of the French General Staff, Alfred Dreyfus, an assimilated Jew, was accused of giving military secrets to the Germans.

    b. He was quickly tried by a military court and found guilty solely on the basis of one military document called the *bordereau*, the handwriting of which somewhat resembled that of Dreyfus.

    c. Only three of the five experts hired by the military court testified that there was a similarity between the two handwritings.

    d. On the basis of this dubious evidence, Dreyfus was convicted, stripped of his rank, and sentenced to life imprisonment on Devil's Island.

    e. During the course of the trial proceedings, the press made much of the fact that Dreyfus was a Jew.

2. The affair was quickly forgotten until Bernard Lazare created a furor in 1896 (see Chapter XLIa, "The Zionist Dream").

    a. He was a young literary critic hired by the Dreyfus family to research the ordeal of Captain Dreyfus.

    b. Lazare researched the affair for one and a half years and then presented his case to important officials.

    c. He managed to convince August Scheurer-Kestner, a member of the French Senate, and Lt. Col. Georges Picquart, head of the French Intelligence Service, that Dreyfus was innocent and a victim of an anti-Semitic plot.

    d. Emile Zola wrote an open letter to the president of France with the headline "J'accuse!" in which he demanded that justice take its course.

    e. A retrial was demanded. This elicited violent reactions from anti-Semites and antirepublicans.

    f. Even the discovery that the *bordereau* was a forgery made by a Major Ferdinand Esterhazy did not stop the anti-Jewish feeling.

    g. Esterhazy, who had been working secretly for the German government, committed suicide and became a martyr among the enemies of the Jews.

3. With the advent of a Liberal coalition government in 1899, the Dreyfus case was again brought to court.

a. Again it was a military court which handled the case, and the evidence of Dreyfus's guilt was even scantier than that of the first trial.

b. The court pronounced Dreyfus "guilty of treason," but because of "extenuating circumstance," his sentence was reduced to ten years imprisonment.

c. The absurdity of the verdict was brought to the attention of the president of the Republic who granted Dreyfus a pardon; a few years later a civil court pronounced him innocent.

d. No French military court, however, cleared Dreyfus's name of the treason accusation.

4. The Dreyfus affair had numerous ramifications.

a. The affair represented the first open threat to the legal and physical status of the Jews in France after the French Revolution.

b. It spawned many anti-Semitic movements such as Charles Maurras' *L'Action Française*, and made anti-Semitism a tool of the anti-republican reaction.

c. After the Dreyfus affair, the French socialist parties rejected anti-Semitism as part of their ideology, deleting such images of Jews as capitalists and reactionaries.

d. The affair pointed to the fragility of the Jewish position, even in such a cultured, progressive, and enlightened country as France.

e. This state of affairs provided, perhaps, the strongest impetus for the founding of a permanent Zionist movement.

f. Theodor Herzl, a young correspondent covering the Dreyfus trial for the Viennese newspaper the *Neue Freie Presse*, became the founder of modern Zionism.

C. *Historical Background: Russia and Poland*

1. Russia and Poland were both under the rule of the Russian czars during the nineteenth century.

2. During the reign of Czar Nicholas I (1825-1855), the Jewish community was weakened by much anti-Jewish legislation.

 a. "Jewish" schools were established with the intention of eventual assimilation and conversion of their Jewish students to Christianity.

 b. Jewish community organizations were abolished.

 c. The notorious *Cantonist System* was established. Under this system Jewish children (usually twelve years old and from the poorer strata of the community) were conscripted into the Czarist military for twenty-five years of service. Most of these cantonists were baptized (many times forcibly) or forgot their Judaism and Jewish origins.

3. The reign of Alexander II (1855-1881), a more liberal czar, saw the repeal of some of the earlier anti-Jewish decrees, notably the Cantonist Laws. Limited political and civil rights were granted to the Jews, although some of these laws were revoked by the end of this reign.

4. The reign of Czar Alexander III (1881-1894) brought brutal anti-Jewish persecutions because the Jews were identified as the cause of all the problems plaguing Russia.

 a. These attacks occasioned one of the most extensive emigrations in Jewish history.

 b. Jews were expelled from Moscow, from many villages, and from the universities (to which they had been admitted in limited numbers).

 c. It was in these years that government-inspired pogroms (violent attacks on Jews) were initiated.

D. *The Russian Pogrom*

1. *Pogrom* is the Russian word for "violence." The word was given to the attacks: ransacking, looting, and massacres officially instigated or officially ignored by the Russian government from 1881 until the Russian Revolution (1917).

2. These riots took place in such communities as Yelizavetgrad and Kiev.

a. Mobs of peasants, civil servants, farmers, laborers, and off-duty soldiers ransacked property and murdered Jews, while the local police and government troops watched idly.

b. This wave of attacks soon spread to other cities and villages in the Pale of Settlement, a special area in the western region of the Russian Empire where Jews were allowed to settle.

c. Large numbers of Jews were expelled from Moscow and Kiev, thereby increasing the population of the Pale of Settlement.

d. Many impoverished Jews, in reaction to pogroms, emigrated from Russia settling mainly in England, France, Germany, Argentina, Canada and the United States.

E. *More Harshness*

1. The accession to the throne of Czar Alexander III's son, Nicholas II (1894-1917), did not improve the status of the Jews in the Russian Empire.

   a. After the Revolution of 1905, some concessions such as the formation of the Duma (parliament) and the reinstatement of some civil liberties were granted.

   b. The Czar, however, supported reactionaries who had founded the "Union of the Russian People."

   c. They held the Jews responsible for the ills of "Mother Russia"; e.g., the defeat in the Russo-Japanese War, economic turmoil, and revolutionary activity. They also felt that Jews had been among the instigators of the 1905 Revolution.

   d. The "Black Hundreds," the general name given to members of the Union of the Russian People, and other nationalistic anti-Jewish groups, took their revenge on the Jews by staging pogroms aided by Czarist troops.

   e. The most notable of these pogroms were at Kishinev (1903), Odessa (1905), and Bialystok (1906) (see Chapter XLIIIa, "H. N. Bialik").

    f. These massacres were the most devastating in a long series of massacres throughout Russia.

2. As persecutions continued, emigration to the West increased and new solutions to the Jewish problem were being explored.

F. *The Beilis Case*

1. Background

    a. In September 1911, the body of a Christian child was found on the outskirts of Kiev, Russia.

    b. Police investigation showed that the child was murdered by a gang of thieves.

    c. An anti-Semitic campaign was launched by the Black Hundred blaming the Jews for killing the child, thus reviving accusations of ritual murder (see Chapter XXX, "Jewish Communities in Medieval Europe").

    d. Mendel Beilis was accused of the crime on the evidence that the dead child was last seen near a brick foundry where Beilis was a foreman.

    e. Protests were made to the Czar to stop this travesty of justice, but were of no avail.

2. The Trial

    a. In the trial, the prosecutor employed overt anti-Semitic remarks in his arguments and used the Talmud to substantiate his claim.

    b. The defense, nevertheless, disproved all evidence brought against Beilis.

    c. Beilis was acquitted and later moved to Israel, eventually settling in the United States.

G. *Conclusion*

Anti-Semitic outbursts in France and Russia illustrated to Europe's Jews that anti-Semitism was a fact and one hundred years of emancipation was not going to make it extinct. During the latter half of the nineteenth century, Jews began seeking radical alternatives to alleviate their condition. Many fled from Europe and settled in the United States, Canada, Argentina, South Africa, and other lands. Some saw revolutionary activities as a solution to the "Jewish Question" ; with the elimination of capitalism, anti-Semitism, which is a feature of this system, would also be eliminated. Some retreated into or rediscovered their Judaism. Others embraced the Zionist ideal of a Jewish state in Palestine.

XLI

THE ZIONIST DREAM

During the years of exile, the messianic hope for the restoration of the Jewish homeland in Palestine was kept alive through prayer, literature, and popular mass movements. With the failure of *Emancipation* (see Appendix D, "Glossary") to destroy the hostility toward the Jews of the Diaspora and the concurrent rise of modern European nationalism in the nineteenth century, the idea of the renewed Jewish homeland reappeared in concrete form. This time, however, the messianic hope did not die a premature death. The Jewish state conceived by Hess, Pinsker, Herzl, and other Zionist thinkers was to be built by men and not resurrected at some later date by a divine declaration. Their ideas formed the foundation of modern Zionism.

A. *Historical Background*

1. The nineteenth century brought a great improvement in the physical situation of west European Jews. They received political rights as citizens and made great strides in the fields of the arts, literature, philosophy, politics, business, and finance.

2. In the Russian Empire, which in the nineteenth century included Poland, Lithuania, and parts of southeastern Europe, Jews received limited civil rights during the reign of Czar Alexander II. A small segment of Jews entered the tiny class of educated people in Russia, while others enjoyed business success.

3. Many members of the revolutionary movements in Russia at the close of the nineteenth century included Jews like Leon Trotsky (Lev Bronstein, 1879-1940).

4. Despite attempts by Jews to assimilate through conversion or adoption of the native culture, anti-Semitism flourished.

5. With the assassination of Alexander II in Russia (1881) and the ascension of Czar Alexander III, the Russian Jews suffered from a series of anti-Jewish pogroms, massacres, and ritual murder trials, as well as retraction of many of their civil rights.

6. In Germany, Jewish civil rights were not really threatened, although it was almost impossible for a Jew to advance to a high position in the civil service or the military without conversion.

   a. By the end of the nineteenth century anti-Semitism and racism were very fashionable in some elements of German society.

   b. The Imperial Court chaplain, Adolf Stoecker, had a large following of anti-Semitic supporters in the Court and in other nationalistic groups.

   c. Influential scholars, journalists, and publicists, as well as the nationalist thinkers, cast their scorn upon Jews and Judaism.

7. In France, the Land of the "Enlightenment" where Jews had first been emancipated, Alfred Dreyfus (a Jewish officer on the Army General Staff) was convicted of treason on the basis of forged evidence (see Chapter XL, "Jewish Nightmares").

8. The resultant furor and anti-Semitic riots over the frame-up of Dreyfus were one of the catalysts for Theodor Herzl's book *Der Judenstaat* ("The Jewish State," 1896).

B. *Three Jewish Nationalistic Thinkers*

1. Moses Hess (1812-1875)

   a. In Moses Hess, we see all the nationalist trends which would later come to the fore in Zionist ideology.

   b. During his early years he had rejected Jewish tradition, being at different times in the socialist and anarchist camps.

   c. In 1842 he helped found the newspaper *Rheinische Zeitung* with Karl Marx and Friedrich Engels.

   d. Because of his participation in the abortive revolution of 1848, he was forced to flee from Germany.

   e. Taking refuge in Paris, he slowly returned to his Jewish roots and wrote a book *Rome and Jerusalem* (1862), which proposed Jewish national self-realization.

    (1) Hope in a political rebirth of the Jewish nation should be awakened and sustained.

    (2) As soon as political conditions in the Middle East would permit, colonization, financed with the help of Jewish businesses in France, should proceed.

f. For Hess, obedience to Jewish ceremonial law was the sign of Jewishness.

g. He wrote that all people of the Jewish *race* (he believed it was ethnic background, not citizenship or political belief, which made a people into a nation) were to be welcome to the new Jewish state.

h. Concerning the settlement of baptized Jews (those who had forsaken the foundation of Jewish life), Hess believed that once these stray Jews are in a homeland, they will find that the rigid forms necessary for the survival of Jewish national traditions will fall away, leaving a vital, spiritually revived Jewish tradition and culture.

i. Once this happens, these assimilated Jews will see how Jewish law is the source of all modern enlightenment and humanitarianism, the purest and finest expression of humanism.

j. Because of this humanism, the new Jewish homeland would have the just social order that socialism dreams of.

k. This state would be based on an agrarian economy. Everything (economics, social principles, laws) would flourish in accordance with Mosaic-socialistic principles.

l. Within this state, Jews could carry out their historical mission of bringing to the world the "Sabbath of history," a time of universal peace and justice.

2. Leo Pinsker (1821-1891)

a. While Hess was a relatively passive political theoretician, Leo Pinsker was more of an activist and propagandist, who succeeded in spreading the idea of Jewish nationalism among the people.

b. Pinsker was a doctor living in Odessa, Russia; he had been active in the Haskalah movement (see Chapter XXXVIII, "Haskalah").

c. Following the pogroms of 1881, he replaced his assimilationist beliefs with Jewish nationalism.

d. He expressed his new ideas in his pamphlet, *Auto-Emancipation*, published in 1881.

e. Pinsker had read *Rome and Jerusalem* and shared Hess's view that emancipation was insufficient to improve the Gentiles' opinion of the Jews; however, he went further than Hess.

    (1) Anti-Semitism is a psychopathic illness and Jews should not expect Gentiles to change their attitudes even with the emancipation and assimilation of the Jews.

    (2) Jews should not and could not expect help from Gentiles in founding a state.

    (3) Pinsker and Hess both believed that despite the Jewish desire to escape the suffering of European society, the new state would be a combination of Jewish and European culture.

    (4) They both saw the necessity of establishing a just society without private property in Palestine.

f. Pinsker was immediately attacked by Orthodox rabbis for having no religious basis for his nationalism and by liberals who criticized his lack of faith in human moral progress.

g. The publication of *Auto-Emancipation* placed Pinsker in contact with people desiring to create a Jewish homeland in Palestine.

h. In 1884, Pinsker became the head of the *Hibbat Zion* ("Lovers of Zion") movement, which was created in order to establish colonies in Palestine.

i. Because of interparty quarreling and lack of funds the organization slowly dissolved. However, the *Hibbat Zion* movement had a lasting effect among Zionist circles in Europe and Palestine.

3. Theodor Herzl (1860-1904)

   a. Theodor Herzl is regarded as the key figure in the early history of Zionism.

   b. Through the influence of one pamphlet and the results of tremendous organizational efforts, Herzl provided a permanent, lasting Zionist movement which exists to this day.

   c. Herzl came from an assimilated family; his father was a wealthy Budapest merchant who later moved to Vienna.

   d. He was a playwright and a literary editor of the Vienna newspaper *Neue Freie Presse*; in his writings he almost never discussed Jewish topics.

   e. An experience during his assignment as Paris correspondent for the paper, however, changed his stance toward Jewish topics.

      (1) While covering the Dreyfus trial in 1895, he became very sensitive to the anti-Semitic harangue of the French crowd.

      (2) As a result of the trial, he went through a period of reevaluation and in 1896 published his pamphlet *Der Judenstaat* ("The Jewish State"), which proposed the establishment of a political Jewish state.

   f. In this pamphlet, Herzl called anti-Semitism real, intolerable, and impossible to escape while living with the Gentiles.

   g. Yet, he claimed, amongst the anti-Semites there were reasonable men, and these reasonable men of the Gentile nations would see it in their interest and to their advantage to help provide a homeland for the Jews.

   h. The Jewish question was a national question, and the first thing to do was to establish it as an international political problem.

   i. The envisioned state would be a European, liberal, democratic type of state.

   j. This was a totally political conception; there was no talk of the racial nation or national mission as in *Rome and Jerusalem*.

k. *Der Judenstaat* ("The Jewish State") made a big impression on many readers. Many were drawn to Herzl's ideas while other considered him a madman.

l. In any case, Herzl spent the last years of his short life forming a viable movement for the Jewish settlement.

   (1) In August 1897, the First World Zionist Congress was called in Basle, Switzerland.

   (2) Eventually various Zionist periodicals such as *Die Welt* ("The World") and *Flambeau* ("Torch") were published.

   (3) A bank was founded (Anglo Palestine Company) and other organizational apparatus established.

m. As president of the World Zionist Congress, Herzl undertook many diplomatic efforts to gain recognition and land for the Jews in Palestine.

   (1) He met with Kaiser Wilhelm II of Germany, Von Plehve, the Russian Minister of Interior, and a representative of the Turkish sultan.

   (2) He also established contact with the French and English governments in order to espouse his views and gain guarantees for Jewish rights in Europe and Palestine.

n. Herzl did not meet with success, except when the British government offered a large parcel of land in Uganda for Jewish colonization.

o. When Herzl proposed Uganda to the Third Zionist Congress (1903), a storm of protest erupted which almost destroyed the movement; eventually the plan was dropped.

p. On July 3, 1904, Herzl died due to an aggravated heart condition and overwork. Forty-four years after his death, his dream of a Jewish state came to fruition.

C. *Intellectual Challenges Within Early Zionism*

1. Herzl had believed in a liberal, political solution because, as he wrote in *The Jewish State*, the Jews were a "bourgeois people" who were steeped in Western culture.

2. Herzl's conception of Zionism was from the perspective of an assimilated Jew.

3. Among the many thinkers who dealt differently with the problem of the Zionist movement were Bernard Lazare and Ahad Ha-am, who challenged political Zionism.

   a. Bernard Lazare (1865-1903)

      (1) Bernard Lazare's emphasis upon social justice as the foundation of a *secular* Jewish nation was later repeated by many who never heard of Lazare's name.

      (2) Lazare's conception of Jewish nationalism is important in that it represents the first socialistic challenge to Herzl's Zionist movement.

      (3) Lazare was a French author and literary critic. Advocating assimilation as the solution for the Jewish question, he preached a form of economic anti-Semitism.

      (4) His thinking was changed during the Dreyfus trial when he was hired by the Dreyfus family as a legal counsel and he helped uncover the anti-Semitic conspiracy.

      (5) He evolved into a Jewish nationalist, advocating a doctrine of Jewish nationalism that accused the wealthy and assimilated Jews of being traitors to their suffering brethren around the world.

      (6) Although he believed that Jews around the world were united by a common culture, tradition, and history, being a socialist, he adhered to the belief that religion was an antiquated relic of the past. For him, Judaism was justice and morality.

      (7) Despite the fact that he was a member of the Zionist Congress for several years and edited the Zionist periodical, *Flambeau*,

he was noncommittal about the idea of a homeland. He was personally more committed to defeating anti-Semitism in France.

(8) Toward the end of his short life he held that the Jewish nation would be one of many small groups within a coming European anarchist society and that the Jews would be the voice of justice and morality within this new social order.

(9) Before he could resolve the discrepancies and inconsistencies in his thought, he died of cancer at the age of 38. Some of his books are *Anti-Semitism, Job's Dungheap*, and *The Jews in Rumania*.

b. Ahad Ha-am (Asher Hirsch Ginsberg, 1856-1927).

(1) Careful colonization and spiritual rebirth were the keywords of Ahad Ha-am's Zionism.

(2) Asher Ginsberg, the "agnostic rabbi," was born in Russia and at an early age became involved in the Haskalah movement.

(3) His studies, both traditional and secular, led him to abandon his religious beliefs and practices.

(4) After the bloody anti-Jewish campaign of Czar Alexander III turned the young Ginsberg to Jewish nationalism, he joined Pinsker's Hibbat Zion movement.

(5) He soon became a critic of Hibbat Zion's hasty efforts at colonization; instead, he stressed an educational program to enlighten members so that when they could settle in Palestine it would be a more dedicated and enduring community.

(6) He began writing articles in Hebrew under the pen name of Ahad Ha-am, "one of the people."

(7) He was a brilliant critic who proposed an intellectual's solutions to the problem of rebuilding the Jewish nation; however, he was not always consistent in his philosophy.

(8) He belonged to organizations working for the settlement of Palestine, including Herzl's Zionist Congress, but he also wrote articles opposing this notion.

(9) He stated that before a mass Zionist community could be established, there must be "preparation of the hearts," an education of the national movement in attitudes and values.

(10) This colony must have a sense of sincere purpose and mission in settling in Palestine. Such an attitude would create a stronger and more successful state.

(11) The Jewish state would become a spiritual fountain of knowledge and strength for the Jews of the Diaspora and for the world as a whole.

(12) For orthodox Jews, the essence of Judaism was strict adherence to the law revealed by God and interpreted by the rabbis. For the agnostic Ahad Ha-am, the essence of Jewishness and the Jewish mission was "spirit," which he left undefined— spirit which was manifest in Jewish morality and the prophetic tradition.

(13) In "This is Not the Way" (1891) and in his later writings Ahad Ha-am stressed this moral code as central to a Jewish nationality.

D. Conclusion

Early Zionist thinkers tried to develop a secular, common bond of Jewish nationhood. Most rejected divine revelation and organized religion, thus forcing them to create a new and "different" form of Judaism. To many of these thinkers a reestablished Judaism would insure the success and growth of a homeland. They accepted the premise that assimilation had failed and that anti-Semitism was a reality of European society. To them the future of the Jewish people was not in Europe, but in a land they could call their own, Palestine.

THE REVIVAL OF THE HEBREW
LANGUAGE AND LITERATURE

The revival of the Hebrew language and literature was first attempted during the Haskalah period (see Chapter XXXVIII, "Haskalah"). For centuries Hebrew had been a written language (mostly religious-oriented writings); the language which was spoken by the Jews varied from place to place. During the Haskalah there was a renewed interest in Judaism and we see a simultaneous revival of the Hebrew language and literature along with a revival of the Yiddish language and literature (see Chapter XLII, "Yiddish Culture"). There was an urgent need to modernize the Hebrew language because biblical Hebrew was too outdated to express many of the new ideas and terminologies of the Maskilim. Hebrew writers of the nineteenth century coined new words, adopted from many current trends in European literature, translated works into Hebrew, and introduced many new ideas into the Jewish world.

A. *The Beginnings*

1. After the pogroms in Russia during the nineteenth century, many Jews settled in Palestine. Hebrew became the language of communication in Palestine between these Ashkenazic and Sephardic Jews, as it was the only language the two groups shared in common.

2. At this time, a number of foreign languages were spoken in Palestine, primarily German, Turkish, English, and French.

B. *The Father of Modern Hebrew*

1. Eliezer Ben Yehudah (born Eliezer Yitzhak Perlman, 1858-1922) dreamed of restoring Hebrew as a modern spoken language.

   a. Ben Yehuda published an article in the magazine *Havatzelet* ("Daffodil") in 1880, attacking the influence of foreign language in Palestine.

   b. He quit medical school in Paris and settled in Palestine in 1881.

   c. In 1883, he accepted a teaching position at an Alliance school in Jerusalem where he had Hebrew recognized, to some extent, as the medium for instruction.

    d. By 1888, all students in the Rishon le-Zion Jewish colony were taught in Hebrew.

2. Ben Yehuda faced massive obstacles in his task. For example, there were those skeptics who thought it impossible to adapt Hebrew for modern usage. Also there was opposition from the orthodox extremists who regarded Hebrew as too sacred for common usage.

3. Ben Yehuda is remembered for his selfless devotion to the revival of Hebrew. To illustrate his intensity of purpose, the story is often told how Eliezer refused to speak any language besides Hebrew in his home. The result, of course, was that the language of his family soon became Hebrew, thereby proving that the language could be used in familiar social intercourse.

C. *The Vaad ha-Lashon (The Language Committee)*

1. Vaad ha-Lashon, an important institution for the revival of Hebrew, was founded in Jerusalem in 1890 by such prominent men as Ben Yehuda, David Yellin, Hayyim Hirschenson, and A. M. Luncz.

2. The committee disbanded in 1891, but reorganized in 1904.

3. The task of the committee was to standardize the Hebrew spoken in Palestine.

4. In 1907, the committee declared that the Sephardic pronunciation of Hebrew was to be adopted as standard.

5. An important function of the committee was to coin new words whenever necessary.

D. *The Struggle for Acceptance of Hebrew as the Language of Palestine*

1. In 1912, when the Technion was founded in Haifa, there was a proposal to use German as the language of instruction in that institution and in the secondary schools in Palestine.

2. This proposal instigated a "war of languages," as there were other bodies who were pressing for the use of particular languages such as English and French.

3. Ben Yehuda persuaded Herbert Samuel (see Chapter XLIV, "Palestine: Turkey and Great Britain") to declare Hebrew as one of the official languages of the mandate.

4. Ultimately, Hebrew was accepted, and today is the official language of the State of Israel.

E. *The National Revival of Hebrew Literature*

1. By the 1880s a new period of Hebrew literature had begun, which was in many respects a reaction to the assimilatory features of the Haskalah.

2. This new form of Hebrew literature was imbued with a nationalism not very different from the various forms of nationalism which were popular in Europe.

3. Just as Hebrew writers of the Haskalah period were influenced by European Romanticism, so the Hebrew writers of the late nineteenth century adopted new trends in European literature such as naturalism and realism.

4. These new literary trends were based on a more realistic view of the world and were not clouded by the idealistic beliefs of the previous generation.

5. This shift of interest by many of the writers aided in the attempts to rehabilitate the Jewish communities of eastern Europe and to strengthen the Zionist movement, which was slowly gaining popularity

F. *Personalities*

1. Peretz Smolenskin (1842-1885) was one of the leading figures in the national revival of the Hebrew language.

   a. In 1869, he founded the monthly Hebrew journal *Ha-Shahar* ("The Dawn"), which was published in Vienna.

    b. He advocated an affirmation of Jewish nationalism that rejected assimilation and alienation from Judaism.

    c. In his writings he called for the return of the Jews to their roots— to Judaism and to Palestine.

    d. Smolenskin held an idealistic view of Jewish history.

        (1) The Jews were a nation which was united through history via the Hebrew language

        (2) Hebrew was the substitute for the land of Israel as long as they lacked a national state.

        (3) The Torah is not only a set of religious laws; rather, it is the stimulus for the spiritual and creative genius of the Jewish people.

    e. In *Ha-Toeh be Darkhei haHayyim* ("The Wanderer in the Paths of Life") he presented a kaleidoscope of Jewish life in eastern and western Europe.

    f. His numerous novels and essays attempted to express his views of trying to free Hebrew literature from what he believed was its antiquated Haskalah tendencies. He wanted to make Hebrew literature an end in itself rather than a means of conveying certain ideas.

2. Mendele Mokher Sefarim (Shalom Jacob Abramovitz, 1835-1917) wrote his novels and short stories in Hebrew, later translating them into Yiddish and vice versa.

    a. He was able to convey through his writings a description of a Jewish world which was economically and spiritually degenerating, yet was still able to retain its dignity.

b. Though many of his stories dealt with the poverty and misery of the Jews living in the Pale of Settlement, he was able to interject his sarcastic humor into his anecdotes and phraseology, thus allowing the reader to smile and laugh despite the wretched conditions.

c. Mendele's writing reflects a love for humanity and a firm belief in the eventual victory of justice. This conviction wasn't shaken even after the events in Russia at the end of the nineteenth century.

d. *Sefer ha-Kabtsanim* ("The Beggars' Book") is a tragic-comical narrative about the daily life of Jewish beggars in the *Shtetl*.

e. In *Masaot Binyamin haShlishi* ("Travels of Benjamin the Third") which is based on Cervantes' *Don Quixote*, the hero sets out on a quest for glory and adventure because he is bored with the present sterile condition.

f. In *Susati* (*Di Kliatshe*, or "The Nag"), Mendele uses the allegory of a beaten, overworked horse to symbolize the condition of the Jewish people.

3. David Frischmann (1839-1922) never allied himself with any of the contemporary currents in Jewish thought or literature. He was always the critic and objective observer, seldom taking upon himself the role of interpreter.

a. In *Ish U Miktarto* ("Man and his Pipe"), he describes a rabbi who is so addicted to his pipe that he profanes the Sabbath in order to smoke.

b. *Tithadesh* ("Wear it Well") is a story about a tailor's apprentice who succumbs to his inner desires and tries on the new suit he is supposed to deliver. The apprentice is caught and is dismissed from his position. The unemployed youth eventually dies in poverty.

c. *Ha-Mekoshesh* ("The Wood Gatherer") is based on the biblical story about the Israelite who was caught gathering wood on the Sabbath and is sentenced to death by stoning (cf. Num. 15:32-36).

G. *Conclusion*

Through the efforts of various scholars, authors, poets, and concerned individuals, the Hebrew language slowly transformed from a language used exclusively by rabbis and religious scholars into a "living" language of the people. The efforts of these Hebraists paid off, for by the beginning of the twentieth century, Hebrew was recognized and accepted as a modern language. The revival of Hebrew coincided with the revival of Yiddish, both being spawned by the Haskalah. Unfortunately, the rich Yiddish culture of eastern Europe eventually perished in the Holocaust, but Hebrew language and literature continued to grow and flourish in the land of Israel.

XLII

YIDDISH CULTURE

Yiddish is a spoken and written language derived from Middle High German (approximately 1200-1300 C.E.) and combined with Hebrew, Slavic, and other languages. It was the language used in everyday life among the Ashkenazic Jews of eastern and central Europe. Through the centuries, Hebrew remained the language of scholarship and prayer, while Yiddish became the everyday language of the masses. In the late nineteenth century a substantial literature developed, which became the core of a Yiddish culture that flourished until the Second World War and, to a considerable extent, still exists in the United States.

A. *Historical Background*

1. Although Yiddish culture flourished in the nineteenth and twentieth centuries, the language itself developed over many centuries.

   a. Yiddish appeared as a Judaeo-German dialect in the twelfth and thirteenth centuries.

   b. This language began to take on its present form with the migration of German Jews to eastern Europe. Many Slavic words and expressions were integrated into the language.

      (1) It was the abandonment of "Western" Judaeo-German in Germany which made the language particular to eastern Europe. In the West, the Jews adopted the vernacular in everyday speech.

      (2) Nevertheless, this "Western" Yiddish continued to be spoken in Jewish communities of Germany, the Netherlands, and France.

2. In response to the Russian Haskalah, a large body of secular Yiddish literature developed.

   a. Yiddish newspapers, publishing houses, and theatres flourished.

   b. Schools and institutes of higher learning were set up with Yiddish as the language of instruction.

3. In response to pogroms and persecutions in eastern Europe, thousands
   of Jews fled and established themselves in America (see Chapter
   XXXIX, "Jews in America").

   a. Despite the fact that English eventually displaced Yiddish as the
      language of most American Jews, a Yiddish literature and culture
      persisted and survives today.

   b. On the European continent, events took a different turn. Due to the
      efforts of both the Nazi and Communist regimes, only a small
      remnant of a Yiddish culture remains today in the Soviet Union and
      eastern Europe.

B. *Early Literature*

1. General Characteristics

   a. The bulk of the literature produced up to the 1860s was didactic in
      nature. Stories were aimed at raising the intellectual, cultural, and
      moral state of the people.

   b. Hebrew and German were traditionally accepted as language of
      elevated expressions of sentiments and ideas. Yiddish was
      considered the language of the masses and was looked down upon
      by many scholars and intellectuals.

2. Didactic Literature

   a. At the beginning of the nineteenth century, several *Maskilim*
      (advocates of the Haskalah movements) devoted themselves to the
      task of spreading secular knowledge among the people.

      (1) An early Maskil was Menahem Mendel Leffin (or Lewin)
          (1749-1826), who, for purposes of instruction, translated
          several books of the Bible into Yiddish. He also wrote popular
          Hebrew books on medicine, science, and ethics.

      (2) Heikel Hurwitz (c. 1750-1822) published a three-volume work
          written in Yiddish about the discovery of America entitled
          Tsofnas Paneakh ("Discovery of the Hidden Things").

   b. Most prevalent among the Haskalah writers were those who
      attacked the narrowness of Jewish education, religious piety, and

especially Hasidism, which they considered an extreme form of fanaticism. This approach was characteristic of Isaac Baer Levinsohn's work (1788-1860). Levinsohn, who was also known as a Hebrew author, wrote *Die Hefker Welt* ("World of Anarchy") in Yiddish as an expedient means to reach the masses. It is a play about the meeting of two leading Jews in a Russian community and a visiting Lithuanian Jew, in which the evils of the community are discussed.

3. Moral Fiction: Axenfeld, Ettinger, and Dick

    a. These authors wrote books which were more literary in style and content than those of earlier writers.

    b. While these authors had moral points to make, these points were made by means of plot movement rather than by polemical castigations.

    c. Israel Axenfeld (1781-1866) of Odessa wrote many novels in this style, as well as several melodramas with moralistic intent. His novels such as *Der Ershter Yiddisher Rekrut* ("The First Jewish Recruit") and his plays like *Die Genarte Welt* ("The Deceived World") are sentimental, moralistic, and shallow, with grotesque plots. These works present an exaggerated depiction of ghetto life.

    d. The works of Solomon Ettinger (1803-1856), which include his drama *Serkele*, published after his death, and his earlier volumes of fables, have a light, graceful style abundant with humor, which presents an idealistic view of the Haskalah movement.

    e. Isaac Meir Dick (1814-1893) of Vilna wrote many short stories which enjoyed great popularity. Dick's style was graceless, satirizing such familiar targets as the narrow scope of traditional Jewish education and forced marriage. His use of humor and the attention he gave to the tastes of his audience are noteworthy. He also wrote popular stories.

    C. *Yiddish Culture From the End of the Nineteenth Century*

1. General Characteristics

    a. The rise of Jewish nationalism helped to free Yiddish culture from the moral preachments of the Haskalah critics, in favor of positive action in order to strengthen Jewish culture, a culture in which the Yiddish language was an essential part.

b. This appreciation of the Jewish and Yiddish heritage can be seen in the works produced during this period.

c. The liberal policies of Czar Alexander II made living conditions slightly easier for the Jews of Russia and Poland, thus helping spread Yiddish culture. The writing of fiction improved in quality, newspapers gradually appeared, and new ideas slowly became popular and widespread among the masses.

2. I. L. Peretz

a. Novelist, dramatist, and socialist Isaac Leib Peretz (1852-1915) is one of the towering figures in Yiddish literature.

b. Peretz depicted the poverty of persons living in the Pale of Settlement. Through his writings he tried to draw out "the beauty of man and his soul" from the ugly world in which he was living. Unlike other Maskilim, he admired the Hasidic movement. He saw it as one method of liberating the Jew from his dismal environment.

c. In his writings, Peretz concerned himself with the individual as a distinct personality, rather than with society as a whole.

d. An intellectual, he championed the poor and became involved with the movement to make Yiddish, previously the folk language of the Jewish masses, into the language of all Jewry.

e. Although he was a Jewish nationalist, he was dissatisfied with the Zionist movement's purely political conception of the nation.

f. His early writings of the 1870s and 1880s attacked religious fanaticism and outworn religious and political beliefs. He used legend and folk story as the vehicles for his message.

(1) Among these early works are *The Golem, Die Frume Katz* ("The Pious Cat"), and *Der Brilliant* ("The Diamond").

(2) Peretz also concerns himself with hatred between men and the tragedy of poverty, as in *Die Fier-Farbige Lantern* ("The

Four-Colored Lantern"), *In Keler* ("In the Cellar"), and especially the story of the pitiful suffering of *Bontzye Schweig*.

g. At the turn of the century, Peretz began writing Hasidic stories. These stories stressed *nigun* (melody) as the harmony of the soul with God and life. Among these stories are *Mishnat Hassidim* ("The Teaching of Hassidim"—in Hebrew), *Zwischen Zwei Berg* ("Between Two Mountains"), and *A Gilgul fun a Nigun* ("The Metamorphosis of a Melody").

3. Shalom Aleichem (1859-1916)

   a. Shalom Rabinovich wrote under the pen name "Shalom Aleichem," Hebrew for "peace be with you," a common greeting used by Jews.

   b. Rabinovich is best remembered for his humorous and sentimental stories such as *Tevye der Milchiger* ("Tevye the Dairyman"), which was the inspiration for the Broadway musical *Fiddler on the Roof, Motl Peyse dem Hazon's* ("Motl the Son of Cantor Peyse"), and the *Menahem Mendel* stories. In these stories, the Jewish condition in the *shtetls*, the small villages of Russia, are treated with self-mocking irony and humor, and fantastic plotting, yet are at the same time realistic depictions of the life of the Jews of Russia and Poland. Tragedy is at the heart of all these stories, the subject matter being pogroms, poverty, and persecutions. Rabinovich's irony and humor reflect an optimism and an inward power in the Jews to overcome this harsh environment.

   c. Shalom Aleichem wrote a large number of plays, mostly comedies. It is generally believed that they are not of the high caliber of his short stories.

   d. He was also the publisher of the literary annual *Die Yiddishe Folksbibliotek* ("The Jewish People's Library"), the first literary venture of its kind in Yiddish. In it were published the works of many young, unknown writers, among them was I. L. Peretz.

4. Yiddish Journalism and Politics

   a. *Die Yiddishe Folksbibliotek*, inaugurated in 1888, was not only a vehicle of expression for young writers, but a forum for articles, essays, and criticisms.

b. Periodicals of this type had existed before, but were less organized and widespread.

c. Other periodicals appeared after the publication of *Die Yiddishe Folksbibliotek*. Among them were I. L. Peretz's *Der Yiddishe Bibliotek* ("The Jewish Library") and *Der Yiddisher Folksblatt* ("The Jewish People's Paper"), first appearing in the 1880s. They were filled with stories written for popular taste and articles of varied topics, including pre-Herzl Zionism. Indeed, these journals could not keep themselves aloof from political developments, for language and culture were becoming issues of a newly awakened Jewish nationalism.

d. In 1897, the Bund (Jewish Worker's League) was formed in Vilna by Jewish socialists.

(1) Yiddish was used as the language to politicize the Jewish workers of the Russian Empire because most of the Jews understood Yiddish.

(2) They agitated among the Jewish workers and staged many successful strikes.

(3) In 1904, the Bund walked out of the Second Congress of Russian Social Democrats in London where their demand for the autonomy of the Bund within the Russian Social Democratic Party was rejected.

(4) This rejection by the Russian Social Democrats spurred a rebirth of Jewish nationalism and demands for Jewish cultural autonomy as part of Bundist ideology.

(5) Because of the success of the Bolshevik Revolution the Bund eventually declined. However, in interwar Poland, the Bund played an important role within the Jewish community.

D. *Yiddish Culture in the United States*

1. General Characteristics

a. As in eastern Europe, there were two stages in the development of Yiddish culture in the United States.

(1) The first period extended form the beginning of the great immigration of the 1880s until approximately 1905. Very little creative literature was written, and most Yiddish writing was in a journalistic style (see Chapter XXXIX, "Jews in America").

(2) The second period, which tapered off after World War II, saw the quality of the literature improve, with Yiddish poetry becoming popular. This was a literary form which did not flourish in Europe.

b. The element of social reform and socialist tendencies appeared earlier in American Yiddish literature than in the European, largely because many of the poor immigrants were put to work in the oppressive sweatshops of New York soon after their arrival.

c. Over the years, Yiddish culture had gradually died out because of the assimilation of Jews into the American society, public education, and mass communication, and the increasing affluence among large numbers of Jews.

2. The First Period

a. The 1880s saw a massive migration of Jews from eastern Europe. The vast majority of these Jews, being extremely poor and unskilled, earned their livelihood by working as laborers in such trades as the clothing industry and peddling.

b. There was a large Jewish urban proletariat; many socialistic and anarchistic ideas became very popular among the workers.

c. Between 1886 and the end of the next decade, many Yiddish newspapers were published, among them the *Arbeiter Zeitung* ("Worker's Newspaper"), *Die Freie Arbeiter Shtimme* ("The Free Worker's Voice"), and *The Abendblatt* ("The Evening Paper"). Only *Der Forverts* ("The Forward"), founded in 1897 by Abraham Kahan, still exists today.

(1) Along with articles on current events, science, sociology, and the inevitable political polemics, came the fictional prose and poetry of the new immigrants.

(2) The fiction was often melodramatic, usually with strong social indictments. It often reflected ideas found in the writings of such novelists as Emile Zola, Leo Tolstoy, and Upton Sinclair.

(3) Authors who wrote this kind of fiction for the workers' press were I. Hurwitz (1872-1955), who wrote under the pen name of Z. Libin and who depicted lurid scenes of poverty and sweat shops, and Leon Kobrin (1873-1946), whose stories *Yankel Boile* and *Wos Is Er* ("What Is He") dealt with the preservation of Jewishness in the face of assimilation and class war.

d. The beginnings of an American Yiddish poetry date from this period, and include the works of David Edelstadt (1866-1892) and Morris Rosenfeld (1862-1923).

(1) Edelstadt's poetry, exemplified by his long poem, *Mein Zawoeh* ("My Testament"), is not of a very high standard, but is, nevertheless, a good example of the type of proletarian protest poetry which was popular at the turn of the century.

(2) Rosenfeld was a proletarian poet, reflecting life as he found it; e.g., *Die Sweat Shop*. His poetry was much more lyrical than the other Yiddish poets of his time. His interest moved outside the factory, as seen in his tragic poems, *Zu A Borweser Meidele* ("To a Barefoot Girl") and *Bei Die Horwes fun Delancy Street* ("On the Ruins of Delancy Street"), and his nationalistic poems, *Der Eibiger Funk* ("The Eternal Spark") and *Der Iddisher Mai* ("The Jewish May").

3. The Second Period

a. After the turn of the century, the poverty of the immigrant Jews abated to an extent, and the immigrants became more attuned to American life and customs. Accordingly, socialist propaganda became less intense. However, Jews did not forsake socialism, and an abiding and active interest in labor movements persisted.

b. In fiction, the historical novel appeared: *In Poilishe Velder* ("In the Polish Woods") and *Hebrew* by Joseph Opatoshu (1886-1954). Psychological insights and personal struggles began to enter into novels such as *Der Zurissiner Mensch* ("The Beaten Man") by

David Pinski (1872-1959). This novel deals with the relations between wealthy Jews during the First World War.

c. In time, the proletarian poems became scarcer; however, there was an increase in the number of Yiddish poetic themes dealing with such diverse topics as grief, communion with nature, love, life in America, and contemplation of beauty. Among the major poets in the twentieth century were Solomon Bloomgarden (1870-1927) who used the pen name Yehoash, Abraham Liessin (1872-1938), and H. Leivick (pseudonym, Leivick Halpern, 1886-1962).

d. Yiddish journalism expanded and daily Yiddish newspapers were published in such American cities as New York, Chicago, and St. Louis.

(1) *Der Forverts* ("The Forward") expanded its circulation and influence during the first three decades of this century under the editorship of Abraham Kahan (1860-1951). It originally published economic essays by M. Zametkin and K. Forenberg and anti-religious socialist polemics by Philip Kranz and Benjamin Feigenbaum. Today, it has taken a more nationalistic stand and is a supporter of the State of Israel. It still publishes Yiddish novels in serial form by such authors as I. B. Singer and Chaim Grade.

(2) Gedaliah Bublik's *Yiddishes Tageblatt* (New York) and M. Katz's *Iddisher Courier* (Chicago) flourished during the first half of the century, publishing essays on Jewish nationalism, problems in adjustment to modernity, and other matters directly or indirectly affecting Jews.

e. Some essayists and critics published outside the periodicals. Two such writers were Baruch Rivkin, author of *Die Grendendenzen fun der Literatur in America* ("The Fundamental Tendencies of Yiddish Literature in America"), and William Nathanson, who set out to popularize philosophy and Western literature for the Yiddish-speaking masses in *Kultur un Zivilizazie* ("Culture and Civilization") and *Intelligenz, Kunst un Kinstler* ("Intelligence, Art, and Artists").

f. With the immigration quotas of the 1920s and the rapid assimilation into American society, Yiddish culture as a separate entity began to die a gradual death. Although *Der Forverts* is still being published, most of the Yiddish newspapers in this country are now defunct. The only sizable groups of people speaking Yiddish as their everyday tongue are in New York, Buenos Aires, Paris, the Soviet Union, and Israel.

g. Though the number of Yiddish speakers has declined, there has been a resurgence of interest in Yiddish in the last few years.

   (1) Scholarly work in the field of Yiddish linguistics, literature and culture is carried on at the YIVO Institute for Jewish Research in New York and in other institutions around the world.

   (2) Yiddish language and literature courses are being offered by many universities.

   (3) Jewish student groups have published Yiddish magazines and news sheets.

E. *Yiddish Culture in the Soviet Union*

1. Background

a. The success of the Bolsheviks in the Russian Revolution of 1917 ushered in a new era for Yiddish culture.

b. The *Yevsektsiya* (Jewish section of the Communist Party) was created in 1918, its function being to propagandize the ideals of the revolution to the Jewish masses.

   (1) Yiddish became the official language of the Soviet Jews, whereas Zionism and Hebrew, initially supported by the government, were later suppressed.

      (a) Hayyim Nahman Bialik and Saul Tschernichowsky left Russia (see Chapters XLIVa and XLIVb, "Bialik" and "Tschernichowsky") to settle in Israel.

      (b) The Habimah Theatre Company was established in 1917, but later left Russia in 1926. It reestablished itself in Israel.

(2) Religious life was crushed, yeshivot were closed down, religious customs such as circumcision were banned, and many religious leaders were imprisoned.

c. Achievements of the Russian Revolution

(1) A Yiddish school system was established throughout the Soviet Union.

(2) The government gave financial support for Yiddish newspapers and journals, which helped propagandize the new doctrines of the regime among the Jews.

(3) Jewish theatre companies were established and supported with government money.

(4) Faculties for Jewish culture were introduced in various Soviet universities.

(5) Courts of law were set up that were conducted in Yiddish.

(6) The Soviet government established Birobidzhan as an autonomous Jewish state in 1928. Thousands of Jews came to settle there, but most left because of harsh conditions.

d. Purges and the War Years

(1) During the purges of the 1920s and 1930s many Jewish institutions were closed and thousands of Jews were imprisoned or executed.

(a) These purges were not specifically anti-Semitic.

(b) This was an attempt to eliminate all opposition to the regime. As it turned out, many of these opponents happened to be Jewish.

(c) Many Jews had supported Leon Trotsky or were affiliated with the Mensheviks and other parties which had opposed the Bolsheviks before the revolution.

   (2) World War II brought about the destruction of the major areas of Jewish settlement in western Russia (see Chapter XLVI, "The Holocaust").

   (3) The Jewish Antifascist Committee was created in order to propagandize the Soviet Cause in the Western world. Notable Soviet personalities, such as the actor Shlomo Mikhoels, the poet Itzhak Fefer, and the writer Ilya Ehrenberg, were involved in this group.

e. "Black Years," 1948-1952

With the advent of the Cold War, Jews were singled out for being supporters of the West because of the "international," "cosmopolitan" nature of the Jewish people.

   (1) The Jewish Antifascist Committee was dissolved.

   (2) The Yiddish press and other Yiddish cultural institutions were closed down.

   (3) Major Soviet Jewish personalities were imprisoned or executed.

   (4) On August 12, 1952, thirty Yiddish writers and poets were executed.

f. Soviet Union Today

   (1) The condition of Soviet Jewry improved slightly after the death of Stalin in 1953.

   (2) However, the Soviet government hasn't as yet reestablished Yiddish schools or revived Yiddish cultural institutions to any extensive degree.

   (3) The relations between the Soviet Union and Israel and the Arab states have had repercussions on the treatment of Soviet Jewry.

   (4) Following the Six-Day War, there has been a revival of Jewish life which has precipitated the demands by many Soviet Jews to emigrate to Israel.

2. Personalities

a. David Bergelson (1884-1952) was a novelist, poet, dramatist, and journalist who originally wrote both in Hebrew and Yiddish. After the revolution he adapted his writing style to the demands of socialist realism. He was among the Yiddish writers executed on August 12, 1952.

b. Shlomo Mikhoels (1890-1948) was a prominent actor and director of the Moscow State Jewish Theatre. During World War II, he was chairman of the Jewish Antifascist Committee. He was considered to be the spokesman of Soviet Jewry and traveled in the United States, Canada, and Mexico in order to gain support for the Soviet Union. On January 13, 1948, he was killed in a car accident. It was later revealed that this was a political assassination.

c. Peretz Markish (1895-1952) was a prominent Yiddish poet. He wrote such epic poems as *Milkhome* ("War") which described the horrors of the Holocaust. His poetry describes life in the Soviet Union, praising the success of industrialization, collectivization, and the achievements of Stalin. Markish was among the Yiddish poets and writers executed on August 12, 1952.

d. Itzhik Fefer (1900-1952) was a Soviet Yiddish poet. In his poem *Stalin* he praises the achievements of the Soviet leader. In his poem *Ich bin a Yid* ("I Am a Jew") he reaffirms his loyalty to his people. During World War II he was cochairman of the Jewish Antifascist Committee. He was also executed on August 12, 1952.

e. Aaron Vergelis (1918-   ) is a Yiddish poet and journalist who was raised in Birobidzhan. He is presently the editor of the *Sovietisch Heimland* ("Soviet Homeland"), which is a Yiddish literary monthly that began publication in 1961. Vergelis is considered to be the official Soviet spokesman on all issues concerning Soviet Jewry.

F. *Conclusion*

Yiddish culture is a folk culture which catered towards the spiritual and emotional needs of the Jews of eastern Europe. It was secular in nature, concerning itself with daily life and political activity. It was also a language of scholars and academicians. YIVO (Institute for Jewish Research), which was originally established in Vilna and relocated in New York after World War II, is involved in researching the myriad areas of Yiddish culture, literature, history, demography, linguistics, and folklore. Though the number of people speaking Yiddish has declined because of genocide and assimilation, there has been a renewed interest in keeping alive and spreading this important component of Jewish cultural history.

XLIII

HAYYIM NAHMAN BIALIK

One of the features of the Haskalah movement was the revival of the Hebrew language and literature. Among the most widely read of the modern Hebrew poets was Hayyim Nahman Bialik, who displayed a thorough command of the Hebrew language. Bialik was able to liberate Hebrew poetry from many of its biblical influences and to create a modern form of Hebrew poetry. He was one of the first Hebrew poets to use the prose form of Hebrew poetry and to experiment with Sephardic Hebrew in contrast to the Ashkenazic Hebrew of eastern Europe. The extent of his achievement is still being measured by literary scholars who find it difficult to reduce his genius to textual criticism. Bialik was not only capable of poignant personal poetic expression, but was inspired to tackle more general issues concerning Jewish life in the Diaspora and in Palestine. Often referred to as the "National Jewish Poet," Bialik is still widely read by students, school children, the man in the street, and members of literary circles.

A. *Life*

1. Early Years

   a. Bialik was born in 1873 in Radi, a small village in the Ukraine, Russia.

   b. The first six years of his life were happily spent admiring and exploring the natural surroundings.

   c. When he was six, Bialik's family moved from Radi to a suburb near Zhitomir, where the father, who had been unable to support the family of seven children as a forest clerk, operated an inn and tavern.

   d. Bialik was sent to *heder* (a one-room religious school), leaving him little time to enjoy the outdoor activities he so loved.

   e. When the child was seven, his father, broken by poverty and misfortune, died, leaving his family penniless.

   f. Bialik's mother peddled in the marketplace all day and knitted stockings at night in order to support her children.

   g. The burden was too heavy for her and she was forced to send Bialik to live with his grandfather, a learned talmudist. The stern grandfather did not understand the boy and the two did not get along well.

2. Middle Years

   a. The next ten years that Bialik spent at his grandfather's home were miserable, but it was there that his ideology developed. He studied the Talmud, the Kabbalah, the philosophical works of Judah Halevi and Maimonides, and other sacred writings. He also read the forbidden modern Hebrew books, which inspired his first attempts to express himself in writing.

   b. At the age of sixteen, Bialik had a chance to escape from his grandfather's home when he was sent to a yeshiva (talmudical academy) at Volozhin, near Vilna.

   c. At the yeshiva he soon joined a secret group called *Nezakh-Israel* ("Eternity of Israel"). These were students who tried to synthesize Jewish nationalism, Haskalah, and orthodoxy.

   d. The more Bialik read the "enlightened" literature, the more he became convinced that there must be a different life somewhere, a life of activity and meaning.

3. Later Years

   a. After a short stay at the yeshiva, Bialik left for Odessa, the center of new Jewish learning.

   b. There he met Ahad Ha-am and Yehoshua Ravnitsky, two leading figures in the Haskalah.

   c. Ahad Ha-Am and Ravnitsky were impressed by Bialik's poetry and helped him publish his first poem *El ha-Zippor* ("To the Bird"), which appeared in *Pardes*, a Hebrew literary magazine in 1892.

   d. A few years after the Russian Revolution, Bialik left Russia and settled in Berlin.

e. In 1921, he established the Hebrew publishing house, Dvir.

f. In 1924, Bialik moved to Palestine. There he directed the activities of Dvir, by then the world's largest Hebrew publishing house.

g. His poetic productivity decreased, and he became involved in collecting anthologies of Jewish literature and translating classics from foreign languages into Hebrew.

h. He also wrote folksongs, children's jingles, and folk legends.

i. In 1934, at the age of sixty-one, Bialik died in Vienna. Bialik had been recognized as the Hebrew "poet laureate" of the twentieth century.

B. *Ideology*

1. Bialik grew up in strict Orthodox surroundings. Though he escaped from this environment, he never abandoned traditional Judaism and was always close to the Jewish people. Like Ahad Ha-Am, Bialik believed that the old ways must be changed and yet assimilation must be avoided. A middle way was needed.

2. This idea was the driving force behind modern Jewish literary trends, Hebrew culture, Jewish nationalism, and Zionism. Bialik was one of the major figures in this movement. He devoted his writing to the development of modern Jewish life.

3. Unlike many writers before him, Bialik was not caught between the opposing forces of the Haskalah and traditional Judaism. For though he sought enlightenment and later renounced some of his religious beliefs, he had no bitterness toward Judaism—only love and admiration.

C. *Literary Traits*

1. In addition to folk songs, short stories, and legends, Bialik wrote a vast amount of poetry in Hebrew and Yiddish. Though his themes varied, his major works can be classified into three general categories: poems of woe and suffering, poems of hope and rebellion, and poems of nature.

   a. The poems of woe and suffering are highly autobiographical. These poems deal with Bialik's childhood, which was one of misery and poverty, and his adolescence, a period when Bialik was trapped in the monotony of the heder and yeshiva. The poems are personal, yet mirror the collective experience of the Jewish people of that time and place. Tears, widowhood, orphanage, poverty, and national decay were common elements in the lives of many eastern European Jews at the turn of the century.

   b. In the poems of hope and rebellion Bialik, the nationalist, emerges. He praises the Jewish people's determination and stamina in the face of a hostile environment, and at the same time rebukes them for not rallying to the support of Zionism and for not attempting to defend themselves from anti-Semitic attackers. In these poems Bialik bewails the plight of his people and wonders when better days will come. As a result of the influence exerted on Jewish youth by these poems, self-defense groups were organized in Russia.

   c. The nature poems, written after the turn of the century, recall Bialik's early childhood, before his spirit was stifled by the heder. They describe the days when he used to spend many hours in the forests, communing with nature. Bialik praises the joy and beauty of nature and often contrasts it to the monotony and gloominess of heder and yeshiva. In later life, he remarked that the only period in his life during which he was completely happy was his early childhood, when he and nature were companions.

   d. Few writers before or after Bialik have had such a complete and thorough command of the Hebrew language. Bialik's use of biblical and liturgical expressions in his poetry and short stories and his appealing style make him the most well-known and popular Hebrew poet.

D. *Major Works*

Bialik's literary output was extensive and varied and many of his poems are considered literary masterpieces.

  1. *El ha-Zippor* ("To the Bird")

   a. This poem, written while Bialik was a student in the Volozhin yeshiva, was his first published work.

b. In this poem, Bialik talks to a bird, who, upon returning from Israel, has come to sing at his window. Bialik asks the bird to tell him stories and news from Israel. He asks her about the valleys, the hills and mountains, the Jordan River, and about his brothers who are working the soil.

c. Bialik contrasts the freedom of Israel with the misery of Russia. He is wondering if his brothers in Israel, who are so happy, realize that he is full of sorrow and that troubles pursue him.

d. The poem ends with Bialik's realization that lamentations and tears will not heal his sorrow, and he requests the bird to sing again.

e. Upon its appearance the poem immediately became popular, for Bialik's longing to return to Israel was shared by thousands of his fellow Jews.

2. *Ha-Matmid* ("The Talmud Student")

a. In this poem, one of his best known narrative pieces, Bialik lashes out at the restrictiveness and narrowness of the yeshiva and its suffocation of the spirit of Jewish students.

b. The poem describes the daily life of a yeshiva student who for six years, from before dawn till late at night, studies the Talmud. In his solitude, he never realizes or enjoys the beauty of nature. The student stands in his dark corner for hours with his only friends: his stand, his candle, and his Talmud.

c. Swaying back and forth, chanting the verses aloud, the student dreams of the day when he will be a great rabbi and will return to his home to be greeted by the proud smiles of his parents and friends.

d. Bialik expresses his sympathy for the student questioning the value of these years of sacrifice. Still, Bialik feels a sense of love and pride toward this student, comparing him to a nail rooted in its place, and his spiritual strength to granite.

e. Bialik ends this poem with regret over such a waste: "A seed that is withered in its soil."

3. *Mete Midbar* ("The Dead of the Wilderness")

    a. This poem, Bialik's great historical narrative, is considered by many to be his literary masterpiece.

    b. It is based on a legend in the Talmud which tells that, because of their rebelliousness against God, the generation of the Exodus perished in the desert and lie sleeping in the sand.

        (1) The first part of the poem describes the dead nation. It is an army of giants, clad in armor and ready for battle. Their faces and breasts are bronze and solid as anvils, and from their heads tangled manes of hair and matted beards flow.

        (2) The second part describes the effect of the splendor of those in the desert. So magnificent is their silent pride and rage that the eagle, the serpent, and the lion, poised for attack, retreat from this solemn scene.

        (3) In the third part of the poem, the giants resurrect and rebel against God's decree of eternal sleep. "To Arms!" they roar; "We are the mighty! The last generation of slaves and the first generation of freemen," they say as they march to battle, the desert about them a raging storm.

        (4) In the conclusion, the storm ceases and the desert is silenced. Vanquished, the giants once more lie in the desert, again to become a legend.

    c. A significant aspect of this poem is Bialik's magnificent description of the desert and its animals.

4. *Be-Ir ha-Harega* ("In the City of Slaughter")

    a. This poem was written after the pogrom (an organized massacre directed against Jews) of Kishinev in 1903 during which forty-seven Jews were killed and two thousand Jewish families were displaced.

    b. Bialik was sent by the Jewish community of Odessa to report on the pogrom.

c. After his return he wrote this long narrative, one of the most bitter and vehement poems ever written in Jewish literature.

   (1) The first part of the poem is a chilling description of the gruesome scenes at the aftermath of the pogrom: Spattered blood and dried brains, piles of bodies and limbs, a babe clinging to the cold breast of its dead mother, a Jew and his dog—both beheaded—are but a few scenes of the horror. The description is a tearless one, yet full of grief and rage.

   (2) The second and longer part of the poem is a bitter chastisement of the Jews who "fled like mice and died like dogs." Bialik lashes out at the "sons of the Maccabees" who lay hidden as they watched their wives, daughters, and lovers being defiled by the murderers.

d. Never before has a poem had such an enormous effect on a whole people. As a direct result of this stinging invective and condemnation, Jewish self-defense groups were organized in eastern Europe, and in subsequent pogroms and attacks, Jewish blood was not spilled as easily as in Kishinev.

5. *Ha-Brekha* ("The Pond")

a. This is generally considered to be Bialik's outstanding nature poem. It is a description of a pond in the middle of the forest which is described in four different phases: during the morning, under the moonlight, in a storm, and at dawn.

b. In the second part of the poem, Bialik reflects upon the natural beauty of the pond and its surroundings. He sees two worlds: the real world and the one reflected in the pond; it is while sitting near the pond that he understands its language of beauty.

c. This poem, which is heralded for its superb imagery and unusually detailed descriptions, is a record of Bialik's memories of the times when, as a child, he wandered through those woods and sat by that same pond.

6. *Shirati* ("My Song")

    a. This is one of Bialik's most touching autobiographical poems. It is here that we may find the personal source of much of the sadness in his poetry.

    b. The poem is a description of the poverty and hardships of Bialik's home during childhood. It tells of hunger, of the gloomy spirit in which the Sabbath was celebrated, of cold winter nights, and of the father feeling guilty about his poverty, yet unable to do anything.

    c. The second part of the poem describes Bialik's mother at the time she was widowed. This very moving description portrays his mother as a weak yet determined woman, gathering up her strength in order to support her family. From dawn till midnight she labored at the marketplace and at home. The sight of his mother suffering had a great effect on his life.

    d. At the end of the poem Bialik symbolically divulges the source of the melancholy in his songs. In the morning, when his mother baked bread for her children, a tear fell into the dough. Later when Bialik ate the bread, he swallowed the tear, and his mother's sigh became a part of him.

7. Bialik also wrote folk songs, children's poems, legends, and short stories.

    a. His folk songs involve such themes as a young woman in search of her lover. Most of these songs were written in Israel and incorporate the natural beauty of the country.

    b. The children's poems view the world as a child would see it— simply and sincerely and full of wonder.

    c. Most of Bialik's short stories are based on childhood memories, and some are semi-autobiographical. They tell about Jewish life in eastern Europe: poverty, ghetto life, relationships with the Gentile neighbors, and daily incidents. Some of the stories convey a feeling of sorrow and pity, while others are humorous.

    d. Bialik translated Schiller's *William Tell*, Cervantes's *Don Quixote*, and Anski's *Dibbuk* into Hebrew. These translations exhibit a rich style.

e. Along with his colleague Y. Ravnitsky, Bialik edited and published the *Book of Legends*, a collection of legends from the Mishnah, and books with a collection of the poetry and writings of Solomon Ibn Gabirol and Moses Ibn Ezra.

E. *Conclusion*

Bialik was and still is the national Jewish poet. His poetry reflects the feelings of the Jewish people, the common experience of a whole nation. His poetry is read widely in Jewish as well as in non-Jewish circles. Bialik's personality evoked and earned him the adoration and love of his people. The eminence he attained and influence he exerted in his own lifetime have persisted even to this day.

SAUL TSCHERNICHOWSKY

Saul Tschernichowsky is considered along with Hayyim Nahman Bialik to be among the most popular of the modern Hebrew poets. Tschernichowsky, who was very much concerned with the aesthetic form and structure of his poetry, adopted many literary techniques and ideas from Hellenistic and European literature and culture. His poems and translations of other authors and poets have been widely read. Tschernichowsky hoped to revitalize what he considered to be a decaying Jewish culture. He wanted to create a "new Jew" who was an heir to the Maccabees and Zealots of old. He was attracted to the Zionist movement and saw in it the path towards the resurrection of the Jewish people.

A. *Life*

1. Early Years

    a. Saul Tschernichowsky was born in 1875 in the village of Mikhailovka, Russia.

    b. His parents, though Orthodox Jews, were influenced by the Haskalah movement and Saul grew up under its influence.

    c. In his childhood, Tschernichowsky was tutored in Russian and Hebrew. His early education included sacred as well as secular literature, and he was especially fond of the poetry of Micah Joseph Lebenson (see Chapter XXXVIII, "Haskalah").
    d. Tschernichowsky was an avid reader of the Greek classics and Shakespearean plays; he also was interested in the natural sciences.

    e. At the age of fourteen, Tschernichowsky left home to enroll at the High School of Commerce in Odessa. There he was introduced to the Hebrew literary circles and a few of his poems were published in various Hebrew periodicals.

2. Later Years

    a. In 1898, the first collection of Tschernichowsky's poetry was published.

b. The years between 1899 and 1903 were spent in Heidelberg, Germany, where Tschernichowsky studied medicine. It was there, too, that he met his future wife, a Polish Christian.

c. From 1903 to 1910, Tschernichowsky practiced medicine in rural Switzerland and Russia, writing many poems and idylls about the local Jewish populace.

d. In 1910, Tschernichowsky moved to St. Petersburg where he practiced medicine.

e. In 1914, he was drafted into the Russian army to become a military physician.

f. The postwar years were difficult ones for Tschernichowsky because the Russian Revolution had a detrimental effect on Jewish life, especially on Hebrew literature.

g. In 1922, Tschernichowsky left Russia and settled in Berlin. Unable to practice medicine, he devoted most of his time to translating classics into Hebrew and writing original works.

h. In 1931, Tschernichowsky settled in Palestine where he worked as a public school physician.

i. An ardent nationalist, Tschernichowsky was politically active and wrote several poems protesting British policies. He also edited a medical dictionary, and in 1942 published a book of children's tales.

j. He was honored several times during this period. He represented the Hebrew branch of the P. E. N. Club (International Association of Poets, Playwrights, Editors, Essayists and Novelists).

k. On October 13, 1943, Tschernichowsky died at the age of 68.

B. *Ideology*

Tschernichowsky's ideology can be characterized as a nationalistic universalism. He was a lover of nature, beauty, and life; an admirer of strength and glory; and a firm believer in the freedom of the spirit and the faith of many.

1. Tschernichowsky glorified and admired the culture of the early Greeks.

    a. He believed that the early Hebrews and Greeks had much in common, and therefore identified strongly with the early Hebrews, the generation of the Exodus, and the conquerors of Canaan. He believed that the true Jewish God is the God of war, the conquering God who led his children to victories against their enemies.

    b. Despite the gap between the two cultures, he wanted to synthesize Judaism with Hellenism, and attempted to bring about rapprochement between the two.

2. Tschernichowsky was opposed to the contemporary state of Judaism.

    a. He felt that it stifled the spirit of the Jew, and that the form of Judaism that existed in his day was not what God or the early Hebrews had desired.

    b. Nevertheless, unlike many of his predecessors and contemporaries, Tschernichowsky did not strongly rebuke the Jews for their way of life. Quite the opposite, he idealized their lifestyle with love and tenderness in many of his narratives.

3. Tschernichowsky was an ardent nationalist and Zionist and a believer in the spirit of pioneering.

    a. He cried out for revenge against the oppressors of the Jews; in his later years in Palestine he was a supporter of the policy of retaliation against Arab attacks.

    b. As an admirer of the early Hebrews, Tschernichowsky believed that the true Jewish character should be in the spirit of the Maccabees and the Zealots, who fought for their rights and independence.

C. *Literary Traits*

1. Tschernichowsky's poems and stories were written in Hebrew.

    a. Because his knowledge of religious literature was limited compared to many of his contemporaries, his writing took on a new and different form.

b. He wrote in a revolutionary style, utilizing few biblical and liturgical phrases, and replacing them with many of the new words which were being introduced into the Hebrew language.

2. Tschernichowsky, who has been given the esteemed title "the first modern Hebrew poet," was a great innovator in Hebrew poetry. He was familiar with the forms and meters of Greek literature and incorporated them in his poetry.

   a. Though many sonnets had been written by Hebrew poets before Tschernichowsky, he was the most original Hebrew sonneteer.

   b. Many of his early sonnets use the nature motif. Tschernichowsky wrote many ballads whose themes are based mostly on Jewish history and legends. Especially interesting are the ballads which he wrote about King Saul, whom he admired greatly. Tschernichowsky's ballads also deal with Jewish martyrdom through the ages; the Crusades, the Black Death, the massacres of the sixteenth and seventeenth centuries, and the Russian pogroms.

   c. Tschernichowsky is best known for his idylls, which were his favorite form of poetry. Modeling himself after Homer, Tschernichowsky introduced the idyll into Hebrew literature. His idylls are, for the most part, serene and calm, describing Jewish life in southern Russia. There, Jew and Gentile live in peace and harmony. The idylls describe the melancholy, moody landscapes of the Crimean steppes.

3. Tschernichowsky's literary output was quite extensive and varied. He was a poet of nature. He was also a poet of nationalism and revolt, crying out for revenge and justice against the tormentors of the Jews. Tschernichowsky wrote love poems, historical narratives, Zionistic poems, and poems describing the Jewish pathos and environment. He is also one of the better known Hebrew writers of children's poetry.

D. *Major Works*

Tschernichowsky wrote stories, children's poems, scientific articles, a play, and translated many classical works into Hebrew. It is for his poetry, however, that Tschernichowsky is best known.

1. *Le-Nokhah Pesel Apollo* ("Before a Statue of Apollo")

This poem is an outstanding example of Tschernichowsky's love of life and scorn of the narrowness and stifling effect of Orthodox Judaism.

a. In the poem, Tschernichowsky praises Apollo, who is the symbol of life, valor, beauty, and strength. Tschernichowsky says that he is the first to burst the chains of traditional Judaism and to embrace the type of life for which Apollo stands.

b. Tschernichowsky accuses the rabbis of going against God's will by imposing unnecessary rituals and observances on Judaism.

c. When this poem was published, it caused a controversy. Tschernichowsky was accused of being a Hellenist and of abandoning Judaism. In reality, however, Tschernichowsky's expression of his admiration of the Greek culture was an attempt to infuse Judaism with the beauties of Hellenism.

2. *Brit Milah* ("Circumcision")

This long narrative, or idyll, is a delightful description of the lives of the Crimean Jews.

a. The poem is the tale of Rabbi Eliakim's trip to a neighboring village to perform a circumcision. In it is a description of the feast following the circumcision.

b. The poem is typical of Tschernichowsky's other idylls in its detailed description of nature, the local populace, and their customs. This poem describes the lighter and happier side of Jewish life, for in that area, Jews and Gentiles lived together in peace.

c. Outstanding in this narrative and Tschernichowsky's other idylls is the fine description of the life and detailed portraits of the Jews.

3. *Baruch mi-Magenza* ("Baruch of Mayence")

This poem is based on a legend about the Crusades. It is a long monologue in which a Jew, Baruch, returns to his wife's grave three days after the massacres by the Crusaders to tell her all that has happened to him.

a. He killed their two daughters so that they would not fall into the hands of the mob, and though he meant to kill himself as well, he weakened and consented to conversion.

b. Baruch recounts the days when he celebrated his bar mitzvah (ceremony marking the initiation of a boy at the age of 13 into the Jewish community) and expresses his bitterness at his betrayal of the religion of his fathers.

c. Baruch spills out his fury at the murderers in a torment of venomous curses and phrases of anger unrivaled in Hebrew literature.

d. Driven to near madness by his bitterness and guilt, Baruch sets fire to the church and town, and runs through the streets in ecstasy watching the fire destroying his enemy.

e. Often considered to be Tschernichowsky's masterpiece, *Baruch mi-Magenza* is a landmark in Hebrew literature. It is a masterly, beautiful, and at times touching commentary on Jewish tragedy and suffering throughout the centuries.

4. *Be-Ein-Dor* ("Endor")

a. Tschernichowsky admired and had an affinity to King Saul. He wrote five poems about King Saul, of which *be-Ein-Dor* was the first.

b. Based on a story in I Samuel 28:7-25, Tschernichowsky recreates that terrible night when Saul visited the sorceress of Endor to learn of his fate in the ensuing battle with the Philistines.

c. Sensing his impending doom, Saul reminisces about his youth, before he was king and burdened with responsibilities.

d. The sorceress resurrects the prophet Samuel with whom Saul has a dialogue. Saul complains bitterly to Samuel for taking away his contentment and innocence and making him king. Samuel's reply is that on the morrow, Saul will be killed.

e. Saul leaves the house of the sorceress, tired and depressed, yet there is no fear in his heart, for he is resigned to his fate.

(1) Perhaps because they shared the same first name, Tschernichowsky himself remarked that he always like King Saul and was on his side against his adversaries.

5. *Zot Tehi Nikmateynu* ("This Will Be Our Revenge")

This poem was dedicated to the victims of the Ukrainian massacres of 1918-1920 during the Russian Civil War. As the title implies, the poem tells how the Jews will avenge the massacre of their people.

a. The first part of the poem details what kind of revenge it will not be. The Jews will not kill, beat, crush, or burn their tormentors. Instead, they will be avenged by their own blood; for the more their oppressors kill, the more their hearts will be turned to rock and they will become beasts. Then, when their souls are poisoned with the blood they shed, they will turn on each other as wild animals, and man will slaughter his brother and son will beat his father.

b. Though Tschernichowsky admired courage and strength, he realized that his people were too weak to seek physical revenge. Therefore he chose the more realistic and noble revenge—the one that the tormentors will inflict upon themselves.

6. *Shirim le-Illil* ("Songs for Illil")

This cycle of poems is a fine example of a phase of Tschernichowsky's works that is not well-known: his love poems.

a. These poems are charming tales of the happiness and disappointment of love.

b. Many of the poems introduce the nature motif and include exquisite descriptions of the human body.

7. Children's Poems

Tschernichowsky was more successful than most other Hebrew poets in the field of children's poetry. Because of their simplicity, charm, and briefness, these poems have a natural appeal to children.

a. The poems do not talk down to the child, but are written on an innocent and simple level.

8. Translations

Tschernichowsky's masterful knowledge of Hebrew, Greek, Latin, Russian, Ukrainian, Serbian, German, Yiddish, French and English made him a great translator.

a. His translations into Hebrew include the Babylonian "Gilgamesh" epic, the Finnish epic "Kalevala," Homers *Iliad* and *Odyssey*, Longfellow's "Hiawatha" and "Evangeline," Shakespeare's *Macbeth* and *Twelfth Night*, Molière's *Le Malade Imaginaire*, as well as numerous other works.

b. Some were more successful than others; however, these translations alone would have secured for Tschernichowsky a place in Hebrew literature, for they helped enrich the modern Hebrew language and extended the growing list of classics available in the Hebrew language.

E. *Conclusion*

Saul Tschernichowsky is often referred to as the "second greatest Hebrew poet"—second only to Hayyim Nahman Bialik. Since the turn of the century, numerous comparisons and studies of these great Hebrew poets have been made. While for a time Bialik's fame cast a shadow on the reputations of all other Hebrew poets, Tschernichowsky succeeded in acquiring a prominent place for himself beside Bialik. Tschernichowsky symbolized the beginning of a new era: the hopes and aspirations of the Jew; his relationship to the universe and life. He wrote of the beauties of life, love, and nature, and expressed admiration for the glory of other cultures, especially that of ancient Greece. Yet he never abandoned Judaism. He was a zealous nationalist, writing of his people with love and taking the banner in their defense. Tschernichowsky was, more than anything else, a humanist.

SHMUEL YOSEF AGNON

Hebrew fiction reached new peaks with writings of S. Y. Agnon. By using the simple narrative, Agnon was able to reach a new level in modern Hebrew prose. His works dealt with the fading Jewish community of Europe, attempting to examine their lifestyles, beliefs, and customs by exploring such topics as loss of faith and identity crisis. In contrast to Europe and the "old way of life," Agnon wrote about life in Palestine and Israel. He wrote about the idealistic generation which came from Europe to resurrect the Jewish state. Agnon has been acclaimed as the greatest modern Hebrew prose writer. His career has been marked with many literary awards which culminated with his acceptance of the Nobel Prize for Literature in 1966.

A. *Life*

1. Shmuel Yosef Agnon (Shmuel Joseph Czaczkes) was born in 1888 to a prosperous Jewish family in Buczaz, Galicia (a region in Austria-Poland).

2. His family was Hasidic, his father being a follower of the Chortkov Rebbe.

3. Traditional Judaism as well as modern European culture permeated the household.

4. Agnon's early education included studies of the Bible, the Talmud, and the writings of Maimonides, as well as the literature of the Haskalah and modern German authors.

5. Agnon began to write at an early age, and his Hebrew and Yiddish poems and short stories appeared in various local publications.

6. When he left for Palestine in 1907, Agnon had already started on the path to becoming a great author. He spent the next six years of his life in Jaffa and Jerusalem, finding employment as a clerk and a tutor, while continuing his writing.

7. In 1913, Agnon left Palestine for Germany where he lived for the next eleven years. Germany was then a center for Hebrew writers and Jewish philosophers and thinkers.

8. Agnon met Martin Buber (with whom he worked on an anthology of Hasidic tales), Hayyim Nahman Bialik, and Gershom Scholem, as well as many Zionist leaders.

9. During this period he married Esther Marx, a member of a respected Jewish family, and wrote some of his best stories.

10. In 1924 a fire burned down his house and destroyed most of the manuscripts of his writings. That same year he returned to Israel, settling in Jerusalem.

11. In 1931, a four-volume set of Agnon's collected works was published and enthusiastically received by the reading public and critics.

12. From then on, he continued to produce great works in Hebrew literature. In 1966 in recognition of his contributions to world literature, Agnon received the Nobel Prize for literature.

13. Agnon died in Jerusalem in 1970.

B. *Literary Traits*

1. Agnon's themes are based on Jewish life in Europe and Palestine.

   a. He writes about the pious Jews, beggars, and scholars in their struggle to earn a livelihood in Europe.

   b. Palestine plays an important role in many stories, either as the object of a pious Jew's cherished dream or as the setting for idealistic Jewish youths.

   c. Such elements as poverty, pain, humiliation, hypocrisy, and irony are major factors in these stories.

2. Agnon's stories, especially the more modern ones, are often a psychological examination of characters.

   a. The world of dream and reality are often combined and intertwined in a manner which leaves the reader in doubt as to which world the character is actually in.

   b. The world which emerges is at times nightmarish and often nostalgic for the disappearing European way of life. It is also unsure of which direction the present life would take. There is a search, sometimes unsuccessful, for a home, a place in society, a meaning in life, and a sense of time.

   c. The names of Agnon's characters are carefully chosen to reflect their personalities.

3. Even though the characters and themes are often tragic, Agnon's writing has a touch of satirical humor and comedy.

4. Agnon's stories are written in modern Hebrew prose, incorporating many quotations and phrases from the Talmud and the Aggadah.

C. *Major Works*

Agnon's literary output consists of hundreds of poems, folk tales, legends, and short stories, as well as novels.

1. *Hakhnasat Kallah* ("The Bridal Canopy")

This novel, published in 1937, is a series of loosely connected tales, legends, and fables relating the adventures of Yudel Hasid, a wandering Galician Jew.

   a. The story tells of Yudel, whose poverty leads him to travel in order to collect a dowry for his three daughters. In the end, he could not collect enough, but his wife miraculously discovers treasure and all ends well.

   b. The beauty of this novel is its portrayal of the inner and external life of the Galician Jew. It is an examination of Jewish traditions, customs, and behavior.

   c. The novel gives a beautifully quaint, if somewhat comic, portrayal of the many Jewish characters one would expect to meet on such a trip.

   d. This novel depicts a lifestyle that once flourished but has slowly faded with time, a culture that was totally annihilated in the coming years.

2. *Ore'ah Nata Lalun* ("A Wayfarer Who Stayed for a Night")

This novel published in 1939 is a chronicle of the decay and extinction of Jewish life in the small towns of Europe

a. The narrator leaves his home in Jerusalem for a short visit to his hometown in Europe. The town, in the narrator's imagination, was always a symbol of traditional Jewish life, of a flourishing Jewish community. Upon his return, the visitor's childhood memories are shattered, for he discovers that his shtetl is collapsing and decaying.

b. The visitor is nostalgically reaching for a past and a home, both of which have crumbled and cannot be restored.

c. The decay of the post-World War I town is conveyed through the characters rather than through the plot. The few Jews who remained in the town are poverty stricken, and many are afflicted with physical and mental illness. They suffered a tragic past and are experiencing a decaying present.

d. The novel is filled with fantasies and dreams. The visitor, unable to find his memories and the security of his childhood, is overcome with self-pity and guilt.

e. Though the intended visit of a few days was prolonged to almost a year, the visitor never quite feels at home in the town.

f. In the end, realizing that there is no hope for Jewish life in the shtetl, the visitor returns to his home in Jerusalem.

g. As opposed to *Hakhnasat Kallah*, *Ore'ah Nata Lalun* is a tale of the spiritual death of European Jewry. The Jewish home in Europe has decayed, and Israel has become the new home.

3. *Temol Shilshom* ("Yesteryear")

Temol Shilshom, the third book of what is sometimes referred to as Agnon's trilogy, is a search for a new life and for a meaning to that life in Israel.

a. It tells the story of Yitzhak Kummer, an idealistic young pioneer, who leaves his home in Galicia and settles in Palestine. He dreams of working the soil and reviving the country, but, unable to find a job as a farmer, he becomes a mediocre house painter in Jaffa.

b. He falls in love with a young intellectual, Sonia, but when she tires of the charm of his innocence, she leaves him. Depressed and heartbroken, Yitzhak moves to Jerusalem in search of something new. There he gradually returns to Orthodox Judaism, which he had rejected upon his arrival in Palestine, and marries Shiphra, the daughter of a religious fanatic.

c. Shortly after his marriage he is bitten by a dog on whom he had previously painted the words "mad dog" in jest. He dies as a result of the bite.

d. The problems examined in this novel are common ones in Agnon's writings: religion, home, identity, and meaning of life. The hero's quest for these is a failure. He becomes progressively more disillusioned with his former ideals and hopes of self-fulfillment slowly melt. When, after his marriage, it appears that Yitzhak has overcome many of his problems and is on the road to spiritual fulfillment, he dies a violent and meaningless death.

e. The symbol of the dog has been discussed in detail by many critics. Their conclusions have ranged from the opinions that the dog symbolizes the Jewish people, to the theory that the dog is Yitzhak.

f. *Temol Shilshom* takes place during the years of the Second Aliyah (1905-1910) and is a chronicle of that period. Yitzhak is by no means typical of the many young pioneers who came to settle in Palestine during that time. However, the problems and ambiguities which confront him, especially the relationship between Zionist ideology and the realism in Palestine, religion, and identity, are problems common to many of his peers.

D. *Conclusion*

S. Y. Agnon's long literary career, spanning more than sixty-five years, has earned him the distinction of being the most popular and widely read modern Hebrew author. Since winning the Nobel Prize for Literature in 1966, translations of his works have been published in many languages. These translations of his works have introduced Agnon to worldwide literary circles. Young and old, secular and traditionalist have been attracted to Agnon's writings, for he writes both about the old way of life and about life in the modern world.

XLIV

PALESTINE: TURKEY AND GREAT BRITAIN

Palestine, which was a part of the Ottoman Empire from 1517 to 1917, was one of the areas of economic and political confrontation between the major European powers. This conflict hindered Zionist attempts to establish permanent Jewish settlements in Palestine. The Zionists were seen by the Ottoman regime as agents of European imperialism, one of the forces which was destroying the rapidly deteriorating Ottoman Empire. During the twentieth century, the Jewish return to Palestine coincided and clashed with the rise of Arab nationalism. After World War I Great Britain was given control over Palestine, where it used a "divide and rule" concept in order to administer the mandate. By playing Jew against Arab, they further aggravated the tense and volatile situation. This situation continued until the future of the mandate was given over to the United Nations, which decided to divide the Palestinian mandate into Jewish and Arab states.

A. *Historical Background*

1. The rampant anti-Semitism of eastern Europe expedited the acceptance of Zionism among many of the Jews. Other reactions to this anti-Semitism included mass emigrations to the United States, Canada, South Africa, Argentina, and other lands; assimilation; revolutionary activity; and attempts to create Jewish autonomies in Europe.

2. The overwhelming majority of the members of the various Zionist organizations insisted that the Jewish homeland was to be established in Palestine. However, there were groups who believed that a Jewish state could be established in some other parts of the globe. These groups never received much popular support or financial backing.

3. Palestine was located at the commercial crossroads of three continents and was considered a geographically strategic position. Because of the decline of the Ottoman Empire in the early part of the nineteenth century, the major European powers began to vie for control of this area.

   a. Britain, France, and Germany competed with each other for economic and political control of this area.

b. In 1882, Britain seized control of Egypt, thereby exerting its influence over the area and assuring itself of having free access to the Suez Canal, which was built in 1869.

c. To offset British commercial influences, Germany constructed the Berlin-Baghdad Railway through the northern part of the Turkish Empire.

d. Because Russia had very few year-round ice-free ports, it desired access to a port city on the Mediterranean Sea.

e. Turkey (or the Ottoman Empire) nominally controlled most of the Levant and Maghrib. It was once a world power but because of corruption, decentralization of government, and nationalism among its minorities, it had fallen into decay. It was given the nickname "the old man of the East." Because of the political necessity of maintaining a balance of power in Europe, the Ottoman Empire was not carved up by the major European powers.

(1) Britain wanted complete control of Palestine in order to protect the Suez Canal, which was important for control of her overseas empire.

(2) Germany needed Turkey's friendship in order to combat Britain's interests in the area. This was one of the reasons that led to its military alliance with Turkey prior to World War I.

4. The political situation at the end of the nineteenth century until the outbreak of World War I made progress of Zionism very slow. Issues such as which side the World Zionist Organization should support during the war split Zionists, who backed their respective countries.

B. *Palestine and Zionism Until the Outbreak of World War I*

1. Jewish Settlements in Palestine Under the Ottoman Turks

a. When the Ottoman Turks conquered Palestine from the Mamluks in the beginning of the sixteenth century, the Jewish population of Palestine was approximately 5,000.

b. Some of the Jews living in Palestine had immigrated from Europe and North Africa, while others were the descendants of Jews who never left Palestine.

c. Safed and Jerusalem became centers of Jewish learning. Also, the teachings of the various messianic and mystical movements attracted many Jews to these places (see Chapter XXXIII, "Joseph Nasi and Manasseh ben Israel" and Chapter XXXVa, "Great Kabbalists").

d. Although the Jews of Palestine were usually not subject to physical persecution, they had to pay a special tax imposed on non-Muslims.

e. Most of the Jews lived in poverty and were supported by a special charity called *chalukah*, which was donated by the Jews in the Diaspora.

2. The Efforts of Theodor Herzl (1860-1904)

a. Herzl was not the first to propose colonization in Palestine. An attempt already had been made by the Hibbat Zion movement in setting up small agricultural settlements in Rishon LeZion and Petach Tikvah with the help of Baron Edmond de Rothschild (1845-1934), who had given them financial support.

b. Herzl, however, attempted to put colonization on a firmer footing by establishing the Jewish Colonial Trust and the Jewish National Fund as a means of permanent support for new settlements.

c. In order to give these settlements some political security and opportunity to expand, Herzl attempted to establish diplomatic relations with Turkey and other European powers, a concerted effort to get assurances for the establishment of a Jewish state.

(1) Herzl had an audience with a representative of the Turkish Sultan, who gave no firm commitment.

(2) He met with Kaiser Wilhelm II of Germany, who was friendly but was also noncommittal.

(3) The British Colonial Secretary gave a firm offer of land in Uganda. While the British offer of Uganda might be termed a diplomatic success of a sort, the members of the Zionist Congress of 1903 did not feel this way and overwhelmingly rejected the proposal after much heated debate.

(4) Herzl also made diplomatic overtures to von Plehve, the anti-Semitic Russian Minister of Interior who played a behind-the-scenes role in the massacre of the Jews in Kishinev, but received no commitment from him either.

3. Emigration to Palestine

a. In 1880, the Jewish population of Palestine was 20,000 to 25,000. The resurgence of anti-Semitism in Europe stimulated an increase in emigration to Palestine.

b. The first *aliyah* occurred in 1882 as a result of the 1881 pogroms in Russia. Most of the immigrants were members of the Hibbat Zion ("Lovers of Zion") movement whose aim was the creation of a land suitable for mass Jewish settlement.

(1) Within a few years, several agricultural settlements were established by the new arrivals.

(2) Due to lack of experience, these settlements were at first unsuccessful and were financially dependent on the contributions of Baron Edmond de Rothschild of Paris.

(3) The immigration continued in the 1890s with new settlements being founded in various parts of the country.

(4) Unable to find work as agricultural laborers, many Jews moved to the cities and became involved in commerce and trade.

(5) The Hebrew language was incorporated into the schools of the Jewish settlement, and became the spoken language of the settlers. (see Chapter XLIb, "Revival of the Hebrew Language and Literature").

c. The second *aliyah* began in 1904 and lasted until the beginning of World War I; the approximately 40,000 Jews who came to Palestine increased the total Jewish population to 85,000.

(1) New agricultural settlements were established.

(2) Tel Aviv was founded in 1909 as a Jewish suburb of Jaffa.

(3) This period saw the beginning of industrialization in Palestine with many factories being set up.

(4) Many of the future leaders of Israel came during this *aliyah*.

4. Opposition to Emigration

   a. The Turkish government viewed Jewish emigration to Palestine as a source of political danger and attempted to stop it.

   b. In 1882, a law was enacted forbidding European Jews from settling in Palestine.

   c. Laws were passed restricting Jews from purchasing land or constructing buildings without special permission.

   d. With the rise of Arab nationalism in the late nineteenth century came Arab opposition to Jewish settlement in Palestine. The Arabs demanded that the Turkish government place restrictions on Jewish emigration and land purchase.

   e. During World War I, the Turkish policy became increasingly unfavorable to the Jews in Palestine. Zionist organizations were banned and several Zionist leaders were deported from the country. During this time, 11,300 Jews left the country.

5. World War I and the Balfour Declaration

   a. The outbreak of the First World War changed the situation in the area. With the major European powers at war, the question of control of the eastern Mediterranean would be settled after the conclusion of the war.

   b. Turkey was allied with Germany and Austria-Hungary (Central Powers), while Britain, France, and Russia had formed an alliance (Allied Powers). The alliance that won the war would eventually decide the fate of Europe and the Middle East.

   c. The First World War also disrupted the Zionist movement.

      (1) The movement had large membership from countries on opposite sides of the conflict. Internal feuding arose when it

could not be decided what position the World Zionist Organization should take in the conflict.

(2) Many Jewish volunteers fought in Allied and Central armed forces.

(3) A battalion of Jewish volunteers that fought in the British army was organized in the Jewish Legion under the leadership of Vladimir Jabotinsky. Such notables as David Ben-Gurion and Itzhak Ben-Zvi fought in the Jewish Legion.

d. Between July 1915 and March 1916, promises of independent Arab states were made in correspondences between Sir Henry McMahon, British High Commissioner for Egypt, and Hussein ibn Ali, Sherif of Mecca. It was later claimed by the British that Palestine was not included in these promises.

e. In May 1916, the Sykes-Picot agreement was ratified. This was an agreement between France and Great Britain to divide up the yet-unconquered territories of the Ottoman Empire.

f. Zionist leader Chaim Weizmann worked successfully for a British commitment to secure a Palestinian homeland for Jews in exchange for Jewish support of the Allied war effort.

(1) This commitment from Britain came in the form of a letter from the British Foreign Secretary Arthur Balfour to Lord Rothschild (dated November 2, 1917) saying that "His Majesty's government views with favour the establishment in Palestine of a national home for the Jewish people." This letter became known as the Balfour Declaration.

(2) The Balfour Declaration had a great impact upon the public. The Declaration represented a victory for Zionism and gained Jewish support for the British.

g. In December 1917, General Allenby of Great Britain conquered Jerusalem, thus establishing British claim for control over Palestine.

C. *Problems Under the British Mandate*

1. Under the various peace agreements following the war, the area encompassing much of modern Israel and Jordan was awarded to Great Britain, while the area of Syria and Lebanon was awarded to France.

2. In June 1920, the British replaced its military government with a mandatory government headed by Sir Herbert Samuel, a Jew, who served as the British High Commissioner for Palestine.

   a. Samuel attempted to satisfy the Arab population by appointing Arab nationalist municipal officials and community leaders.

   b. He placed restrictions on land sales to Jews, while placing no such restrictions on Arab purchases of land.

   c. In 1922, the Jewish Agency was established as the mediating body between the British administration and the Jewish population in Palestine.

3. The third *aliyah* (1919-1923) brought approximately 35,000 Jews to Palestine. Most of these immigrants were young people with strong Zionist convictions. Many left Russia because of their disillusionment with the Russian Revolution.

   a. Many new kibbutzim (collective agricultural settlements) were established.

   b. Construction in the cities was increased and industry was expanded.

4. In the 1920s and 1930s, Arab riots against the Jews increased because of the sudden economic and social change in the country.

   a. Arab nationalist leaders, whose numbers had increased since the fall of the Ottoman Empire at the end of the First World War, demanded a limit to the emigration of Jews to Palestine and the creation of an independent Arab Palestine.

   b. The *Haganah*, a Jewish self-defense organization, was formed in June 1920 to protect Jewish settlements from Arab attacks.

5. The fourth *aliyah* (1924-1928) brought approximately 62,000 Jews to Palestine. Many of these Jews were middle-class merchants and artisans who preferred to settle in cities. They had fled Europe because of the rise of anti-Semitism in postwar Europe, especially in Poland.

   a. In 1925, the Hebrew University in Jerusalem was established.

   b. Construction of cities increased and many new settlements, whose main crop was citrus fruit, were established.

6. The Arab nationalists felt threatened by the increased Jewish emigration to Palestine and demanded that restrictions be placed on emigration.

   a. Arab terrorist gangs sporadically attacked Jewish settlements and cities, inflicting heavy damage on the Jewish community.

   b. Arab groups attacked Jews living in Jerusalem, Hebron, and Safed, killing and wounding many.

   c. Arab extremists intimidated other Arabs in order to prevent them from selling land to Jews or from cooperating with Zionist endeavors.

   d. In 1936, the Arab Higher Committee called a general strike in Palestine, demanding an end to Jewish immigration and the prohibition of Jewish acquisition of land. The following three years were marked by violence and disorder.

   e. During this period attacks on Jewish settlements increased and a campaign of terror was initiated against the Jews.

7. The fifth *aliyah* (1929-1939) occurred because of Hitler's rise to power in Germany in 1933; approximately 200,000 central European Jews came to Palestine to escape the Nazi reign of terror (see Chapter XLVI, "The Holocaust"). Many of these new settlers were professionals and merchants.

8. The Haganah, which was the official military force of the Jewish Agency, evolved into an effective military organization, successfully repulsing many of the Arab attacks on Jewish settlements.

a. Extremist elements were opposed to the policy of self-restraint adopted by the Haganah and formed an underground group known as the *Irgun Tzevai Leumi* (I.Z.L. or "National Military Organization"). The *Irgun* and *Lehi* (Israel Freedom Fighters "Stern Group") engaged in activities against the Arabs as well as the British authorities.

9. Faced with rising internal disorder, Prime Minister Neville Chamberlain issued a White Paper on May 17, 1939.

   a. This limited Jewish immigration into Palestine to 15,000 Jews for the next five years, at which time Jewish immigration would be dependent upon Arab agreement.

   b. The White Paper stated that it was not Britain's intention to change Palestine into a Jewish state.

   c. The 1939 White Paper closed off a safe harbor for immigration at the hour of the Jews' greatest peril.

      (1) In Nazi-dominated countries, organized campaigns of terror and legislation were beginning.

      (2) By the end of the year, the Germans had extended their dominion into Poland, center of the largest concentration of Jews in the world.

D. *World War II and Its Aftermath*

1. Although Winston Churchill was quick to condemn the White Paper when he was out of the cabinet, he did not change the White Paper policy during his tenure in office.

   a. One of his reasons for not changing policy lay in protecting the oil supply. In the early stages of the war, the German and Italian armies occupied much of North Africa, thus threatening to destroy Britain's domination of the area and cutting off oil supplies to the Allies.

   b. Another reason was that it was important to placate the more vocal segments of Arab Palestine, who were antagonistic to the Allies and might (as many did) support the Axis powers.

2. Despite the White Paper, the *moshav* ("Jewish settlement in Palestine") expressed its willingness to help in the British war efforts. Approximately 26,000 Palestinian Jews served with the British army, many of whom saw action in North Africa and Europe. In 1944, the Jewish Brigade was formed as part of the British army.

3. Immigration of Jews continued "illegally" under the most perilous of circumstances.

   a. Emigrants sailed at night in unseaworthy, overcrowded ships, many of which exploded or sank because of faulty equipment.

   b. Most ships never reached Palestine. The British navy often intercepted these ships and sent their human cargo to Cyprus and Mauritius.

4. The Jews hoped that after the war British policy would change favorably toward Jewish immigration and settlement in Palestine. The hopes, however, were not realized.

   a. Despite preelection promises, the postwar Labor government with Ernest Bevin as Foreign Secretary cut the flow of emigrants to Palestine to an even lower rate than the 1939 White Paper permitted.

   b. Thousands of survivors of the Nazi death camps were interned in allied-run D.P. (displaced persons) camps in Europe and Cyprus. The Jewish response was an intensification of active resistance as well as continuation of the risky illegal immigration.

5. The British government rejected proposals by a joint Anglo-American commission for the removal of restrictions on land purchases by Jews and the immediate admission of 100,000 Jewish war refugees.

   a. Arab attacks against kibbutzim and cities were countered by retaliatory attacks by the *Haganah* (the Jewish Agency's self-defense organization) and other Jewish military organizations.

   b. In 1947, a renewed Jewish campaign of violence, headed by the *Irgun Tzevai Leumi* (National Military Organization) and *Lehi* (Israel Freedom Fighters) attacked not only centers of Arab terrorist activity, but also the headquarters of the British mandate and various opposing Jewish groups.

c. The country was on the brink of civil war by the beginning of 1947 when the United Nations entered the picture (see Chapter XLVIIIa, "The Emergence of Israel").

E. *Conclusion*

After World War II the British control over the Palestinian mandate rapidly deteriorated. The position of Great Britain as a world power was shaken because of economic problems in the postwar period. The rise of nationalism and demands for independence from her colonies shrunk her overseas holdings, which were so vital to her economy. Great Britain was unreceptive to the demands of admitting thousands of survivors of Hitler's death camps into Palestine. On the pretext of being neutral she allowed Palestine to become the site of a civil war between Arabs and Jews. By 1947 the situation in Palestine had deteriorated to such an extent that Great Britain finally consented to allow the United Nations to settle the question of Palestine.

XLV

NEW THINKING: ROSENZWEIG, BUBER, AND HESCHEL

In nineteenth- and twentieth-century Western society, emancipation and assimilation have been a constant threat to the continuum of the Jewish way of life. The relevance of Jewish thought and tradition in a modern, rapidly changing society was being questioned and more often than not rejected in favor of assimilation. Franz Rosenzweig, Martin Buber, and Abraham Joshua Heschel attempted, through their various writings and activities, to propose a vibrant and relevant understanding of Judaism which could confront the problems of our modern, and alienating, society.

A. *Franz Rosenzweig (1886-1929)*

1. Life

a. Rosenzweig was born in 1886 into an assimilated Jewish family in Berlin.

b. He studied philosophy, history, and literature at various German universities.

c. In 1913, he was on the verge of converting to Christianity when he had a revelatory experience at an Orthodox Yom Kippur service. Henceforth, he devoted himself to Jewish scholarship and learning.

d. While serving in the German army during World War I, he began writing his views on religious philosophy.

e. After the war, his writings and activities were primarily devoted to Jewish philosophy.

f. In 1920, Rosenzweig founded the *Freies Jüdisches Lehrhaus* in Frankfurt. Both Buber and Heschel were involved in teaching at this institution. During this period, Rosenzweig translated and commented on ninety-two poems by Judah Halevi and in collaboration with Buber, worked on a new German translation of the Bible.

g. From 1922 till the end of his life, Rosenzweig suffered from paralysis which confined him to bed. Nevertheless, he remained the guiding spirit of the *Freies Jüdisches Lehrhaus* and continued writing until his death in 1929.

2. Works

    a. *Stern der Erlösung* ("The Star of Redemption")

        (1) Published in 1921, this work deals with his concept of redemption, which is vital for any understanding of Rosenzweig's philosophy of education.

        (2) We know the essence of God is infinite; however, it is unknown to us.

        (3) We know that despite the fact that man is different from God, man still tries to be one with God; that is, man desires immortality.

        (4) We thus have three separate entities: God, man, and soul, that constitute Judaism.

        (5) Rosenzweig has posited a relationship between these three entities through the conceptions of creation, revelation, and redemption.

            (a) *Creation* is an ongoing process, in which man is provided for in God's scheme of things.

            (b) *Revelation* helps man become aware of his creator and establishes an "I-Thou" relationship between creator and creation.

            (c) *Redemption* is attained by obedience to God's revealed commandments. It is the means by which man raises himself to the immortal plane of God, while still remaining human.

        (6) In this theological context, we can see the foundation of Rosenzweig's philosophy of education, which would be the guide by which man can find redemption.

b. *Zeit Ist's* ("It is Time")

   (1) Originally written in 1917 as a letter to the German-Jewish philosopher Hermann Cohen, *Zeit Ist's* explained why a new system of Jewish education was necessary in Germany.

   (2) The majority of German Jews had only a few years of "religious training," if any at all. They also lacked an understanding of the requirements of a Jewish life; in his eyes, the Jewish homelife was rapidly disappearing.

   (3) Rosenzweig stressed the importance of a thorough understanding of the various books related to Judaism such as the prayer books and the Bible.

   (4) He sketched out a basic course of Jewish study for children in primary and secondary schools, introducing them to the various holidays of the Jewish year, stories and moral concepts selected from Scripture, and various topics in history and literature.

   (5) This program was the prototype for countless "Sabbath schools," or "Sunday schools," in Germany and the United States, which exist and thrive until this day.

c. Rosenzweig also wrote other books of note.

   (1) In *Hegel and the State* he repudiates the German idealism of his times.

   (2) *Kleinere Schriften* ("Minor Writings") is a collection of essays on the theme of Jewish adult education.

3. Freies Jüdisches Lehrhaus ("The Free Jewish Academy")

a. This institution was founded by Rosenzweig with the aim of bringing Jews back to their roots and to an understanding of Judaism within a modern framework,

b. Rosenzweig believed that the Bible is the basis of Jewish survival, but realized that the old style of studying was impotent against the influx of new ideas such as Bible criticism which had permeated the intellectual atmosphere since the Emancipation.

    c. Orthodoxy generally refused to accept the challenge of modernity. Though Reform Judaism had accepted the challenge, it lost many of its Jewish concepts and principles.

    d. The FJL aimed to entice Jews back to their roots and to see their heritage within a modern context. "Return to the sources" became the key phrase of FJL. The distinction between teaching and learning was to be eliminated. Most of those at the FJL, including Rosenzweig, were or had been laymen and not rabbinic scholars. Those who taught the works of the prophets, scribes, and sages were themselves being educated while in the process of teaching.

B. *Martin Buber (1878-1965)*

1. Life

    a. Born in Vienna to a Galician family, Buber received a traditional Jewish education from his grandfather, Solomon Buber, a noted midrashic scholar.

    b. During his youth, Buber was introduced to Hasidism, which was a formative influence in his life.

    c. He studied philosophy and art history at the universities in Berlin and Vienna.

    d. In 1898, he joined the Zionist movement, becoming the editor of its weekly periodical, *Die Welt* ("The World"), in 1901.

    e. Through this organ, Buber criticized Herzl's purely political conception of Zionism. Instead, Buber advocated the idea of rebirth of a unified Jewish culture.

    f. This innovative idea was championed in *Der Jude* ("The Jew"), a journal which Buber founded in 1916.

    g. In the late 1920s, he taught religion and ethics at the University of Frankfurt and at Rosenzweig's *Freies Jüdisches Lehrhaus*.

    h. During this period, he edited a journal concerned with social problems, *Die Kreatur* ("The Creature"), worked on a translation of the Bible with Rosenzweig, and wrote about religious philosophy.

i. When the Nazis came to power in 1933, Buber took over as director of Jewish education in Germany. He helped raise hope and spirit in a rapidly deteriorating community.

j. In 1938, he emigrated to Palestine. A fervent advocate of Jewish-Arab understanding, he helped form the *Brith Shalom* ("Peace Treaty") organization, which was started to further Jewish-Arab relations in Palestine.

k. Buber became a professor of sociology, religion, and social philosophy at the Hebrew University in Jerusalem.

2. Philosophy

a. *I and Thou*, Buber's major work, is an explanation of his understanding of the relationship of God to man and of humans to each other.

   (1) Buber claims there are two ways by which man sees himself vis-a-vis the outer world. "I-It" is the attitude of detachment. Man treats the object of his consciousness as a thing separated from him; it becomes a means to an end, which should be examined and, if possible, manipulated.

   (2) "I-Thou" is the relationship toward another human being. It encompasses all human relationships. Through the I-Thou relationship the deeper meaning of existence is discovered. I-Thou relationships are experienced through love, friendship, and possibly, like the Romantics, through communion with nature.

   (3) This type of relationship, says Buber, leads to an awareness of "a breath from the eternal Thou; in each Thou we address the eternal Thou," which is God.

   (4) The conception of the eternal Thou is influenced by Hasidic thought, which he tries in his writings to link with modern religious thought.

b. Buber's philosophical thought finds expression in his nationalistic writings, such as *Drei Reden über das Judentum* ("Three Speeches on Judaism") and *Die Jüdische Bewegung* ("The Jewish Movement").

(1) Here, as in *I and Thou*, there is an assertion of strong emotion and intuitive thought, rather than logical reasoning or systematic thinking.

(2) Buber extends his conception of the "I" by applying the objective (I-It)—subjective (I-Thou) dichotomy to large groups of people.

(3) Everyone experiences the objective and subjective feelings of belonging to a group, a common land, language, etc.

(4) In most nations the objective and subjective feelings are in harmony. The Jews, however, without a homeland, lack an objective group consciousness.

(5) Buber thus calls for a strengthening of the subjective consciousness through a reassertion of Jewish heritage, as well as political efforts to regain a Palestinian homeland.

(6) In this way, the subjective Jewish consciousness can resist the dangerous lack of a subjective foundation (homeland) which menaces the reconstruction of a real, spiritual Jewish national life.

(7) Through a subjective Jewish consciousness, Jews can come into contact with the eternal Thou.

(8) Jewish life, according to Buber, strives for a unity of divine precept with daily action; it works for the unity of individual and group under the Law of God, and visualizes a brighter future. Buber thus makes the Jewish people the means of human dialogue with God.

c. Buber retold many Hasidic tales and legends, inserting into them his own philosophy.

(1) He chose from the folk stories and legends about famous Hasidic masters, reshaping and embellishing them with poetic German.

(2) *Die Legende des Baal Shem* ("The Legend of the Baal Shem") and *Der grosse Maggid und seine Nachfolger* ("The Great Maggid and His Followers") are drawn directly from folk

sources. *Die Geschichten des Rabbi Nahman* ("The Stories of Rabbi Nahman") retells stories told orally by Rabbi Nahman (a Hasidic master) to his followers, who recorded them in writing (see Chapter XXXVII, "Hasidism").

(3) In all of these works, Buber puts oral tradition into literary form.

C. *Abraham Joshua Heschel (1907-1972)*

1. Life

   a. Born in 1907 in Warsaw, Heschel was a direct descendant of such Hasidic luminaries as Dov Baer of Mezhrich and Levi Isaac of Berdichov.

   b. After years of traditional rabbinical studies, he enrolled at the University of Berlin to study philosophy (1927).

   c. Heschel also enrolled at the *Hochschule für die Wissenschaft des Judentums* ("High School for the Science of Judaism"), where he later held a teaching position from 1932 to 1933.

   d. He receive his doctorate from the University of Berlin in 1933.

   e. Heschel succeeded Martin Buber at the *Freies Jüdisches Lehrhaus* in 1937, but along with other Polish Jews residing in Germany, was deported to Poland by the Nazi regime a year later.

   f. He left Poland in 1939, shortly before the German invasion, and in 1940 he accepted an invitation to occupy the chair of Jewish Philosophy and Rabbinics at the Hebrew Union College, the Reform rabbinical seminary in Cincinnati.

   g. From 1945 until his death in 1972, he occupied the chair of Jewish Ethics and Mysticism at the Jewish Theological Seminary, the Conservative rabbinical seminary in New York.

   h. He also spent time at other major institutions in the capacity of visiting professor.

   i. He wrote many books and was an outspoken advocate for civil rights and peace causes.

2. Philosophy

   a. God

      (1) For Heschel, God is encountered not as an object, but as a *dimensional reality.*

      (2) In *Man is Not Alone*, Heschel speaks of God's being as omnipotent and omniscient.

      (3) Like Buber, he has separated mysticism from pantheism (the belief that nature or the universe *is* God) because God is above and beyond all things.

      (4) Heschel places himself in the line of the prophetic tradition.

      (5) In *The Prophets*, Heschel explains the conflict between the two conceptions of God:

         (a) The *mystical* strain has been seen as "other-worldly," striving to realize unity with the divine.

         (b) The *prophetic* strain has normally been seen as concerned with this world, with an emphasis upon submission to God.

      (6) In *The Prophets*, Heschel refuses to reduce prophetic inspiration to a subjective experience because he believes the two traditions are complementary.

      (7) In *God in Search of Man* he attempts to resolve the two traditions: "It is within man's power to seek Him; it is not within his power to find Him." Man may, as the mystic does, seek unity with God through prayer; however, the "Divine Word" which inspired the prophets, is also necessary.

   b. Man

      (1) Man must go beyond a generalized conception of himself as a "what," a physical, political, psychological, or like entity. He must view himself as a "who," a uniquely centered self.

(2) Heschel believes that God is a presence that meets us in ineffable, indefinable dimensions.

(3) The only way one can respond to such a presence is with humility. Humanity begins with humility, which leads to a kind of "reverence" similar to Buber's I-Thou relationship.

(4) Knowledge of our smallness makes us conscious that we are creatures, products of a Creator, while at the same time, awareness of our sordidness makes us aware of the evil within us.

(5) Heschel stressed the importance of the messianic hope and the necessity to strive for redemption on earth.

c. Tradition

(1) Heschel points to the Baal Shem Tov as the one who "banished melancholy from the soul and uncovered the ineffable delight of being a Jew."

(2) To the Baal Shem Tov, obedience to God's law was not a burden, but a foretaste of heaven. In the face of suffering and bewilderment, it is this ecstatic obedience to God's law which brings hope and meaning to human existence.

(3) Every human being, in his heart, desires something which "outlasts life, strife, and agony."

(4) It is Jewish tradition, cemented by Divine Law, which gives us "intimations of the lasting," the eternal covenant. It is the Sabbath which characterizes this form of intimation. In the ceremonial Jewish observance of the Sabbath we receive a weekly foretaste of the world to come, resurrection of the soul of man.

D. *Conclusion*

These scholars tried to come to grips with a modern, alienating society, a society which threatened to isolate and destroy Jewish life. In their own ways they hoped to rekindle the divine spark that is found in all persons. They never rejected modernity or the "ideals" of the Enlightenment; however, they believed that there is much one can learn from the past.

Whether through a reeducation program, the setting up of a dialogue between man and God, or through a rediscovery of mysticism and Hasidism, the same goal was achieved: the birth of a "new" Jew, a Jew who could be proud of his heritage and could triumph over the destructive forces of modern society.

XLVI

THE HOLOCAUST

The term *holocaust* is used as a description of the systematic destruction of European Jewry. This slaughter was perpetrated by the National Socialist (Nazi) regime and their accomplices in the various German-occupied countries during the Second World War. Through a well-planned program of economic and social legislation, expropriation of capital, concentration, enslavement, deportation, and finally extermination, the once-vibrant Jewish communities of Europe were totally destroyed. The destruction of approximately six million Jews and tens of millions of other European peoples exemplified the degeneration and collapse of centuries of European civilization. No past crimes and injustices in history could match the barbarity and brutality with which Nazis and their followers carried out their "final solution." The Holocaust was not only a tragedy for the Jewish people; rather, it was a tragedy for all of mankind who allowed the slaughter to continue without protesting.

A. *Historical Background*

1. Anti-Semitism had existed in Germany since the Middle Ages (see Chapter XXX, "Jewish Communities in Medieval France, Germany, and Italy"). Until the nineteenth century the hostility of the Church (Catholic and Protestant) against Jews manifested itself in various anti-Jewish legislation (ghettos, economic restrictions, etc.).

2. The growth of nationalism in Germany, during and after the Napoleonic Wars, manifested itself in a different way from other forms of European nationalism.

   a. One of the foundations of nineteenth-century German nationalism was not only the allegiance and subservience to the state, but also a notion of a community of blood, which included a belief in superiority of the (fictitious) Aryan race.

   b. As might be expected with the gradual development of this concept, anyone not of pure German stock was considered an "enemy," regardless of allegiance to the political organs of the German state or importance in German economic and public life.

c. Among these "foreigners" in Germany were the Jews. By the twentieth century, the Jews had received citizenship and most civil rights and were assimilating into German life (see Chapter XL, "Haskalah").

d. Many Jews had completed their assimilation by being baptized because many areas such as university positions and government jobs were barred to Jews. These anti-Jewish restrictions were abrogated during the period of the Weimar Republic (1919-1933).

e. In racial theories a Jew remained a Jew even if he was baptized; since one's "Jewishness" is in the blood no change can possibly occur.

f. Although there were occasional anti-Semitic outbreaks in nineteenth-century Germany, anti-Semitism did not openly enter politics until such men as Adolf Stöcker and Otto Boeckel made it an integral part of their short-lived, but influential, political movements. In 1881, Stöcker, who was the Protestant chaplain at the Prussian Imperial Court, introduced into the Reichstag (Parliament) an anti-Semitic bill, which advocated a limitation on Jewish influence in German life.

3. After the German defeat in World War I (1918), many small nationalist political parties sprang up.

a. Political leaders tried to find a scapegoat upon whom they could attribute the defeat and the ensuing chaos that was a result of the First World War.

b. The scapegoat was found in the foreign element in their midst—the Jews, Poles, Gypsies, and Bolsheviks.

c. Adolf Hitler's National Socialist German Workers (Nazi) party had been one of the many right-wing extremist parties on the fringes of the German political scene.

(1) According to the Nazis, the worldwide depression in the 1920s and 1930s was to be blamed on the Jews and the Bolsheviks, who were destroying the economy.

(2) By January 1933 the Nazis gained control of the German Reichstag. Within a short time an unopposed dictatorship was established under the leadership of Adolf Hitler.

(3) He regarded the Jewish "race" as the source of all evil, and therefore declared a campaign against the Jewish communities, first in Germany and later in all of Europe.

B. *Harassment, Terror, and Destruction*

1. Reasons

    a. In Hitler's political testament, *Mein Kampf* ("My Battle", 1923), his hatred for the Jews and his wish to do away with them are openly expressed.

    b. He wrote that during World War I the Jew had "stabbed" the invincible German army in the back, causing them to be defeated in the war.

    c. Hitler stated that the Jews were the source of all modern evil, ranging from the Jewish capitalist banking interests of the Rothschilds to the bolshevism of Leon Trotsky and Rosa Luxemburg.

    d. Baptism could not change this Jewish "evil" because it was in the blood, and every Jew had this "evil" in him.

    e. The Jews were to be removed from German life, in order to "purify" the German economy and culture and to protect the German "race" from being defiled by the inferior Jews.

2. The Beginning: Removal of Jews from Public Life

    a. Having attained power, Hitler lost no time in putting his anti-Semitic program into effect.

    b. During the years 1933-1934, Jews were removed from the German civil service and expelled from the universities.

    c. The Nazis instituted a major boycott of all Jewish shops and businesses, forcing many of them into bankruptcy.

d. Many large Jewish enterprises were expropriated. This economic move was not directed against Aryan big business concerns, which were needed for the rearming of the "New Germany."

e. Thousands of Jews were deprived of their livelihoods and were forced to leave Germany.

f. Officially organized attacks by mobs against Jewish shops and individuals were common.

g. Hitler instituted various laws which were intended to drive the Jews out of Germany.

   (1) These regulations dominated the life of the German Jews.

   (2) It was impossible for Jews to enter any profession; those already in a profession were forbidden to administer services to Aryans.

   (3) There was enforced economic and social discrimination.

   (4) Jews became liable to arbitrary imprisonment for undefined crimes. Thousands of Jews were imprisoned in concentration camps which were erected immediately after Hitler's rise to power.

h. Although many German Jews emigrated (some 300,000 out of a population of approximately 500,000), many were still unable or unwilling to leave the land of their birth.

3. Terror Increases and the Net Widens

   a. The Jews were able to emigrate to a limited number of countries.

      (1) The number of countries accepting Jewish refugees became fewer with the expansion of German territory under Hitler.

      (2) Few nations wished to resettle these impoverished refugees who had been stripped of most of their property. One of the arguments used for limiting immigration was that these nations were still recovering from the economic depression and new immigrants would upset the economic order.

(3) The United States and Great Britain admitted some immigrants. They received a large proportion of ousted scientists and intellectuals who were forced to flee Nazi persecutions.

(4) Before 1939 some German Jews were able to emigrate to Palestine, but because of the White Paper of 1939 this immigration was limited (see Chapter XLIV, "Palestine: Turkey and Great Britain").

(5) Small numbers of refugees went to South America, North Africa, and the Far East.

(6) Others left for west European countries that the Nazis eventually conquered after 1939.

b. After the murder of Ernst vom Rath, a German official in Paris, by a Jew, the Nazis staged the infamous *Kristallnacht* ("Crystal Night") on November 9-10, 1938.

(1) A pogrom was staged in every German and Austrian city, destroying many of the synagogues and businesses of the Jewish community.

(2) After the pogrom was over, the Nazis presented the Jewish communities with a collective fine of billions of marks to pay for repairs of the damage caused by the Nazis during the *Kristallnacht*.

(3) It was later made illegal for a German insurance company to pay an insurance claim to a Jew, because German insurance companies paid for most of the damages which were a result of *Kristallnacht*.

c. The Nazis expanded across Europe.

(1) After the annexation of Austria in March 1938, Nazi anti-Semitic policies were introduced in Austria, thus adding 200,000 Jews to the number of victims in the growing web of tyranny.

(2) After the Munich "peace conference" in March 1938, Czechoslovakia and Bohemia were added to the lands of the German Reich.

(3) After the outbreak of the Second World War on September 1, 1939, Poland, Holland, Belgium, Denmark, Norway, and France were occupied by German forces.

(4) In addition, Germany forced racial laws upon her allies: Italy, Hungary, Croatia, Bulgaria, and Rumania. In these lands which came under Nazi control, Jews found themselves faced with a concerted program of terror and death.

4. Extermination

    a. It had been the Nazi policy to expropriate Jewish capital and force Jews out of all aspects of German life, hoping for the eventual emigration of Jews from Germany.

    b. After the German conquest of Poland in August 1939, a systematic program of concentration of the Jewish communities was introduced.

        (1) In the conquered areas Jews were forced to live in specified areas and were governed by laws and regulations imposed on them by the Nazis.

        (2) Jews living in smaller towns were deported to the larger cities and towns.

        (3) Many Jews died or were murdered during these deportations.

        (4) Ghettos in such cities as Warsaw, Vilna, Lvov, Lodz, and Lublin had Jewish self-governments called *Judenrat*, which was controlled by the Nazis.

        (5) These Judenrat were set up by the Germans to regulate life in the ghettos. Under the control of the Judenrat, businesses, factories, schools, hospitals, kitchens, and theatres operated on a day-to-day basis.

(6) Because the ghettos were densely populated and food and medicine were scarce, disease, starvation, and death were common.

c. Concentration camps were built at Auschwitz, Bergen-Belsen, Buchenwald, Treblinka, and other places.

(1) They were originally intended to house political prisoners and those who opposed the Nazi government, but eventually, captured Russians, Jews, Gypsies, and other "undesirables" were imprisoned there.

(2) German industrial concerns opened armament factories that employed thousands of slave laborers.

(3) The concentration camps were later expanded and transformed into death camps.

d. In January 1942 at the Wannsee Conference the "Final Solution" to the "Jewish problem" was proposed. This was a plan for the extermination of European Jewry.

(1) Jews living in western Europe were deported to the east where they were either used for slave labor or were exterminated.

(2) The ghetto administrations had to supply a specified quota of Jews for supposed "resettlement" in the east.

(3) Adolf Eichmann, who was in charge of the "Final Solution," told the court at his trial in Jerusalem in 1961, that approximately 4,000,000 Jews were killed in the death camps and approximately 2,000,000 Jews died in other ways (starvation, disease, etc.).

e. The question of resistance and rebellion was discussed in the ghettos. It was argued that even if a German were killed, the reprisals on the Jewish community would be tremendous.

(1) Jews resisted German domination by carrying on their everyday lives. In the ghettos, children studied in school, theatre groups performed, and young people married. This in itself should be considered resistance.

(2) Those working in armament plants or German-run factories and shops resisted by sabotaging their work or by not working fast enough.

(3) Jews staged armed rebellions in the Warsaw ghetto, Lublin ghetto, and in Auschwitz and Treblinka death camps. Though these were heroic acts, they were doomed to failure because of lack of arms, manpower, and support from the various non-Jewish resistance groups. Despite lack of success, the ghetto uprisings proved to the Nazis that the Jews did know how to fight.

(4) Jews who escaped from the Nazis organized or joined anti-Nazi partisan groups. Unfortunately, many of the partisan groups who were anti-Nazi were also anti-Jewish. Many Jews escaped the Nazis only to fall into the hands of anti-Semitic partisans (this was especially true in Poland).

D. *After the Holocaust*

1. The Holocaust, considered by many to be man's most monstrous crime against his fellowman, was a well-planned program of extermination which had the active support of the citizens of the occupied countries.

2. The Allied Powers tried and convicted the major Nazi leaders during the Nuremberg Trials, 1946-1948.

   a. Many Nazis have escaped capture and have found refuge in South American and Arab countries.

   b. Many of those convicted were later given lesser sentences or pardoned after serving some time in prison.

   c. Many former Nazis assumed important positions in the governments of East and West Germany.

   d. The West German government signed a $1,500,000,000 agreement with Israel for restitution for damages incurred to the Jewish people.

   e. Many Germans live under a burden of collective guilt for their active participation in, or apathetic indifference to, the genocide of millions of civilians.

3. Jews in Europe still had many problems after the war.

   a. The end of fighting did not bring peace to the fragment of European Jewry which had survived the war (approximately 3,000,000 out of a population of approximately 9,000,000). In Poland there was an upsurge of anti-Semitism, as many Poles blamed the Jews for the war.

   b. Realizing that east Europe was no longer a desirable place to live, many Jews fled to the English, French, and American sectors of Occupied Europe.

   c. These refugees were interned in displaced persons' camps while waiting for some decision to be made about their fate.

   d. Support for efforts predating the Holocaust to establish a Jewish state was seen as the only solution to alleviate the problem of the Jewish refugees in Europe (see Chapter XLVIIIa, "Emergence of Israel").

E. *Conclusion*

Man's inhumanity to man has rarely been so overt as in the decimation of Europe's Jews, which will forever remain a bloody stain in history. In retrospect, the murderers and their accomplices were not the only guilty parties: The silence and apathy of presidents, prime ministers, popes, Christians, and Jews must also be included among the factors responsible for the genocide. A Jewish state was created a few years after the Holocaust, which was seen by some as a form of atonement for the crime which Europe felt obligated to pay the Jewish people for their suffering or as an expedient solution to a refugee problem. The Holocaust has left its impact on religious thought, literature, and politics. However, we are still too close to the event to comprehend fully the effects of this tragedy on the Jewish people and on the world.

XLVII

AMERICAN JEWRY IN THE TWENTIETH CENTURY

We can see the results of emancipation and assimilation in the development of the American Jewish community in the twentieth century. Because there were no legal or economic restrictions placed upon the Jews, they had the opportunity for self-development and advancement. In the span of eight decades Jews have become an integral part of the American society, yet at the same time they have remained a separate and distinct group.

A. *Cultural Activities*

1. The mass migration of east Europeans Jews created a vibrant Yiddish cultural life in America (see Chapter XLII, "Yiddish Culture").

    a. An American Yiddish press developed which catered to the various political and religious factions among the immigrants.

    b. Yiddish literature and poetry reached new heights in the new country.

    c. The Yiddish theatre flourished.

    d. Lecture series were sponsored by various organizations to help "Americanize" the new immigrants.

    e. Community centers were established to help provide cultural and social activities for the immigrants.

    f. An after-public school system was set up using Yiddish as the language of instruction.

2. As the children of the immigrants became integrated into the society, they saw no need to speak Yiddish or be involved in "European" activities.

    a. Many children of immigrants spoke only English, refusing to speak Yiddish, which they considered to be "Old Worldly."

    b. Many Jews Americanized their names.

3. American Jews played a major role in the development of the twentieth-century American novel. A number of authors have written about their experiences growing up as a Jew in America. In many respects, the "Jew" took over the stereotype of the "Yankee" in American literature. The Jew became the symbol of the rags-to-riches get-rich-in-America story.

4. American Jews became prominent in the entertainment field. Some began as actors and actresses in the Yiddish theatre, eventually moving onto the English stage and screen. Jews can be found today in all areas of the entertainment business.

5. Many Jewish intellectuals fled to America after the Nazi takeover in Germany and Austria. Many became instructors in universities and were influential in shaping American thought. They contributed their knowledge in such fields as philosophy, literature, physics, chemistry, art, music, and medicine.

B. *Economics*

1. The new immigrants settled in the larger eastern cities where they lived in lower income areas. They settled there because they originally landed in eastern harbor cities. These areas were usually older and because of this, the rent was cheaper. Other new immigrants also lived there, giving areas an ethnic flavor.

2. The new immigrants began working in the garment industry and in other unskilled trades. They organized unions in order to receive higher wages, safer working conditions, shorter hours, and other benefits. These Jewish unions were part of the foundation of the labor movement in America.

3. In time, the Jews shifted from being employed as manual workers, eventually entering business and professional fields.

   a. There was the motivation to advance and raise one's social and economic status. Education was seen as one method of advancement in society.

   b. Professionals were admired because of the steady income and status attached to such professions.

c. As their income rose, they eventually became involved in the post-World War II migration from the city to the suburbs.

d. One of the reactions to this way of life that was based on materialism was the "counterculture" of the 1960s.

C. *Religion*

1. Many Jews tried to retain their traditional orthodox practices.

   a. The conditions and customs in America, however, forced many religious Jews to cut their beards and work on the Sabbath. Some succumbed to economic demands and complied, while others were able to remain orthodox in America.

   b. A "modern orthodoxy" developed in America where one could remain an Orthodox Jew and still be integrated into American society.

2. After World War II many Hasidim came to New York where they set up insular communities (see Chapter XXXVII, "Hasidism").

3. The children of the immigrants learned English and adopted American customs. Many of the children felt alienated from their parents, whom they identified as immigrants and not "Americans." This alienation led to a gradual rejection of Judaism by some first- and second-generation American Jews. Those who remained observant Jews tended to become members of Conservative and Reform congregations, which were more adaptable to the American lifestyle.

4. The three major branches of Judaism (Orthodox, Conservative, and Reform) organized school systems, summer camps, youth groups, leadership programs, rabbinical seminaries, and teachers institutes in order to strengthen their respective movements.

5. Despite the erection of many new synagogues there was a general trend of laxity in religious observance. The various branches of Judaism have been trying to bring back uninterested Jews to the synagogue in order to worship and to become involved in Jewish affairs. Youth and adult groups were established by congregations in order to strengthen the community. Many congregational facilities have also been used as Jewish centers where communal functions and activities other than worship can be quartered.

D. *Education*

1. Many of the early immigrants were socialists and disregarded religious practices and beliefs. They were not interested in setting up religious schools for their children.

2. Many of the immigrants discarded their "old world" ways in order to assimilate into American society. They stressed a public school secular education as being the most important means to achieve this end.

3. Immigrants who wanted to maintain Judaism set up after-school religious classes which were usually held in the local synagogue.

4. Teaching institutes were set up to train qualified teachers in Hebrew, Yiddish, and Jewish studies.

5. Yeshivot and Jewish day schools were established in which Jewish and secular subjects could be taught in the same institution.

6. Today there are Jewish religious institutions of higher learning which offer undergraduate and graduate degrees. Secular universities across the country offer courses and degrees in Judaic studies, Hebrew, and Yiddish.

E. *Communal Affairs*

1. The American Jewish community did not have the power of their European predecessors because, in America, Jews could disassociate themselves from the community with impunity and still remain Jewish, while in Europe the community could enforce social controls on its members.

2. With the immigration of east European Jews at the end of the nineteenth century, German Jews feared that nativist anti-Semitism might increase because of the influx of "foreigners." They established organizations to help integrate the new immigrants into American society.

3. The immigrants also set up their own organizations. Natives of the same town started organizations which helped each other in times of need. They also provided a social and cultural center in order to meet fellow townsmen. These fraternal organizations helped provide

funeral arrangements, insurance, and pensions for members and their families.

4. National organizations were established to protect Jewish legal rights, provide for communal needs, give aid in times of emergency, combat anti-Semitism, and promote better relations between Jews and non-Jews. These include such organizations as the American Jewish Congress, American Jewish Committee, the United Jewish Appeal, Anti-Defamation League of B'nai B'rith, ORT, and HIAS.

F. Political Trends

1. The German Jews were generally wealthier, more conservative, and tended to vote Republican. The east European Jews were mainly working class. Many of them were anarchists and socialists, who voted for the various labor parties. Eventually, the Democratic party received the overwhelming support of the Jewish population.

2. During the Depression some Jews became completely frustrated with the system, were radicalized, and joined the Communist party and other socialist parties.

3. Jews viewed Franklin Roosevelt as "a defender of the Jews" in America's battle against fascism. Revelations about his lack of action to help Jews during World War II (refusing to bomb the railways to death camps) have destroyed much of the "Roosevelt mythology," which was prevalent in the Jewish community.

4. Because of their experience as a persecuted people, Jews are very sensitive to injustice. This is one of the reasons why many Jews tended to support such movements as civil rights and the campaign against the Vietnam War.

5. Many Jews were found in the various "new left" groups of the 1960s and 1970s. Young Jews became frustrated with the current system and wanted to see a drastic change, so they became involved with anti-establishment activity.

G. Anti-Semitism

1. Anti-Semitism was one of the features of the nativist antiforeigner movements of the nineteenth century. Jews were restricted from joining exclusive clubs and fraternities, or dining in certain restaurants

or hotels. As a reaction against this, Jews created their own clubs, fraternities, and resorts.

2. After World War I, there was a rise of antiforeigner sentiment. Foreigners were seen as socialists, Bolsheviks, and anarchists who wanted to destroy the American way of life.

   a. Immigration restriction laws were passed in 1921 and 1924.

   b. The U.S. isolationist policy of the 1920s and 1930s was a result of this distrust of foreigners and of affairs which didn't directly concern the United States.

   c. This American nationalism had many anti-Semitic overtones. The Jews were seen by some of these isolationists as the corrupters and destroyers of the American way of life.

3. World War II and the Holocaust helped lessen anti-Semitic thought and behavior.

4. In the last decade there has been an upsurge of anti-Semitism by blacks. The Jew is seen as an exploiter and oppressor because many of the black areas in the larger urban centers were areas in which Jews formerly lived. Many Jews still own buildings or have businesses in the area. There are a high number of Jews working in the black community, holding such jobs as teachers, social workers, and welfare inspectors. The Jew is stereotyped as the symbol of the "white" who has been the major cause of the poverty in the black community.

5. In recent years many outbursts of anti-Semitic rhetoric have taken on the guise of anti-Zionism.

H. *Zionism*

1. East European Jews brought the idea of Zionism to America.

2. Reform Judaism opposed Zionism until World War II because of its views about the role of the Jews (see Chapter XXXVIII, "Haskalah"). However, it has since changed its position and Zionism is an essential part of Reform Judaism.

3. Jews on the Left (both "old" and "new") viewed Zionism as a reactionary, nationalistic belief.

4. American Jewry has been an active supporter of the State of Israel. Because of the Holocaust, American Jews have felt a need to keep the Jewish state alive.

  a. American Jews play an important role in supplying money to Israel.

  b. American Jewish lobbies try to get pro-Israeli bills and allocations passed in Congress.

  c. Thousands of American Jews visit Israel annually, thus helping the Israeli economy.

  d. The emigration of American Jews to Israel has been minimal. This is because most major emigrations occur when the Jew feels threatened in his present environment.

I. *Conclusion*

The American Jewish community is the largest and most influential Jewish community in the Diaspora. After a relatively short "transitional" period, the new immigrants and their children were able to integrate and assimilate themselves into American society. Many of the Jewish ideals, traditions and customs which were brought over from Europe have been redefined, expanded, and reapplied to become relevant in light of the American-Jewish experience. Despite many changes in the makeup of the community, the American Jew has been able successfully to retain his distinct and separate identity in that "melting pot" called America.

XLVIII

THE EMERGENCE OF ISRAEL

On May 14, 1948, the State of Israel was proclaimed. The new Jewish homeland became the refuge for hundreds of thousands of Jewish refugees who survived the Nazi Holocaust, the persecutions in Arab lands, and cultural repression in the Soviet Union. The creation of the Jewish state also created the displacement of thousands of Palestinian Arabs. The act of a Jewish settlement in Palestine has resulted in the present Middle East conflict, which has involved the major world powers. Hampered by the necessity to maintain security, the government has not been able to resolve many pressing economic and social problems. Within three decades there have been four wars. Both the Arab states and Israel have suffered from the consequences of their seemingly irreconcilable differences.

A. *Historical Background*

1. World War II changed world power politics. The United States, which before the war had had little interest in the Middle East, was now the world's greatest military and economic power.

   a. The United States was dependent upon the Middle East for its oil.

   b. As the Cold War progressed, Israel's proximity to the Soviet Union was important for security reasons.

2. Britain emerged victorious from World War II, but the war had proved very costly to it.

   a. Enormous war debts and economic problems that were a result of the war made it difficult for England to retain its colonial empire.

   b. Nationalism and the struggle for independence was growing among the populace of various British colonies in Asia and Africa. Britain's economy was dependent upon trade with its colonies and commonwealth partners. England could not afford to lose control of the Suez Canal, which was vital for its economy.

B. *Israel, Its Neighbors, and the Great Powers*

1. Creation of the State of Israel

   a. British Foreign Secretary Ernest Bevin rejected the Truman administration's suggestion to admit 150,000 Jewish refugees to Palestine.

   b. Tension mounted in the area with both sides resorting to violence.

      (1) Arab attacks upon Jewish settlements increased.

      (2) Jewish military groups had already been organized and many clashes between Arab and Jewish groups ensued.

   c. Thousands of European Jewish refugees who survived the Nazi death camps were interned in British concentration camps on Cyprus.

   d. In May 1947, the United Nations stepped in and set up the Special Committee on Palestine (UNSCOP). The commission suggested a plan which would partition Palestine into two autonomous states:

      (1) A Jewish state, along the coastal plain extending southward through a narrow strip of desert to the Gulf of Aqaba.

      (2) An Arab state comprising the remainder of the Palestine mandate.

   e. The UN General Assembly passed the proposal on November 29, 1947, with a vote of thirty-three for, thirteen against, and ten abstentions.

   f. Although Britain had said that it would follow the decision of the United Nations, it obstructed the implementation of this decision.

      (1) The hostilities and terrorism which had been going on since the end of the Second World War deteriorated into civil war.

      (2) The officially neutral British administration supplied arms and leadership to the newly formed Arab League while failing to supply defense forces to besieged Jewish communities and to supply convoys.

g. In the spring of 1948, the British prepared to withdraw from Palestine and on May 15, 1948, they left, ending the 28-year old Palestine mandate.

h. On the previous day (May 14, 1948), David Ben-Gurion, chairman of the Jewish Agency Executive, proclaimed the creation of the new State of Israel.

i. The Arab forces who outnumbered the Jews and possessed better armaments attacked almost immediately.

j. A temporary armistice on June 11, 1948, was proclaimed by the UN envoy, Count Folke Bernadotte, after which fighting broke out again.

k. Eventually the Arab forces were repulsed by the Israelis.

l. By July 1949 an armistice with the surrounding Arab state had been signed under the mediation of Dr. Ralph Bunche. This ended the War of Liberation with an Israeli victory.

m. A peace treaty with the Arab states, which would recognize the State of Israel and its borders, was expected, but was never concluded.

2. Early Development of Israel

a. The absence of a peace treaty and the defense of the borders of the new state were the most pressing problems for Israel in its early existence.

(1) An army, navy, and air force were developed. This required heavy taxation and generous financial assistance from Jewish organizations and individuals throughout the world.

(2) Despite the enormous military expenditures, the building of a nation continued at a rapid pace.

b. In February 1949, during the War of Liberation, the Israeli parliament, Knesset, was formed. Chaim Weizmann was elected the new president and David Ben-Gurion served as prime minister.

c. With the proclamation of independence, the British White Paper was annulled, thus allowing the unrestricted immigration of Jews to Israel.

(1) In 1950, the Knesset passed the Law of Return, which automatically gave a Jew the right to emigrate to Israel and be immediately eligible for citizenship.

(2) Within a period of five years, the population of Israel doubled.

(3) The absorption of European Jews and Jews from Arab countries resulted in immense economic and social problems, which were partially alleviated through the financial assistance of Jews around the world and by the German government war restitutions (see Chapter XLVI, "The Holocaust").

d. New towns were built, agricultural settlements established, and desert areas irrigated and reclaimed for agricultural use.

e. Educational institutions of all types were established. The Hebrew University, whose campus was located in Jordan, was reestablished in the Israeli section of the city of Jerusalem.

f. A constant effort was made to move the new state towards self-sufficiency in agriculture and industry.

g. Increased immigration and the end of the war reparations payments by the West German government in 1966 were some of the factors that contributed to a major inflation and economic crisis during the late 1950s and 1960s.

3. Wars with the Arabs: 1956, 1967, and 1973.

a. No peace treaty was ever signed between Israel and the Arab states that might have brought an end to the fighting. Instead the area has been in a constant state of "cease fire."

b. After Colonel Nagib overthrew the regime of King Farouk in Egypt (1952), guerilla activity along the Israeli-Egyptian border increased. Gamal Abdul Nasser, who had become the new leader of Egypt, proclaimed himself dedicated to Arab unity and the destruction of the State of Israel. He undertook rather shaky alliances with other Arab states, notably Iraq, Syria, and Jordan.

c. Since its establishment by the United Nations as an Egyptian-controlled territory in 1949, the Gaza Strip had been a staging area for guerilla attacks upon Israel. By 1955, these attacks had become more frequent and severe, and were openly supported by the Egyptian government.

d. In November 1956, the Israeli army, hoping to destroy the home bases of the marauders, invaded the Gaza Strip.

   (1) In a few days they occupied the entire Sinai Peninsula, except for a strip of land along the Suez Canal.

   (2) Israel was allied with the British and French who were trying to repossess the Suez Canal, which Nasser had expropriated.

   (3) Due to pressure from the United Nations and the United States, Israel was forced to withdraw from the Sinai and the Gaza Strip in exchange for a UN security guarantee.

   (4) Israeli ships were denied access to the Suez Canal, but the Gulf of Aqaba was opened to Israeli shipping after years of blockade, thus providing free access to the Indian Ocean.

e. This state of affairs lasted until the next outbreak of war in June 1967.

   (1) In May 1967, Nasser put Egyptian troops in Sinai and demanded that the UN observation forces be removed immediately.

   (2) The United Nations complied with Nasser's demand, and Egypt cut Israeli access to the Gulf of Aqaba.

   (3) The Six-Day War erupted in which Israel was victorious, defeating Egypt, Syria, and Jordan. Israel occupied the Sinai Peninsula, the Gaza Strip, the entire West Bank of Jordan, and the Golan Heights.

   (4) After the end of the war, the United Nations passed a resolution condemning Israel and called for her withdrawal to the prewar boundaries.

(5) No peace treaty was concluded, and the United Nations sent Gunnar Jarring, the Swedish ambassador, to Moscow to work out a permanent settlement.

f. Border clashes and terrorist activity continued until October 1973, when a fourth Arab-Israeli war broke out.

(1) On October 6, 1973, on the Jewish holiday of Yom Kippur (Day of Atonement), Egyptian forces crossed the Suez Canal and gained a foothold on the Sinai Peninsula.

(2) Syrian forces invaded the Golan Heights.

(3) After recovering from the initial shock, the Israeli forces were able to halt the Arab advance and were able to push them back in certain areas.

(4) After weeks of fighting, U. S. Secretary of State Henry Kissinger was able to negotiate a temporary cease fire.

(5) Preliminary peace talks began in Geneva between the various parties in the conflict.

(6) In 1977, a peace process began between Egypt and Israel resulting in the Camp David Accord; the only peace treaty between and Arab state and Israel.

4. Palestinian Refugees

a. Perhaps the most serious problem facing Israel today is the Palestinian refugee problem. There are approximately one million Palestinian Arabs who have remained in Israel or who have fled the country because of the wars.

b. Although some of the Arab community of Palestine remained in Israel after 1948, most of the Palestinian Arabs responded to the commands of Arab leaders to leave Palestine. Others were forced out of their homes by Jewish military forces or were afraid of the prospects of living in a Jewish state and fled Palestine.

c. Thousands settled in UN-run refugee villages situated in Lebanon, Jordan, Egypt, and Syria.

(1) They were not accommodated by Arab countries, which could not afford to add thousands of people in an economy that had difficulty supporting its own people.

(2) Despite Israel's claims that it was looking for a solution to the Palestinian refugee problem, it was unable to make a settlement with people who were openly hostile to the Jewish state.

d. Membership in various Palestinian guerilla groups was drawn from these bitter, neglected refugees.

e. Palestinian guerilla groups have been supported and created by several Arab governments in their struggle to "liberate" Palestine.

C. *Conclusion*

Despite many setbacks, Israel has developed rapidly since its creation as a state. It has faced many internal and external problems, but has managed to survive and prosper. Because of the constant threat of war, security allocations have taken priority over much-needed economic and social reforms. The Arab-Israeli conflict has drained both sides, physically and mentally. Both sides have found themselves in the midst of an international conflict involving the superpowers who have vested interests in the area. The search for a solution continues. Talks between the belligerent parties have begun and it is to be hoped that peace will come to the area.*

MODERN HEBREW LITERATURE

In the last forty to fifty years the main center of Hebrew literature has unquestionably been Israel. Poets and authors writing in Hebrew have reflected in their works the emotions and experiences created by the revival of a nation and building of a new life in an ancient land. Some have used life in the Diaspora as their subject matter, while others have turned to Jewish history for their source material. The various periods of immigration in the earlier part of the century and the successive influxes of immigrants have continually supplied and enriched the country with new literary talents. With the emergence of the State of Israel, a new generation

---

*In November, 1977, Egypt's Prime Minister Anwar Sadat arrived in Israel to negotiate peace and addressed the Knesset in Jerusalem. In September 1978, the Camp David Peace Agreement between Israel and Egypt was signed.

of young writers whose mother tongue was Hebrew gave Hebrew literature a new vitality and life. Beginning with questions and problems which were unique to Israel, such as the Holocaust, independence, and absorption of immigrants, these writers soon broadened their scope to take a more universalistic approach to the problems shared by all mankind.

A. *The First Generation*

1. The first group includes those who began writing in the Diaspora. They came to Palestine imbued with the spirit of national revival and the desire to rebuild the homeland (see Chapter XLIV, "Palestine: Turkey and Great Britain").

2. Foremost among these writers were Hayyim Nahman Bialik and Saul Tschernichowsky who were quite influential in the Hebrew literary scene. Bialik established a school of thought which emphasized a new form of Jewish nationalism drawn from the Bible and the prophetic writings. In addition, he attempted to establish a vibrant literary community in Palestine. He organized the Dvir Publishing House and the Hebrew Writers Association and assumed undisputed leadership of the literary community (see Chapter XLIIIa, "Bialik").

3. Tschernichowsky introduced a new element into Hebrew literature. He contended that Jewish life in the Diaspora ceases to be a natural and wholesome one because it was divorced from nature. Through his poetry he tried to reawaken this sense of love of nature in Jewish life (see Chapter XLIIIb, "Tschernichowsky").

4. J. H. Brenner (1881-1921) began his literary career in Russia.

   a. In 1909, he moved to Palestine where he continued writing, as well as being active in various labor and pioneer organizations.

   b. Much of Brenner's work is autobiographical, and explicitly expresses the sense of isolation that plagued him throughout his life.

   c. The main characters of his novels are idealists and intellectuals who vainly attempt to flee from the Jewish society against which they are revolting.

d. Brenner is a realist whose honest writing depicts a tragic and helpless world which has no future.

    (1) In his writing, he rejects any positive identification with the old Jewish values and ideals, discarding the view that the Jewish experience of the Zionist movement is a key to the solution of this dilemma.

    (2) He regards the return to the land of Israel as neither a continuation of past traditions nor as a move towards fulfilling a future destiny; rather it is an attempt to make life meaningful in the present.

e. His works can be divided according to their location: pre-World War I Russia, London, and Palestine.

    (1) Among the best of these works is *Mi-Saviv la-Nekudah* ("Around the Point"), the story of an impoverished yeshivah student who comes to the big city and undertakes secular studies with the aim of becoming a Hebrew writer.

    (2) *Me-Ever la-Gevulim* ("Over the Borders") is a similar story, but this time in the setting of the urban London ghetto.

    (3) *Mi-Kan u-mi-Kan* ("From Here and There") is set in Palestine. The eventual outcome of the struggles between the protagonists is the discovery that the solution to the problem of alienation and despair is working and tilling the soil of Palestine.

    (4) *Shekhol ve-Khishalon* ("Breakdown and Bereavement") describes the anguish of a new immigrant who couldn't succeed in adjusting to working on the land or living in Jerusalem.

5. Rahel Bluwstein lived from 1890 to 1931.

a. Bluwstein was born in Russia and came to Palestine in 1909, where she worked in various agricultural settlements.

b. During World War I, she was stricken with tuberculosis. Because of the illness, she was forced to spend the rest of her life in hospitals and sanitariums.

    c. Most of her poetry was written while she was in the hospital.

       (1) It reflects her desperate struggle to cling to life, which she saw as slowly fading away.

       (2) Her poetry is a reflection of her personal situation, be it sadness or joy.

    d. While stylistically lacking, the poems of the dying woman were very popular among the early pioneers and succeeding generations. Her poetry is at times monotonous, but Rahel was quite aware of her limitations and spoke of them in her poetry.

    e. Her poem *Kinneret* has become a popular folksong. In it, she glorifies her beloved lake and exults in the joy of living a free and creative life in Palestine.

B. *The Second Generation*

1. In the second period of Palestinian Hebrew literature, the writings reflect the yearnings for the building of the land of Israel and the creation of the new life that was to come about by this rebuilding.

    a. There was a definite continuum both thematically and literally, from the first period to the second.

       (1) While the influence of authors such as Bialik continued throughout this and later periods, it is important to note the emergence of a new generation of writers during this time.

       (2) These young writers, who emigrated to Israel in the 1920s, not only challenged the authority of Bialik's literary leadership,but also presented their generation's diametrically opposed views concerning social and political issues of the period.

       (3) These radical views developed as a natural consequence of the trauma and upheaval which these writers had experienced after the First World War and the Russian Revolution.

2. The two leading prose writers of this period were S. Y. Agnon (1888-1970) and Haim Hazaz (1898-1973).

a. Agnon's literary achievements and influence on other writers have been great. In 1966, he received the Nobel Prize for Literature (see Chapter XLIIIc, "Shmuel Yosef Agnon").

b. Hazaz has made some very important contributions to Hebrew literature.

   (1) With the introduction of the prose writing of Hazaz, Hebrew fiction reached new heights.

   (2) Hazaz allows his characters to show their emotions. He has allowed the reader to see how the characters eat and drink, what they talk about, how they mourn, and how they rejoice.

   (3) His early writings describe the revolutionary period in the Ukraine and the changes which took place vis-a-vis Jewish life in the small towns of that time.

      (a) Several important works of that period in his life are *Pirkei Mahpekhah* ("Chapters of the Revolution") and *Be-Yishuv shel Ya'ar* ("In a Forest Settlement"). Both describe Jewish life in the Ukraine during the prerevolutionary period.

c. Hazaz arrived in Palestine in 1931, where he concerned himself with Israel's Yemenite community, both in Israel and in Yemen.

   (1) Examples of these concerns are seen in the following stories: *Ha-Yoshevet Ba-Ganim* ("The Dweller in the Garden") and *Mori Sa'id*, which takes place in Israel, and *Ya'ish*, which is set in Yemen.

d. The central theme of Hazaz is that of the redemption of the Diaspora Jew. This messianism was in opposition to Zionism; redemption would mean the end of Judaism; and thus Zionism became the negation of Diaspora Judaism.

e. Like Agnon, Hazaz's style is literary and his vocabulary and syntax differ considerably from the Hebrew of his time.

f. Though Hazaz's Hebrew is basically mishnaic or talmudic, he displays great talents for changing the language for the sake of realism. He Ukrainized the Hebrew of the Ukrainian peasants and Arabicized the speech of the Yemenite Jews.

3. There are five outstanding poets of this period.

   a. Abraham Shlonsky, Nathan Alterman, Leah Goldberg, Uri Zvi Greenberg, and Shin Shalom best exemplify the period. This group of writers has attempted to disassociate itself from the previous generation.

      (1) They are opposed to Bialik's preoccupation with classical structure and language which they believe was not in tune with the changing trends in writing.

      (2) Many of them expressed their new ideas in *Ketuvim* ("Writings"), a magazine published by the Hebrew Writers Association in 1926.

   b. Abraham Shlonsky (1900-1973), as the editor of *Ketuvim* and later editor of another literary journal, *Turim*, openly challenged Bialik's literary authority, a challenge that made a great impact on the literary community.

      (1) He demanded the acceptance of spoken Hebrew and even slang as legitimate forms of poetic expression.

      (2) He called for a modern, "de-theologized" Hebrew poetry in contrast with the rationalistic, nationalist-oriented poetry of the older generation.

      (3) His poems express a feeling of despair and agony for his generation of Jews, who had suffered so much from war, revolution, and pogroms. This is seen in *Be-Elleh ha-Yamim* ("In These Days"), which he wrote about the Arab riots in Palestine in the 1920s, or in *Shirei ha-Mappolet ve-ha-Piyyut* ("Songs of the Downfall and Elegy"), where he describes his loneliness and alienation in a Europe that has gone mad.

      (4) In his later works, he treats themes in a more mature fashion. He attempts to strike a balance between symbolistic influences and the more blatant surrealistic and expressionistic imagery. This is seen in *Avnei Gevil* ("Unhewn Stones"), which reflects the poet's resignation to the fate of humanity in facing its

inevitable doom. In *Mi-Shirei ha-Perozedor ha-Arokh* ("From Poems of the Long Corridor"), he reflects about life and death.

c. Nathan Alterman (1910-1970) continued and extended Shlonsky's experiments with new forms of rhyme and syntax taken from the spoken language.

   (1) Although he did succeed in using what was at the time considered a slangy vocabulary, he actually did not stray very far from the common usages in the language.

   (2) The reason for this is clear: Spoken Hebrew was not developed enough in the twenties and thirties for Alterman, or Shlonsky, to utilize it freely in their writings.

   (3) However, Alterman's work is certainly very important and unique in its own ways. Almost from the beginning, there appear different strains in his works which would occasionally intermingle.

      (a) There is his ballad type of verse which was published weekly in the Hebrew newspaper *Haaretz*.

      (b) He later had a weekly column in the newspaper *Davar* called *Ha Tur ha-Shevi'i* ("The Seventh Column"). This became a running poetic commentary on the turbulent forties and played a role in expressing and shaping the moods and attitudes of a people simultaneously witnessing their nation's rebirth and their own destruction.

      (c) On the other hand, there is his lyrical poetry which utilizes his expressional metaphors and slangy neologisms, which can be seen in his first book *Kohavim ba-Hutz* ("Stars Outside").

d. Leah Goldberg (1911-1970) was also active in Shlonsky's circle and was closely associated with the modernistic movement in Hebrew literature of the thirties.

   (1) Leah Goldberg shunned the verbal extravagance of the others and tended to use traditional verse forms.

(2) Her brand of modernism is reflected in the conversational style of her works and the reflection of both the rhetorical forms of her predecessors and the expressionistic style of her contemporaries.

(3) Her themes are universal and deal with such matters as childhood, love, aging, and death.

(4) She uses a simple language which has a lot of symbolism in it. This is seen in her poem *Mi-Shirei ha-Nahal* ("The Songs of the Stream") where she uses nature to help represent the problems of an artist.

e. Uri Zvi Greenberg (1894-1981) rejected the rational, humanistic ideals which were popular among contemporary writers. He replaced them with a mystical antirationalism which professed a quasi-racial conception of the history and destiny of the Jewish people.

(1) Though he rejects Europe and its literary traditions, he frequently uses poetic techniques which are found in European literature.

(2) He draws most of his inspiration and style from biblical and kabbalistic literature.

(3) His poetry expresses his horror at the fate of the Jews. This is seen in *Rehovot ha-Nahar* ("Streets of the River") where he concluded that the Holocaust was the logical consequence of Judaeo-Christian relations. In this poem he condemns God for not saving his people.

f. Shin Shalom (1904-1990) has expressed in his writings a strong nationalism combined with a mystical individualistic mission.

(1) He writes about the conflict and tension between man and the world he is living in.

(2) In *Panim el Panim* ("Face to Face") he describes a magical journey into one's soul.

(3) In his novel *Ha-Ner lo Kavah* ("The Candle Was Not Extinguished") he depicts the struggle of a poet in his battle against allowing his creativity to be destroyed.

C. *The Third Generation**

1. This period of modern Hebrew literature in Palestine is generally known as the State of Israel period. Though the year 1948 stands as a convenient date for the beginning of this period, its beginnings are actually earlier. The leading figures of this generation are quite different from their predecessors in that they are all native Palestinians or arrived in Palestine at a very early age.

   a. Not only is Hebrew their native tongue, or at least a language of their early childhood years, but their view and relationships with the land of Israel and Zionism are quite different from others before them.

   b. They view the land in a much more realistic way, and can understand the Zionistic dreams of their fathers.

   c. This change of geographical emphasis also has changed the Hebrew style of the writers.

      (1) Because these writers have had secular educations, they do not have many rabbinic or medieval allusions in their work.

      (2) Their writings are not influenced by eastern or central European literature, nor are there carry-overs from Yiddish and eastern European Jewish culture.

      (3) This group is influenced by British and American literature and emphasizes either primary biblical references or modern colloquial expressions.

   d. Many of these young writers are members of kibbutzim and are associated with various leftwing socialistic movements.

      (1) One name given to the early members of this school, the Palmach generation, comes from the fact that many of these people served in the *Palmach*, the crack army units of the War of Independence whose membership consisted of many kibbutzniks.

---

*Authors and writers living in 1991 are not included in this work.

(2) The members of the Palmach generation have been imbued with an idealistic enthusiasm which soon gave way to the harsh reality of building the new state.

(3) Immigration, the unresolved conflict with the Arabs, the shift of foreign policies on the part of the great powers, and the always increasing necessity to compromise ideals in order to survive are biting realities of the times.

e. As the utopian ideologies gradually erode, the Israeli writers have begun to question the possibility of creating a new form of Zionist ideology.

(1) The prose and poetry of the late fifties and sixties have taken individualistic, existential, and even surrealistic tones of expression.

(2) Except for their cultural or geographical contexts, this literature has rarely dealt with the parochial Jewish problems which have previously been so prevalent in Hebrew literature.

(3) No matter how much they reject ideologies, these writers have never been able to escape the ethical imperatives of the Jewish tradition.

2. Many of the leading poets of this period have been connected with the Palmach, including such figures as Amir Gilboa, and Abba Kovner.

a. Amir Gilboa (b. 1917) set the stage for the new group of poets by creating in his poetry a unique blend of traditional and colloquial elements.

(1) His poetry is permeated with the tragedy of the Holocaust, not only because his family perished in it, but also because as a soldier in the Jewish Brigade he experienced many of the horrors of war.

(2) In his later works a surrealistic atmosphere of dreams and childhood experiences appear and his poetry becomes more complicated. He has been experimenting with Hebrew sounds and has created a surrealistic atmosphere of images and events.

b. Abba Kovner (1918-1990) differs from the other poets because he was brought up in a European Zionist environment and because he was a survivor of the Holocaust.

   (1) He was one of the leaders in the Vilna Ghetto. After the ghetto was destroyed he became a partisan.

   (2) After the war ended he was active in organizing *Berihah* ("Escape"), which was the illegal immigration of Jews to Israel.

   (3) He eventually settled in Israel, joining Kibbutz Yad Mordechai.

   (4) His poetry repeatedly uses the themes of the Holocaust and the struggle for Israel's survival.

   (5) Throughout his works he uses a lot of symbolism and conjures images which provoke us with a complex and horrifying picture of war and death.

3. The Palmach generation also produced realistic prose literature dealing with the problems which the new state was encountering: the Holocaust, War of Independence, immigration, changing life on the kibbutz, and the Israeli-Arab issues.

E. *Conclusion*

In the last 150 years, the Hebrew language has been transformed from a language used exclusively for clerical and religious functions to a "living" language used by Jews around the world. Novelists, poets, essayists, journalists, satirists, and playwrights who write in Hebrew reflect in their work the anguish, joy, and confusion of contemporary Jewish history. One finds in their works the developments and advances which were occurring in Zionism, Israel, Europe, and America. Their writings pose many questions as they try to solve the problems which arise in their respective generation: dignity of manual labor, British mandatory policy, Holocaust, illegal immigration, Arab-Israeli wars, absorption of immigrants, social and economic ills, occupied territories, guerilla activities, and the Jews vs. Israeli dichotomy. In spite of years of constant fighting, a generation has arisen which has reacted to its environment and living condition by producing many sensitive and introspective pieces of literature.

APPENDIX A

HISTORY OF THE JEWS*

The following article by Dr. Ellis Rivkin, a noted Jewish historian, is a review of material that was covered in this work. Dr. Rivkin's article will also offer you a different perspective on certain aspects of Jewish history. By this time, you should have some definite ideas concerning Jewish history and thought. Therefore, this article should serve as a stimulus to you to consider the different aspects of Jewish history and to begin to see how modern Jewish history has developed.

Jewish history is a complex phenomenon that resists a simple and concise summary. Its beginnings are to be traced back to the early civilizations of the ancient Near East; while its development involves an interaction with many empires and civilizations. It displays a bewildering array of contradictory manifestations that defy facile generalizations. Jewish history is the history of a people, living in its own land and enjoying independence; it is also a history of a people living on its own land, subject to the sovereignty of powerful empires. It is the history of religious communities affirming their viability in a world-wide diaspora (dispersion), long after the land of Israel had ceased to be a major area of Jewish settlement. Yet it is also the history that includes the emergence of the modern state of Israel. Wherever one turns, Jewish history confronts the historian with diverse and contradictory phenomena. Jews have created tribal, monarchial, theocratic, aristocratic, oligarchial, republican, and democratic forms of self-government. They have espoused secularistic and nationalistic ideologies. Jews have been nomads and peasants, shepherds and craftsmen, warriors and scholars, statesmen and pariahs, slaveowners and slaves, creditors and debtors, capitalists and proletarians, rich and poor. They have been literate and illiterate, provincial and cosmopolitan, naive and sophisticated, rationalistic and mystical, legalistic and moralistic, heretical and traditional, liberal and reactionary, nationalistic and universalistic. Such a welter of diverse and conflicting manifestations would present formidable problems for the historian even if they followed one upon the other, but they almost defy generalization when they are continuously intermingling, resisting neat classifications and categories.

To find our way through this bewildering maze, we shall approach Jewish history as a process displaying two major features:

*This article was prepared for the *New International Encyclopedia* and is reproduced with permission of its author, Dr. Ellis Rivkin, Professor of Jewish History, Hebrew Union College, Jewish Institute of Religion, Cincinnati, Ohio.

(1) An evolution of interdependent forms in the direction of greater and greater complexity. This evolution accounts for the differentiated character of Jewish history—that which makes it distinct and separate, and which justifies the giving of a single name, Jewish, to so contradictory a process.

(2) A relationship with larger societies, cultures, and civilizations which is so interlocked in character that every phase in the history of the Jews bears the ineradicable stamp of these larger units. Yet the impress of the larger world is so absorbed and reworked by the prevailing Jewish forms that the end result is the maintenance of a distinctively Jewish pattern. Jewish history can thus be thought of as a process that elaborates ever more complex and interdependent forms through an intellectually selective interaction with the larger social, cultural, and civilizational complexes within which this history developed.

Ancient Near Eastern Phase (2000-332 B.C.E.)

Patriarchal Period (2000-1020 B.C.E.). The history of the Jews had its origins in the migration of seminomadic Amorite tribes into the Fertile Crescent, c. 2000 B.C.E. Some of these tribes, under their patriarchal chief Abraham, maintained their tent-dwelling culture in Canaan (Palestine), a land viewed as promised to them by their protector-God, El-Shaddai.

Compelled by famine to seek food in Egypt (c. 1700), some of the tribes settled in Goshen. Reduced to servile status, they responded to the leadership of Moses, fled from Egypt c. 1280, and at Mount Sinai covenanted themselves to Yahweh, the God whom Moses identified with Shaddai. They swore exclusive loyalty to Him and accepted legislation that Moses promulgated in His name.

Taking advantage of the weakening of Egyptian imperial control in Canaan, the tribes, under the leadership of Joshua, conquered a considerable part of Canaan c. 1250-1200. A century of semianarchy followed these exploits. It was marked by occasional coalitions against external enemies, led by military chieftains, such as Gideon, called Judges.

Monarchial Period (1020-587 B.C.E.). The emergence of an agricultural-urban society transformed the seminomadic tribal structure, and ushered in a monarchical order. Confronted by the Philistine menace and the need for dependable state power, the prophet-priest Samuel first selected Saul (1020-1005 B.C.E.) and then David (c. 1004-965) to unify the tribes under a monarchical system. David's son Solomon (c. 965-926) consolidated the structure through heavy taxation, a bureaucratic hierarchy, a mercenary army, and an elaborate cultus in the Temple that he built at Jerusalem.

Resentful of the despotic system, the 10 northern tribes rebelled in 929 and established the kingdom of Israel. In contrast to the stable Davidic dynasty of the kingdom of Judah, the kingdom of Israel's history was marked by violent dynastic changes.

The cementing of commercial relations by the dynasty established by King Omri (882-871) with Tyre evoked the wrath of Elijah, who denounced Ahab (871-852) for introducing the Tyrian Baal. Elijah's insistence on the exclusive worship of Yahweh bore fruit when his successor Elisha supported Jehu's bid for the throne.

The Elijah-Elisha type of guild prophet was gradually superseded by a new kind of prophet. Amos was the first of these. Dissatisfied with the limited vision of the Yahweh exclusivists, he denounced the elaborate Yahwistic cult patronized by Jeroboam II (787-747) of Israel. He insisted that Yahweh was the God of justice, who abhorred the exploitation of the lower classes, and who would punish both Judah and Israel. The new prophetic message was spread in Israel by Hosea (c. 747-735) and in Judah by Isaiah (c. 740-701), Micah (745-700), and Jeremiah (626-585).

The rise of Assyria brought an end to the kingdom of Israel in 721, while the triumphant Babylonians destroyed Jerusalem and its Temple in 587. The Judeans, however, were spared the fate of the lost Ten Tribes, for though exiled to Babylonia, they were not annihilated.

Since these catastrophic events had been predicted by the new prophets, the Jews accepted them as evidence of Yahweh's anger and not His weakness.

Exile and Restoration (587-445 B.C.E.). This notion was fortified by Ezekiel (c. 592-c. 570) who interpreted the destruction and exile as deserved punishment for disloyalty to Yahweh and for the profanation of His house by an impure priesthood. He prophesied a glorious reconstruction of the Temple cult. The Second Isaiah (c. 550), however, placed greater emphasis on the cosmic power of Yahweh and conceived the restoration as an opportunity to spread His teachings throughout the world.

Persia's imperial successes were followed by Cyrus's permission for a restored Judaea in 538 B.C.E. Although the Temple was rebuilt around 516, the restored society remained unstable until a durable system— associated with the leadership of Nehemiah and Ezra and based on the canonization of the Pentateuch—was achieved (c. 445).

Persian Domination (445-332 B.C.E.). As Persian imperial governor, Nehemiah set up a society that was centered around the Temple priesthood. Power was concentrated in the hands of the Aaronide priesthood, presided over by a high priest of the Aaron-Eleazar-Phineas-Zadok line, which sought its support from a free peasant class.

The authority for such far-reaching structural changes was the canonized Pentateuch. This remarkable document has for millenniums been accepted as divine revelation by Jews, Christians, and Muslims. Although modern scholars hold it to be a composite consisting of a least three distinct strata, it functioned from the time of its canonization (445 B.C.E.) as a unified work. As such, it stresses the efficacy of a sacrificial cultus, and it accords the Aaronides supreme authority. Though never attaining the rank of the Pentateuch, other writings, such as those of the prophets, were also venerated.

The newly established hierocracy proved to be a very durable system till the reign of Antiochus IV Epiphanes (175-163 B.C.E.).

Greco-Roman Phase (332 B.C.E-425 C.E.)

Hellenistic Domination (332-142 B.C.E.). Alexander the Great and his successors, the Ptolemies and the Seleucids, radically transformed the structural patterns of the Near East, primarily through the introduction of the Greek city-state and the Greek culture that accompanied it. Though the Aaronide hierocracy easily accommodated itself first to Alexander (336-323) and later to the Ptolemies (323-197) and Seleucids (Antiochus III, 197-187), it could not but be affected by the quickened tempo of trade, commerce, urbanization, and cultural change. The integrity of the priesthood was severely undermined when Hellenistically oriented priests (Jason, Menelaus) vied with one another to buy the high priestly office from Antiochus IV Epiphanes. Favoring the extension of Hellenistic forms, Antiochus attempted to obliterate Judaism in 168 B.C.E. The majority of the Jews, however, were stirred to revolution, and rallied around the priest Mattathias, the Hasmonean. Under the effective military leadership of his sons Judas Maccabeus, Jonathan, and Simon, they were able to purify the Temple and secure independence in 142 B.C.E.

Hasmonean Dynasty (142-63 B.C.E.). Simon the Hasmonean, in becoming high priest and ethnarch, ushered in not only a period of independence, but also a new high priestly dynasty. This was a momentous change, for hitherto the high priest had been from the family of Zadok, which traced its right to Phineas, to whom God (Num. 25:10-13) had promised the high priesthood as an everlasting possession.

The legitimists (that is, Zadokites, whence "Sadducees") at first rejected the Hasmonean line, but subsequently they modified their opposition and supported the Hasmonean John Hyrcanus (135-104 B.C.E.) when he broke with the Pharisees.

The Pharisees were a revolutionary scholar class that had supported the claims of the Hasmonean high priesthood. This they were able to do because they posited the ultimate authority of an oral law that had been revealed by God simultaneously with the written law. Since this affirmation of an oral law subordinated the Zadokite hierocracy to a non-Aaronide scholar class, it was rejected by the Sadducees, who denounce these Sopherim ("scholars") as Perushim ("separatists," "heretics"; whence the name "Pharisees").

The masses, however, enthusiastically supported the Pharisees, the oral law, and the legitimacy of the Hasmonean high priesthood. Indeed, they sided with the Pharisees when the rupture occurred with John Hyrcanus, and they violently resisted Alexander Jannaeus' (103-76) attempt to consolidate a monarchy with Sadducean support. Only after Salome Alexandra (76-67) restored authority to the Pharisees and their oral law did the masses acquiesce in the monarchy. Thenceforth the Pharisees and their successors, the rabbis, were sovereign in the realm of Jewish law.

Roman Domination (68 B.C.E.-425 C.E.). Judean independence was brief (142-63 B.C.E.). The collapse of the Hellenistic monarchies enabled Rome to take over the Near East, and Rome maintained imperial control over Palestine after the destruction of Jerusalem, either through puppet kings (Hyrcanus II, 63-40; Herod 37-4 B.C.E.; Agrippa I, 41-44 C.E.), procurators (7-36 C.E., 44-66), through the scholar class (Sanhedrin, 70-132), or the patriarchate (145-425).

Heavy taxation coupled with provocative acts by the Roman authorities twice threw the Jews into bloody rebellion (66-70 C.E. and 132-35 C.E.). The first of these ended with destruction of the Second Temple.

The turbulent years 7 to 70 C.E.encouraged a variety of dissident movements within Judaism, one of which grew up around Jesus of Galilee (c. 4 B.C.E-c. 30 C.E.), who preached the imminent coming of the kingdom of God, and was himself deemed by his most devoted disciples to be the Messiah. Although the Procurator Pontius Pilate crucified Jesus (c. 30) for the challenge to Roman sovereignty that a messianic "King of the Jews" implied, a small handful of Jesus' disciples, led by Peter, believed that he would return to usher in the kingdom. The movement made little headway among the Jews, but Paul, by rejecting the law, offered the message of the redemptive power of Christ, which had great appeal to the Gentiles. The rupture with Judaism, however, could not eradicate the historical consequence of the umbilical relationship.

Triumph of Oral-Law Judaism (70 C.E. on). The destruction of the Temple ended once and for all the cultus and the power of the Aaronides, and elevated to supremacy the Pharisaic scholar class. In the following centuries the majority of the Jews accepted the leadership of the scholar classes, whose authority was rooted in the concept of a twofold law, written and oral. Also, the synagogue form of religious expression made the cultus unnecessary.

The leadership of the scholar class was recognized by Rome when it permitted the reconstruction of its legislative body, the Beth Din Ha-Gadol (now called Sanhedrin), under the aegis of Johanan ben Zakkai (70). Although the participation of some members of the scholar class in the unsuccessful Bar Kokhba revolt against Hadrian (132-135) induced Rome temporarily to declare the ordination of scholars, the Antonine emperors underwrote the authority of a strong patriarch, Judah ha-Nasi ("the Prince") (170-217). The latter effectively curbed the independence of individual members of the scholar class by curtailing ordination and by promulgating in the Mishnah an authoritative rendition of the oral law. Although the Mishnah, the patriarch's lawbook, bears—in its systematization and its logical-deductive mode of thought—the impress of Greco-Roman forms, it came to enjoy a sanctity almost equal to that of the Pentateuch.

The patriarchal absolutism of Judah ha-Nasi coincided with the last decades of Roman imperial splendor. The disastrous 3rd century spelled not only mighty changes for the structure of empire but also for the viability of Palestinian Jewry. Although the patriarchate continued under Judah's progeny until the 5th century, it held sway over growing poverty and disintegration. The development of Rome into a Christian state encouraged further deterioration. Palestinian leadership steadily eroded, so that the Palestinian Talmud, unlike the Mishnah, never came to enjoy uncontested authority. With the abolition of the patriarchate, Palestinian Jewry played a relatively insignificant role until the Islamic period.

The Diaspora or Dispersion (from 586 B.C.E.)

With the decline of the patriarchal system in Palestine in the 3rd century C.E., the history of the Jews shifts to other parts of the world. Indeed, except for very brief interludes (in the 10th, 16th, and 17th centuries), Palestine is only peripherally involved in Jewish history until the emergence of the Zionist movement at the turn of the 20th century.

As early as the destruction of the First Temple in 587 B.C.E., viable Jewish communities were set up by exiles in Babylonia and refugees in Egypt. With the Hellenization of the Near East, Jews settled in all major cities. An especially virile community developed in Alexandria under the Ptolemies which produced a durable literature (for instance, the Septuagint, the Letter of Aristeas, and Philo) and enjoyed a vigorous life until the pogroms of the Roman period (38 C.E.). By the time of Paul's journeys, Jews were living throughout the cities of the Roman and Parthian worlds.

Jews in the Sassanian World (225-650 C.E.). The Babylonian Jewish community of the Sassanian period, however, was the first Diaspora Jewry to dominate Jewish historical development for any substantial length of time.

Two Babylonian Jewish scholars, Rav (219-247) and Samuel (219-254), brought back with them from Palestine the patriarchal lawbook, the Mishnah, and adopted it as the fundamental law for the Babylonian Jewish scholar class. The decline in Palestinian fortunes, coupled with the favor shown the Jewish scholar class by the Persian Sassanian Emperor Shapur I (241-271), enabled Rav and Samuel to free themselves from Palestinian authority, establish academies for the thorough study of the Mishnah, and determine the laws by which Babylonian Jewry was to be ruled.

The disintegration of Sassanian power brought with it deterioration of Jewish status, and led two scholars, Rav Ashi (374-427) and Rabina (474-499), to collect all the discussions (called Gemara) of the Babylonian Jewish scholar class into a massive work known as the Babylonian Talmud—no simple lawbook like the Mishnah, but a compendium of everything that the scholars had uttered. Though the Mishnah serves as its text, the Talmud contains not only complex legal debates over the meaning of the Mishnah but also homilies, folklore, anecdotes, and much else. Though never meant to be a code, the Talmud attained an authority among Jews paralleled only by the Mishnah and the Bible.

Jews in the Islamic World (650-1024 C.E.). Islam fell heir to Babylonian Jewry—as well as to the Jewries of the Byzantine Empire. Although Mohammed himself was hostile to the Jews, his successors accorded them autonomous rights. Under both the Umayyads (to 750) and the Abbasids (750-10th century), the Jews were ruled by an exilarch of Davidic descent and by a scholar class (called the Gaonate) whose authority rested on the Babylonian Talmud. Forced out of agriculture by the discriminatory land tax, many Jews, especially in the Abbasid period, undertook an active role in the expanding international trade and finance. Most of the Jews entered a variety of urban occupations. This shift represented a significant economic change, for until the 8th and 9th centuries the majority of Jews had earned their living from agriculture.

The fragmentation of the Abbasid empire in the 10th century undermined the hegemony over Islamic Jewry and wielded by the exilarchate and the Gaonate from Baghdad. Jewish centers sprang up in Egypt, North Africa (Kairouan), and Andalusia, freed themselves from exilarchical and Gaonic controls, and developed their own autonomous communities on the basis of Talmudic law.

The Jews of Andalusia had an especially illustrious development (9th-12th centuries). Under the benign rule of the Umayyads (8th-10th centuries) and then under the various Emirs (11th century), Jews engaged in all occupations (including agriculture), attained high public office (even that of vizier), and produced works of the highest quality in philosophy, grammar, lexicography, and poetry. The invading Almohads (1148), however, made a shambles of Andalusia and compelled the Jews either to accept Islam or to flee.

Among those fleeing was young Moses ben Maimon (Maimonides) (1135-1204), who settled in Egypt under the more tolerant rule of Saladin and wrote two works of enduring impact: the Mishneh Torah (1180), a systematization of Talmudic Jewish law, and the Guild of the Perplexed (1195), a brilliant adaptation of Aristotle to Judaism. With the death of Maimonides, the Jewries of Islam lumbered through a stagnant existence until the rise of the Ottoman power in the 16th century.

Jews in Christian Europe (8th-18th Centuries). The patterns of medieval Jewish history in Christian lands were an outcome of the relationship of the various Jewries to the vicissitudes of feudalism. Since these relationships varied from area to area, the historical experience of the Jews differed greatly. For this reason only one generalization can be made: in each Christian country the Jews enjoyed the positive status so long as their services were utilizable by the ruling classes, a negative status when disintegrative forces in society undercut their usefulness.

Germany, France, England. Because of their values as international merchants (8th-10th centuries), as town builders (10th-11th), and as large-scale moneylenders (11th-12th), the Jews enjoyed a protected status in Germany, France, and England (from 1066). Even the church in these centuries utilized their services. In Germany, although the First Crusade (1096) was accompanied by violent pogroms, the Jewish communities continued to flourish throughout the 12th century.

A basic shift in policy occurred at the end of the 12th century in all three countries. Heavily indebted to Jewish financiers, the king, nobility, and church sought to escape repayment by subjecting the Jews to confiscatory taxation, debasement of legal status, and ideological vilification. This last was launched by Innocent III (1198-1216), who insisted that the Jews be reduced to servile status because of their rejection of Christ. As church policy (Fourth Lateran Council, 1215), this doctrine encouraged the masses to pillage and pogrom the Jews as alleged Christ-killers, desecrators of the Host, and murderers of Christian children for ritual purposes (the Blood Libel). This reversal of policy was most decisive in England and France where, after being divested of much of their wealth, they were expelled (England, 1291; France, 1205, 1322, 1394). Such a fate did not befall them in Germany only because the weakness of the emperor precluded a single act of expulsion. Instead, they were reduced to the status of serfs of the emperor (1235) and were bought, sold, bartered, and pawned by the ruling class (13th-15th centuries).

During the years of privileged status, autonomous Jewish communities produced a highly creative scholar class. Rabbi Solomon ben Isaac of Troyes (Rashi, 1040-1105) wrote a commentary on the Talmud that was never equaled in lucidity and a commentary on the Bible which became a classic. Adopting Rashi as their model, his disciples (the Tosaphists) brought to perfection the casuistic-dialectic (pilpul) approach to the Talmud. With the decline of the Jewish communities, however, the quality of learning deteriorated.

Christian Spain. When the Jews were expelled from England and France, many found a welcome in Christian Spain. Here Christian rulers granted charters to the Jewish communities (aljamahs) and appointed Jews to responsible posts in recognition of their valuable economic services.

The bitter class struggles of the 14th century, however, in undermining the stability of society, unleashed a wave of anti-Semitic violence (1391) that made the aljamahs a shambles. The economic and social fate of the Jews was sealed soon thereafter (decrees of 1412), and finally they were expelled (1492).

During the 1391 pogroms thousands of Jews, especially of the wealthy courtier class, had adopted Christianity. Accepted as bona fide converts (conversos, New Christians), they had intermarried freely with the nobility, and occupied high positions in church and state. Accused (1449) of being secret Jews and attacked violently (1470s), the conversos soon found themselves subjected to the Inquisition (1480), established to investigate their Christian loyalty. Many were burned at the stake; many more were imprisoned and deprived of their wealth; all were stripped of the positive appellation converso and vituperatively renamed marranos ("pigs"). Some of these marranos returned to Judaism and became the founders of western Jewish communities in the 17th century.

Italy. The Italian states of the north that had previously excluded Jews (10th-12th centuries) permitted them from the 13th century to establish loan banks. As long as their services were essential, these bankers were protected and prospered; the communities that grew up enabled their more gifted members to reflect the Renaissance in their writings.

The decline of the Italian city-states (16th-18th centuries), accompanied as it was by a renewal of the papal denunciation of the Jews (bull Cum nimis absurdum), spelled economic stagnation and ghettoization for the Jews. Except for a brief respite in Venice (till 1648), the Jewries of Italy steadily deteriorated till the Risorgimento.

Poland. In the 13th and 14th centuries Poland, too, offered a haven for German Jews. Such Christian Polish Kings as Casimir the Great (1333-1370) offered Jews charters of privilege and protection in return for the services the Jews rendered as fiscal agents, as administrators of the estates of the King and nobility, and as town dwellers. Jews fared well till 1648, developing effective institutions of self-government (the Kahal; the Council of Four Lands), and creating academies (yeshivot) that produced legal minds of rare brilliance (for example, Moses Isserles, 1530-1572).

The economic disintegration of Poland in the 17th century was ushered in by the slaughter of the Jews (Khmelnitsky massacres, 1648). Left in a state of desperation, the Jews were easily victimized by the pseudo-Messiah of Izmir, Turkey, Shabbetai Zevi (1626-1676). After the failure of this movement the Jews responded in large numbers (especially in Volhynia and Podolia) to the spontaneous piety of a new movement, Hasidism, ushered in by Israel Baal Shem Tob (1700-1760). In emphasizing the inner spirit, it appealed not only to poor and semi-illiterate Jews of the towns and villages but to a segment of the scholar class itself. The desperate attempt of Elijah, the Gaon of Vilna (1720-1797), to arrest the movement was only partially successful.

Jews in the Ottoman Empire (16th-17th Centuries). When the Jews were expelled from Spain, they were encouraged to settle in the Ottoman Empire, where their financial and commercial know-how could be utilized. Joined subsequently by marranos, the Iberian Jews engaged in international trade and in the 16th century developed the cloth industry in such Palestinian cities as Safed. The thriving Jewries of Jerusalem, Constantinople, and Salonika proved to be fertile soil for major developments in Jewish law, the most towering of which was a compendium, the Shulhan Arukh, by Joseph Karo (1488-1575), that came to be recognized by Jews the world over as definitive. Paralleling the achievements in law was the elaboration of the mystical doctrines (cabala) of the 13th century Spanish work, the Zohar, by such brilliant mystics as Isaac Luria (1534-1572) of Safed.

The decline of Ottoman power in the 17th century proved disastrous to the Jews. Wracked by the consequences of dissolution, the majority of Ottoman Jewry—joined by large numbers elsewhere—fervently accepted the messianic claims of the Jewish mystic Shabbetai Zevi (1626-1676). His conversion to Islam (1666) at the sultan's insistence plunged myriads of his followers into despair and condemned Ottoman Jewry to stagnation.

The Modern World (17th-20th Centuries)

The key to the history of the Jews in the modern world is to be found in (1) the development of capitalism, (2) the emergence of constitutionally grounded nation-states, and (3) the growth of secular scientific thought. Wherever these phenomena gained ascendancy, the precapitalist, medieval status of the Jews was radically altered for the better (Holland, England, France, United States, Germany, Austria, and Italy); wherever they were unsuccessful or only partially so (Russia-Poland, the Balkans, and Turkey) their degraded status continued; whenever they were challenged, as in France, in the Dreyfus case (1894-1906), anti-Semitism bared its fangs; wherever they were discarded (Nazi Germany, Soviet Russia) the survival of the Jews was jeopardized.

The triumph of Westernization brought about the dissolution of self-governing Jewries and weakened the millennial authority of the Bible and the Talmud. Jews as citizens were free to associate with or disassociate from other Jews and Judaism. Many were attracted to new Western forms of Judaism (Reform, Conservative, Neo-Orthodox), or to secular ideologies (liberalism, nationalism, socialism).

Western Europe and America. The Jewish communities of the West were new communities founded (from the end of the 16th century) by merchant capitalist marranos from Spain and Portugal. The communities were relatively small and lacking in complexity of social structure and in a previous history. As the various nations of their domicile adopted representative systems of government, the Jews gained citizenship rights (France, 1791; Holland, 1796; England, 1847). Although such status was challenged from time to time by anti-Semitic movements (especially in connection with the Dreyfus case in France), it proved durable.

The Westernization process manifested itself most clearly in the United States. Uncluttered by medieval legal restraints on the Jews, and unencumbered by precapitalistic modes and institutions, the United States was in a position to offer the Jews of Europe rare opportunities. Whether these Jews were from the Iberian mercantile background (1654-1820), from the cities, towns, and villages of Germany (1820-1870), or from eastern Europe (1870-1914), they engaged in a variety of economic and professional activities and developed communities and institutions in keeping with the structure of American life. This adjustment was achieved, in part, through the growth of Reform Judaism, launched in the United States by Isaac Mayer Wise (1819-1900), and the later Conservative movement championed by Solomon Schechter (1850-1915). Though a large Jewish proletarian element sustained a strong labor union and socialist interest at the beginning of the 20th century, and an even larger number of

Jews clung to the orthodox-rabbinic Judaism of their east European origins, the steady rise of Jews into the middle class, especially after 1918, encouraged the acculturation process.

Central and Eastern Europe. Westernization in central and eastern Europe had to cope with Jewish communities which were an outgrowth of precapitalistic economic and political systems. As a consequence, there was stubborn conflict between the advocates of Westernization (Haskalah) and the upholders of traditionalism. In Germany a small group of Court Jews (17th century) emerged as wealthy merchant capitalists (18th century) and supported the "enlightened" Judaism of Moses Mendelssohn (1729-1786). Though the Napoleonic conquest briefly emancipated the Jews from their degraded status, the Congress of Vienna (1815) restored the old order, and anti-Semitic riots (1818) stunned the Westernized Jews. Although many converted to Christianity, most Jews sought a solution through the Westernizing of Judaism, either radically through the Reform Judaism of Abraham Geiger (1810-1874) or more traditionally through the Conservative Judaism of Zacharias Frankel (1801-1875) and the Neo-Orthodoxy of Samson Raphael Hirsch (1808-1888) and through the efforts at political emancipation as proclaimed by Gabriel Riesser (1806-1863). The unification of Germany by Bismarck ushered in full emancipation, and the Jews of Germany responded with a flush of creativity in all endeavors.

A somewhat similar development occurred in Austria-Hungary. The intellectual spokesmen for Westernization (Haskalah) in Galicia in the 1820s and 1830s had to fight bitter battles with the followers of Hasidism. Emancipation, in 1868, represented a great victory for the Westernizers, and Vienna became a center of Jewish intellectual and artistic ferment.

The slow arrival of capitalism in eastern Europe precluded emancipation. The tsarist regime, except for some short-lived reforms under Alexander II (1855-1881), treated the Jews with extreme harshness and in 1882 expelled the Jews from the villages, restricting their residence to a Pale, or Settlement. Consequently, the Westernizers abandoned hopes for emancipation held by Judah L. Gordon (1831-1892), and turned to the nationalism of J. L. Pinsker (1821-1891) and Peretz Smolenskin (1842-1885) as a solution.

The rise of Jewish nationalism in the East was paralleled by a similar awakening in the West. Theodor Herzl (1860-1904), an emancipated Western Jew of Vienna, was convinced by the persistence of anti-Semitism in the West (for example, the Dreyfus case, 1894) that the Jews were a nation and that anti-Semitism would come to an end only when the Jews had a national home of their own , preferably in Palestine, as he explained in his book, *The Jewish State* (1896). His own strenuous efforts bore fruit, especially among the Jews of Russia-Poland, and he organized the World

Zionist Congress in 1897. The hopes of the movement were especially heightened by the Balfour Declaration of 1917, in which the British government expressed itself as favoring a Jewish homeland in Palestine after the war.

The Crisis Years (1918-1945). World War I left crises of such great severity that they spawned totalitarian societies in Russia, Italy, Germany, and Spain, and threatened to overwhelm all but the most durable Westernized nations.

These developments proved to be fraught with danger to Jews. In Russia the Soviet regime offered Bolshevik conformity to the Jews, and not emancipation. Precapitalist Jews, capitalist Jews, socialist Jews, and Zionist Jews—all suffered hardships.

In Poland the Jews were persistently subjected to discriminatory legislation, even though their status as a national minority was guaranteed by the Versailles Peace Treaty.

Even in the West the Jews found anti-Semitism to be highly popular when the depression of the 1930s brought into question the viability of capitalism and constitutional government.

The Jewish settlers in Palestine did not have an easy time either. The policies of the British mandatory administration raised painful obstacles to the construction of a national home, for these policies were anything but firm against rising Arab nationalism. The fate of the hardy Jewish settlement on the eve of World War II was very uncertain.

All these difficulties faded into minor problems in the face of Hitler's determination to exterminate the Jews. Crushed by the economic collapse of Germany (1929-1932), millions of Germans accepted Hitler's analysis of the disaster: the Jews as international capitalists and international Bolsheviks had deliberately ruined Germany. Attaining the chancellorship, Hitler set about creating a totalitarian society free of Jews. He stripped them of their wealth and humiliated them (Nuremberg Laws, 1934). With anti-Semitic ideology thoroughly entrenched, the Nazi system used the mantle of war to wipe out the Jews of Europe. Systematically and efficiently about 6,000,000 Jews were destroyed.

The Postwar World. Only the previous history of the Jews spared them total annihilation, for it had spread them among many lands (England, Canada, the United State, South and Central America, North Africa, South Africa, Palestine and the Middle East, India, and the Soviet Union). In the postwar world only the Soviet Union took a negative attitude toward the Jews, and their position there steadily deteriorated.

It was otherwise elsewhere. The murder camps, the pitiful survivors, the Nuremberg trials—all documented the reality of the extermination process and discredited anti-Semitism in the eyes of the Western world.

The decline of imperial controls in the Near East afforded the Jews in Palestine the opportunity of winning their independence in 1948. Opening the doors wide to Jews the world over, the new state of Israel proved to be a haven for survivors of concentration camps and for the Jews of North Africa and the Near and Middle East. These new settlers found themselves in a complex industrialized country with modern political institutions, the fruit of the years of Zionist adherence to their ideal of a viable nation.

In the United States, where more than 5,000,000 Jews live, they have enjoyed the freedom which the Constitution made possible. As citizens they have taken full advantage of the opportunities afforded them and have for the most part achieved middle class status. They have developed a variety of philanthropic, communal, and scholarly institutions; they support three major religious denominations; they are active in government, politics, business,the professions, and the arts. And, with the exception of the Soviet Union and its satellites, conditions are now much the same for Jews the world over.

If, then, historical patterns are meaningful, it would seem that the well-being of the Jews once again reflects the well-being of the societies in which they live.

Consult Roth, Cecil, *A Short History of the Jewish People* (1948); *The Westminster Historical Atlas to the Bible*, ed. by G. E. Wright and F. V. Filson (1956); Rivkin, Ellis, "A Decisive Pattern in American Jewish History", *Essays in American Jewish History* (1958); Bright, John, *A History of Israel* (1959); Rivkin Ellis, "Modern Trends in Judaism," *Modern Trends in World Religions* (1959); Roth, Cecil, *The Jews in the Renaissance* (1959); Tcherikover, V. A., *Hellenistic Civilization and the Jews* (1959); Marcus, J. R., *The Jew in the Medieval World* (1960); Baer, Y. F., *A History of the Jews in Christian Spain* (1961).

APPENDIX B

CHRONOLOGICAL CHART

All dates are B.C.E. unless otherwise indicated.

c. 2000-c. 1750	Age of the patriarchs: Abraham, Isaac, and Jacob
c. 1750-c. 1400	Sojourn in Egypt
c. 1400-c. 1250	Exodus from Egypt
c. 1250-c. 1050	Conquest of Canaan; period of the Judges
c. 1050-c. 1000	Samuel, the last Israelite Judge
c. 1030-c. 1006	Saul, the first Israelite king
c. 1006-c. 965	David rules over Israel
c. 965-c. 930	Solomon rules over Israel; the first Temple built in Jerusalem
c. 925	Division of the United Kingdom
721	Fall of the Northern Kingdom
604-561	Nebuchadnezzar II rules Babylonian Empire
586	Fall of the Southern Kingdom; mass deportation to Babylonia
538	First return under Sheshbazzar
529-522	Cambyses II rules Persian Empire
522-486	Darius I rules Persian Empire
520-515	Temple in Jerusalem rebuilt
486-465	Xerxes rules Persian Empire
465-424	Artaxerxes I rules Persian Empire
c. 458	Second return under Ezra
c. 445	Walls of Jerusalem reconstructed under Nehemiah; Ezra reads the Torah
336-323	Alexander the Great rules Macedonia
c. 332	Alexander the Great overthrows the Persian Empire and establishes Greek rule throughout the Near East
323	Alexander dies and his newly founded empire breaks up into a series of rival Greek kingdoms. The Ptolemies rule in Egypt, the Seleucids in Syria, and the Antigonids in Macedonia
320	Ptolemy I conquers Jerusalem
320-200	Ptolemies rule Palestine
285-246	Reign of Ptolemy II Philadelphius
c. 250	Beginnings of the Septuagint
c. 223-187	Antiochus III (The Great) of Syria annexes Palestine and makes it a province of the Seleucid Empire

c. 200	Hebrew Bible standardized and divided into Torah, Prophets, and Writings
c. 200-70 C.E.	Period of Sadducee activity
c. 200	Antiochus III conquers Jerusalem
c. 200-100 C.E.	Apocryphal and Apocalyptic Literature
187-175	Seleucus IV, beginning of Hellenistic infiltration, resisted by the Zadokite High Priest, Onias III
175-163	Antiochus IV (Epiphanes) rules
168	Antiochus IV begins his persecution of the Jews
168-165	Maccabean Revolt
c. 165	Judas Maccabeus rededicates the Temple (Feast of Hanukkah)
163-150	Demetrius I reigns as king of Syria
160	Death of Judas Maccabeus; independent Maccabean Kingdom established (Hasmonean dynasty)
c. 160-142	High priesthood of Jonathan, son of Mattathias
c. 150	Jonathan, son of Mattathias, becomes governor of Palestine
145-138	Demetrius II reigns as king of Syria
145-134	High priesthood of Simon, son of Mattathias
141	Judea an independent state
134-104	High priesthood of John Hyrcanus, son of Simon; opposed by Pharisees
c. 130-200 C.E.	Activity of Pharisees
c. 104-103	Aristobulus I, high priest and king
103-76	Alexander Yannai, son of John Hyrcanus, is high priest and king
76-67	Salome Alexandra, widow of Alexander Yannai, rules as regent
67	Alexander's two sons, Hyrcanus II and Aristobulus II, fight over succession
63	Romans intervene and occupy Jerusalem; Roman rule of Palestine begins; Hyrcanus II made high priest; Pompey in Jerusalem
37-4	Herod governs Judea; end of Hasmonean dynasty; Shemaiah and Avtalion
30-10 C.E.	Hillel president of Sanhedrin
c. 30-45 C.E.	Philo Judeas of Alexandria
19	Herod rebuilds Temple
27-14 C.E.	Emperor Augustus
4	Jesus born in Bethlehem

All dates are C.E. unless otherwise indicated

6-41	Judea, Samaria, and Idumea formed into a Roman province
6-15	Annas, high priest
26-36	Pontius Pilate procurator of Judea
29	Jesus crucified by Romans in Jerusalem
c. 38-100	Josephus Flavius
c. 40-150	The beginning of the New Testament; origin of Christianity
54-68	Emperor Nero
64-66	Florus, last Roman procurator in Palestine
66	First Jewish Revolt against Rome; Zealots capture Masada
68	Qumran community destroyed
69-79	Emperor Vespasian
70	Fall of Jerusalem, Temple destroyed; Sanhedrin established at Jabneh by Johanan ben Zakkai
73	Fall of Masada, end of Jewish revolt
97-117	Emperor Trajan
115-117	Jews in Diaspora revolt against Rome
117-138	Emperor Hadrian
132-135	Second Jewish Revolt against Rome, led by Simeon Bar Kokhba
135	Fall of Betar; Rabbi Akiva executed; Aelia Capitolina established
c. 200	*Targumim* of Onkelos and Jonathan
c. 220	Death of Judah ha-Nasi
303	Roman Empire divided under Emperor Diocletian
313	Constantine issued Edict of Milan; Christianity tolerated
c. 390	The Jerusalem Talmud compiled
339	Constantius forbids marriage of a Jew with a Christian woman
392	Christianity becomes the official religion of the Roman Empire under Theodosius
c. 400	Jerome completes the Vulgate (Latin) translation of the Bible
418	Jews excluded from all public offices and dignities in the Roman Empire
c. 500	Babylonian Talmud completed
570-635	Muhammad founds Islam
589	Beginning of the period of Geonim

590-604	Pope Gregory openly tries to convert the Jews
614-617	Jewish rule established in Jerusalem under the Persians
627	Emperor Heroclius forbids Jews to enter Jerusalem
638	Jerusalem conquered by the Arabs
640	Omar banishes all Jews from Arabia; the "Pact of Omar" imposes restrictions upon the Jews in the Muslim world
711	Spain conquered by the Muslims
786-809	The Khazars embrace Judaism
762-767	Anan ben David founds the Karaite sect
768-814	Charlemagne rules the Franks
942	Death of Saadyah Gaon
960	Hasdai Ibn Shaprut receives a response to his letter from the Khazar king
998-1938	Last of the Geonim
1056	Death of Solomon Ibn Gabirol
1066	Jews settle in England
1078	Jerusalem conquered by the Seljuks
1083	End of the Khazar Kingdom
1096-1099	First Crusade
1096	Crusader massacre of the Jews of the Rhineland
1040-1105	Rashi
c. 1050-1120	Bahya Ibn Pakuda
1055-1138	Moses Ibn Ezra
1075-1141	Judah Halevi
1089-1164	Abraham Ibn Ezra
1147-1149	Second Crusade
1180	Death of Abraham Ibn David
1182	Jews expelled from France
1135-1204	Maimonides
1189-1192	Third Crusade
1215	Lateran Council
1233	The writings of Maimonides burned in Paris
1244	Talmud burned in Paris
1254	Louis IX expels Jews from France
1194-1270	Nahmanides
1290	Jews expelled from England
1250-1305	Moses de Leon
1348-1349	Persecution of Jews in Europe as a consequence of the Black Death
1380-1435	Joseph Albo

1415	Bull of Pope Benedict XIII against Talmud or any Jewish book attacking Christianity
1454	Gutenberg Bible
c. 1470-1520	Obadiah of Bertinoro travels from Italy to Palestine and records events
1475	First Hebrew book printed
1480	The Inquisition against the Marranos comes to Spain; Judah Ibn Verga of Seville records the Persecutions in the "Road of Judah"
1490-1537	David Reuveni claims to be ambassador from the Jewish King in Arabia
1492	Conquest of Moors completed
	Jews expelled from Spain
	Columbus discovers America
1432-1508	Isaac Abravanel
1497	Jews expelled from Portugal
1488-1575	Joseph Caro
1520-1579	Joseph Nasi
1534-1572	Isaac Luria
1604-1657	Manasseh Ben Israel
1654	First Jewish settlement in New Amsterdam
1656	Jews allowed to live openly in England
1648	Chmielnicki Revolt
1626-1676	Shabbetai Tzevi
1632-1677	Baruch Spinoza
1700-1760	The Baal Shem Tov
1720-1797	The Gaon of Vilna
1726-1791	Jacob Frank
1772, 1793, 1795	Partitions of Poland
1729-1786	Moses Mendelssohn
1776	American Revolution
1782	Joseph II's Edict of Toleration
1786	French Revolution
1791	Jews of France declared full citizens
	Pale of Settlement instituted in the Russian Empire
1785-1840	Nahman Krochmal
1788-1860	Isaac Baer Levinson
1814-1815	Congress of Vienna
1848	Revolutionary activity in various countries in Europe
	Large German emigration to America
1794-1886	Leopold Zunz
1801-1875	Zechariah Frankel
1810-1874	Abraham Geiger

1808-1867	Abraham Mapu
1812-1875	Moses Hess
1806-1828	Isaac Leeser
1819-1900	Isaac Meyer Wise
1873	Hebrew Union College founded
1881	Czar Alexander II assassinated
	Widespread pogroms in Russia
1882	Beginning of First Aliya (BILU)
1885	1,300,000 Jews emigrate to United States
1821-1891	Leo Pinsker
1842-1885	Perez Smolenskin
1835-1917-	Mendele Mokher Sefarim
1852-1915	Isaac Leib Peretz
1859-1916	Shalom Aleichem
1856-1927	Ahad Ha-Am
1858-1922	Eliezer Ben Yehuda
1894	Dreyfus Affair
1860-1904	Theodor Herzl
1897	First Zionist Congress at Basel
	Bund founded in Vilna
1886	Jewish Theological Seminary founded
1896	Rabbi Isaac Elhanan Theological Seminary established (later to merge as Yeshivah University)
1911	Beilis Case
1914-1918	World War I
1917	Balfour Declaration
	Russian Revolution
1886-1929	Fran Rosenzweig
1878-1965	Martin Buber
1873-1934	Hayyim Nahman Bialik
1875-1943	Saul Tschernichowsky
1880-1970	Shmuel Yosef Agnon
1933	Hitler becomes Chancellor of Germany
1939	British White Paper
1939-1945	World War II
	The Holocaust:Approximately 6,000,000 Jews exterminated
1947	UN Resolution on Partition of Palestine
	Discovery of Dead Sea Scrolls
1948	State of Israel proclaimed
1956	Suez Campaign
1967	Six-Day War, Jerusalem re-unified
1973	Yom Kippur War

1977	Egypt's Prime Minister Anwar Sadat arrived in Jerusalem in November.
1978	Camp David Peace Agreement. Signed in Washington D.C. in September

APPENDIX C

GENERAL BIBLIOGRAPHY

I. BIBLIOGRAPHY OF WORKS CONSULTED

Abraham, I., ed. *Hebrew Ethical Wills*. 2nd edition. 2 vols. Philadelphia: Jewish Publication Society, 1948.

Agnon, Shmuel Y. *The Bridal Canopy*. New York: Schocken Books, 1937.

Agnon, Shmuel Y. *Days of Awe*. New York: Schocken Books, 1965.

Alter, R. "The Kidnapping of Bialik and Tschernichowsky," *Midstream*. June, 1964.

Amichai, Y. *Poems*. New York: Harper and Row, 1969.

Antonious, George. *The Arab Awakening*. London: Hamish Hamilton, 1938.

Arnold, T. W. and A. Guillaume, eds. *The Legacy of Islam*. Oxford: Clarendon Press, 1931.

Baer, Y. F. *A History of the Jews in Christian Spain*. 2 vols. Philadelphia: Jewish Publication Society, 1966.

Bamberger, Bernard J. *The Story of Judaism*. New York: Schocken Books, 1970.

Band, Arnold. *Nostalgia and Nightmare*. Los Angeles: University of California Press, 1968.

Bauer, Yehuda. *Flight and Rescue: Brichah*. New York: Random House, 1970.

Belkin, S. *Philo and the Oral Law*. Cambridge, MA: Harvard University Press, 1940.

Ben Amos, D. *In Praise of the Baal Shem Tov*. Bloomington: University of Indiana Press, 1970.

Bentwich, N. *Josephus*. Philadelphia: Jewish Publication Society, 1914.

Bildersee, A. *Jewish Post-Biblical History*. Cincinnati, OH: Union of American Hebrew Congregations, 1918.

Birnbaum, P. *Daily Prayer Book*. New York: Hebrew Publishing Co., 1949.

Blau, J. *The Story of Jewish Philosophy*. New York: Random House, 1961.

Block, J. *Israeli Stories*. New York: Schocken Books, 1962.

Bokser, Ben Zion. *The Legacy of Maimonides*. New York: Philosophical Library, 1950.

Bowker, J. *The Targums and Rabbinic Literature*. London: Cambridge University Press, 1969.

Brenner, I. H. *Breadkown and Bereavement*. Ithaca: Cornell University Press, 1971.

Bright, J. *A History of Israel*. Philadelphia: Westminster Press, 1959.

Bonner, L. *Sects and Separatism during the Second Jewish Commonwealth*. New York: Bloch Publishing Co., 1967.

Browne, L. *The Wisdom of Israel*. New York: Random House, 1956.

Bruce, F. F. *Israel and the Nations*. Grand Rapids, MI: Eerdmans, 1963.

Buber, Martin. *Hasidism and Modern Man*. New York: Horizon Press, 1958.

Buber, Martin. *I and Thou*. New York: Scribner, 1970.

Buber, Martin. *Tales of Rabbi Nachman*. New York: Horizon Press, 1956.

Buber, Martin. *Tales of the Hasidim*. 2 vols. New York: Schocken Books, 1961.

Burnshaw, S. *The Modern Hebrew Poem Itself*. New York: Holt, Rinehart, and Winston, 1965.

Burrows, M. *The Dead Sea Scrolls*. New York: Viking Press, 1955.

Burrows, M. *More Light on the Dead Sea Scrolls*. New York: Viking Press, 1958.

Butwin, Frances. *The Jews of America*. New York: Behrman House, 1973.

Byrnes, R. F. *Anti-Semitism in Modern France*. New Brunswick, NJ: Rutgers University Press, 1950.

Caro, Joseph. *Code of Jewish Law*. New York: Hebrew Publishing Co., 1927.

Charles, R. H. *Religious Developments Between the Old and New Testaments*. New York: Henry Holt, 1914.

Charles, R. H., ed. *The Apocrypha and Pseudepigrapha of the Old Testament*. London: Oxford University Press, 1963.

Chavel, C. *Rambam, His Life and Teachings*. New York: P. Feldman, 1960.

Chomsky, W. *Hebrew: the Eternal Language*. Philadelphia: Jewish Publication Society, 1957.

Cohen, Elie A. *Human Behavior in the Concentration Camp*. New York: Norton, 1953.

Cohen, Norman. *Warrant for Genocide*. New York: Harper and Row, 1967.

Collins, Larry and Dominique Lapierre. *O Jerusalem*. London: Weidenfeld and Nicholson, 1972.

Dentan, R. C. *The Apocrypha, Bridge of the Testaments.* Greenwich, CN: Seabury Press, 1954.

Dentan, R. C. *Saul Tschernichowsky, Poet of Revolt.* Ithaca, NY: Cornell University Press, 1968.

Diamond, Malcolm L. *Martin Buber: Jewish Existentialist.* New York: Oxford University Press, 1968.

Dimont, Max. *The Jews in America.* New York: Simon and Schuster, 1978.

Dimont, Max. *Jews, God and History.* New York: Simon and Schuster, 1962.

Druck, D. *Saadya Gaon, Scholar, Philosopher, Champion of Judaism.* New York: Bloch Publishing Co., 1942.

Druck, D. *Yehuda Halevi, His Life and Works.* New York: Bloch Publishing Co., 1941.

Dubnow, S. *History of the Jews in Russia and Poland.* 3 vols. Philadelphia: Jewish Publication Society, 1916.

Efros, I. *Complete Poetic Works of Hayyim Nahman Bialik.* New York: The Histadruth Ivrith of America, Inc., 1948/1974.

Efros, I. *Hayyim Nahman Bialik.* New York: Hebrew Pen Club of the U. S., 1940.

Encyclopedia Judaica. 16 vols. Jerusalem: Keter Publishing House, 1972.

Federbush, S., ed. *Rashi, His Teachings and Personality.* New York: Cultural Department of the World Jewish Congress, 1958.

Finkelstein, L., ed. *Rab Saadia Gaon, Studies in His Honor.* New York: Jewish Theological Seminary of America, 1944.

Freehof, Solomon. *Preface to Scripure.* Cincinnati, OH: Union of American Hebrew Congregations, 1950.

Freehof, Solomon. *The Responsa Literature.* Philadelphia: Jewish Publication Society, 1955.

Freundlich, C. H. *Peretz Smolenskin.* New York: Bloch Publishing Co., 1965.

Friedland, A. H. *Selections from the Works of Chaim Nachman Bialik.* Cleveland: Bureau of Jewish Education, 1955.

Gay, R. *Jews in America.* New York: Basic Books, 1965.

Ginzberg, Louis. *On Jewish Law and Lore.* Philadelphia: Jewish Publication Society, 1955.

Goodspeed, E. *The Story of the Apocrypha.* Chicago: University of Chicago Press, 1939.

Graetz, H. *A History of the Jews in Moslem Times.* New York: Hebrew Publishing Co., 1949.

Grayzel. Solomon. *A History of the Jews*. Philadelphia: Jewish Publication Society, 1968.

Grene, Marjorie. *Spinoza*. Garden City, NY: Anchor Books, 1973.

Guttmann, J. *Philosophies of Judaism*. New York: Holt, Rinehart and Winston, 1963.

Halasz, N. *Captain Dreyfus: The Story of a Mass Hysteria*. New York: Simon and Schuster, 1968.

Halevi, Judah. *The Kuzari*. New York: Schocken Books, 1964.

Halkin, A. *Modern Hebrew Literature: Trends and Values*. New York: Schocken Books, 1950.

Handlin, Oscar. *Adventures in Freedom*. New York: McGraw-Hill, 1954.

Handlin, Ocsar. *Children of the Uprooted*. New York: G. Brazwiller, 1966.

Handlin, Oscar. *The Uprooted*. Boston: Little, Brown and Co., 1973.

Harrison, R. K. *Introduction to the Old Testament*. Grand Rapids, MI: Eerdmans, 1969.

Herberg, Will. *Four Jewish Existentialist Theologians*. New York: Doubleday, 1958.

Hertz, J. *Liturgy and Ritual: Daily Prayers*. New York: Bloch Publishing Co., 1948.

Hertzberg, A. *The Zionist Idea: A Historical Analysis and Reader*. New York: Doubleday, 1959.

Heschel, Abraham Joshua. *God in Search of Man*. Philadelphia: Jewish Publication Society, 1955.

Hilberg, Raul. *The Destruction of Europe's Jews*. Chicago: Quadrangle Press, 1967.

Hitler, Adolf. *Mein Kampf*. Boston: Houghton Mifflin, 1970.

Howe, Irving and Eliezer Greenberg, eds. *A Treasury of Yiddish Poetry*. New York: Holt, Rinehart, and Winston, 1972.

Howe, Irving and Eliezer Greenberg, eds. *Voices from the Yiddish: Essays, Memoirs, Diaries*. Ann Arbor: University of Michigan Press, 1972.

Husik, I. *A History of Medieval Jewish Philosophy*. Philadelphia: Jewish Publication Society, 1946.

Idelsohn, A. *Jewish Liturgy and Its Development*. New York: Sacred Music Press, 1932.

Josephus, Flavius. *Antiquities*. Vols, IV-VX, works of Josephus. Loeb Classical Library. London: William Heinemann, Ltd.

Josephus, Flavius. *The Jewish War*. Baltimore: Penquin Books, 1969.

Kadushin, M. *The Rabbinic Mind*. New York: Jewish Theological Seminary, 1952.

Kastein, J. *The Messiah of Ismir, Shabbatai Zevi.* New York: Viking Press, 1931.

Keller, Werver. *Diaspora: the Post-Biblical History of the Jews.* New York: Harcourt, Brace and World, Inc., 1966/1969.

Kenyon, F. *Our Bible and the Ancient Manuscripts.* London: Eyre and Spottiswoode, 1958.

Kochan, L. *The Jews in the Soviet Union Since 1917.* New York: Oxford University Press, 1970.

Kovner, A. *A Canopy in the Desert.* Pittsburgh: University of Pittsburgh Press, 1973.

Laqueur, U., ed. *Israel-Arab Reader.* London: Pelican Books, 1969.

Learsi, R. *The Jews in America.* Cleveland: World Publishing Co., 1954.

Leviant, C., ed. *Masterpieces of Hebrew Literature.* New York: KTAV, 1969.

Levy, Hans, Alexander Altman, and Isaac Heinemann, eds. *Three Jewish Philosophers.* New York and Philadelphia: Meridian Books and Jewish Publishing Society, 1960.

Mansoor, Menahem, trans. *The Book of Direction to the Duties of the Heart,* London: Routledge and Kegan Paul, 1973.

Marcus, J. R. *The Colonial American Jews, 1492-1776.* 3 vols. Detroit: Wayne State University Press, 1970.

Marcus, J. R. *The Jew in the Medieval World.* Cincinnati: Union of American Hebrew Congregations, 1938.

Margolis, M. *The Story of Bible Translations.* Philadelphia: Jewish Publication Society, 1917.

Margolis, Max L. and Alexander Marx. *A History of the Jewish People.* Philadelphia: Jewish Publication Society, 1927.

Metzger, B. M. *An Introduction to the Apocrypha.* New York: Oxford University Press, 1957.

Millgram, A. E. *Jewish Worship.* Philadelphia: Jewish Publication Society, 1971.

Mintz, R. *Modern Hebrew Poetry.* Berkeley: University of California Press, 1966.

Moore, G. *Judaism in the First Centuries of the Christian Era.* 2 vols. Cambridge, MA: Harvard University Press, 1927.

Morse, Arthur. *While Six Million Died.* New York: Random House, 1968.

Mosse, George. *The Crisis of German Ideology.* New York: Grosset and Dunlop, 1964.

Mosse, George. *Nazi Culture.* New York: Grosset and Dunlop, 1966.

Neuman, A. *The Jews in Spain*. Philadelphia: Jewish Publication Society, 1942.

Neusner, Jacob. *A History of the Jews in Babylonia*. 5 vols. Leiden: E. J. Brill, 1965-1970.

Neusner, Jacob. *Understanding American Judaism*. 2 vols. New York: KTAV, 1975.

Noth, M. *The History of Israel*. London: Adam and Charles Black, 1960.

Noveck, Simon, ed. *Great Jewish Personalities in Ancient and Medieval Times*. New York: Farrar, Straus, and Cadahy, 1959.

Patterson, D. *Abraham Mapu*. London: East and West Library, 1964.

Penueli, S. Y. *Anthology of Modern Hebrew Poetry*. 2 vols. Jerusalem: Institute for the Translation of Hebrew Literature, 1966.

Pfeiffer, C. F., *Between the Testaments*. Grand Rapids, MI: Baker Book House, 1961.

Pfeiffer, C. F. *The Dead Sea Scrolls*. Grand Rapids, MI: Baker Book House, 1957.

Pfeiffer, R. H. *History of New Testament Times with an Introduction to the Apocrypha*. New York: Harper and Brothers, 1949.

Pfeiffer, R. H. *Introduction to the Old Testament*. New York: Harper and Brothers, 1948.

Poliakov, Leon. *Harvest of Hate*. Syracuse: Syracuse University Press, 1954,

Poll, S. *The Hasidic Community of Williamsburg*. New York: Free Press, 1961.

Rabinovich, I. *Major Trends in Modern Hebrew Literature*. Chicago: University of Chicago Press, 1968.

Ratner, J. *The Philosophy of Spinoza*. New York: The Modern Library, 1954.

Regelson, A. *Israel's Sweetest Singer, Yehuda Halevi*. New York: The Hebrew Poetry Society of America, 1943.

Reitlinger, Gerald. *The Final Solution*. London: Valentine Mitchell, 1968.

Ribalow, M. *The Flowering of Modern Hebrew Literature*. New York: Twayne Publishers, 1959.

Ringelblum, Emmanuel. *Notes from the Warsaw Ghetto*. New York: McGraw-Hill, 1958.

Rose, Peter. *The Ghetto and Beyond*. New York: Random House, 1959.

Rosenzweig, Franz. *On Jewish Learning*. New York: Schocken Books, 1955.

Rosenzweig, Franz. *The Star of Redemption*. Boston: Holt, Rinehart, and Winston, 1971.

Roth, Cecil. *A History of the Jews*. New York: Schocken Books, 1970.

Roth, Cecil. *A History of the Marranos*. New York: Harper and Row, 1966.

Roth, Cecil. *The House of Nasi*. Philadelphia: Jewish Publication Society, 1948.

Roth, Cecil. *A Life of Manasseh ben Israel*. Philadelphia: Jewish Publication Society, 1934.

Roth, Philip. *Good-bye Columbus*. New York: Modern Library, 1966.

Rowley, H. H. *The Relevance of Apocalyptic*. rev. ed. New York: Harper and Brothers, 1944.

Russell, D. S. *Between the Testaments*. Philadelphia: Fortress Press, 1965.

Russell, D. S. *The Method and Message of Jewish Apocalyptic*. London: S. C. M. Press, 1964.

Samuel, Maurice. *Selected Poems of Chaim Nahman Bialik*. New York, 1926.

Scholem, Gershom. *Major Trends in Jewish Mysticism*. New York: Schocken Books, 1971.

Scholem, Gershom. *Shabbatai Zevi*. Princeton: Princeton University Press, 1973.

Selzer, M. *Zionism Reconsidered*. New York: Macmillan, 1970.

Sherman, Franklin. *The Promise of Heschel*. Philadelphia: Lippencott, 1970.

Silberschlag, E. "Saul Tschernichowsky: Poet of Myths," *Commentary I*. New York, 1946, pp, 46-57.

Singer, I. B. *The Family Moskat*. New York: Farrar, Straus and Giroux, 1950.

Singer, I. B. *Yoshe Kalb*. New York: Random House, 1971.

Sklare, Marshall. *America's Jews*. New York: Random House, 1971.

Snaith, N. H. *The Jews from Cyrus to Herod*. New York: Abingdon Press, 1956.

Snowman, L. V. *Tschernichowsky and His Literature*. London: Hassefer, 1929.

Stein, Leonard. *The Balfour Declaration*. London: Valentine Mitchell, 1961.

Suhl, Y. *They Fought Back*. New York: Crown Publishing, 1967.

Thackeray, H. *Josephus, the Man and the Historian*. New York: KTAV, 1967.

Trachtenberg, Joshua. *The Devil and the Jews*. New York: Harper, 1966.

Trepp. Leo. *A History of the Jewish Experience*. New York: Behrman House, 1973.

Trunk, Isaiah. *Judenrat*. New York: Macmillan, 1972.

Twersky, I., ed. *A Maimonides Reader*. New York: Behrman House, 1972.

Vermes, Geza. *The Dead Sea Scrolls: a New Perspective.* Philadelphia: Fortress Press, 1976.

Vermes, Geza. *The Dead Sea Scrolls in English.* 3rd revised edition. Middlesex: Penguin Books, 1987.

Wallenrod, R. *The Literature of Modern Israel.* New York: Abelard-Schuman, 1957.

Wasserstein, A., ed. *Flavius Josephus: Selections from His Works.* New York: Viking Press, 1974.

Waxman, M. *A History of Jewish Literature.* 6 vols. New York: Thomas Yoseloff, 1960.

Weizmann, Chaim. *Trial and Error.* New York: Schocken Books, 1966.

Wiesel, E. *Night.* New York: Hill and Wang, 1960.

Weisel, E. *Souls on Fire.* New York: Random House, 1972.

Yadin, Y. *Bar Kokhba: the Discovery of the Legendary Hero of the Last Jewish Revolt Against Imperial Rome.* London: Weidenfeld and Nicolson, 1971.

Yadin, Y. *Masada.* New York: Random House, 1966.

Yadin, Y. *The Message of the Scrolls.* London: Weidenfeld and Nicolson, 1957.

Zborowski, Mack and Elizabeth Herzog. *Life is with People.* New York: Schocken Books, 1967.

II. BIBLIOGRAPHIES IN JEWISH HISTORY AND THOUGHT

A. General Comprehensive Works

Agus, Jacob B. *The Evolution of Jewish Thought from Biblical Times to the Present.* London: Abelard-Schuman, 1959.

Agus, Jacob B. *The Meaning of Jewish History.* 2 vols. London: Abelard-Schuman, 1963.

Bamberger, Bernard. *The Story of Judaism.* 3rd rev. ed. New York: Schocken, 1964.

Baron, Salo W. *A Social and Religious History of the Jews.* 2nd rev. ed. 17 vols. New York: Columbia University Press, 1952-.

Ben-Sasson, Haim H., ed. *A History of the Jewish People.* London: Weidenfeld and Nicolson, 1976.

Ben-Sasson, Haim H. and Shmuel Ettinger, eds. *Jewish Society Through the Ages.* London: Vallentine and Mitchell, 1971.

Blau, Joseph L. *The Story of Jewish Philosophy.* New York: Random House, 1962.

Bokser, Ben Zion. *Judaism: Profile of a Faith.* New York: A.A. Knopf, 1963.

Comay, Joan. *Who's Who in Jewish History After the Period of the Old Testament.* London: Weidenfeld and Nicolson, 1974.

Dubnov. Simon. *A History of the Jews.* 5 vols. South Brunswick: T. Yoseloff, 1967-1973.

Epstein, Isidore. *Judaism: a Historical Presentation.* Harmondsworth, Middlesex: Penguin, 1959.

Finkelstein, Louis, ed. *The Jews: Their History, Culture and Religion.* 4th rev. ed. 3 vols. New York: Schocken, 1970-1971.

Fleg, Edmond A., ed. *The Jewish Anthology.* New York: Harcourt, Brace, and Co., 1925.

Gilbert, Martin. *Jewish History Atlas.* 2nd rev. ed. London: Weidenfeld and Nicolson, 1976.

Graetz, Heinrich. *History of the Jews.* 6 vols. Philadelphia: Jewish Publication Society, 1891-1898.

Grayzel, Solomon. *A History of the Jews from the Babylonian Exile to the Present.* 2nd rev. ed. Philadelphia: Jewish Publication Society, 1968.

Goldberg, David J. and John D. Rayner. *The Jewish People: Their History and Their Religion.* London: Viking-Penguin, 1987.

Guttman, Julius. *Philosophies of Judaism: The History of Jewish Philosophy from Biblical Times to Franz Fosenzweig.* New York: Holt, Rinehart, and Winston, 1964.

Hertzberg, Arthur, ed. *Judaism.* New York: George Braziller, 1961.

Johnson, P. *A History of the Jews.* New York: Harper and Row, 1987.

Keller, Werner. *Diaspora: The Post-Biblical History of the Jews.* London: Pitman, 1971.

Margolis, Max L. and Alexander Marx. *A History of the Jewish People.* Philadelphia: Jewish Publication Society, 1927.

Noveck, Simon, ed. *Great Jewish Personalities in Ancient and Medieval Times.* New York: Farrar, Straus, and Cudahy, 1959.

Parkes, James. *A History of the Jewish People.* London: Weidenfeld and Nicolson, 1962.

Roth, Cecil. *A History of the Jews.* New York: Schocken Books, 1970.

Sachar, Abram L. *A History of the Jews.* 5th rev. ed. New York: A. A. Knopf, 1965.

Schwarz, Leo W., ed. *Great Ages and Ideas of the Jewish People.* New York: Modern Library, 1956.

Seltzer, Robert M. *Jewish People, Jewish Thought: The Jewish Experience in History.* New York and London: Macmillan and Collier, 1980.

Silver, Daniel, and Bernard Martin. *A History of Judaism.* 2 vols. New York: Basic Books, 1974.

Waxman, Meyer. *A History of Jewish Literature.* 6 vols. New York: T. Yoseloff, 1960.

Zinberg, Israel. *A History of Jewish Literature.* 12 vols. Cleveland: Case Western Reserve University, 1972-1978.

B. Encyclopedias

Bridger, David, ed. *The New Jewish Encyclopedia.* New York: Behrman House, 1962.

Bromiley, G. W., ed. *International Standard Bible Encyclopedia.* 4 vols. Grand Rapids, MI: Eerdmans, 1979-1988.

Buttrick, G. A., ed. *The Interpreter's Dictionary of the Bible.* 4 vols. and Supplement. New York: Abingdon, 1962, 1976.

Encyclopedia Judaica. 16 vols. Jerusalem: Keter Publishing House, 1972.

The Jewish Encyclopedia. 12 vols. New York and London: Funk and Wagnalls Co., 1901- 1906.

Roth, Cecil and Geoffrey Wigoder, eds. *The New Standard Jewish Encyclopedia.* Jerusalem: Massada, 1970.

Werblowsky, R. J. Zwi and Geoffrey Wigoder, eds. *The Encyclopedia of the Jewish Religion.* Jerusalem: Massada, 1966.

C. Sources in English Translation

Abrahams, Israel, ed. *Hebrew Ethical Wills.* 2 vols. Philadelphia: Jewish Publication Society, 1948.

Ackerman, Walter, ed. *Out or Our People's Past: Sources for the Study of Jewish History.* New York: United Synagogue Commission on Jewish Education, 1977.

Adler, Elkan, ed. *Jewish Travellers: ATreasury of Travelogues from Nine Centuries.* London: George Routledge and Sons, Ltd., 1930.

Ahad Ha'am. *Essays, Letters, Memoirs.* Translated and edited by L. Simon. Oxford: East and West Library, 1946.

Ahad Ha'am. *Selected Essays.* Translated and edited by L. Simon. Philadelphia: Jewish Publication Society, 1912.

Arad, Yitzhak, Israel Gutman, and Abraham Margalion, eds. *Documents on the Holocaust: Selected sources on the Destruction of the Jews of Germany and Austria, Poland, and the Soviet Union.* Jerusalem: Yad Vashem, 1981.

The Babylonian Talmud. 35 vols. Edited by I. Epstein. London: Soncino Press, 1935-1948.

Barnett, Richard D. *Illustrations of Old Testament History.* 2nd rev. ed. London: British Museum Publications, 1977.

Bauer, Yehuda and Nili Keren. *The Holocaust: a History.* New York: New Viewpoints, 1982.

Benjamin of Tudela. *The Itinerary of Benjamin of Tudela.* Translated and edited by M. N. Adler. London: H. Frowde, Oxford University Press, 1907.

Beller, Jacob. *Jews in Latin America.* New York: I. David, 1969.

Beyerlin, Walter et al., eds. *Near Eastern Religious Texts Relating to the Old Testament.* London: SCM Press, 1978.

Browne, L. *The Wisdom of Israel.* New York, 1945.

Buber, Martin. *Tales of the Hasidim.* 2 vols. New York: Schocken, 1947-1948.

Chazan, Robert, ed. *Church, State and Jew in the Middle Ages.* New York: Behrman, 1980.

Chazan, Robert, and Marc Lee Raphael, eds. *Modern Jewish History: a Source Reader.* New York: Schocken Books, 1974.

Cohen, Arthur A., ed. *Arguments and Doctrines: A Reader of Jewish Thinking in the Aftermath of the Holocaust.* New York: Harper and Row, 1970.

Cohen, Jacob X. *Jewish Life in South America: a Survey for the American Jewish Congress.* New York: Bloch Publishing Co., 1941.

Dawidowicz, Lucy S., ed. *The Holocaust Reader.* New York: Behrman House, 1976.

Dawidowicz, Lucy S., ed. *The Golden Tradition.* New York: Holt, Rinehart, and Winston, 1967.

Dawidowicz, Lucy S. *The War Against the Jews, 1933-1945.* New York: Holt, Rinehart, and Winston, 1975.

Ehrmann, Eliezer L. *Readings in Modern Jewish History.* New York: KTAV, 1977.

Freehof, Solomon, ed. *A Treasury of Responsa.* Philadelphia: Jewish Publication Society, 1969.

Glatzer, Nahum N., ed. *The Dynamics of Emancipation: The Jew in the Modern Age.* Boston: Beacon Press, 1965.

Glatzer, Nahum N., ed. *Faith and Knowledge: the Jew in the Medieval World.* Boston: Beacon Press, 1963.

Glatzer, Nahum N., ed. *A Jewish Reader in Time and Eternity.* 2nd rev. ed. New York: Schocken, 1961.

Glatzer, Nahum N., ed. *Modern Jewish Thought: a Source Reader.* New York: Schocken Books, 1977.

Glatzer, Nahum N., ed. *The Rest is Commentary: a Source Book of Judaic Antiquity.* Boston: Beacon Press, 1961.

Glatzer, Nathan. *The Judaic Tradition.* Boston: Beacon Press, 1969.

Grayzel, Solomon. *The Church and the Jews in the XIIIth Century.* Detroit: Wayne State University Press, 1989.

Goitein, Shlomo Dov, ed. *Letters of Medieval Jewish Traders.* Princeton: Princeton University Press, 1973.

Hertzberg, Arthur, ed. *The Zionist Idea: A Historical Analysis and Reader.* Garden City, N.Y.: Doubleday and Herzl Press, 1959.

Hilberg, Raul, ed. *Documents of Destruction: Germany and Jewry, 1933-1945.* Chicago: Quadrangle, 1971.

Holtz, Barry W., ed. *Back to the Sources.* New York: Summit Books, 1984.

Hoexter, Julius and Moses Jung, eds. *Sourcebook of Jewish History and Literature.* London: Shapiro, Vallentine, and Co., 1938.

In Praise of the Baal Shem Tov (Shivhei ha-Besht). Translated and edited by D. Ben-Amos and J. R. Mintz. Bloomington: Indiana University Press, 1970.

Jacobs, Louis, ed. *Hasidic Thought.* New York: Behrman House, 1976.

Jacobs, Louis, ed. *Jewish Mystical Testimonies*. Jerusalem: Keter, 1976.

Kobler, Franz, ed. *Letters of the Jews Through the Ages: From Biblical Times to the Middle of the Eighteenth Century*. 2 vols. London: Ararat, East and West Library, 1952.

Mahler, Raphael, ed. *Jewish Emancipation: A Selection of Documents*. New York: American Jewish Committee, 1941.

Marcus, Jacob. *The Jew in the Medieval World: A Source Book*. Cincinnati: UAHC, 1938.

Mendes-Flohr, Paul R. and Jehuda Reinharz, eds. *The Jew in the Modern World: A Documentary History*. New York and Oxford: Oxford University Press, 1980.

Meyer, Michael A., ed. *Ideas of Jewish History*. New York: Behrman, 1974.

Midrash Rabbah. Edited by H. Freedman and M. Simon. 10 vols. London: Soncino Press, 1939.

The Mishnah. Edited and Translated by H. Danby. Oxford: Clarendon Press, 1933.

Montefiore, Claude G. and Herbert Loewe, eds. *A Rabbinic Anthology*. London: Macmillan., 1938.

Newman, Louis I., ed. *The Hasidic Anthology: Tales and Teachings of the Hasidim*. New York and London: Scribners, 1934.

Patai, Raphael, ed. *Encyclopedia of Zionism and Israel*. 2 vols. New York: Herzl Press and McGraw-Hill, 1971.

Pritchard, James B., ed. *The Ancient Near East: An Anthology of Texts and Pictures*. 2 vols. Princeton: Princeton University Press, 1958-1975.

Schappes, Morris U., ed. *A Documentary History of the Jews in the United States, 1654-1875*. New York: The Citadel Press, 1950.

Scholem, Gershom, ed. *Zohar, the Book of Splendor*. New York: Schocken Books, 1949.

Synan, Edward. *The Popes and the Jews in the Middle Ages*. New York and London: Macmillan, 1965.

The Talmud. Soncino English Translation. Edited by I. Epstein. 35 vols. London: Soncino Press, 1935-1948.

Thomas, David W., ed. *Documents from Old Testament Times*. London: Thomas Nelson and Sons, Ltd., 1958.

Twersky, Isadore, ed. *A Maimonides Reader*. New York: Behrman House, 1972.

Views of the Biblical World. 5 vols. Jerusalem, New York, and Chicago: Jordan Publications, 1959-1961.

Yogev, Gedalia, ed. *Political and Diplomatic Documents: December 1947 - May 1948*. 2 vols. Jerusalem: State of Israel, Israel State Archives and the World Zionist Organization, Central Zionist Archives, 1979.

The Zohar. 5 vols. London: Soncino Press, 1931-1934.

Zuckerman, Nathan, ed. *The Wine of Violence: an Anthology on Anti-Semitism*. New York: Association Press, 1947.

D. The Biblical Period

Ackroyd, Peter R. *Continuity: A Contribution to the Study of the Old Testament Religious Tradition*.

Ackroyd, Peter R. *The People of the Old Testament*. London: Christophers, 1959.

Albright, William F. *The Biblical Period from Abraham to Ezra*. New York: Harper and Row, 1963.

Albright, William F. *From the Stone Age to Christianity: Monotheism and the Historical Process*. 2nd rev. ed. Garden City, N.Y.: Doubleday, 1957.

Anderson, George W. *The History and Religion of Israel*. London: Oxford University Press, 1966.

Avi-Yonah, Michael and Yohanan Ahroni. *The Macmillan Bible Atlas*. New York: Macmillan, 1968.

Bright, John. *A History of Israel*. 2nd ed. Philadelphia: Westminster Press, 1972.

Buber, Martin. *The Prophetic Faith*. New York: Macmillan, 1949.

Cassuto, Umberto. *The Documentary Hypothesis and the Composition of the Pentateuch*. Jerusalem: Magnes, 1961.

Cornfeld, Gaalyagu, ed. *Pictoral Biblical Encylopedia: A Visual Guide to the Old and New Testaments*. New York: Macmillan, 1964.

Eissfeldt, Otto. *The Old Testament: An Introduction*. Oxford: B. Blackwell, 1965.

Fohrer, Georg. *Introduction to the Old Testament*. Nashville: Abingdon Press, 1968.

Gordon, Cyrus H. *The World of the Old Testament*. Garden City, N.Y.: Doubleday, 1958.

Hermann, Siegfried. *A History of Israel in Old Testament Times*. London: SCM Press, 1975.

Kaufmann, Yehezkel. *The Religion of Israel: From its Beginnings to the Babylonian Exile*. Chicago: University of Chicago Press, 1960.

Kraeling, Emil G. *Rand Mcnally Bible Atlas*. New York: Rand McNally and Co., 1956.

Lods, A. *Prophets and the Rise of Judaism*. London: Routledge and Kegan Paul, 1961.

Malamat, Avraham, "Origins and the Formative Period," in *A History of the Jewish People*. Edited by H. H. Ben-Sasson. London: Weidenfeld and Nicolson, 1976, pp. 1-87.

Noth, Martin. *The History of Israel*. 2nd revised edition. London: A. and C. Black, 1960.

Pfeiffer, Robert H. *Introduction to the Old Testament*. New York: Harper and Brothers, 1941.

Segal, Moses H. *The Pentateuch, Its Composition and Its Authorship and Other Biblical Studies*. Jerusalem: Magnes Press, 1967.

Tadmor, Haim, "The Period of the First Temple, the Babylonian Exile and the Restoration," in *A History of the Jewish People*. Edited by H. H. Ben-Sasson. London: Weidenfeld and Nicolson, 1976, pp. 91-182.

E. The Second Temple Period

The Oral Law: the Mishnah and the Talmud

Adler, Morris. *The World of the Talmud*. Washington, D. C.: B'nai B'rith Hillel Foundations, 1958.

Alon, Gedalyahu. *The Jews in Their Land in the Talmudic Age: 70-640 C.E.* Jerusalem Magnes Press, 1980.

Avi-Yonah, Michael, and Zvi Baras, eds. *Society and Religion in the Second Temple Period. The World History of the Jewish People*. First Series, vol. 8. Jerusalem: Massada Publishing Co., 1977.

Bickermann, Elias. *From Ezra to the Last of the Maccabees: Foundations of Post-Biblical Judaism*. New York: Schocken, 1962.

Box, George H. *Judaism in the Greek Period: From the Rise of Alexander the Great to the Intervention of Rome (333 to 63 B.C.)*. Oxford: Clarendon Press, 1932.

Charles, R. H., ed. *The Apocrypha and Pseudepigrapha of the Old Testament*. 2 vol. Oxford: Clarendon Press, 1913.

Cohen, Abraham. *Everyman's Talmud*. London: J. M. Dent, 1934.

Finkelstein, Louis. *Pharisaism in the Making: Selected Essays*. New York: KTAV, 1972.

Foerster, Werner. *From the Exile to Christ: A Historical Introduction to Palestinian Judaism*. Philadelphia: Fortress Press, 1964.

Ginzburg, Louis, ed. *The Legends of the Jews*. 7 vols. Philadelphia: Jewish Publication Society, 1909-1938.

Gutmann, Joseph, ed. *The Synagogue: Studies in Origins, Archaeology, and Architecture*. New York: KTAV, 1975.

Neusner, Jacob. *From Politics to Piety. The Emergence of Pharisaic Judaism.* Englewood Cliffs, NJ: Prentice-Hall, 1973.

Neusner, Jacob. *A History of the Jews in Babylonia.* 5 vol. Leiden: E. J. Brill, 1965-1970.

Neusner, Jacob. *Invitation to the Talmud.* New York: Harper and Row, 1973.

Oesterley, William O. *A History of Israel.* vol. 2. from *The Fall of Jerusalem, 586 B.C. to the Bar-Kokhba Revolt, A. D. 135.* Oxford: Clarendon Press, 1932.

Pfeiffer, Robert H. *History of New Testament Times with an Introduction to the Apocrypha.* New York: Harper and Brothers, 1949.

Smallwood, E. Mary. *The Jews Under Roman Rule: From Pompey to Diocletian.* Leiden: E. J. Brill, 1976.

Strack, Hermann. *Introduction to the Talmud and Midrash.* Philadelphia: Jewish Publication Society, 1931.

Vermes, Geza. *The Dead Sea Scrolls: Qumran in Perspective.* London: Collins, 1977.

Zeitlin, Solomon. *The Rise and Fall of the Judean State: A Political, Social and Religious History of the Second Commonwealth.* 3 vols. Philadelphia: Jewish Publication Society, 1968-1978.

F. The Medieval Period

Baron, Salo W. *Ancient and Medieval Jewish History: Essays by Salo Wittmayer Baron.* New Brunswick, N. J.: Rutgers University Press, 1972.

Chazan, Robert, ed. *Medieval Jewish Life: Studies from the Proceedings of the American Academy for Jewish Research.* New York: KTAV, 1976.

Efros, Israel. *Studies in Medieval Jewish Philosophy.* New York: Columbia University Press, 1974.

Epstein, Isidore, ed. *Moses Maimonides 1135-1204: Anglo-Jewish Papers in Connection with the Eighth Centenary of His Birth.* London: Soncino, 1935.

Flannery, Edward H. *The Anguish of the Jews: Twenty-three Centuries of Anti- Semitism.* New York: Macmillan, 1965.

Geiger, Abraham. *Judaism and Islam.* Madras, India: M. D. C. S. P. C. K. Press, 1898.

Goitein, Shlomo Dov. *Jews and Arabs: Their Contacts Through the Ages.* New York: Schocken, 1955.

Husik, Isaac. *A History of Medieval Jewish Philosophy.* Philadelphia: Macmillan, 1916.

Isaac, Jules. *Jesus and Israel.* New York: Holt, Rinehart, and Winston, 1971.

Katz, Jacob. *Exclusiveness and Tolerance: Studies in Jewish-Gentile Relations in Medieval and Modern Times*. London: Oxford University Press, 1961.

Levy, Hans, Alexander Altmann, and Isaac Heinemann, eds. *Three Jewish Philosophers*. New York and Philadelphia: Meridon Books and the Jewish Publication Society, 1960.

Nemoy, Leon, ed. *Karaite Anthology: Excerpts from the Early Literature*. New Haven and London: Yale University Press, 1952.

Poliakov, Leon. *The History of Anti-Semitism*. 3 vols. London: Routledge and Kegan Paul, 1974-1975.

Rosenthal, Erwin. *Judaism and Islam*. London and New York: Thomas Yoseloff, 1961.

Roth Cecil, ed. *The Dark Ages: Jews in Christian Europe 711-1096. The World History of the Jewish People*. Second Series. vol. 2. Tel Aviv: Massada Publishing Co., 1966.

Scholem, Gershom. *Kabbalah*. Jerusalem: Keter, 1974.

Scholem, Gershom. *Major Trends in Jewish Mysticism*. 3rd rev. ed. New York: Schocken, 1954.

Silver, Abba Hillel. *A History of Messianic Speculation in Israel: From the First to the Seventeenth Centuries*. New York: Macmillan, 1927.

Werblowsky, R. J. Zwi. *Joseph Karo: Lawyer and Mystic*. London: Oxford University Press, 1962.

G. Rennaissance and Modern Periods

Agus, Jacob B. *Modern Philosophies of Judaism*. New York: Behrman's Jewish Book House, 1941.

Ashtor, Eliyahu. *The Jews of Moslem Spain*. 2 vols. Philadelphia: Jewish Publication Society, 1973-1979.

Avineri, Shlomo. *The Making of Modern Zionism: the Intellectual Origins of the Jewish State*. New York: Basic Books, 1981.

Baeck, Leo. *The Essence of Judaism*. New York: Schocken, 1967.

Baer, Yitzhak. *A History of the Jews in Christian Spain*. 2 vols. Philadelphia: Jewish Publication Society, 1961-1966.

Bauer, Yehuda. *From Diplomacy to Resistance: A History of Jewish Palestine, 1939-1945*. Philadelphia: Jewish Publication Society, 1970.

Bein, Alex. *Return to the Soil: a History of Jewish Settlement in Israel*. Jerusalem: Youth and Hechalutz Department of the Zionist Organization, 1952.

Ben Horin, Meir. *Common Faith, Uncommon People: Essays in Reconstructionist Judaism*. New York: Rexonstructionist Press, 1970.

Blau, Joseph L. *Modern Varieties in Judaism*. New York: Columbia University Press, 1966.

Blau, Joseph L., ed. *Reform Judaism, A Historical Perspective: Essays from the Yearbook of the Central Conference of American Rabbis*. New York: KTAV, 1973.

Buber, Martin. *Hassidism and Modern Man*. New York: Horizon Press, 1958.

Buber, Martin. *The Origin and Meaning of Hassidism*. New York: Horizon Press, 1960.

Cohen, Israel. *The Zionist Movement*. Edited and revised with a supplemental chapter on Zionism in the United States by Bernard G. Richards. New York: Zionist Organization of America, 1946.

Dawidowicz, Lucy S. *The War Against the Jews, 1933-1945*. New York: Holt, Rinehart, and Winston, 1975.

Dicker, Hermann. *Wanderers and Settlers in the Far East: A Century of Jewish Life in China and Japan*. New York: Twayne Publishers, 1962.

Dubnov, Simon. *History of the Jews in Russia and Poland: From the Earliest Times to the Present Day*. 3 vols. Philadelphia: Jewish Publication Society, 1916-1920.

Elbogen, Ismar. *A Century of Jewish Life*. Philadelphia: Jewish Publication Society, 1944.

Encyclopedia of Zionism and Israel. Edited by Raphael Patai. 2 vols. New York: Herzl Press and McGraw Hill, 1971.

Epstein, Melech. *Jewish Labor in U.S.A.: An Industrial and Cultural History of the Jewish Labor Movement*. 2 vols. New York: Trade Union Sponsoring Committee, 1950-1953.

Fackenheim, Emil L. *Encounters Between Judaism and Modern Philosophy: A Preface to Future Jewish Thought*. New York: Basic Books, 1973.

Fishman, Priscilla, ed. *The Jews of the United States*. Jerusalem: Keter Publishing House, 1974.

Freid, Jacob, ed. *Jews in the Modern World*. 2 vols. New York: Twayne , 1962.

Gilbert, Martin: *Exile and Return: the Emergence of Jewish Statehood*. London: Weidenfeld and Nicolson, 1978.

Goldman, Lazarus M. *The History of the Jews in New Zealand*. Wellington: A. H. and A. Reed, 1958.

Graupe, Heinz. *The Rise of Modern Judaism: An Intellectual History of German Jewry: 1650-1942*. Huntington, NY: R. E. Krieger, 1979.

Grayzel, Solomon. *History of the Contemporary Jews: From 1900 to the Present.* Philadelphia: Jewish Publication Society, 1960.

Gruenbaum, Isaac. *The History of Zionism.* 2 vols. Tel Aviv: Lion, 1943-1946.

Grunwald, Max. *History of the Jews in Vienna.* Philadelphia: Jewish Publication Society, 1936.

Handlin, Oscar. *Adventure in Freedom: Three Hundred Years of Jewish Life in America.* New York: McGraw-Hill, 1954.

Herberg, Will. *Judaism and Modern Man: An Interpretation of Jewish Religion.* Philadelphia: Jewish Publication Society, 1951.

Herzl, Theodore. *The Jewish State.* New York: Herzl Press, 1970.

Heschel, Abraham J. *God in Search of Man: a Philosophy of Judaism.* Philadelphia: Jewish Publication Society, 1955.

Hilberg, Raul. *The Destruction of the European Jews.* Chicago: Quadrangle, 1961.

Hirschberg, Haim Z. *A History of the Jews in North Africa.* 2 vols. Leiden: E. J. Brill, 1974-1980.

Howe, Irving. *World of Our Fathers: The Journey of the East European Jews to America and the Life They Found and Made.* New York and London: Harcourt, Brace, and Jovanovich, 1976.

Hyamson, Albert M. *History of the Jews in England.* 2nd rev. ed. London: Methuen and Co., Ltd., 1928.

The Jewish Communites of the World. 3rd rev. ed. London: A. Deutsch, 1971.

Kaplan, Mordechai M. *Judaism as a Civilization: Toward a Reconstruction of American-Jewish Life.* New York: Macmillan, 1934.

Katz, Jacob. *Out of the Ghetto: the Social Background of Jewish Emancipation, 1770-1870.* Cambridge, MA: Harvard University Press, 1973.

Klausner, Joseph. *A History of Modern Hebrew Literature: 1785-1930.* London: M. L. Cailingold, 1932.

Koestler, Arthur. *Promise and Fulfillment: Palestine 1917-1949.* London: Macmillan, 1949.

Lapierre, Dominique and Larry Collins. *O Jerusalem.* Jerusalem: Weidenfeld and Nicolson, 1972.

Laqueur, Walter. *A History of Zionism.* New York: Holt, Rinehart, and Winston, 1972.

Laqueur, Walter, ed. *The Israel-Arab Reader: A Documentary History of the Middle East Conflict.* 2nd revised edition. New York: B. L. Mazel Inc., 1969.

Lipman, Vivian D., ed. *Three Centuries of Anglo-Jewish History*. Cambridge: W. Heffer, 1961.

Marcus, Jacob R. *The Rise and Destiny of the German Jew*. Cincinnati: American Hebrew Congregations, 1934.

Marcus, Jacob R. *Early American Jewry*. 2 vols. Philadelphia: Jewish Publication Society, 1951-1953.

Marcus, Jacob R. *Israel Jacobson: The Founder of the Reform Movement in Judaism*. 2nd rev. ed. Cincinnati: Hebrew Union College Press, 1972.

Minkin, Jacob S. *The Romance of Hassidism*. New York: Macmillan, 1935.

Mosse, George L. *The Crisis of German Ideology: Intellectual Origins of the Third Reich*. New York: Grosset and Dunlap, 1964.

Mosse, George L. *Towards the Final Solution: A History of European Racism*. New York: H. Fertig, 1978.

Neusner, Jacob. *Understanding American Judaism: Toward the Description of a Modern Religion*. 2 vols. New York: KTAV, 1975.

Noveck, Simon, ed. *Great Jewish Personalities in Modern Times*. New York: B'nai Brith, 1960.

Noveck, Simon, ed. *Great Jewish Thinkers of the 20th Century*. New York: B'nai Brith Department of Adult Education, 1963.

Parkes, James. *A History of Palestine from 135 A. D. to Modern Times*. London: Victor Gollancz, 1949.

Parkes, James. *Anti-Semitism*. London: Vallentine-Mitchell, 1963.

Pollak, Michael. *Mandarins, Jews and Missionaries: The Jewish Experience in the Chinese Empire*. Philadelphia: Jewish Publication Society, 1980.

Porath, Yehoshua. *The Palestinian Arab National Movement: From Raids to Rebellion*, London: Cass, 1977.

Preuss, Walter. *The Labor Movement in Israel: Past and Present*. Jerusalem: Reuven Mass, 1965.

Price, Charles A. *Jewish Settlers in Australia*. Canberra: Australian National University, 1964.

Rosenberg, Stuart E. *The Jewish Community in Canada*. 2 vols. Toronto: McClelland and Stewart, 1970-1971.

Roth, Cecil. *The History of the Jews of Italy*. Philadelphia: Jewish Publication Society, 1946.

Roth, Cecil. *A History of the Jews in England*. 3rd rev. ed. Oxford: Clarendon Press, 1964.

Rudavsky, David. *Modern Jewish Religious Movements: A History of Emancipation and Adjustment.* New York: Behrman House Inc., 1967.

Sachar, Howard M. *The Course of Modern Jewish History.* New York: World Publishing Co., 1958.

Sachar, Howard M. *A History of Israel: From the Rise of Zionism to our Time.* Jerusalem: Steinmatzky, 1976.

Sack, Benjamin. *History of the Jews in Canada: From the Earliest Beginnings to the Present Day.* Montreal: Canadian Jewish Congress, 1945.

Saron, Gustav and Louis Htz, eds. *The Jews in South Africa: A History.* Cape Town, London, and New York: Oxford University Press, 1955.

Sassoon, David S. *A History of the Jews in Baghdad.* Letchworth: S. Sassoon, 1949.

Scholem, Gershom. *Shabbatai Sevi: the Mystical Messiah 1626-1676.* Princeton, N. J.: Princeton University Press, 1973.

Sklare, Marshall. *Conservative Judaism: an American Religious Movement.* New York: Schocken, 1972.

Sokolow, Nahum. *History of Zionism: 1600-1918.* 2 vols. London: Longmans, Green, and Co., 1918.

Stein, Leonard. *The Balfour Declaration.* London: Vallentine-Mitchell, 1961.

Stillman, Norman. *The Jews of Arab Lands: A History and Source Book.* Philadelphia: Jewish Publication Society, 1979.

Strizower, Schifra. *Exotic Jewish Communities.* London: Thomas Yoseloff, 1962.

Weisbrot, Robert. *The Jews of Argentina: From the Inquistion to Peron.* Philadelphia: Jewish Publication Society, 1979.

Wiznitzer, Arnold. *Jews in Colonial Brazil.* Morningside Heights, NY: Columbia University Press, 1960.

APPENDIX D

GLOSSARY

ACADEMY OF SURA. See **SURA.**

ACROSTICS. A literary device found in the Bible and in many medieval liturgical compositions. The alphabet is used in a variety of combinations to spell out the author's name, verses from the Bible, etc. Acrostics are of special importance in the Kabbalah.

AELIA CAPITOLINA. Name given by the Romans to Jerusalem when they rebuilt it after the Bar Kokhba revolt (135 C.E.). Jews were forbidden to enter the city except on the Ninth of Av. The city was named after Emperor P. Aelius Hadrianus (Hadrian) and the god Jupiter Capitolinus, in whose honor a temple was erected in the city.

AGGADAH. Hebrew: "telling, narration." The nonlegal portions of the Talmud, which include homilies, parables, maxims, ethical sayings, and general folklore.

AGGADIC EXEGESIS. Interpretation of the Scriptures involving the homiletic method of *Derash* ("investigation") which attempted to show religious and ethical teachings from the texts and to find scriptural evidence for existing traditions and customs.

ALLEGORY. A method of literary analysis wherein nonliteral meaning is desired or implied. It is similar to an extended metaphor.

ALIYAH. Hebrew: "ascent." The pilgrimage to Israel, particularly to Jerusalem, which is considered in rabbinic literature to be the highest point in the world. In contemporary times it refers to the emigration of Jews to Israel.

AMIDAH. Hebrew: "standing." Also called the Eighteen Benedictions. Group of prayers in the Jewish liturgy recited while the congregation is standing.

AMORAIM. Those rabbis from c. 200 to 500 C.E. who discussed and interpreted the Mishnah; authors of the Gemara.

ANTI-SEMITISM. Term used since the later part of the nineteenth century for the overt and hidden hatred toward Jews and Judaism.

APOCALYPTIC LITERATURE. A type of writing that flourished in Judaism and early Christian thought (165 B.C.E. to 120 C.E.), with the purpose of encouraging the faithful to stand firm under persecution. The encouragement was in the form of a promise of speedy deliverance from current evils by the intervention of God, which would bring about the end of the present world order, the resurrection, and the eternal reward of the righteous and damnation of the unrighteous.

APOCRYPHA. Greek: "hidden, stored away." The Apocrypha refers to the fourteen books found in the Greek Septuagint (LXX) but not in the canonical Hebrew Scriptures. These books are important for the development of Jewish religious thought in the Second Temple period.

APOLOGETICS. Literary works written in defense of Jews and Judaism. Examples of these works are Josephus's *Contra Apion*, Judah Halevi's *Kuzari*, and Moses Mendelssohn's *Jerusalem*.

ARAMAIC. The language spoken by various northwest Semitic peoples from the eighth century B.C.E. up through the first few centuries of the present era. Large portions of Daniel, Ezra, the Talmud, and the Midrash are written in Aramaic.

ASHKENAZ (pl., **ASHKENAZIM**). The generic term used to refer to German Jews since the ninth century and those Jews who immigrated to Eastern Europe during the time of the Crusades. Their ritual differs from their Sephardic counterparts in the pronunciation of Hebrew, their reliance on the Palestinian Talmudic tradition, and their use of Yiddish (a Judeo-German dialect).

ASSIMILATION. The loss of an individual's or a group's cultural, religious, or national identity through an absorption into another society or environment.

ASSIDEANS. See Hasidim.

AUTO-DA-FÉ. Portuguese: "act of faith." The ceremony in which the Inquisition announced the sentence of those accused of heresy. The sentenced person was then handed over to secular authorities, who then carried out the execution or punishment.

BABYLONIAN EXILE. A period of time between the destruction of the kingdom of Judah by Nebuchadnezzar in 586 B.C.E. and the return from captivity in 538 B.C.E. During this epoch, a small group of Jews remained in Palestine, although the majority of the Jews were exiled to Mesopotamia. The Babylonian Exile is important for the development of the synagogue and the beginnings of the organized prayer book and canonization of the Scriptures. In 538 B.C.E. the Persian king, Cyrus, permitted the Jews to return to Palestine.

BALFOUR DECLARATION. Letter sent by Arthur James Balfour, British foreign secretary, to Lord Rothschild, on November 2, 1917, declaring that the British government viewed with favor the establishment of a Jewish national home in Palestine.

BAR MITZVAH. Hebrew: "Son of the Commandment." The ceremony commemorating a Jewish boy's thirteenth birthday and his initiation into the Jewish community.

BEN SIRA, WISDOM OF. See ECCLESIASTICUS.

BETAR. Ancient town near Jerusalem which was the last stronghold of Simeon Bar Kokhba (134-135 C.E.).

BETH MIDRASH. Hebrew: "House of Study." It is a place of study, discussion, and prayer.

BILU. *Bet Yaakov lekhu ve-nelkhah*, Hebrew: "House of Jacob, come, let us go." Zionist pioneer movement founded in Russia in 1882. Members of this group helped found the settlements of Rishon Le-Zion (1882) and Petakh Tikvah (1883).

BIUR. Moses Mendelssohn's German translation of the Pentateuch with Hebrew commentaries, completed in 1783.

BLACK DEATH. An epidemic which swept Europe (1348-1349). The populations of the affected countries accused the Jews of causing the plague and began murderous attacks on the Jewish populations of these lands. The Jews themselves were relatively unaffected by the epidemic due to their forced segregation from the general population and their sanitary habits.

BLACK HUNDREDS. Popular name for members of the Sayuz Russkav Naroda ("Union of the Russian People"), which was a Russian anti-Semitic, reactionary organization in the early part of the twentieth century.

BLOOD LIBEL. Also referred to as blood accusation, and ritual murder accusation—the accusation that the Jews murdered Christians in order to use their blood for use in the Passover service.

BUND. Abbr. of *Allgemeiner Yiddisher Arbeterbund in Liter, Polen un Russland.* Yiddish: "General Federation of Jewish Workers in Lithuania, Poland, and Russia." A Jewish socialist party founded in Vilna in 1897.

BYZANTINE EMPIRE. The eastern part of the Roman Empire established in the fourth century C.E. Until 637 the Byzantine Empire, with its capital in Constantinople, included Palestine.

CAIRO GENIZAH. See **GENIZAH.**

CALIPH. The traditional spiritual leader of a Moslem community or empire.

CANAAN. In pre-Biblical times this referred to the area of Syria. However, in a more restricted sense, it was also applied to the coastal area of Palestine.

CANON. The name given to the holy books of the Bible.

CANTONIST SYSTEM. The forced conscription of Jewish children into the Czarist army for twenty-five years of military service. This system was abolished by Czar Alexander II in 1856.

CHALUKAH. Hebrew: "distribution." The distribution of funds which were collected to support the poor Jews living in Palestine.

CHURCH FATHERS. Those teachers and authors of the Christian Church who lived from the era following the composition of the New Testament until the Dark Ages. Pope Gregory the Great, who died in 604 C.E., is usually considered to be the last of the Church Fathers.

CODEX. A leaf book, as distinguished from a roll or scroll, invented and used first by the Romans; a handwritten manuscript in book form.

COHEN. Hebrew: "priest." The chosen intermediary between man and God. The hereditary title given to the firstborn son of an Israelite family. After the construction of the Golden Calf the title became suspect, and the Levites were chosen for guardianship of the Tabernacle and the family of Aaron took upon itself the responsibility for sacrifices.

COMMON ERA. Term used by Jews and others to refer to the period of time from the beginning of the first millenium. Equals A.D. (*Anno Domini*).

CONCENTRATION CAMPS. Prison camps set up by the Nazis for the detention of opponents of the regime.

CONSERVATIVE JUDAISM. Religious movement which developed in the United States as a middle road between Orthodox and Reform Judaism. It recognizes a divine inspiration to the Torah, but has adapted Jewish law to modern life on the basis of principles of change inherent in traditional Judaism. These changes in the law can be brought about by the decision of vested religious authorities.

COUNCIL OF TRENT (1545-1563). Inspired the movement known as the Counter-Reformation. It was a part of the anti-Semitic reaction of the Catholic Church.

CREATIO EX NIHILO. Belief held by philosophers such as Philo that the world was created out of nothing. This is in opposition to the belief that God created the world out of existing formless matter.

CRUSADES. Term which refers to the series of religious wars from 1096 to 1300. These wars were fought by the Christian rulers against the Moslems for control of the Holy Land. During this period medieval Jewry suffered under severe persecutions.

DAY OF JUDGMENT. Time when God will decide the fate of nations or individuals. Relates to the doctrine of eschatology.

DAYYAN. Hebrew: "Judge." Specifically refers to those rabbis qualified to serve on a rabbinical court, not only for religious matters, but also for those financial or civil suits brought before a Jewish court.

DEAD SEA SCROLLS. The body of literature discovered in 1947 near the Dead Sea, containing parts of the library of a Jewish community living before and during the time of Jesus. Some of the fragments contain parts of the Bible, while others are the rules by which the sect who composed the scrolls lived. The scrolls were written between 200 B.C.E. and 200 C.E. and it is a generally accepted fact that the authors of the scrolls were the Essenes.

DERASH. The literary method of Biblical interpretation to discover new meaning other than the literal ones appearing in the Scriptures.

DESECRATION OF THE HOST. Accusation that the Jews defiled, mutilated, or destroyed the wafer used in Catholic mass that symbolizes the body of Jesus.

DEVEKUT. Hebrew: "cleave, or devotion." An intense love of God which is the ultimate goal of a Jew's religious and spiritual endeavors.

DIASPORA. Traditionally, this word, which is derived from the Greek word meaning "dispersion," has referred to all Jewish settlement outside of the land of Israel, or Palestine. Jews began to live outside the Holy Land during the decline of the First Temple period. After the first large exile of residents of Judah by the Babylonians in the sixth century B.C.E., many Jews did not return to Palestine when they were permitted to do so in subsequent centuries. They became scattered throughout the existing kingdoms. Since the creation of the State of Israel, the idea of the Diaspora has been altered from one of "exile" to one of "voluntary decentralization."

DISPUTATION. Debates between representatives of opposing religions. In the Middle Ages, these theological debates involved representatives of the Jewish community and the Church where the differences of the two faiths were discussed. Many times these debates resulted in the burning of Jewish books, particularly the Talmud.

DOCUMENTARY THEORY. A theory popularized by Julius Wellhausen (1844-1918) and his school attempting to document the authorship of the Torah and the Book of Joshua. This theory is based on the use of different names for God, linguistic and stylistic variations, as well as other signs of a composite structure.

DONMEH. A Judeo-Moslem sect living in Turkey, whose members are the descendants of the followers of Shabbetai Tzevi, who had embraced Islam.

D. P. Displaced Persons. Term applied to those people who were forcibly removed from their homes and resettled in other locations during and after World War II.

DREYFUS AFFAIR. Scandal in the nineteenth century in which Captain Alfred Dreyfus of the French army was accused of selling military secrets to the Germans. It was later revealed that this was an anti-Semitic plot involving high-ranking French officers.

EBIONITES. A Judeo-Christian sect which flourished from the second through fourth centuries C.E. Members of the sect adhered to the Jewish law even though they believed in Jesus as the Messiah.

ECCLESIASTICUS. Also called the *Wisdom of Ben Sira.* This work was translated into Greek in 132 B.C.E. by the grandson of Simeon, Joshua (in Greek: "Jesus") Ben Sira, who lived around 170 B.C.E. The book is similar to the Book of Proverbs, containing wise sayings, moral teachings, and urging moderation. The book's form is also similar to Proverbs. Until the discovery of the Cairo Genizah in late nineteenth century the original Hebrew text had been lost.

EDICT OF EXPULSION. Proclamation of Queen Isabella of Spain which went into effect on July 30, 1492 (supposedly the Ninth of Av on the Jewish calendar). This edict ordered all those who professed Judaism to leave Spain and the Spanish dominions, including Sicily and Sardinia.

EDICT OF MILAN. Declaration made by Constantine (Roman emperor from 312 to 337 C.E.) in 312 which served to establish Christianity as the supreme religion in the Roman Empire. This edict seriously affected Jewish rights.

EDICT OF TOLERATION. Imperial decree by Joseph II of Austria-Hungary in 1782 which removed some of the restrictions imposed on the Jewish community. However, it insisted on a reform of the communal and educational system of the Jewish community.

EDOM. The portion of land in southeast Palestine traditionally given to Esau. The inhabitants lived by hunting. Traditionally, the Edomites were enemies of the Children of Israel. In the Talmud, the term *edomite* refers to any oppressive government, particularly Rome. Later, in the Middle Ages, it referred to Christian Europe.

EIN GEDI. Oasis on the shores of the Dead Sea.

EIN SOPH. Hebrew: "eternal, never ending God." In kabbalistic terminology, the name for the "eternal God" which is beyond human comprehension. Man, however, can understand the Ein Soph via the sephirot, which were derived from it.

EL, ELOHIM Hebrew: God. It has the same meaning in all other Semitic languages.

EMANCIPATION. The legislative freeing of Jews from restrictions in daily life. This usually involved a granting of equal civil, economic, and religious rights, abolition of various restrictions, and the granting of citizenship.

ESCHATOLOGY. The study of the doctrine of "last things," that is, the nature of such future events as the end of the present world order, the final judgment of all men, and the future state of both the just and the unjust.

ESSENES. A Jewish sect which flourished during the Second Commonwealth and whose members lived an ascetic and sometimes mystical life in monastic communities. See **DEAD SEA SCROLLS.**

ETHICAL WILLS. See **TSAVAOT.**

ETHICS (or SAYINGS) OF THE FATHERS. Hebrew: *Pirke Avot.* Tractate of the Mishnah containing a collection of ethical and religious precepts of the rabbinic sages which has been incorporated into the Jewish prayer book.

EXEGESIS. Interpretation and exposition of the Scriptures.

EXILARCH. Refers to the head of the Babylonian Jewish community in exile. It was an hereditary office held traditionally by a member of the House of David. He was chief tax collector for the Jews. This office came into existence in the second century C.E. and lasted, at least nominally, until the thirteenth century.

FEDAYEEN. Arabic: "self-sacrificers." Arab commando squads who launched attacks into Israeli territory from their bases in the Gaza Strip during the 1950s.

FINAL SOLUTION. Term referring to the physical destruction of European Jews during World War II.

FRANKISTS. The followers of Jacob Frank, an eighteenth-century false messiah. In 1756 Frank and his followers were baptized as Catholics. The descendants of this group were absorbed into Polish society.

FREIES JÜDISCHES LEHRHAUS. German: "The Free Jewish Academy." Academic institution founded in 1920 in Frankfort by Franz Rosenzweig. Its aim was to help Jews understand their Judaism within a modern framework. Its staff included such notables as Martin Buber and Abraham Joshua Heschel.

GAON (pl., GEONIM). Hebrew: "eminence, excellency." The title of the intellectual leaders of the Babylonian Jewish community from the sixth through the eleventh centuries C.E. They were the leaders of the two major academies in Sura and Pumbedita. Their influence affected most of world Jewry in the post-Talmudic period.

GEMARA. Discussions and interpretations of the Mishnah, mainly in Aramaic. The Gemara and the Mishnah together make up the Talmud.

GEMATRIA. The method of biblical exegesis based on the interpretation of words via the computation of the numerical values of the Hebrew letters.

GENIZAH. Hebrew: "hiding." Refers to one of the rooms of a synagogue used exclusively for permanently storing discarded and worn holy writings. Such a room, full of ancient scrolls, was found in Cairo, Egypt, just prior to the start of the twentieth century. It yielded thousands of manuscripts and texts.

GHETTO. In general, any Jewish quarter or section of a city, although specifically used to refer to an area restricted by law to Jews alone. The first ghetto, or "foundry," was established in Venice in 1517, although Jewish segregation began with Church legislation in the twelfth century.

GILGAMESH EPIC. Refers to the ancient Babylonian creation myth which has several parallels to the narrative in the Bible. In contrast to the monotheistic view in the Biblical version, the Gilgamesh Epic is highly polytheistic.

GNOSTICISM. Greek: "knowledge." Belief system of Hellenistic origin in the second to third centuries C.E. Gnostics held that the world was the result of an intermediary of God fallen from the Divine Sphere. This system greatly influenced the ideas of the Kabbalists in the twelfth and thirteenth centuries.

GOLAH. See DIASPORA.

GOLDEN AGE OF SPAIN. The period in Spain from about 900-1200 during which Jewish culture flourished. Under the tolerant rule of the Moslems, many Jews rose to high government positions. During this period, much poetry, philosophy, and religious writing was produced.

GOLEM. Hebrew: "shapeless mass." In Jewish mysticism and folklore, a human-like robot created by pronouncing the Holy Name. In folklore, this creation was summoned to protect the Jews during periods of persecution.

GOSPELS. Refers to the four books of the New Testament which relate the life and teaching of Jesus. The Gospels of Matthew, Luke, and Mark, called the Synoptic Gospel, all relate material from approximately the same point of view. The Gospel of John is probably the most recent creation.

GUR ARYEH. Hebrew: "lion's cubs." The disciples of Rabbi Isaac Luria (the "Ari": Ashkenazi Rabbi Isaac).

HABAD. (Initials of *Hokhman Binah vaDaat*) Hebrew: "wisdom, understanding, knowledge." The name for the Hasidic school of thought founded by Shneour Zalman of Lyady. Another name for this Hasidic group is Lubavitch.

HAGANAH. Hebrew: "defense." The Jewish defense force of the Jewish Agency during the Palestinian mandate. With the creation of the State of Israel it was incorporated into the I.D.F. (Israel Defense Force).

HAGGADAH. See AGGADA.

HAGIOGRAPHA. The Greek (Christian) term for all the canonical books of Jewish Scripture which are not included in the Law or in the Prophets. In Hebrew these works are called *Ketuvim* ("Writings").

HALAKHAH. Hebrew: "law" (derived from *halakh*, meaning "to go"). Usually refers to the legal part of Talmudic and later literature of the Jews. This contrasts to the other type of Talmudic literature referred to as *aggadah*, which is nonlegal.

HALUTZIM. Hebrew: "pioneers." Young Jews who came to Palestine in the late nineteenth and twentieth century to rebuild the Jewish homeland.

HAPAX LEGOMENA. Greek term used to refer to those words which only occur once in the Bible. Many studies were made on the origins of these words and their later usage by medieval grammarians.

HAPHTARAH. Hebrew: "conclusion." Selection derived from the prophetic books of the Bible and read after the weekly portion of the Scriptures on Sabbaths, festivals, and afternoons of fast days.

HASIDIM. Hebrew: "pious ones, saints." Refers to a group of Jews that formed during the fourth century B.C.E. for the purpose of promoting the observance of Jewish ritual and study of the Law. The Pharisees developed largely from this group.

HASIDISM. Religious and social movement started by Israel Baal Shem Tov in the eighteenth century in Poland. Its philosophy stressed the equality of all before God, the importance of piety, spiritual exultation, the concept of joy as an integral part of worship, and *devekut*. After the death of the Baal Shem, Hasidic dynasties under the leadership of tzaddikim developed. Today the majority of the Hasidim are living in Israel and the United States.

HASMONEANS. Also called Maccabees. The ruling family of the Jewish nation in the second and first centuries B.C.E. which led a successful rebellion against the Syrian Hellenists (168-163 B.C.E.).

HAVDALAH. Hebrew: "distinction." The ceremonial conclusion of the Sabbath. The use of wine, spices, and a candle flame signify the differentiation of the Sabbath from the weekdays, the sacred from the profane, the light from the darkness, the people of Israel from other nations.

HAZZAN. Hebrew word for cantor which was probably derived from the Assyrian *hazannu*, meaning governor or overseer. Originally, the *hazzan* served as the overseer of the synagogue, but he also helped in leading prayers. He eventually took charge of leading the prayers and thus achieved his cantorial role.

HELLENISM. Amalgam of Greek and Oriental civilization (language and ideas) which flourished in the ancient world after Alexander the Great (d. 323 B.C.E.). Jewish thought and life was affected most by Hellenism at Alexandria, Egypt. The conflict that developed between it and Judaism came to a head with the Maccabean Revolt (165 B.C.E.), which checked the spread of Hellenism in Judea.

HEXAPLA. The polyglot Bible compiled by Origen (c. 184-c. 253 C.E.). The work contained the original Hebrew, a Greek transliteration of the Hebrew, and the Greek translations of Aquila, Symmachus, the Septuagint, and Theodotion.

HEXATEUCH. The Pentateuch and the Book of Joshua.

HIBBAT ZION. Hebrew: "Love of Zion." Zionist organization founded in Russia in 1882 by Leo Pinsker.

HIJRA. Arabic: "flight, emigration." Concerns a flight from country and friends. Often refers to the flight of Mohammed from Mecca to Medina in the year 622 C.E.

HOLOCAUST. Term referring to the physical, cultural, and spiritual destruction of the European Jewish community from 1939 to 1945 by the Nazis and their accomplices.

HOLY OF HOLIES. The inner sanctum of the Temple which contained the Ark. Only the high priest was permitted to enter the Holy of Holies—and then only on special occasions.

HYKSOS. A loose confederation of western Asian people that dominated Egypt between the twelfth and sixteenth dynasties. About 1580 B.C.E. Amosis finally expelled them and inaugurated a new empire. Some feel that Joseph may have served a Hyksos Pharaoh.

"I AND THOU." Philosophical concept popularized by Martin Buber; explains the relationships of man to God and of man to other people. This involves a closer, more compassionate "I-Thou" form of relationship instead of an impersonal, detached "I-It" form of relationship.

INQUISITION. The Church tribunal which attempted to impose punitive measures against all forms of heresy against the Catholic Church. In Spain, under the auspices of the Church and the control of Queen Isabella (1478-1492), the Inquisition dealt with those "converted" Jewish Marranos. The result of the movement was the expulsion of Jews from Spain in 1492.

INTERTESTAMENTAL PERIOD. The period during which the apocryphal literature was composed; also called the Second Temple period.

IRGUN TZEVAI LEUMI. Hebrew: "National Military Organization." Rightwing Jewish military organization during the Palestinian mandate, founded in 1931 as a break-off from the Haganah.

ISLAM. A monotheistic belief system developed by Mohammed and given to the Arabs as their religion c. 610. The religion incorporates several important personalities and events from the New and Old Testaments. The three holy cities to the Islam religion are Mecca, Medina, and Jerusalem.

ISRAELITE. Generically refers to nonpriestly members of the Children of Israel.

JABNEH. An ancient Palestinian city located just south of Jaffa. After the destruction of the Second Temple in 70 C.E., Rabbi Johanan ben Zakkai established a rabbinical academy in this city and the Sanhedrin was relocated there. The town remained important as the seat of the Sanhedrin until the Bar Kokhba revolt. During the Middle Ages Jabneh was an important commercial center.

JEWISH AGENCY. During the mandate period, the official representative body of the Jewish community in Palestine. After the establishment of the State of Israel it continued to function as a nongovernmental agency in charge of coordinating Israel and Zionist activity in the Diaspora.

JEWISH LEGION. Jewish military units organized as part of the British Army during World War I.

JEWISH SECTS. Religious controversies since the composition of the Bible have resulted in the formation of religious sects, including the Samaritans, Pharisees, Sadducees, and Karaites. There have been other dissident religious groups within the structure of Judaism since the Middle Ages, such as the Sabbetaians, the Frankists, the Hasidim, and the Reform Jews.

JOSEPHUS, FLAVIUS. Jewish historian, writer, and military leader of the Jews in Palestine when they revolted against the Romans. After the fall of Jerusalem he accompanied the Roman Emperor, Titus, to Rome. Josephus's historical writings—which include *The Jewish War, The Antiquities of the Jews,* and *Autobiography*—are the principal knowledge of Jewish history of that period, although not always accurate or reliable.

JUSTINIAN CODE. Edict proclaimed by Justinian (Byzantine emperor) regulating the Jewish synagogue service and forbidding rabbinic expositions in the Byzantine Empire over which he ruled from 527 to 565 C.E.

KABBALAH. Hebrew: "tradition." The system of Jewish philosophical mysticism which began about 1200 and expressed itself in various movements up to modern times. The *Zohar,* a mystical commentary of the Bible written in the thirteenth century, is its great classic. It also exerted a profound influence on the Hasidism of the eighteenth century.

KADDISH. Hebrew: "consecration." Aramaic prayer incorporated into the Jewish liturgy praising the greatness of God's name and His creation. More recently recited as a mourner's prayer.

KALAM. Arabic: "speech, reason." General term for Islamic scholastic theology which stressed a rational approach to religion. The various schools of Islamic thought had a great impact on medieval Jewish philosophy.

KARAITES. A Jewish sect which flourished in the Near East, principally in Babylonia and Egypt, from the ninth to twelfth centuries C.E. This sect adhered exclusively to the Hebrew Scriptures, rejecting the Talmud. Some twelve thousand Karaites supposedly still exist, most of them in Russian Crimea.

KAVANAH. Hebrew: "intention." Spiritual concentration which usually accompanies the performance of a commandment or prayer.

KELIPOT. Hebrew: "husks." In Jewish mysticism, the outer shells which encase the sparks of the Divine which are within everything. The task of man is to liberate these sparks from these husks in order to try to achieve a unity with God.

KHAZARS. Turkish or Finnish tribe which settled in the Ural Mountain region of Russia. In 786-809, their king, Bulan, with approximately four thousand of his nobles, converted to Judaism. Later kings corresponded with Spanish Jews such as Hasdai Ibn Shaprut. The narrative of their conversion forms the philosophical book by Judah Halevi.

KIBBUTZ. Israeli collective agricultural settlement, where the members live and work communally.

KIDDUSH. Hebrew: "Sanctification." Denotes the benediction pronounced upon the wine at the commencement of the Sabbath and holidays.

"KOINE" GREEK. The common Greek language used for the first translations of the Hebrew Bible and the New Testament.

KOL NIDREI. Hebrew for "all vows." It was written in Aramaic more than a thousand years ago. This Aramaic formula, recited on the eve of Yom Kippur, calls for the dispension of vows and obligations made by an individual for himself alone. It acquired intense significance particularly during the period of persecutions in Spain. The stirring tune of *Kol Nidrei* was composed in Germany in early 16th century.

KORAN. The holy book for the Islam religion. It records the ideas and speeches of the religion's founder, Mohammed. The book is strongly influenced by Hebrew Biblical literature and tradition.

KRISTALLNACHT. The outbreak of mass anti-Jewish rioting in Germany from November 9 to 10, 1938. This was in reaction to the assassination of Ernst vom Rath, an official of the German embassy in Paris, by Herschel Grynspan.

KUZARI. Philosophical work by Judah Halevi (written in the twelfth century) which describes a debate between representatives of Judaism,

Christianity, Islam, and Aristotelian philosophy. This preceded the conversion of the Khazar king to Judaism.

LADINO. Fifteenth-century Spanish mixed with various Mediterranean languages written in Hebrew characters which is spoken by Sephardic Jews.

LEHI. Hebrew: Lohamei Herut Yisrael. "Fighters for the Freedom of Israel." Also referred to as the "Stern Gang," an underground Jewish military group formed during the mandate. It was founded in 1940 as a splinter group of the Irgun.

LETTER OF ARISTEAS. Pseudepigraphic work giving the legend surrounding the writing of the Septuagint. It also praises Judaism and Jerusalem in the light of the Hellenistic world. Supposedly written by Aristeas, a Greek official of Ptolemy II of Egypt (285-246 B.C.E.), it is now generally recognized as the composition of an Egyptian Jew in the second century B.C.E.

LEVANT. Countries bordering on the eastern part of the Mediterranean Sea.

LEVITES. Descendants from the tribe of Levi who became the guardians of the Tabernacle in Temple rites.

LOGOS. Greek: "word." Term used to represent the personified speech of God, especially in the New Testament, but also in Proverbs.

LURIANIC KABBALAH. Also referred to as "practical Kabbalah." System of thought in Kabbah developed by Rabbi Isaac Luria in which one's kavanah is capable of bringing a person to a closer understanding of God and creation. This can be attained through repentance, self-affliction, observance of the Law, and the study of the mystical writings. It had a great impact on the Shabbati Tzevi and Hasidic movements.

MAARIV. Hebrew: "who brings in the evening." The evening prayer.

MAASEH BERESHIT. Hebrew: "mystery of creation." In kabbalistic literature, the mystical concepts connected to the creation of the world described in Genesis 1.

MAASEH MERKAVAH. Hebrew: "mystery of the Divine Chariot." In kabbalistic literature, the mystical concepts connected to the chariot and throne of God described in Ezekiel 1.

MACCABEES. Also Hasmoneans. They worked for the restoration of Jewish political and religious life.

MAGGID. Hebrew: "preacher." An itinerant preacher who wandered from town to town teaching Torah and moral values. In Jewish mysticism, a heavenly agent, usually an angel, who communicated with the mystics.

MAGHARIANS. Arabic name of a Jewish sect called "men of the caves." The sect is so called because its books were found in a cave. It is believed to have originated during the first century B.C.E.

MAHZOR. Hebrew: "cycle." Refers to the prayer book used for the festivals. Initially the *mahzor* included the prayers for the whole year, including the Sabbath and weekdays. Later, however, the Sabbath and weekday prayers were put into the *siddur*.

MAKOM. Hebrew: "place." Refers to the designation of God.

MARRANO. Spanish: "swine." Word applied to those descendants of Spanish and Portuguese baptized Jews who secretly continued to practice their Judaism after their conversion. The Inquisition in Spain (1480) attempted to purge the country of these heretics.

MASADA. Fortified stronghold located on the lofty cliffs near the Dead Sea. Masada served as a refuge for Herod's family in 40 B.C.E. Until 72 C.E., Masada served as a fortress for various groups, last of all the Zealots, who committed mass suicide in 73 C.E. in order to escape capture by the Romans. Extensive excavations have been completed at the location.

MASHAL. A fable, usually in the form of an ethical allegory in which animals, plants, etc., are anthropomorphized to convey a moral.

MASKIL. Hebrew: "illuminated." Adherent of the Haskalah movement.

MASORAH. The traditions surrounding the alterations in spellings, writings, and reading of the Bible.

MASORETIC TEXT. The traditional Hebrew text of the Old Testament which was given vowels and copious marginal notations by the Masoretes, mostly between 500 to 900 C.E. This group of men preserved, remarkably well, the text of the Hebrew Scriptures from before the Christian era.

MATZAH. Unleavened bread, eaten during the holiday of Passover.

MEGILLOT. Hebrew: "scrolls." Refers to the five Biblical Hagiographa read on special Jewish holidays—Passover, Song of Songs; Feast of Weeks, Ruth; *Purim*, Esther; Feast of Tabernacles, Ecclesiastes; and Ninth of Av, Lamentations.

MELTING POT. Popular term referring to the assimilatory nature of American society.

MEN OF THE GREAT SYNAGOGUE. The period dating from about 450 to 200 B.C.E. The Men of the Great Synagogue added to the Jewish liturgy, preserved the Scriptures, and began formulation of the Oral Law.

MIDRASH. Hebrew: "exposition." The collection of rabbinical homiletical interpretations of the Scriptures verse by verse, the purpose of which is to popularize the essence of Scripture in its particular and universal application.

MINHAG. Hebrew: "custom." It is applied to any old and general usage or religious practice among Jews, and in particular to the ritual of the synagogue which varies at different periods and from one Jewish community to another.

MINHAH. Hebrew: "offering." The daily late-afternoon prayer, instituted instead of the afternoon Temple meal offering which is referred to in Leviticus.

MINYAN. Hebrew: "number." The minimum of ten Jewish adult males required for communal prayer. A Jewish male can enter the *minyan* after his Bar Mitzvah, at the age of thirteen.

MISHNAH. The compilation of Jewish laws made by Rabbi Judah the Patriarch (c. 135-200 C.E.). The Mishnah also contains additions and modifications by other scholars. With the Gemara, this forms the Talmud.

MISHNEH TORAH. Hebrew: "Repetition of the Torah." Also known as the *Yad Hazakah* ("Strong Hand"), it is a religious work written by Maimonides between 1166 and 1176. In it is the code of Jewish law, which is divided into fourteen books, covering various areas of Jewish law and thought.

MITNAGDIM. Hebrew: "opponents." Opponents of the Hasidic movement in the eighteenth and nineteenth centuries. The leader of this group was Rabbi Elijah ben Solomon, the Gaon of Vilna.

MITZVAH. Hebrew: "commandment." The name given to the 613 affirmative and prohibitive obligations or duties arranged by Maimonides. It was traditionally regarded as a means of expressing the immeasurable love of the Jews for God. A person is said to have "earned a *mitzvah*" by performing a good deed.

MOREH NEVUKHIM. Hebrew: "Guide for the Perplexed." Philosophical work completed by Maimonides in 1190. It was an attempt to interpret the Torah in light of Greek philosophy.

MOSHAV. In Israel, an agricultural settlement where the inhabitants own their own homes and possessions, but cooperate in working, purchasing, and selling their produce.

MUSAPH. Additional prayer recited on Sabbaths and festivals which replaces the additional sacrifices that were offered in the Temple on these special days.

MYTHOPOEIA. Myth-forming, myth-making.

NABATEAN LANGUAGE. Language of the people of Arab extraction that occupied Edom in the sixth century B.C.E.

NAGID. Hebrew: "prince." In the Middle Ages, the leader of the Jewish community in Moslem countries.

NASI. Hebrew: "prince." Honorary term used in the Talmud for the president of the Sanhedrin. The Nasi was not only the spiritual leader of the community but also political representative of the Jews.

NAZI PARTY. Acronym for National Socialist German Workers Party. A reactionary German political party which gained control of the German government in 1933 under the leadership of Adolf Hitler. Upon ascension to power, Nazis eliminated political opponents and established a dictatorship on the premise that the party controlled all aspects of German life. Principles of the party included anti-Semitism, anti-Communism, anti-liberalism, "Aryan" supremacy, the regaining of German land lost in World War I, and the acquisition of adequate living space for Germany's overcrowded population.

NEOPLATONISM. A late Greek philosophy represented by Plotinus (205-270 C.E.). Includes the idea of Divine emanation. This philosophical system had great influence on medieval Jewish writers and on later writings, particularly the Kabbalah.

NUMERUS CLAUSUS. Latin: "closed numbers." Restrictions on the number of Jews admitted to educational institutions, professions, etc.

NEW TESTAMENT. The body of literature canonized by the Church which relates the life and teaching of Jesus of Nazareth and includes the apocryphal literature.

NINTH OF AV. Hebrew: *Tishah be-Av.* Traditionally, a fast day commemorating the destruction of the First and Second Temples, both on approximately this date. This date is customarily observed as the anniversary of the fall of Betar in 135 C.E., the expulsion of the Jews from Spain in 1492, and numerous other national calamities.

OLD TESTAMENT. Christian terminology used to refer to that body of literature included in the Jewish Bible. See TANAKH.

ORAL LAW. The tradition of interpretation and analysis of the Written Law, handed down orally from generation to generation. Its importance was based on the tradition that it was likewise given to Moses on Sinai and represented an amplification of the Written Law. It became the whole body of the Talmudic legislation and hence the core of Jewish practice.

ORIENTAL JEWS. Term for the non-Ashkenazic and non-Sephardic Jewish communities of North Africa, Middle East, Central Asia, Caucasus, Ethiopia, and Southern Arabia who have developed a religious and cultural tradition of their own.

ORTHODOX JUDAISM. Adherence to traditional Judaism which is based on the acceptance of the Divine Law in its written and oral forms (Torah and Talmud, respectively). These are considered binding on all

Jews for all times. Modification of the Law can be made by decision of acknowledged rabbinic scholars if they are based on certain principles established by the rabbis for biblical exegesis.

OTTOMAN EMPIRE. After the Jewish expulsion from Spain in 1492, the Ottoman Empire served as an important Jewish center, since the sultans allowed the Jews to freely enter the empire. The Jewish community flourished there until after the sixteenth century, when conditions worsened somewhat. Even after this deterioration, however, Jews in the Ottoman Empire were not persecuted to the degree that they suffered persecution in other countries.

PACT OF OMAR. Legislation of the Caliph Omar guaranteeing Jews and Christians certain security in exchange for payment of a poll tax, restricting them from holding public offices, and limiting their clothing to distinctive garb.

PALE OF SETTLEMENT. Twenty-five provinces in the western part of the Czarist Russian Empire in which Jews were permitted to reside. This system of settlement instituted in 1791 was finally abolished in 1917.

PALEOGRAPHY. The study of describing or deciphering ancient writings with the purpose of placing each inscription in its proper cultural and chronological context.

PALESTINIAN MANDATE. The British colonial administration of the former Ottoman territory of Palestine from 1920 to 1947.

PALESTINIANS. The native Arab population of Palestine, many of whom fled the country after the State of Israel was proclaimed in 1948.

PANTHEISM. Philosophical belief that the presence of God is in everything, or that the universe as a whole is God.

PAPAL STATES. States which were governed by the papacy.

PAPYRUS. A water plant, most abundant in Egypt, whose pith was cut into slices, laid side by side, and pressed together into 10- or 12-inch square sheets. When dry, these sheets were glued together and constituted a 25- to 30-foot roll used for writing, usually only on one side. This was the regular material used by the Greeks in antiquity.

PARDES. Hebrew: "orchard, field." Mnemonic word formed from the initials of four methods of scriptural exegesis: *Peshat* ("literal meaning"); *Remez* ("allusion"); *Deerash* ("investigation"); *Sode* ("mystical").

PASSOVER Hebrew: *Pesach*. One of the three pilgrim festivals commemorating the event that God passed over the houses of the Jews when he killed the firstborn sons of the Egyptians before the exodus from Egypt. During this eight-day festival (seven days in Israel) no leavened products are eaten.

PATRIARCHS. Hebrew: *avot*. Traditionally refers to the founding fathers of the Jewish religion: Abraham, Isaac, and Jacob.

PENTATEUCH. Also called Torah. It is generally the Five Books of Moses.

PENTECOST. Hebrew: *Shavuot* ("The Feast of Weeks"). One of the three pilgrim festivals commemorating the wheat harvest. In ancient times, during the existence of the Temple, pilgrims would bring offerings of the first fruits. The term *pentecost* comes from the Greek word for fifty, signifying that the holiday represented the end of the fifty-day period after the Feast of Passover.

PESHAT. The simple, literal meaning of the Bible and the primary level of exegesis.

PESHITTAH. Syriac: "simple." Refers to the Syriac translation of the Bible during the second century C.E.

PHARISEES. Emerged as a distinct group during or after the Maccabean Revolt (c. 165 B.C.E.). They believed in the authority of the Written Law, along with the Sadducees; but they also held the Oral Law to be authoritative. As the latter was an interpretation of the Written Law from the viewpoint of each successive generation, the Pharisees represented the mass of Jewish people in religious and social outlook, and Pharisaism became the foundation of later rabbinical Judaism.

PHILISTINES. A Mediterranean people, originating from Asia Minor and Greece, who settled eventually in Palestine. From the name of this nation the Romans, under Hadrian, gave the name Palestine to the former land of Judah.

PHILO JUDAEUS. Jewish philosopher and writer of Alexandria, Egypt. Philo (20 B.C.E.-40 C.E.) attempted to reconcile, in true diasporic style, Greek philosophy and Jewish faith. His most important work was an interpretation of Hebrew Scriptures allegorically, so as to transform history into abstract principles that are universally applicable. His writings also have much historical value.

PHYLACTERIES. Two small boxes of leather containing parchment slips on which are inscribed Deuteronomy 6:4-9, 11:13-21, and Exodus 13:1-10, 13:11-16. These were worn on the forehead and left arm all day by the Pharisees and rabbis, but today in present Orthodox are limited to morning worship on weekdays by adult males. In Hebrew they are called *tephillin* (Aramaic: "attachment").

PILPUL. Literally: "debate." Usually refers to the clarification of textual material in the Talmud or rabbinical literature. This method became prominent after the sixteenth century.

PITTSBURGH PLATFORM. Program adopted by American Reform rabbis in 1885 which stated that the role of Reform Judaism was to spread ethical values among the people of the world, that some of the rabbinic legislation was no longer applicable, and that Reform Judaism should reject the concept of return to Zion.

PIYYUT (pl., PIYYUTIM). Greek: "poietes." A form of liturgical Hebrew poetry which originated in Palestine (c. 300-500 C.E.). In the early Middle Ages in Europe there was a rebirth of this type of composition.

PLATONISM. Philosophical system founded by the Greek Plato (428/9-347 B.C.E.).

POGROM. Russian: "destruction." Violent attacks on the Jewish communities of eastern Europe which were frequently instigated by the government.

POLEMICS. Records of discussions between two or more scholars.

PROPHETS, FIRST OR FORMER. Includes the historical books of Joshua, Judges, Samuel, and Kings.

PROPHETS, LATER OR LATTER. Includes the books of the Bible of Isaiah, Jeremiah, Ezekiel, and the Twelve Minor Prophets: Hosea, Joel,

Amos, Obadiah, Jonah, Micah, Nahum, Habakkuk, Zephaniah, Haggai, Zechariah, and Malachi.

PROTESTANT REFORMATION. Generic term used to explain the religious movement of the sixteenth century which succeeded in dividing the Catholic Church. Martin Luther was one of the leaders.

PROTOCOLS OF THE ELDERS OF ZION. An anti-Semitic pamphlet purporting to prove that an international Jewish conspiracy existed which planned to disrupt the established systems of government and eventually to take control of the world.

PSEUDEPIGRAPHA. A body of Jewish literature dating from between 200 B.C.E. and 200 C.E. These books were falsely attributed to famous Biblical personages to enhance their authority. They are noncanonical, apocalyptic works which are not part of the Apocrypha.

PTOLEMIES. Name of the rulers of the Macedonian dynasty of Egypt which began in 305 B.C.E. and lasted until 88 B.C.E. Due to the administrative rule of these kings, the governmental operation of Palestine was little changed, despite the rules of the Seleucids and the Hasmoneans.

PURIM, FEAST OF. This festival commemorates the intervention of the Jewess Esther, then Queen of Persia, on the behalf of her people to prevent their annihilation by Haman. The events are recorded in the Book (Scroll) of Esther which is read on this holiday.

QERI U-KHETIV. Hebrew: "read and written." These are the directions for the corrections of the original Biblical text. The actual text was not altered, due to the traditional veneration of the standard version. There are over thirteen-hundred variations, which were finally recorded in the margins by the Masoretes.

QUMRAN. Excavations here, on the northwest shore of the Dead Sea, have uncovered the remains of ancient buildings and a cemetery. The Dead Sea Scrolls were found in the adjacent caves in Wadi Murabbaat.

RABBINIC LITERATURE. The branch of literature formulated after the redaction of the Talmud (c. 500 C.E.). Included in this literature are commentaries on the Talmud, responsa literature, and legal codes. This type of literature continued to be composed throughout the Middle Ages.

RECONSTRUCTIONISM. Religious movement developed by Rabbi Mordecai Kaplan in the 1930s. Its foundations lie on the premise that Judaism is conceived to be a "religious civilization"—that is, a way of life based on various expressions of religion, customs, ethics, history, folklore, language, music, and community. It recognizes Israel as the center of world Jewry but sees the infeasibility of a large immigration there. Jews in the Diaspora must develop a revitalized Judaism and unite together in forming strong organic communities.

REFORMATION. The term is generically applied to the religious movement of the sixteenth century credited with the division of Western Christianity into Catholicism and Protestantism.

REFORM JUDAISM. Religious movement which developed in German in the nineteenth century as a result of the Haskalah movement. It eventually took root and flourished in America. It maintained that modifications must be introduced into Judaism in order to meet the needs of the times. Haskalah is believed to be a human creation and as such, is subject to human modifications and abrogations. These changes include relaxation of various rituals, rejection of some beliefs, and introduction of many changes in synagogue worship. In recent years Reform Judaism has been reevaluating many of these changes and has reintroduced many aspects of traditional Judaism which it had previously rejected.

RESPONSA. Collection of literature, usually in post-Talmudic times, giving the questions (*she'elot*) and written replies (*teshuvot*) to matters dealing with any aspect of Jewish law. These answers were given by qualified Jewish authorities of the time. Noted individuals who codified this body of literature were Moses Maimonides and Joseph Caro.

RESURRECTION. A belief developed by the Pharisees that the bodies of the dead will rise from their graves upon the arrival of the Messiah. Denial of this belief was considered heretical until the modern time. Relates to the doctrine of eschatology.

REVELATION. The act of communication from God to man and the content of that communication. In traditional Jewish belief, man's knowledge of the existence of God came originally from God Himself. Thus, the Mosaic revelation on Mt. Sinai provided Israel with a Written and Oral Law. The relationship between knowledge obtained by revelation (Torah) and knowledge obtained through human reason alone has been discussed by philosophers and theologians down through the ages.

ROSH HA-SHANAH. Hebrew: (literally) "head of the year." A two-day festival commemorating the Jewish New Year. This holiday also marks the start of the ten days of penitence which ends on Yom Kippur (the Day of Atonement). During this period, God judges every man and each man's fate for the coming year is decided upon. The *shofar* (ram's horn) is blown. Rosh Ha-shanah does not necessarily signify a day marking the creation of the world.

SABBATH. Hebrew: *shabbat.* The day of rest, observed by the Jews weekly from sundown Friday until nightfall Saturday. Traditionally, all forms of labor are forbidden on this day.

SABBETAIANS. Followers of Shabbetai Tzevi, a false messiah of the seventeenth century.

SABRA. Native born Israelis.

SADDUCEES. Tracing their ancestry back to Zadok, high priest during the time of David, this Jewish sect, in the Second Commonwealth period, was composed of the Jewish aristocracy, prosperous merchants, and Temple priesthood. In their conservatism, they accepted as religiously authoritative only the Written Law, refusing all Oral tradition of the Pharisees. They also rejected the doctrines of the resurrection of the dead and the existence of angels.

SAMARITANS. A separate religious sect that separated from the Jews about 432 B.C.E. This group uses the Samaritan Pentateuch, which differs greatly from the traditional (Masoretic) version of the Torah.

SAMBATYON. Mythical river which supposedly rests on the Sabbath. It is believed that the Ten Lost Tribes of Israel reside on the other side of this river. Supposedly, upon the appearance of the Messiah, the Ten Tribes will return.

SANHEDRIN. A Hebrew word of Greek origin signifying the assembly of seventy-one ordained scholars, serving as the high court and legislature for the Jews. Prior to the destruction of the Second Temple, the Sanhedrin met in the Hall of Hewn Stone. This court flourished until its decline in the fourth century C.E. Since that time, there have been several unsuccessful attempts to reestablish this governing body, particularly since the creation of the State of Israel.

SECOND COMMONWEALTH. The period in Jewish history from the Maccabean Revolt (165 B.C.E.) to the Fall of Jerusalem (70 C.E.).

SECOND JEWISH REVOLT. 132-135 C.E. Documents recording the events of this era were found among the Dead Sea Scrolls in the caves of Wadi Murabbaat.

SECOND TEMPLE PERIOD. The period in Jewish history during which the Second Temple stood (516 B.C.E.-70 C.E.).

SEDER. Hebrew: "order." Refers to the ceremonial observance on the first two (in Israel and among reform Jews, one) nights of Passover.

SEDRA OR PARASHA. The weekly Torah portion read in the synagogue on the Sabbath. There are fifty-four such divisions which allow the reading of the entire Pentateuch annually.

SELEUCIDS. Name of an Hellenistic royal dynasty. Several of its kings granted favorable rights to the Jews. However, under the rule of Antiochus IV (Epiphanes), the religious and cultural limitations placed upon the Jews led to the Hasmonean revolt, which eventually ended the Seleucid rule over the Jews in 128 B.C.E.

SELIHOT. Hebrew: "penitential prayers." A specific type of lyrical poem requesting forgiveness of sin and a desire for mercy in God's eyes.

SEFARDI OR SEPHARDI (pl., SEPHARDIM). A term first used to refer to the Jews expelled from Spain in 1492. These exiles settled in North Africa, Egypt, Palestine, Syria, the Ottoman Empire, and in small numbers, in Italy. Their descendants still preserve certain ritualistic differences from their Ashkenazic counterparts, the use of Ladino (Judeo-Spanish language and literature), and pronunciation of the Hebrew language. The Sephardic community composes about 15 percent of world Jewry.

SEPHIROT. Hebrew: "numbers." In Jewish mysticism, ten mystical numbers or emanations, through which God manifests Himself.

SEPTUAGINT. The Greek translation of the Hebrew Scriptures done in Alexandria, Egypt, between the third and first centuries B.C.E.

SEVORAIM. Leaders of the Babylonian academies between the Amoraim and the Geonim (six and tenth centuries). They expounded obscure passages in the Talmud and, adding their comments, produced the final redaction of the Talmud.

SHAHARIT. Hebrew: "dawn (prayer)." The initial morning prayer said by traditional Jews daily.

SHEMA. The watchword of the Jewish faith, proclaiming the monotheistic basis of Judaism.

SHOFAR. Horn of any clean animal, except a cow; especially a ram's horn. Traditionally blown to commemorate certain Jewish rituals.

SHTETL. Yiddish: "little town." Small towns and villages of eastern Europe which had large Jewish populations.

SHULHAN ARUKH. Hebrew: "Prepared Table." Code of Jewish law compiled by Joseph Caro in 1565.

SHUT. Hebrew: *she'elot u'tshuvot*, "questions and answers" (see **RESPONSA** literature).

SIDDUR (pl., **SIDDURIM**). Hebrew: "order." The prayerbook for daily and Sabbath usage, as distinguished from the *mahzor*, used for festivals.

SINAI CAMPAIGN. Second Arab-Israeli war which was a result of the Egyptian nationalization of the Suez Canal. In November 1956 the Israel forces occupied most of the Sinai Peninsula. Due to American pressure, the conquered territory was later returned to Egypt.

SIX-DAY WAR. Third Arab-Israeli war precipitated by the Egyptian blockage of the Straits of Tiran. In June 1976 war erupted and Israeli forces occupied the Sinai Peninsula, the West Bank of the Jordan River, and the Golan Heights.

SOPHERIM. Hebrew: "scribes." A group of scholars who were mainly active in the two centuries after Ezra (c. 400-200 B.C.E.). These scholars involved themselves in interpretations of the Torah and the development of the Oral Law. They were the forerunners of the Pharisees.

STELE. An inscribed monument.

STERN GANG. See **LEHI.**

SURA. Scholarly rabbinical academy in Babylonia which was founded by the great Talmudic scholar Rav in the early third century. This academy flourished until the eleventh century. One of the most noted periods for this academy was when Saadyah Gaon headed it from 928 to 942.

SYNOPTIC. Refers to the first three gospels of the New Testament (Matthew, Luke, and Mark) which narrate the story of Jesus' life and teachings from the same viewpoint.

SYRIAC. A Semitic language belonging to the Aramaic branch. The approximate dates of written documentation are the second through the thirteenth centuries. Modern Syriac is still spoken.

TABERNACLES, FEAST OF. Hebrew: *Sukkot*. One of the three pilgrim festivals commemorating the fall harvest. Traditionally, an open booth (*sukkah*) is erected in which religious Jews dwell or eat for the week during which the festival is observed.

TALLIT. A rectangular prayer shawl to whose four corners fringes (*tzitzit*) are attached.

TALMUD. Name applied to each of two major compendia (completed at the end of the fifth century) of the records of discussion, administration, and interpretation of Jewish laws by generations of scholars and jurists in many academies and countries. Containing both the *halakhah* and *aggadah* (law and legendary lore), the Talmud is made up of two basic divisions: the Mishnah—interpretations of Biblical law—and the Gemara—later commentaries. The Oral Law, plus commentaries (Mishnah and Gemara), finally was compiled about 500 C.E. The Palestinian Talmud is the Mishnah and Gemara of the Palestinian rabbinic schools and the Babylonian Talmud is that of the Babylonian schools. The Babylonian Talmud is more important for Jewish studies and includes much more material. This body of literature is the most important spiritual document of the Jewish people after the Bible, summarizing more than six centuries of cultural and religious growth (150 B.C.E.-500 C.E.).

TANAKH. The acronym for the components of the Bible: Torah (the Five Books of Moses), Neviim (Prophets), and Ketuvim (the Writings or Hagiographa).

TANNAIM. The rabbis whose interpretations and opinions are recorded in the Mishnah.

TARGUM (pl., TARGUMIM). Aramaic from the Assyrian *targumanu*, meaning interpreter or dragoman. This refers to the Aramaic translation of the Bible. The practice of reading the Aramaic translation of the Bible at public prayer gatherings goes back to Ezra. There are three major *targumim*: Targum Onkelos, Targum Jonathan, and Targum Yerushalmi.

TARGUM JONATHAN. Refers to the translation of the Bible into Aramaic. Dedicated to the Former and Latter Prophets, the text, named after Jonathan ben Uzziel, mainly paraphrases the teachings of other texts.

TARGUM ONKELOS. Aramaic translation of the Pentateuch done by a Palestinian proselyte in the first century C.E.

TETRAGRAMMATON. Greek: "four-lettered." Word used to represent the name of God, traditionally not pronounced by the Jews, while Christians read the four Hebrew letters as Jehovah or Yahweh.

THERAPEUTAE. A group of Jewish ascetics, both men and women, having their center near Alexandria, Egypt, around the first century C.E. They spent their entire time, according to Philo, studying the Scriptures and contemplating divine realities.

TIKKUN. Hebrew: "restoration." In kabbalistic thought, the repairing of the fallen sparks, by which evil had entered the world. This could lead to the redemption and the coming of the Messiah. This restoration of order could take place through the study of the Torah, Talmud, and mystical writings, and through the observance of the Law.

TORAH. Hebrew: "teaching." Generic term used to cover the Bible, the Talmud, and all later commentaries. Specifically, it refers to the Five Books of Moses.

TOSAPHISTS. Refers to those individuals in France and Germany in the twelfth through the fourteenth centuries, who gave critical and explanatory notes on the Talmud.

TOSEPHTA. A body of literature containing variant opinions and discussions by the Tannaim on the same subjects as the Mishnah. It is generally felt that the Amoraim are responsible for its compilation.

TSAVAOT. Hebrew: "ethical wills." Documents written by prominent Jews bequeathing material or spiritual goods to their descendants.

TUR (pl., TURIM). One of the "rows" used in Jacob ben Asher's codification of Biblical and Talmudic commentaries. Jacob ben Asher lived from 1270 to 1343.

TWELVE TRIBES OF ISRAEL. The twelve family groupings of Israelites coming from the sons of Jacob: Reuben, Simeon, Levi, Judah, Issachar, Zebulun, Joseph, Benjamin, Dan, Naphtali, Gad, and Asher. When Moses assigned the priestly office to the tribe of Levi, he divided the tribe of Joseph into the tribes of Ephraim and Manasseh. This division by tribes was maintained through King Solomon's reign. After Solomon, when the Kingdom was divided into two parts, the Tribes split from the Tribes of Judah, Simeon and most of Benjamin, which formed the Southern Kingdom. Ten of the tribes have been "lost" and presently reside on the opposite side of the mythical River Sambatyon.

TZADDIK. Hebrew: "righteous man." In Hasidic thought an intermediary between man and God. The tzaddik was considered by his followers to be capable of performing miracles. With the growth of Hasidism, many dynasties of tzaddikim developed.

TZAHAL. Hebrew: *Tzva Haganah le-Yisrael*—Israel Defense Force (I.D.F.), the Israeli armed forces founded in 1948.

TZIMTZOM. Hebrew: "contraction." In Lurianic Kabbalah, the process in which God "withdraws" into Himself leaving a vacuum which is filled with the emanations of the Ein Soph. From this process creation took place.

UNSCOP. United Nations Special Committee on Palestine. Special committee formed by the United Nations in April 1947 to investigate a solution to the Palestine question. Their report formed the basis for the partition resolution of November 29, 1947.

USURY. The lending of money at an exorbitant rate of interest. Because it was prohibited by the Catholic Church , many Jews in the Middle Ages became moneylenders, one of the few professions Jews were allowed to practice.

VAAD ARBAH HA-ARATZOT. Hebrew: "Council of the Four Lands." The autonomous representative body of the Jewish communities of Poland, Lithuania, Ukraine, and Volhynia, which was in charge of assessing the state tax owed by the Jewish community, regulating Jewish religious life, etc. It was eventually dissolved in 1764.

VAAD HALASHON HAIVRIT. "Hebrew Language Council." Founded in Jerusalem in 1890, it is charged with the function of coining new Hebrew words, standardizing grammar, and publishing dictionaries, grammar books, journals, etc.

VULGATE. Between 382 and 385 C.E., Jerome (347-420 C.E.) revised the Latin New Testament from Greek manuscripts and later, in Bethlehem, translated the entire Old Testament from Hebrew. This resulted in the Latin Vulgate, which became the standard Biblical text for the Western world throughout the Middle Ages. As many as eight thousand manuscripts exist today.

WADI. An Arabic term for "valley," or "dry stream bed."

WADI MURABBAAT. Location of caves south of Qumran where the Dead Sea Scrolls were first discovered in 1947.

WHITE PAPER of 1939. British policy announced in May 1939 which called for the establishment of a Palestinian state in ten years. It limited Jewish immigration to Palestine to 75,000 for a five-year period, whereafter all Jewish immigration would be contingent upon the approval of the Arabs. In addition the sale of land to Jews was to be limited.

WISSENSCHAFT DES JÜDENTUM. German: "Science of Judaism." In nineteenth-century Germany, the scientific investigation of Jewish history, religion, literature, etc.

WRITINGS. See HAGIOGRAPHA.

WRITTEN LAW. Term referring to the Law received by Moses in written form. Strictly speaking, this is limited to the Pentateuch; but by extension it is also used to denote certain books of the Hagiographa which are also recorded in written form.

YESHIVA. Institution of higher Jewish learning, devoted primarily to the study of the Torah, Talmud, and other rabbinic writings.

YETZER HA-RA. A Hebrew term meaning an evil urge or inclination to the evil, which is opposed to the inclination to the good. It is not considered as evil per se but as a power abused by men. It is a passion in which all human action originates.

YEVSEKTSIIA. Russian: "Jewish section." The Jewish section of the Communist party which was formed in 1918 in order to spread the ideas of the Russian Revolution among the Jews. It was dissolved during Stalin's purges of the 1930s.

YIDDISH. Jewish language derived from medieval German written in Hebrew characters. After the migration of Jews to eastern Europe, many Slavic words were added to the language. In the nineteenth and twentieth centuries a great deal of Yiddish literature was written in eastern Europe and the United States.

YISHUV. The Jewish settlement in Israel.

YOM KIPPUR. Hebrew: "Day of Atonement." Jewish festival on which an individual is commanded to cleanse himself of the past year's sins. Traditionally commemorates the descent of Moses from Mt. Sinai for the second time, after the construction of the Golden Calf.

YOM KIPPUR WAR. Fourth Arab-Israeli war which erupted on October 6, 1973, on the Jewish holiday of Yom Kippur. As a result of this war, the Egyptians regained a foothold on the Sinai Peninsula.

ZEALOTS. A group composed of fanatic Jewish patriots who opposed all foreign political rule and who were zealous for literal and particularistic fulfillment of religious laws. They were most active against Rome from 37 B.C.E. to 70 C.E.

ZIONISM. The movement aimed at the return of the Jewish people to the land of Israel. In the nineteenth and twentieth centuries, it manifested itself as the movement for the establishment of a Jewish state in Palestine, and the maintenance of the existence of the State of Israel.

ZOHAR. Hebrew: "brightness." The fundamental book of Jewish mysticism. It was first published by Moses de Leon in Spain in the thirteenth century. It consists of a mystical interpretation of the Bible.

GENERAL INDEX

Refer to the Glossary for items listed in **boldface** numbers.